MASS CALENDAR

Date

2022

NOVEMBER
27 - 1st Sunday of Advent.....

DECEMBER
4 - 2nd Sunday of Advent...... 116
8 - Immaculate Conception... 121
11 - 3rd Sunday of Advent 127
18 - 4th Sunday of Advent 132
25 - Nativity of the Lord ...136-149

2023

JANUARY
1 - Mary, Holy Mother of God..150
8 - The Epiphany of the Lord..155
15 - 2nd Sun. in Ord. Time...... 162
22 - 3rd Sun. in Ord. Time....... 166
29 - 4th Sun. in Ord. Time....... 171

FEBRUARY
5 - 5th Sun. in Ord. Time....... 176
12 - 6th Sun. in Ord. Time....... 180
19 - 7th Sun. in Ord. Time....... 186
26 - 1st Sunday of Lent........... 191

MARCH
5 - 2nd Sunday of Lent........... 198
12 - 3rd Sunday of Lent 203
19 - 4th Sunday of Lent 213
26 - 5th Sunday of Lent 223

APRIL
2 - Palm Sunday................... 232
6 - Holy Thursday—Chrism... 255
   —Lord's Supper.............. 262
7 - Good Friday.................... 276
8 - Easter Vigil.................... 303
9 - Easter Sunday................. 352
16 - 2nd Sunday of Easter 360
23 - 3rd Sunday of Easter....... 366
30 - 4th Sunday of Easter 372

28 - Pentecost Sunday 398

JUNE
4 - The Most Holy Trinity........ 418
11 - Body and Blood of Christ . 422
18 - 11th Sun. in Ord. Time..... 428
25 - 12th Sun. in Ord. Time..... 433

JULY
2 - 13th Sun. in Ord. Time..... 438
9 - 14th Sun. in Ord. Time..... 443
16 - 15th Sun. in Ord. Time..... 448
23 - 16th Sun. in Ord. Time..... 454
30 - 17th Sun. in Ord. Time..... 459

AUGUST
6 - Transfiguration of the Lord 464
13 - 19th Sun. in Ord. Time..... 470
15 - The Assumption 475
20 - 20th Sun. in Ord. Time..... 485
27 - 21st Sun. in Ord. Time..... 489

SEPTEMBER
3 - 22nd Sun. in Ord. Time.... 494
10 - 23rd Sun. in Ord. Time..... 498
17 - 24th Sun. in Ord. Time..... 503
24 - 25th Sun. in Ord. Time..... 508

OCTOBER
1 - 26th Sun. in Ord. Time..... 513
8 - 27th Sun. in Ord. Time..... 518
15 - 28th Sun. in Ord. Time..... 524
22 - 29th Sun. in Ord. Time..... 529
29 - 30th Sun. in Ord. Time..... 534

NOVEMBER
1 - All Saints 538
5 - 31st Sun. in Ord. Time..... 544
12 - 32nd Sun. in Ord. Time..... 549
19 - 33rd Sun. in Ord. Time..... 554
26 - Our Lord Jesus Christ,
   King of the Universe........... 560

The Value of a Missal

"Hand Missals which are drawn up according to the requirements of the modern liturgical renewal and which contain not only the Ordinary of the Mass but a version of all the liturgical texts approved by the competent authority are still necessary for the more perfect understanding of the total mystery of salvation celebrated during the liturgical year, for drawing meditation and fervor from the inexhaustible riches of the liturgical texts, and for facilitating actual participation.

"This demands not only that the Word of God be proclaimed within the gathered community and attentively listened to by it, but also that the holy people respond to the Word of God which they have received and celebrate the Sacred (Mysteries) by singing or reciting the parts of the Ordinary and Proper [of the Mass], hymns and Psalms.

"[Missals are] especially necessary for . . . those who participate in daily Mass, or who desire to live and pray every day in the spirit of the liturgy; those who because of sickness or inconvenience or other similar reasons cannot assemble with their own liturgical community, so that they may be joined to their prayer more truly and intimately; children who are to be initiated progressively into the mystery of the liturgy."

Postconciliar Commission for the Implementation
of the Constitution on the Sacred Liturgy

This Missal belongs to

....

Year A

For 2022-2023

New *Saint Joseph*

SUNDAY MISSAL

PRAYERBOOK AND HYMNAL

This new Missal has been especially designed to help you participate at Mass . . . in the fullest and most active way possible.

How easy it is to use this Missal

- Refer to the Calendar inside the front cover for the page of the Sunday Mass (the "Proper").

- This arrow (↓) means continue to read. This arrow (→) indicates a reference back to the Order of Mass ("Ordinary") or to another part of the "Proper."

- Boldface type always indicates the people's parts that are to be recited aloud.

ORDER OF MASS (Ordinary) pp. 10-77

MASS TEXT for each Sunday/ Holyday of Obligation pp. 111-565

POPULAR HYMNS pp. 566-617

TREASURY OF PRAYERS pp. 618-659

MAJOR PRACTICES pp. 660-671

*"Take this, all of you, and eat of it, for this is
my Body, which will be given up for you."*

New . . . St. Joseph

SUNDAY MISSAL

PRAYERBOOK AND HYMNAL

For 2022-2023

THE COMPLETE MASSES FOR SUNDAYS, HOLYDAYS, and the SACRED PASCHAL TRIDUUM

With the People's Parts of Holy Mass
Printed in Boldface Type
and Arranged for Parish Participation

IN ACCORD WITH THE THIRD TYPICAL EDITION
OF THE ROMAN MISSAL

WITH THE "NEW AMERICAN BIBLE" TEXT
FROM THE REVISED SUNDAY LECTIONARY,
SHORT HELPFUL NOTES AND EXPLANATIONS,
AND A TREASURY OF POPULAR PRAYERS

Dedicated to St. Joseph
Patron of the Universal Church

CATHOLIC BOOK PUBLISHING CORP.
New Jersey

NIHIL OBSTAT: Rev. Pawel Tomczyk, Ph.D.
Censor Librorum

IMPRIMATUR: ✠ Kevin J. Sweeney, D.D.
Bishop of Paterson

March 15, 2022

Published with the approval of the
Committee on Divine Worship,
United States Conference of Catholic Bishops

The St. Joseph Missals have been diligently prepared with the invaluable assistance of a special Board of Editors, including specialists in Liturgy and Sacred Scripture, Catechetics, Sacred Music and Art.

In this Sunday Missal Edition the musical notations for responsorial antiphons are by Rev. John Selner, S.S.

(T-2023)
ISBN 978-1-953152-83-1
© 2022 by *Catholic Book Publishing Corp.*, N.J.
catholicbookpublishing.com
Printed in the U.S.A.   22 SH 1

PREFACE

IN the words of the Second Vatican Council in the *Constitution on the Liturgy*, the *Mass* "is an action of Christ the priest and of his body which is the Church; it is a sacred action surpassing all others; no other action of the Church can equal its efficacy by the same title and to the same degree" (art. 7). Hence the Mass is a sacred sign, something visible which brings the invisible reality of Christ to us in the worship of the Father.

The Mass is the re-presentation of the Paschal Mystery, which delivers us from sin, death, and the devil and whereby we merit to receive a share in the eternal life of the Resurrected Christ.

"At the Last Supper, on the night when he was betrayed, our Savior instituted the Eucharistic sacrifice of his body and blood. He did this in order to perpetuate the sacrifice of the Cross throughout the centuries until he should come again, and so to entrust to his beloved spouse, the Church, a memorial of his death and resurrection: a sacrament of love, a sign of unity, a bond of charity, a Paschal banquet in which Christ is eaten, the mind is filled with grace, and a pledge of future glory is given to us.

"The Church, therefore, earnestly desires that Christ's faithful, when present at this mystery of faith, should not be there as strangers or silent spectators; on the contrary, through a good understanding of the rites and prayers they should take part in the sacred action conscious of what they are doing, with devotion and full collaboration. They should be instructed by God's word and be nourished at the table of the Lord's body; they should give thanks to God; by offering the immaculate Victim, not only through the hands of the priests but also with him, they should learn also to offer themselves; through Christ the Mediator, they should be drawn day by day into ever more perfect union with God and with each other, so that . . . God may be all in all" (art. 47-48).

Accordingly, this new Sunday Missal has been edited, in conformity with the latest findings of modern liturgists, especially to enable the people to attain the most active participation.

To insure that "each . . . lay person who has an office to perform [will] do all of, but only, those parts which pertain to his office" (art. 28), a simple method of instant identification of the various parts of the Mass, has been designed, using different typefaces:

(1) **boldface type**—clearly identifies all people's parts for each Mass.

(2) lightface type—indicates the Priest's, Deacon's, or reader's parts.

In order to enable the faithful to prepare for each Mass AT HOME and so participate more actively AT MASS, the editors have added short helpful explanations of the new scripture readings, geared to the spiritual needs of daily life. A large selection of hymns for congregational singing has been included as well as a treasury of private prayers.

We trust that all these special features will help Catholics who use this new St. Joseph Missal to be led— in keeping with the desire of the Church—"to that full, conscious, and active participation in liturgical celebrations which is demanded by the very nature of the liturgy. Such participation by the Christian people as a chosen race, a royal priesthood, a holy nation, a redeemed people (1 Pt 2:9; cf. 2:4-5), is their right and duty by reason of their baptism" (art. 14).

THE ORDER OF MASS TITLES

THE INTRODUCTORY RITES
1. Entrance Chant
2. Greeting
3. Rite for the Blessing and Sprinkling of Water
4. Penitential Act
5. Kyrie
6. Gloria
7. Collect **(Proper)**

THE LITURGY OF THE WORD
8. First Reading **(Proper)**
9. Responsorial Psalm **(Proper)**
10. Second Reading **(Proper)**
11. Gospel Acclamation **(Proper)**
12. Gospel Dialogue
13. Gospel Reading **(Proper)**
14. Homily
15. Profession of Faith **(Creed)**
16. Universal Prayer

THE LITURGY OF THE EUCHARIST
17. Presentation and Preparation of the Gifts
18. Invitation to Prayer
19. Prayer over the Offerings **(Proper)**
20. Eucharistic Prayer

21. Preface Dialogue
22. Preface
23. Preface Acclamation
   Eucharistic Prayer
   1, 2, 3, 4
   Reconciliation 1, 2
   Various Needs 1, 2, 3, 4

THE COMMUNION RITE
24. The Lord's Prayer
25. Sign of Peace
26. Lamb of God
27. Invitation to Communion
28. Communion
29. Prayer after Communion **(Proper)**

THE CONCLUDING RITES
30. Solemn Blessing
31. Final Blessing
32. Dismissal

THE ORDER OF MASS

Options are indicated by A, B, C, D in the margin.

THE INTRODUCTORY RITES

Acts of prayer and penitence prepare us to meet Christ as he comes in Word and Sacrament. We gather as a worshiping community to celebrate our unity with him and with one another in faith.

1 ENTRANCE CHANT   `STAND`

If it is not sung, it is recited by all or some of the people.

Joined together as Christ's people, we open the celebration by raising our voices in praise of God who is present among us. This song should deepen our unity as it introduces the Mass we celebrate today.

→ `Turn to Today's Mass`

2 GREETING (3 forms)

When the Priest comes to the altar, he makes the customary reverence with the ministers and kisses the altar. Then, with the ministers, he goes to his chair. After the Entrance Chant, all make the Sign of the Cross:

Priest: In the name of the Father, and of the Son, and of the Holy Spirit.

PEOPLE: **Amen.**

The Priest welcomes us in the name of the Lord. We show our union with God, our neighbor, and the Priest by a united response to his greeting.

A ———————————————————————

Priest: The grace of our Lord Jesus Christ,
and the love of God,
and the communion of the Holy Spirit
be with you all.

PEOPLE: And with your spirit.

B ———————— OR ————————

Priest: Grace to you and peace from God our Father
and the Lord Jesus Christ.

PEOPLE: And with your spirit.

C ———————— OR ————————

Priest: The Lord be with you.

PEOPLE: And with your spirit.

[Bishop: Peace be with you.

PEOPLE: And with your spirit.]

3   RITE FOR the BLESSING and SPRINKLING OF WATER

From time to time on Sundays, especially in Easter Time, instead of the customary Penitential Act, the Blessing and Sprinkling of Water may take place (see pp. 78-81) as a reminder of Baptism.

4   PENITENTIAL ACT (3 forms)

(Omitted when the Rite for the Blessing and Sprinkling of Water [see pp. 78-81] has taken place or some part of the liturgy of the hours has preceded.)

Before we hear God's word, we acknowledge our sins humbly, ask for mercy, and accept his pardon.

Invitation to repent:

After the introduction to the day's Mass, the Priest invites the people to recall their sins and to repent of them in silence:

Priest: Brethren (brothers and sisters), let us acknowledge our sins,
and so prepare ourselves to celebrate the sacred mysteries.

Then, after a brief silence, one of the following forms is used.

A

Priest and **PEOPLE:**

**I confess to almighty God
and to you, my brothers and sisters,
that I have greatly sinned,
in my thoughts and in my words,
in what I have done and in what I have
failed to do,**

They strike their breast:

**through my fault, through my fault,
through my most grievous fault;**

Then they continue:

**therefore I ask blessed Mary ever-Virgin,
all the Angels and Saints,
and you, my brothers and sisters,
to pray for me to the Lord our God.**

B —————————— OR ——————————

Priest: Have mercy on us, O Lord.

PEOPLE: For we have sinned against you.

Priest: Show us, O Lord, your mercy.

PEOPLE: And grant us your salvation.

C —————————— OR——————————

Priest, or a Deacon or another minister:

You were sent to heal the contrite of heart:
Lord, have mercy.

PEOPLE: Lord, have mercy.

Priest or other minister:

You came to call sinners:
Christ, have mercy.

PEOPLE: Christ, have mercy.

Priest or other minister:

You are seated at the right hand of the
Father to intercede for us:

Lord, have mercy.

PEOPLE: Lord, have mercy.

—————————

Absolution:

At the end of any of the forms of the Penitential Act:

Priest: May almighty God have mercy on us,
forgive us our sins,
and bring us to everlasting life.

PEOPLE: Amen.

5 KYRIE

Unless included in the Penitential Act, the Kyrie is sung or said by all, with alternating parts for the choir or cantor and for the people:

℣. Lord, have mercy.

℟. **Lord, have mercy.**

℣. Christ, have mercy.

℟. **Christ, have mercy.**

℣. Lord, have mercy.

℟. **Lord, have mercy.**

6 GLORIA

As the Church assembled in the Spirit we praise and pray to the Father and the Lamb.

When the Gloria is sung or said, the Priest or the cantors or everyone together may begin it:

Glory to God in the highest,
and on earth peace to people of good will.

We praise you,
we bless you,
we adore you,
we glorify you,
we give you thanks for your great glory,
Lord God, heavenly King,
O God, almighty Father.

Lord Jesus Christ, Only Begotten Son,
Lord God, Lamb of God, Son of the Father,
you take away the sins of the world,
    have mercy on us;

you take away the sins of the world,
   receive our prayer;
you are seated at the right hand of the Father,
   have mercy on us.

For you alone are the Holy One,
you alone are the Lord,
you alone are the Most High,
Jesus Christ,
with the Holy Spirit,
in the glory of God the Father.
Amen.

7 COLLECT

The Priest invites us to pray silently for a moment and then, in our name, expresses the theme of the day's celebration and petitions God the Father through the mediation of Christ in the Holy Spirit.

Priest: Let us pray.

→ Turn to Today's Mass

Priest and people pray silently for a while. Then the Priest says the Collect prayer, at the end of which the people acclaim:

PEOPLE: Amen.

THE LITURGY OF THE WORD

The proclamation of God's Word is always centered on Christ, present through his Word. Old Testament writings prepare for him; New Testament books speak of him directly. All of scripture calls us to believe once more and to follow. After the reading we reflect on God's words and respond to them.

As in Today's Mass   **SIT**

8   FIRST READING

At the end of the reading: Reader: The word of the Lord.

PEOPLE: Thanks be to God.

9   RESPONSORIAL PSALM

The people repeat the response sung by the cantor the first time and then after each verse.

10   SECOND READING

At the end of the reading: Reader: The word of the Lord.

PEOPLE: Thanks be to God.

11   GOSPEL ACCLAMATION   **STAND**

Jesus will speak to us in the Gospel. We rise now out of respect and prepare for his message with the Alleluia.

The people repeat the Alleluia after the cantor's Alleluia and then after the verse. During Lent one of the following invocations is used as a response instead of the Alleluia:

(a)   **Glory and praise to you, Lord Jesus Christ!**
(b)   **Glory to you, Lord Jesus Christ, Wisdom of God the Father!**
(c)   **Glory to you, Word of God, Lord Jesus Christ!**
(d)   **Glory to you, Lord Jesus Christ, Son of the Living God!**

(e) **Praise and honor to you, Lord Jesus Christ!**

(f) **Praise to you, Lord Jesus Christ, King of endless glory!**

(g) **Marvelous and great are your works, O Lord!**

(h) **Salvation, glory, and power to the Lord Jesus Christ!**

12 GOSPEL DIALOGUE

Before proclaiming the Gospel, the Deacon asks the Priest: Your blessing, Father. *The Priest says:*

May the Lord be in your heart and on your lips, that you may proclaim his Gospel worthily and well, in the name of the Father, and of the Son, ✠ and of the Holy Spirit. *The Deacon answers:* Amen.

If there is no Deacon, the Priest says inaudibly:

Cleanse my heart and my lips, almighty God, that I may worthily proclaim your holy Gospel.

13 GOSPEL READING

Deacon (or Priest):
>	The Lord be with you.

PEOPLE: And with your spirit.

Deacon (or Priest):

✠ A reading from the holy Gospel according to N.

PEOPLE: Glory to you, O Lord.

At the end:

Deacon (or Priest):
>	The Gospel of the Lord.

PEOPLE: Praise to you, Lord Jesus Christ.

Then the Deacon (or Priest) kisses the book, saying inaudibly: Through the words of the Gospel may our sins be wiped away.

14 HOMILY   SIT

God's word is spoken again in the Homily. The Holy Spirit speaking through the lips of the preacher explains and applies today's biblical readings to the needs of this particular congregation. He calls us to respond to Christ through the life we lead.

15 PROFESSION OF FAITH (CREED) `STAND`

As a people we express our acceptance of God's message in the Scriptures and Homily. We summarize our faith by proclaiming a creed handed down from the early Church.

All say the Profession of Faith on Sundays.

THE NICENE CREED

I believe in one God,
the Father almighty,
maker of heaven and earth,
of all things visible and invisible.

I believe in one Lord Jesus Christ,
the Only Begotten Son of God,
born of the Father before all ages.
God from God, Light from Light,
true God from true God,
begotten, not made, consubstantial with the Father;
through him all things were made.
For us men and for our salvation
he came down from heaven,
and by the Holy Spirit was incarnate of the Virgin
    Mary,   } *bow*
and became man.

For our sake he was crucified under Pontius Pilate,
he suffered death and was buried,
and rose again on the third day
in accordance with the Scriptures.
He ascended into heaven
and is seated at the right hand of the Father.
He will come again in glory
to judge the living and the dead
and his kingdom will have no end.

I believe in the Holy Spirit, the Lord, the giver of life,
who proceeds from the Father and the Son,
who with the Father and the Son is adored and
    glorified,
who has spoken through the prophets.

I believe in one, holy, catholic and apostolic Church.
I confess one Baptism for the forgiveness of sins
and I look forward to the resurrection of the dead
and the life of the world to come. Amen.

OR ——————— APOSTLES' CREED ———————

Especially during Lent and Easter Time, the Apostles'
Creed may be said after the Homily.

I believe in God,
the Father almighty,
Creator of heaven and earth,
and in Jesus Christ, his only Son, our Lord,
who was conceived by the Holy Spirit, ⎫ *bow*
born of the Virgin Mary, ⎭
suffered under Pontius Pilate,
was crucified, died and was buried;
he descended into hell;
on the third day he rose again from the dead;
he ascended into heaven,
and is seated at the right hand of God the Father
   almighty;
from there he will come to judge the living and the dead.

I believe in the Holy Spirit,
the holy catholic Church,
the communion of saints,
the forgiveness of sins,
the resurrection of the body,
and life everlasting. Amen.

16 UNIVERSAL PRAYER   (Prayer of the Faithful)

As a priestly people we unite with one another to pray for today's
needs in the Church and the world.

After the Priest gives the introduction the Deacon or other
minister sings or says the invocations.

PEOPLE: Lord, hear our prayer.
(or other response, according to local custom)
At the end the Priest says the concluding prayer:
PEOPLE: Amen.

THE LITURGY OF THE EUCHARIST

17 PRESENTATION AND PREPARATION SIT OF THE GIFTS

While the people's gifts are brought forward to the Priest and are placed on the altar, the Offertory Chant is sung.

Before placing the bread on the altar, the Priest says inaudibly:

Blessed are you, Lord God of all creation,
for through your goodness we have received
the bread we offer you:
fruit of the earth and work of human hands,
it will become for us the bread of life.

If there is no singing, the Priest may say this prayer aloud, and the people may respond:

PEOPLE: Blessed be God for ever.

When he pours wine and a little water into the chalice, the Deacon (or the Priest) says inaudibly:

By the mystery of this water and wine
may we come to share in the divinity of Christ
who humbled himself to share in our humanity.

Before placing the chalice on the altar, he says:

Blessed are you, Lord God of all creation,
for through your goodness we have received
the wine we offer you:
fruit of the vine and work of human hands,
it will become our spiritual drink.

If there is no singing, the Priest may say this prayer aloud, and the people may respond:

PEOPLE: **Blessed be God for ever.**

The Priest says inaudibly:

With humble spirit and contrite heart
may we be accepted by you, O Lord,
and may our sacrifice in your sight this day
be pleasing to you, Lord God.

Then he washes his hands, saying:

Wash me, O Lord, from my iniquity
and cleanse me from my sin.

18 INVITATION TO PRAYER

Priest: Pray, brethren (brothers and sisters),
        that my sacrifice and yours
        may be acceptable to God,
        the almighty Father.   `STAND`

PEOPLE:

May the Lord accept the sacrifice at your hands
for the praise and glory of his name,
for our good
and the good of all his holy Church.

19 PRAYER OVER THE OFFERINGS

The Priest, speaking in our name, asks the Father to bless and accept these gifts.

→ `Turn to Today's Mass`

At the end, **PEOPLE:**   **Amen.**

20 EUCHARISTIC PRAYER

We begin the eucharistic service of praise and thanksgiving, the center of the entire celebration, the central prayer of worship. We lift our hearts to God, and offer praise and thanks as the Priest addresses this prayer to the Father through Jesus Christ. Together we join Christ in his sacrifice, celebrating his memorial in the holy meal and acknowledging with him the wonderful works of God in our lives.

21 PREFACE DIALOGUE

Priest: The Lord be with you.
PEOPLE: And with your spirit.

Priest: Lift up your hearts.
PEOPLE: We lift them up to the Lord.

Priest: Let us give thanks to the Lord our God.
PEOPLE: It is right and just.

22 PREFACE

As indicated in the individual Masses of this Missal, the Priest may say one of the following Prefaces (listed in numerical order).

No.		Page	No.		Page
P 1:	Advent I	82	P 14:	3rd Sun. of Lent	210
P 2:	Advent II	82	P 15:	4th Sun. of Lent	220
P 3:	Nativity of the Lord I	83	P 16:	5th Sun. of Lent	229
P 4:	Nativity of the Lord II	83	P 19:	Palm Sunday of the	
P 5:	Nativity of the Lord III	84		Passion of the Lord	253
P 6:	Epiphany of Lord	159	P 20:	Holy Thursday	261
P 8:	Lent I	84	P 21:	Easter I	85
P 9:	Lent II	85	P 22:	Easter II	86
P 12:	1st Sun. of Lent	196	P 23:	Easter III	86
P 13:	2nd Sun. of Lent	201	P 24:	Easter IV	86
			P 25:	Easter V	87

No.	Page	No.	Page
P 26: Ascension I	87	**P 48:** Holy Eucharist II	92
P 27: Ascension II	88	**P 50:** Transfiguration	468
P 28: Pentecost Sunday	416	**P 51:** Jesus Christ, King	
P 29: Ordinary Sunday I	88	of the Universe	564
P 30: Ordinary Sunday II	89	**P 56:** Blessed Virgin I	153
P 31: Ordinary Sunday III	89	**P 58:** Immac. Conception	126
P 32: Ordinary Sunday IV	90	**P 59:** Assumption	483
P 33: Ordinary Sunday V	90	**P 71:** All Saints	542
P 34: Ordinary Sunday VI	91	**P 77:** For the Dead I	93
P 35: Ordinary Sunday VII	91	**P 78:** For the Dead II	94
P 36: Ordinary Sunday VIII	91	**P 79:** For the Dead III	94
P 43: Most Holy Trinity	421	**P 80:** For the Dead IV	94
P 47: Holy Eucharist I	92	**P 81:** For the Dead V	95

23 PREFACE ACCLAMATION

Priest and **PEOPLE:**

Holy, Holy, Holy Lord God of hosts.
Heaven and earth are full of your glory.
Hosanna in the highest.
Blessed is he who comes in the name of the Lord.
Hosanna in the highest. `KNEEL`

Then the Priest continues with one of the following Eucharistic Prayers.

EUCHARISTIC PRAYER .... Choice of ten

1 To you, therefore, most merciful Father .. p. 24
2 You are indeed Holy, O Lord, the fount ... p. 31
3 You are indeed Holy, O Lord, and all .... p. 34
4 We give you praise, Father most holy ..... p. 39
R1 You are indeed Holy, O Lord, and from ... p. 44
R2 You, therefore, almighty Father .... p. 49
V1 You are indeed Holy and to be glorified .. p. 53
V2 You are indeed Holy and to be glorified .. p. 58
V3 You are indeed Holy and to be glorified .. p. 63
V4 You are indeed Holy and to be glorified .. p. 68

EUCHARISTIC PRAYER No. 1

The Roman Canon

(This Eucharistic Prayer is especially suitable for Sundays and Masses with proper Communicantes *and* Hanc igitur.*)*

[The words within parentheses may be omitted.]

To you, therefore, most merciful Father,
we make humble prayer and petition
through Jesus Christ, your Son, our Lord:
that you accept
and bless ✠ these gifts, these offerings,
these holy and unblemished sacrifices,
which we offer you firstly
for your holy catholic Church.
Be pleased to grant her peace,
to guard, unite and govern her
throughout the whole world,
together with your servant N. our Pope,
and N. our Bishop,
and all those who, holding to the truth,
hand on the catholic and apostolic faith.

Remember, Lord, your servants N. and N.
and all gathered here,
whose faith and devotion are known to you.
For them, we offer you this sacrifice of praise
or they offer it for themselves
and all who are dear to them:
for the redemption of their souls,
in hope of health and well-being,
and paying their homage to you,
the eternal God, living and true.

In communion with those whose memory we
  venerate,
especially the glorious ever-Virgin Mary,
Mother of our God and Lord, Jesus Christ,
† and blessed Joseph, her Spouse,
your blessed Apostles and Martyrs
Peter and Paul, Andrew,
(James, John,
Thomas, James, Philip,
Bartholomew, Matthew,
Simon and Jude;
Linus, Cletus, Clement, Sixtus,
Cornelius, Cyprian,
Lawrence, Chrysogonus,
John and Paul,
Cosmas and Damian)
and all your Saints;
we ask that through their merits and prayers,
in all things we may be defended
by your protecting help.
(Through Christ our Lord. Amen.)

Therefore, Lord, we pray:*
graciously accept this oblation of our service,
that of your whole family;
order our days in your peace,
and command that we be delivered from eternal
  damnation
and counted among the flock of those you have
  chosen.
(Through Christ our Lord. Amen.)

Be pleased, O God, we pray,
to bless, acknowledge,
and approve this offering in every respect;

† * *See p. 95 for proper* Communicantes *and* Hanc igitur.

1 make it spiritual and acceptable,
so that it may become for us
the Body and Blood of your most beloved Son,
our Lord Jesus Christ.

On the day before he was to suffer,
he took bread in his holy and venerable hands,
and with eyes raised to heaven
to you, O God, his almighty Father,
giving you thanks, he said the blessing,
broke the bread
and gave it to his disciples, saying:

Take this, all of you, and eat of it,
for this is my Body,
which will be given up for you.

In a similar way when supper was ended,
he took this precious chalice
in his holy and venerable hands,
and once more giving you thanks, he said the
    blessing
and gave the chalice to his disciples, saying:

Take this, all of you, and drink from it,
for this is the chalice of my Blood,
the Blood of the new and eternal covenant,
which will be poured out for you and for many
for the forgiveness of sins.

Do this in memory of me.

Priest: The mystery of faith. *(Memorial Acclamation)*

PEOPLE:

A We proclaim your Death, O Lord,
and profess your Resurrection
until you come again.

B When we eat this Bread and drink this Cup,
   we proclaim your Death, O Lord,
   until you come again.

C Save us, Savior of the world,
   for by your Cross and Resurrection
   you have set us free.

Therefore, O Lord,
as we celebrate the memorial of the blessed Passion,
the Resurrection from the dead,
and the glorious Ascension into heaven
of Christ, your Son, our Lord,
we, your servants and your holy people,
offer to your glorious majesty
from the gifts that you have given us,
this pure victim,
this holy victim,
this spotless victim,
the holy Bread of eternal life
and the Chalice of everlasting salvation.

Be pleased to look upon these offerings
with a serene and kindly countenance,
and to accept them,
as once you were pleased to accept
the gifts of your servant Abel the just,
the sacrifice of Abraham, our father in faith,
and the offering of your high priest Melchizedek,
a holy sacrifice, a spotless victim.

In humble prayer we ask you, almighty God:
command that these gifts be borne
by the hands of your holy Angel
to your altar on high

1 in the sight of your divine majesty,
so that all of us, who through this participation at
    the altar
receive the most holy Body and Blood of your Son,
may be filled with every grace and heavenly
    blessing.
(Through Christ our Lord. Amen.)

Remember also, Lord, your servants *N.* and *N.*,
who have gone before us with the sign of faith
and rest in the sleep of peace.
Grant them, O Lord, we pray,
and all who sleep in Christ,
a place of refreshment, light and peace.
(Through Christ our Lord. Amen.)

To us, also, your servants, who, though sinners,
hope in your abundant mercies,
graciously grant some share
and fellowship with your holy Apostles and
    Martyrs:
with John the Baptist, Stephen,
Matthias, Barnabas,
(Ignatius, Alexander,
Marcellinus, Peter,
Felicity, Perpetua,
Agatha, Lucy,
Agnes, Cecilia, Anastasia)
and all your Saints;
admit us, we beseech you,
into their company,
not weighing our merits,
but granting us your pardon,
through Christ our Lord.

1

Through whom
you continue to make all these good things,
  O Lord;
you sanctify them, fill them with life,
bless them, and bestow them upon us.

(Concluding Doxology)

Through him, and with him, and in him,
O God, almighty Father,
in the unity of the Holy Spirit,
all glory and honor is yours,
for ever and ever.

The people acclaim: **Amen.**

Continue with the Mass, as on p. 72.

EUCHARISTIC PRAYER No. 2

(This Eucharistic Prayer is particularly suitable on Weekdays or for special circumstances.)

STAND

℣. The Lord be with you.
℟. **And with your spirit.**

℣. Lift up your hearts.
℟. **We lift them up to the Lord.**

℣. Let us give thanks to the Lord our God.
℟. **It is right and just.**

It is truly right and just, our duty and our salvation,
always and everywhere to give you thanks, Father
    most holy,
through your beloved Son, Jesus Christ,
your Word through whom you made all things,
whom you sent as our Savior and Redeemer,
incarnate by the Holy Spirit and born of the Virgin.

Fulfilling your will
    and gaining for you a holy people,
he stretched out his hands
    as he endured his Passion,
so as to break the bonds of death
    and manifest the resurrection.

And so, with the Angels and all the Saints
we declare your glory,
as with one voice we acclaim:

2

Holy, Holy, Holy Lord God of hosts.
Heaven and earth are full of your glory.
Hosanna in the highest.
Blessed is he who comes in the name of the Lord.
Hosanna in the highest.

KNEEL

You are indeed Holy, O Lord,
the fount of all holiness.

Make holy, therefore, these gifts, we pray,
by sending down your Spirit upon them like the
    dewfall,
so that they may become for us
the Body and ✠ Blood of our Lord Jesus Christ.

At the time he was betrayed
and entered willingly into his Passion,
he took bread and, giving thanks, broke it,
and gave it to his disciples, saying:

Take this, all of you, and eat of it,
for this is my Body,
which will be given up for you.

In a similar way, when supper was ended,
he took the chalice
and, once more giving thanks,
he gave it to his disciples, saying:

Take this, all of you, and drink from it,
for this is the chalice of my Blood,
the Blood of the new and eternal covenant,
which will be poured out for you and for many
for the forgiveness of sins.

Do this in memory of me.

2 Priest: The mystery of faith. *(Memorial Acclamation)*

PEOPLE:

A We proclaim your Death, O Lord,
and profess your Resurrection
until you come again.

B When we eat this Bread and drink this Cup,
we proclaim your Death, O Lord,
until you come again.

C Save us, Savior of the world,
for by your Cross and Resurrection
you have set us free.

Therefore, as we celebrate
the memorial of his Death and Resurrection,
we offer you, Lord,
the Bread of life and the Chalice of salvation,
giving thanks that you have held us worthy
to be in your presence and minister to you.

Humbly we pray
that, partaking of the Body and Blood of Christ,
we may be gathered into one by the Holy Spirit.

Remember, Lord, your Church,
spread throughout the world,
and bring her to the fullness of charity,
together with N. our Pope and N. our Bishop
and all the clergy.

In Masses for the Dead, the following may be added:

Remember your servant N.,
whom you have called (today)
from this world to yourself.

Grant that he (she) who was united with your Son in a
    death like his,
may also be one with him in his Resurrection.

2

Remember also our brothers and sisters
who have fallen asleep in the hope of the
    resurrection,
and all who have died in your mercy:
welcome them into the light of your face.
Have mercy on us all, we pray,
that with the Blessed Virgin Mary, Mother of
    God,
with blessed Joseph, her Spouse,
with the blessed Apostles,
and all the Saints who have pleased you
    throughout the ages,
we may merit to be coheirs to eternal life,
and may praise and glorify you
through your Son, Jesus Christ.

(Concluding Doxology)

Through him, and with him, and in him,
O God, almighty Father,
in the unity of the Holy Spirit,
all glory and honor is yours,
for ever and ever.

The people acclaim: **Amen.**

Continue with the Mass, as on p. 72.

(This Eucharistic Prayer may be used with any Preface and preferably on Sundays and feast days.)

KNEEL

You are indeed Holy, O Lord,
and all you have created
rightly gives you praise,
for through your Son our Lord Jesus Christ,
by the power and working of the Holy Spirit,
you give life to all things and make them holy,
and you never cease to gather a people to yourself,
so that from the rising of the sun to its setting
a pure sacrifice may be offered to your name.

Therefore, O Lord, we humbly implore you:
by the same Spirit graciously make holy
these gifts we have brought to you for
consecration,
that they may become the Body and ✚ Blood
of your Son our Lord Jesus Christ,
at whose command we celebrate these mysteries.

For on the night he was betrayed
he himself took bread,
and, giving you thanks, he said the blessing,
broke the bread and gave it to his disciples,
saying:

Take this, all of you, and eat of it,
for this is my Body,
which will be given up for you.

In a similar way, when supper was ended,
he took the chalice,

and, giving you thanks, he said the blessing,
and gave the chalice to his disciples, saying:

3

Take this, all of you, and drink from it,
for this is the chalice of my Blood,
the Blood of the new and eternal covenant,
which will be poured out for you and for many
for the forgiveness of sins.

Do this in memory of me.

Priest: The mystery of faith. *(Memorial Acclamation)*

PEOPLE:

A **We proclaim your Death, O Lord,**
   and profess your Resurrection
   until you come again.

B **When we eat this Bread and drink this Cup,**
   we proclaim your Death, O Lord,
   until you come again.

C **Save us, Savior of the world,**
   for by your Cross and Resurrection
   you have set us free.

Therefore, O Lord, as we celebrate the memorial
of the saving Passion of your Son,
his wondrous Resurrection
and Ascension into heaven,
and as we look forward to his second coming,
we offer you in thanksgiving
this holy and living sacrifice.

Look, we pray, upon the oblation of your Church
and, recognizing the sacrificial Victim by whose
    death
you willed to reconcile us to yourself,

3 grant that we, who are nourished
by the Body and Blood of your Son
and filled with his Holy Spirit,
may become one body, one spirit in Christ.

May he make of us
an eternal offering to you,
so that we may obtain an inheritance with your elect,
especially with the most Blessed Virgin Mary,
    Mother of God,
with blessed Joseph, her Spouse,
with your blessed Apostles and glorious Martyrs
(with Saint *N*.: the Saint of the day or Patron Saint)
and with all the Saints,
on whose constant intercession in your presence
we rely for unfailing help.

May this Sacrifice of our reconciliation,
we pray, O Lord,
advance the peace and salvation of all the world.
Be pleased to confirm in faith and charity
your pilgrim Church on earth,
with your servant *N*. our Pope and *N*. our Bishop,
the Order of Bishops, all the clergy,
and the entire people you have gained for your
    own.

Listen graciously to the prayers of this family,
whom you have summoned before you:
in your compassion, O merciful Father,
gather to yourself all your children
scattered throughout the world.

† To our departed brothers and sisters
and to all who were pleasing to you
at their passing from this life,
give kind admittance to your kingdom.

There we hope to enjoy for ever the fullness of
    your glory
through Christ our Lord,
through whom you bestow on the world all that
    is good. †

(Concluding Doxology)

Through him, and with him, and in him,
O God, almighty Father,
in the unity of the Holy Spirit,
all glory and honor is yours,
for ever and ever.

The people acclaim: **Amen.**

      Continue with the Mass, as on p. 72.

---

† *In Masses for the Dead the following may be said:*

†Remember your servant *N.*
whom you have called (today)
from this world to yourself.
Grant that he (she) who was united with your Son in a
    death like his,
may also be one with him in his Resurrection,
when from the earth
he will raise up in the flesh those who have died,
and transform our lowly body
after the pattern of his own glorious body.
To our departed brothers and sisters, too,
and to all who were pleasing to you
at their passing from this life,
give kind admittance to your kingdom.
There we hope to enjoy for ever the fullness of your glory,
when you will wipe away every tear from our eyes.
For seeing you, our God, as you are,
we shall be like you for all the ages
and praise you without end,
through Christ our Lord,
through whom you bestow on the world all that is good. †

EUCHARISTIC PRAYER No. 4

℣. The Lord be with you. **STAND**
℟. **And with your spirit.**

℣. Lift up your hearts.
℟. **We lift them up to the Lord.**

℣. Let us give thanks to the Lord our God.
℟. **It is right and just.**

It is truly right to give you thanks,
truly just to give you glory, Father most holy,
for you are the one God living and true,
existing before all ages and abiding for all eternity,
dwelling in unapproachable light;
yet you, who alone are good, the source of life,
have made all that is,
so that you might fill your creatures with blessings
and bring joy to many of them by the glory of your
    light.

And so, in your presence are countless hosts of
    Angels,
who serve you day and night
and, gazing upon the glory of your face,
glorify you without ceasing.

With them we, too, confess your name in exultation,
giving voice to every creature under heaven,
as we acclaim:

Holy, Holy, Holy Lord God of hosts.
Heaven and earth are full of your glory.
Hosanna in the highest.

**Blessed is he who comes in the name of the Lord.
Hosanna in the highest.**

4

`KNEEL`

We give you praise, Father most holy,
for you are great
and you have fashioned all your works
in wisdom and in love.
You formed man in your own image
and entrusted the whole world to his care,
so that in serving you alone, the Creator,
he might have dominion over all creatures.
And when through disobedience he had lost your
    friendship,
you did not abandon him to the domain of death.
For you came in mercy to the aid of all,
so that those who seek might find you.
Time and again you offered them covenants
and through the prophets
taught them to look forward to salvation.

And you so loved the world, Father most holy,
that in the fullness of time
you sent your Only Begotten Son to be our Savior.
Made incarnate by the Holy Spirit
and born of the Virgin Mary,
he shared our human nature
in all things but sin.
To the poor he proclaimed the good news of
    salvation,
to prisoners, freedom,
and to the sorrowful of heart, joy.
To accomplish your plan,
he gave himself up to death,
and, rising from the dead,
he destroyed death and restored life.

4 And that we might live no longer for ourselves
but for him who died and rose again for us,
he sent the Holy Spirit from you, Father,
as the first fruits for those who believe,
so that, bringing to perfection his work in the world,
he might sanctify creation to the full.

Therefore, O Lord, we pray:
may this same Holy Spirit
graciously sanctify these offerings,
that they may become
the Body and ✚ Blood of our Lord Jesus Christ
for the celebration of this great mystery,
which he himself left us
as an eternal covenant.

For when the hour had come
for him to be glorified by you, Father most holy,
having loved his own who were in the world,
he loved them to the end:
and while they were at supper,
he took bread, blessed and broke it,
and gave it to his disciples, saying:

Take this, all of you, and eat of it,
for this is my Body,
which will be given up for you.

In a similar way,
taking the chalice filled with the fruit of the vine,
he gave thanks,
and gave the chalice to his disciples, saying:

Take this, all of you, and drink from it,
for this is the chalice of my Blood,
the Blood of the new and eternal covenant,

4

*which will be poured out for you and for many
for the forgiveness of sins.*

Do this in memory of me.

Priest: The mystery of faith. *(Memorial Acclamation)*

PEOPLE:

A   We proclaim your Death, O Lord,
     and profess your Resurrection
     until you come again.

B   When we eat this Bread and drink this Cup,
     we proclaim your Death, O Lord,
     until you come again.

C   Save us, Savior of the world,
     for by your Cross and Resurrection
     you have set us free.

Therefore, O Lord,
as we now celebrate the memorial of our
    redemption,
we remember Christ's Death
and his descent to the realm of the dead,
we proclaim his Resurrection
and his Ascension to your right hand,
and, as we await his coming in glory,
we offer you his Body and Blood,
the sacrifice acceptable to you
which brings salvation to the whole world.

Look, O Lord, upon the Sacrifice
which you yourself have provided for your Church,
and grant in your loving kindness
to all who partake of this one Bread and one
    Chalice
that, gathered into one body by the Holy Spirit,

4 they may truly become a living sacrifice in Christ
to the praise of your glory.

Therefore, Lord, remember now
all for whom we offer this sacrifice:
especially your servant N. our Pope,
N. our Bishop, and the whole Order of Bishops,
all the clergy,
those who take part in this offering,
those gathered here before you,
your entire people,
and all who seek you with a sincere heart.

Remember also
those who have died in the peace of your Christ
and all the dead,
whose faith you alone have known.

To all of us, your children,
grant, O merciful Father,
that we may enter into a heavenly inheritance
with the Blessed Virgin Mary, Mother of God,
with blessed Joseph, her Spouse,
and with your Apostles and Saints in your kingdom.
There, with the whole of creation,
freed from the corruption of sin and death,
may we glorify you through Christ our Lord,
through whom you bestow on the world all that
   is good.

(Concluding Doxology)

Through him, and with him, and in him,
O God, almighty Father,
in the unity of the Holy Spirit,
all glory and honor is yours,
for ever and ever.

The people acclaim: **Amen.**

Continue with the Mass, as on p. 72.

EUCHARISTIC PRAYER FOR
RECONCILIATION I

℣. The Lord be with you.

℞. **And with your spirit.**

℣. Lift up your hearts.

℞. **We lift them up to the Lord.**

℣. Let us give thanks to the Lord our God.

℞. **It is right and just.**

It is truly right and just
that we should always give you thanks,
Lord, holy Father, almighty and eternal God.

For you do not cease to spur us on
to possess a more abundant life
and, being rich in mercy,
you constantly offer pardon
and call on sinners
to trust in your forgiveness alone.

Never did you turn away from us,
and, though time and again we have broken your
     covenant,
you have bound the human family to yourself
through Jesus your Son, our Redeemer,
with a new bond of love so tight
that it can never be undone.

Even now you set before your people
a time of grace and reconciliation,
and, as they turn back to you in spirit,
you grant them hope in Christ Jesus
and a desire to be of service to all,

43

R
1

while they entrust themselves
more fully to the Holy Spirit.

And so, filled with wonder,
we extol the power of your love,
and, proclaiming our joy
at the salvation that comes from you,
we join in the heavenly hymn of countless hosts,
as without end we acclaim:

Holy, Holy, Holy Lord God of hosts.
Heaven and earth are full of your glory.
Hosanna in the highest.
Blessed is he who comes in the name of the Lord.
Hosanna in the highest.

`KNEEL`

You are indeed Holy, O Lord,
and from the world's beginning
are ceaselessly at work,
so that the human race may become holy,
just as you yourself are holy.

Look, we pray, upon your people's offerings
and pour out on them the power of your Spirit,
that they may become the Body and ✠ Blood
of your beloved Son, Jesus Christ,
in whom we, too, are your sons and daughters.

Indeed, though we once were lost
and could not approach you,
you loved us with the greatest love:
for your Son, who alone is just,
handed himself over to death,

R 1

and did not disdain to be nailed for our sake
to the wood of the Cross.

But before his arms were outstretched between heaven and earth,
to become the lasting sign of your covenant,
he desired to celebrate the Passover with his disciples.

As he ate with them,
he took bread
and, giving you thanks, he said the blessing,
broke the bread and gave it to them, saying:

Take this, all of you, and eat of it,
for this is my Body,
which will be given up for you.

In a similar way, when supper was ended,
knowing that he was about to reconcile all things in himself
through his Blood to be shed on the Cross,
he took the chalice, filled with the fruit of the vine,
and once more giving you thanks,
handed the chalice to his disciples, saying:

Take this, all of you, and drink from it,
for this is the chalice of my Blood,
the Blood of the new and eternal covenant,
which will be poured out for you and for many
for the forgiveness of sins.
Do this in memory of me.

R 1

Priest: The mystery of faith. *(Memorial Acclamation)*

PEOPLE:

A We proclaim your Death, O Lord,
and profess your Resurrection
until you come again.

B When we eat this Bread and drink this Cup,
we proclaim your Death, O Lord,
until you come again.

C Save us, Savior of the world,
for by your Cross and Resurrection
you have set us free.

Therefore, as we celebrate
the memorial of your Son Jesus Christ,
who is our Passover and our surest peace,
we celebrate his Death and Resurrection from the
dead,
and looking forward to his blessed Coming,
we offer you, who are our faithful and merciful
God,
this sacrificial Victim
who reconciles to you the human race.

Look kindly, most compassionate Father,
on those you unite to yourself
by the Sacrifice of your Son,
and grant that, by the power of the Holy Spirit,
as they partake of this one Bread and one
Chalice,
they may be gathered into one Body in Christ,
who heals every division.

R 1

Be pleased to keep us always
in communion of mind and heart,
together with N. our Pope and N. our Bishop.
Help us to work together
for the coming of your Kingdom,
until the hour when we stand before you,
Saints among the Saints in the halls of heaven,
with the Blessed Virgin Mary, Mother of God,
the blessed Apostles and all the Saints,
and with our deceased brothers and sisters,
whom we humbly commend to your mercy.

Then, freed at last from the wound of corruption
and made fully into a new creation,
we shall sing to you with gladness
the thanksgiving of Christ,
who lives for all eternity.

(Concluding Doxology)

Through him, and with him, and in him,
O God, almighty Father,
in the unity of the Holy Spirit,
all glory and honor is yours,
for ever and ever.

The people acclaim: **Amen.**

Continue with the Mass, as on p. 72.

STAND

℣. The Lord be with you.

℟. **And with your spirit.**

℣. Lift up your hearts.

℟. **We lift them up to the Lord.**

℣. Let us give thanks to the Lord our God.

℟. **It is right and just.**

It is truly right and just
that we should give you thanks and praise,
O God, almighty Father,
for all you do in this world,
through our Lord Jesus Christ.

For though the human race
is divided by dissension and discord,
yet we know that by testing us
you change our hearts
to prepare them for reconciliation.

Even more, by your Spirit you move human hearts
that enemies may speak to each other again,
adversaries join hands,
and peoples seek to meet together.

By the working of your power
it comes about, O Lord,
that hatred is overcome by love,
revenge gives way to forgiveness,
and discord is changed to mutual respect.

Therefore, as we give you ceaseless thanks
with the choirs of heaven,

we cry out to your majesty on earth,
and without end we acclaim:

Holy, Holy, Holy Lord God of hosts.
Heaven and earth are full of your glory.
Hosanna in the highest.
Blessed is he who comes in the name of the Lord.
Hosanna in the highest.

You, therefore, almighty Father,   `KNEEL`
we bless through Jesus Christ your Son,
who comes in your name.
He himself is the Word that brings salvation,
the hand you extend to sinners,
the way by which your peace is offered to us.
When we ourselves had turned away from you
on account of our sins,
you brought us back to be reconciled, O Lord,
so that, converted at last to you,
we might love one another
through your Son,
whom for our sake you handed over to death.

And now, celebrating the reconciliation
Christ has brought us,
we entreat you:
sanctify these gifts by the outpouring of your Spirit,
that they may become the Body and ✠ Blood of
 your Son,
whose command we fulfill
when we celebrate these mysteries.

For when about to give his life to set us free,
as he reclined at supper,
he himself took bread into his hands,

R 2

and, giving you thanks, he said the blessing,
broke the bread and gave it to his disciples, saying:

Take this, all of you, and eat of it,
for this is my Body,
which will be given up for you.

In a similar way, on that same evening,
he took the chalice of blessing in his hands,
confessing your mercy,
and gave the chalice to his disciples, saying:

Take this, all of you, and drink from it,
for this is the chalice of my Blood,
the Blood of the new and eternal covenant,
which will be poured out for you and for many
for the forgiveness of sins.

Do this in memory of me.

Priest: The mystery of faith. *(Memorial Acclamation)*

PEOPLE:

A We proclaim your Death, O Lord,
　　and profess your Resurrection
　　until you come again.

B When we eat this Bread and drink this Cup,
　　we proclaim your Death, O Lord,
　　until you come again.

C Save us, Savior of the world,
　　for by your Cross and Resurrection
　　you have set us free.

Celebrating, therefore, the memorial
of the Death and Resurrection of your Son,
who left us this pledge of his love,
we offer you what you have bestowed on us,
the Sacrifice of perfect reconciliation.

R 2

Holy Father, we humbly beseech you
to accept us also, together with your Son,
and in this saving banquet
graciously to endow us with his very Spirit,
who takes away everything
that estranges us from one another.

May he make your Church a sign of unity
and an instrument of your peace among all people
and may he keep us in communion
with N. our Pope and N. our Bishop
and all the Bishops
and your entire people.

Just as you have gathered us now at the table of
    your Son,
so also bring us together,
with the glorious Virgin Mary, Mother of God,
with your blessed Apostles and all the Saints,
with our brothers and sisters
and those of every race and tongue
who have died in your friendship.
Bring us to share with them the unending banquet
    of unity
in a new heaven and a new earth,
where the fullness of your peace will shine forth
in Christ Jesus our Lord.

(Concluding Doxology)

Through him, and with him, and in him,
O God, almighty Father,
in the unity of the Holy Spirit,
all glory and honor is yours,
for ever and ever.

The people acclaim: **Amen.**

Continue with the Mass, as on p. 72.

V 1 EUCHARISTIC PRAYER FOR USE IN MASSES FOR VARIOUS NEEDS I

STAND

℣. The Lord be with you.

℟. **And with your spirit.**

℣. Lift up your hearts.

℟. **We lift them up to the Lord.**

℣. Let us give thanks to the Lord our God.

℟. **It is right and just.**

It is truly right and just to give you thanks
and raise to you a hymn of glory and praise,
O Lord, Father of infinite goodness.

For by the word of your Son's Gospel
you have brought together one Church
from every people, tongue, and nation,
and, having filled her with life by the power of
    your Spirit,
you never cease through her
to gather the whole human race into one.

Manifesting the covenant of your love,
she dispenses without ceasing
the blessed hope of your Kingdom
and shines bright as the sign of your faithfulness,
which in Christ Jesus our Lord
you promised would last for eternity.

And so, with all the Powers of heaven,
we worship you constantly on earth,
while, with all the Church,
as one voice we acclaim:

V
1

Holy, Holy, Holy Lord God of hosts.
Heaven and earth are full of your glory.
Hosanna in the highest.
Blessed is he who comes in the name of the Lord.
Hosanna in the highest.

KNEEL

You are indeed Holy and to be glorified, O God,
who love the human race
and who always walk with us on the journey of life.
Blessed indeed is your Son,
present in our midst
when we are gathered by his love
and when, as once for the disciples, so now for us,
he opens the Scriptures and breaks the bread.

Therefore, Father most merciful,
we ask that you send forth your Holy Spirit
to sanctify these gifts of bread and wine,
that they may become for us
the Body and ✛ Blood
of our Lord Jesus Christ.

On the day before he was to suffer,
on the night of the Last Supper,
he took bread and said the blessing,
broke the bread and gave it to his disciples, saying:

Take this, all of you, and eat of it,
for this is my Body,
which will be given up for you.

In a similar way, when supper was ended,
he took the chalice, gave you thanks
and gave the chalice to his disciples, saying:

V 1

Take this, all of you, and drink from it,
for this is the chalice of my Blood,
the Blood of the new and eternal covenant,
which will be poured out for you and for many
for the forgiveness of sins.

Do this in memory of me.

Priest:　The mystery of faith.　*(Memorial Acclamation)*

PEOPLE:

A　We proclaim your Death, O Lord,
　　and profess your Resurrection
　　until you come again.

B　When we eat this Bread and drink this Cup,
　　we proclaim your Death, O Lord,
　　until you come again.

C　Save us, Savior of the world,
　　for by your Cross and Resurrection
　　you have set us free.

Therefore, holy Father,
as we celebrate the memorial of Christ your Son,
　our Savior,
whom you led through his Passion and Death on
　the Cross
to the glory of the Resurrection,
and whom you have seated at your right hand,
we proclaim the work of your love until he comes
　again
and we offer you the Bread of life
and the Chalice of blessing.

Look with favor on the oblation of your Church,
in which we show forth

the paschal Sacrifice of Christ that has been handed on to us,
and grant that, by the power of the Spirit of your love,
we may be counted now and until the day of eternity
among the members of your Son,
in whose Body and Blood we have communion.

Lord, renew your Church (which is in *N.*)
by the light of the Gospel.
Strengthen the bond of unity
between the faithful and the pastors of your people,
together with *N.* our Pope, *N.* our Bishop,
and the whole Order of Bishops,
that in a world torn by strife
your people may shine forth
as a prophetic sign of unity and concord.

Remember our brothers and sisters (*N.* and *N.*),
who have fallen asleep in the peace of your Christ,
and all the dead, whose faith you alone have known.
Admit them to rejoice in the light of your face,
and in the resurrection give them the fullness of life.

Grant also to us,
when our earthly pilgrimage is done,
that we may come to an eternal dwelling place
and live with you for ever;
there, in communion with the Blessed Virgin Mary, Mother of God,
with the Apostles and Martyrs,

V1 (with Saint *N.*: the Saint of the day or Patron)
and with all the Saints,
we shall praise and exalt you
through Jesus Christ, your Son.

(Concluding Doxology)

Through him, and with him, and in him,
O God, almighty Father,
in the unity of the Holy Spirit,
all glory and honor is yours,
for ever and ever.

The people acclaim: **Amen.**

Continue with the Mass, as on p. 72.

EUCHARISTIC PRAYER FOR USE IN MASSES FOR VARIOUS NEEDS II

V 2

STAND

℣. The Lord be with you.
℟. **And with your spirit.**

℣. Lift up your hearts.
℟. **We lift them up to the Lord.**

℣. Let us give thanks to the Lord our God.
℟. **It is right and just.**

It is truly right and just, our duty and our
    salvation,
always and everywhere to give you thanks,
Lord, holy Father,
creator of the world and source of all life.

For you never forsake the works of your wisdom,
but by your providence are even now at work in
    our midst.
With mighty hand and outstretched arm
you led your people Israel through the desert.
Now, as your Church makes her pilgrim journey
    in the world,
you always accompany her
by the power of the Holy Spirit
and lead her along the paths of time
to the eternal joy of your Kingdom,
through Christ our Lord.

And so, with the Angels and Saints,
we, too, sing the hymn of your glory,
as without end we acclaim:

V 2

Holy, Holy, Holy Lord God of hosts.
Heaven and earth are full of your glory.
Hosanna in the highest.
Blessed is he who comes in the name of the Lord.
Hosanna in the highest.

KNEEL

You are indeed Holy and to be glorified, O God,
who love the human race
and who always walk with us on the journey of life.
Blessed indeed is your Son,
present in our midst
when we are gathered by his love,
and when, as once for the disciples, so now for us,
he opens the Scriptures and breaks the bread.

Therefore, Father most merciful,
we ask that you send forth your Holy Spirit
to sanctify these gifts of bread and wine,
that they may become for us
the Body and ✛ Blood
of our Lord Jesus Christ.

On the day before he was to suffer,
on the night of the Last Supper,
he took bread and said the blessing,
broke the bread and gave it to his disciples, saying:

Take this, all of you, and eat of it,
for this is my Body,
which will be given up for you.

In a similar way, when supper was ended,
he took the chalice, gave you thanks
and gave the chalice to his disciples, saying:

Take this, all of you, and drink from it,
for this is the chalice of my Blood,
the Blood of the new and eternal covenant,
which will be poured out for you and for many
for the forgiveness of sins.

Do this in memory of me.

Priest: The mystery of faith. *(Memorial Acclamation)*

PEOPLE:

A We proclaim your Death, O Lord,
and profess your Resurrection
until you come again.

B When we eat this Bread and drink this Cup,
we proclaim your Death, O Lord,
until you come again.

C Save us, Savior of the world,
for by your Cross and Resurrection
you have set us free.

Therefore, holy Father,
as we celebrate the memorial of Christ your Son,
   our Savior,
whom you led through his Passion and Death on
   the Cross
to the glory of the Resurrection,
and whom you have seated at your right hand,
we proclaim the work of your love until he comes
   again
and we offer you the Bread of life
and the Chalice of blessing.

Look with favor on the oblation of your Church,
in which we show forth

**V
2**

the paschal Sacrifice of Christ that has been
     handed on to us,
and grant that, by the power of the Spirit of your
     love,
we may be counted now and until the day of
     eternity
among the members of your Son,
in whose Body and Blood we have communion.

And so, having called us to your table, Lord,
confirm us in unity,
so that, together with N. our Pope and N. our
     Bishop,
with all Bishops, Priests and Deacons,
and your entire people,
as we walk your ways with faith and hope,
we may strive to bring joy and trust into the world.

Remember our brothers and sisters (N. and N.),
who have fallen asleep in the peace of your Christ,
and all the dead, whose faith you alone have
     known.
Admit them to rejoice in the light of your face,
and in the resurrection give them the fullness of
     life.

Grant also to us,
when our earthly pilgrimage is done,
that we may come to an eternal dwelling place
and live with you for ever;
there, in communion with the Blessed Virgin Mary,
     Mother of God,
with the Apostles and Martyrs,
(with Saint N.: the Saint of the day or Patron)

V 2

and with all the Saints,
we shall praise and exalt you
through Jesus Christ, your Son.

(Concluding Doxology)

Through him, and with him, and in him,
O God, almighty Father,
in the unity of the Holy Spirit,
all glory and honor is yours,
for ever and ever.

The people acclaim: **Amen.**

Continue with the Mass, as on p. 72.

STAND

℣. The Lord be with you.
℟. **And with your spirit.**

℣. Lift up your hearts.
℟. **We lift them up to the Lord.**

℣. Let us give thanks to the Lord our God.
℟. **It is right and just.**

It is truly right and just, our duty and our salvation,
always and everywhere to give you thanks,
holy Father, Lord of heaven and earth,
through Christ our Lord.

For by your Word you created the world
and you govern all things in harmony.
You gave us the same Word made flesh as Mediator,
and he has spoken your words to us
and called us to follow him.
He is the way that leads us to you,
the truth that sets us free,
the life that fills us with gladness.

Through your Son
you gather men and women,
whom you made for the glory of your name,
into one family,
redeemed by the Blood of his Cross
and signed with the seal of the Spirit.

Therefore, now and for ages unending,
with all the Angels,

**V
3**

we proclaim your glory,
as in joyful celebration we acclaim:

Holy, Holy, Holy Lord God of hosts.
Heaven and earth are full of your glory.
Hosanna in the highest.
Blessed is he who comes in the name of the Lord.
Hosanna in the highest.

KNEEL

You are indeed Holy and to be glorified, O God,
who love the human race
and who always walk with us on the journey of life.
Blessed indeed is your Son,
present in our midst
when we are gathered by his love
and when, as once for the disciples, so now for us,
he opens the Scriptures and breaks the bread.

Therefore, Father most merciful,
we ask that you send forth your Holy Spirit
to sanctify these gifts of bread and wine,
that they may become for us
the Body and ✝ Blood
of our Lord Jesus Christ.

On the day before he was to suffer,
on the night of the Last Supper,
he took bread and said the blessing,
broke the bread and gave it to his disciples, saying:

Take this, all of you, and eat of it,
for this is my Body,
which will be given up for you.

V 3 In a similar way, when supper was ended,
he took the chalice, gave you thanks
and gave the chalice to his disciples, saying:

Take this, all of you, and drink from it,
for this is the chalice of my Blood,
the Blood of the new and eternal covenant,
which will be poured out for you and for many
for the forgiveness of sins.

Do this in memory of me.

Priest: The mystery of faith. *(Memorial Acclamation)*

PEOPLE:

A **We proclaim your Death, O Lord,**
and profess your Resurrection
until you come again.

B **When we eat this Bread and drink this Cup,**
we proclaim your Death, O Lord,
until you come again.

C **Save us, Savior of the world,**
for by your Cross and Resurrection
you have set us free.

Therefore, holy Father,
as we celebrate the memorial of Christ your Son,
    our Savior,
whom you led through his Passion and Death on
    the Cross
to the glory of the Resurrection,
and whom you have seated at your right hand,
we proclaim the work of your love until he comes
    again
and we offer you the Bread of life
and the Chalice of blessing.

Look with favor on the oblation of your Church,
in which we show forth
the paschal Sacrifice of Christ that has been
     handed on to us,
and grant that, by the power of the Spirit of your
     love,
we may be counted now and until the day of
     eternity
among the members of your Son,
in whose Body and Blood we have communion.

By our partaking of this mystery, almighty Father,
give us life through your Spirit,
grant that we may be conformed to the image of
     your Son,
and confirm us in the bond of communion,
together with *N.* our Pope and *N.* our Bishop,
with all other Bishops,
with Priests and Deacons,
and with your entire people.

Grant that all the faithful of the Church,
looking into the signs of the times by the light of
     faith,
may constantly devote themselves
to the service of the Gospel.

Keep us attentive to the needs of all
that, sharing their grief and pain,
their joy and hope,
we may faithfully bring them the good news of
     salvation
and go forward with them
along the way of your Kingdom.

V 3

Remember our brothers and sisters (*N.* and *N.*),
who have fallen asleep in the peace of your Christ,
and all the dead, whose faith you alone have known.
Admit them to rejoice in the light of your face,
and in the resurrection give them the fullness of life.

Grant also to us,
when our earthly pilgrimage is done,
that we may come to an eternal dwelling place
and live with you for ever;
there, in communion with the Blessed Virgin Mary,
   Mother of God,
with the Apostles and Martyrs,
(with Saint *N.*: the Saint of the day or Patron)
and with all the Saints,
we shall praise and exalt you
through Jesus Christ, your Son.

(Concluding Doxology)

Through him, and with him, and in him,
O God, almighty Father,
in the unity of the Holy Spirit,
all glory and honor is yours,
for ever and ever.

The people acclaim: **Amen.**

Continue with the Mass, as on p. 72.

EUCHARISTIC PRAYER FOR USE IN MASSES FOR VARIOUS NEEDS IV

STAND

℣. The Lord be with you.
℟. **And with your spirit.**

℣. Lift up your hearts.
℟. **We lift them up to the Lord.**

℣. Let us give thanks to the Lord our God.
℟. **It is right and just.**

It is truly right and just, our duty and our salvation,
always and everywhere to give you thanks,
Father of mercies and faithful God.

For you have given us Jesus Christ, your Son,
as our Lord and Redeemer.

He always showed compassion
for children and for the poor,
for the sick and for sinners,
and he became a neighbor
to the oppressed and the afflicted.

By word and deed he announced to the world
that you are our Father
and that you care for all your sons and daughters.

And so, with all the Angels and Saints,
we exalt and bless your name
and sing the hymn of your glory,
as without end we acclaim:

**V
4**

Holy, Holy, Holy Lord God of hosts.
Heaven and earth are full of your glory.
Hosanna in the highest.
Blessed is he who comes in the name of the Lord.
Hosanna in the highest.

KNEEL

You are indeed Holy and to be glorified, O God,
who love the human race
and who always walk with us on the journey of life.
Blessed indeed is your Son,
present in our midst
when we are gathered by his love
and when, as once for the disciples, so now for us,
he opens the Scriptures and breaks the bread.

Therefore, Father most merciful,
we ask that you send forth your Holy Spirit
to sanctify these gifts of bread and wine,
that they may become for us
the Body and ✜ Blood
of our Lord Jesus Christ.

On the day before he was to suffer,
on the night of the Last Supper,
he took bread and said the blessing,
broke the bread and gave it to his disciples, saying:

Take this, all of you, and eat of it,
for this is my Body,
which will be given up for you.

In a similar way, when supper was ended,
he took the chalice, gave you thanks
and gave the chalice to his disciples, saying:

Take this, all of you, and drink from it,
for this is the chalice of my Blood,
the Blood of the new and eternal covenant,
which will be poured out for you and for many
for the forgiveness of sins.

Do this in memory of me.

Priest: The mystery of faith. *(Memorial Acclamation)*

PEOPLE:

A **We proclaim your Death, O Lord,**
and profess your Resurrection
until you come again.

B **When we eat this Bread and drink this Cup,**
we proclaim your Death, O Lord,
until you come again.

C **Save us, Savior of the world,**
for by your Cross and Resurrection
you have set us free.

Therefore, holy Father,
as we celebrate the memorial of Christ your Son,
    our Savior,
whom you led through his Passion and Death on
    the Cross
to the glory of the Resurrection,
and whom you have seated at your right hand,
we proclaim the work of your love until he comes
    again
and we offer you the Bread of life
and the Chalice of blessing.

Look with favor on the oblation of your Church,
in which we show forth

V 4 the paschal Sacrifice of Christ that has been
handed on to us,
and grant that, by the power of the Spirit of your
love,
we may be counted now and until the day of
eternity
among the members of your Son,
in whose Body and Blood we have communion.

Bring your Church, O Lord,
to perfect faith and charity,
together with *N.* our Pope and *N.* our Bishop,
with all Bishops, Priests and Deacons,
and the entire people you have made your own.

Open our eyes
to the needs of our brothers and sisters;
inspire in us words and actions
to comfort those who labor and are burdened.
Make us serve them truly,
after the example of Christ and at his command.
And may your Church stand as a living witness
to truth and freedom,
to peace and justice,
that all people may be raised up to a new hope.

Remember our brothers and sisters (*N.* and *N.*),
who have fallen asleep in the peace of your Christ,
and all the dead, whose faith you alone have
known.
Admit them to rejoice in the light of your face,
and in the resurrection give them the fullness of
life.

V 4

Grant also to us,
when our earthly pilgrimage is done,
that we may come to an eternal dwelling place
and live with you for ever;
there, in communion with the Blessed Virgin Mary,
    Mother of God,
with the Apostles and Martyrs,
(with Saint *N.:* the Saint of the day or Patron)
and with all the Saints,
we shall praise and exalt you
through Jesus Christ, your Son.

(Concluding Doxology)

Through him, and with him, and in him,
O God, almighty Father,
in the unity of the Holy Spirit,
all glory and honor is yours,
for ever and ever.

The people acclaim: **Amen.**

Continue with the Mass, as on p. 72.

THE COMMUNION RITE

To prepare for the paschal meal, to welcome the Lord, we pray for forgiveness and exchange a sign of peace. Before eating Christ's Body and drinking his Blood, we must be one with him and with all our brothers and sisters in the Church.

24 THE LORD'S PRAYER

`STAND`

Priest: At the Savior's command
and formed by divine teaching,
we dare to say:

Priest and **PEOPLE:**

Our Father, who art in heaven,
hallowed be thy name;
thy kingdom come,
thy will be done
on earth as it is in heaven.
Give us this day our daily bread,
and forgive us our trespasses,
as we forgive those who trespass against us;
and lead us not into temptation,
but deliver us from evil.

Priest: Deliver us, Lord, we pray, from every evil,
graciously grant us peace in our days,
that, by the help of your mercy,
we may be always free from sin
and safe from all distress,
as we await the blessed hope
and the coming of our Savior, Jesus Christ.

72

PEOPLE: **For the kingdom,**
the power and the glory are yours
now and for ever.

25 SIGN OF PEACE

The Church is a community of Christians joined by the Spirit in love. It needs to express, deepen, and restore its peaceful unity before eating the one Body of the Lord and drinking from the one cup of salvation. We do this by a sign of peace.

The Priest says the prayer for peace:

Lord Jesus Christ,
who said to your Apostles:
Peace I leave you, my peace I give you,
look not on our sins,
but on the faith of your Church,
and graciously grant her peace and unity
in accordance with your will.
Who live and reign for ever and ever.

PEOPLE: **Amen.**

Priest: The peace of the Lord be with you always.

PEOPLE: **And with your spirit.**

Deacon (or Priest):
  Let us offer each other the sign of peace.

The people exchange a sign of peace, communion and charity, according to local customs.

26 LAMB OF GOD

Christians are gathered for the "breaking of the bread," another name for the Mass. In Communion, though many we are made one body in the one bread, which is Christ.

The Priest breaks the host over the paten and places a small piece in the chalice, saying quietly:

May this mingling of the Body and Blood
of our Lord Jesus Christ
bring eternal life to us who receive it.

Meanwhile the following is sung or said:

PEOPLE:

> **Lamb of God, you take away the sins of the world,**
> > **have mercy on us.**
> **Lamb of God, you take away the sins of the world,**
> > **have mercy on us.**
> **Lamb of God, you take away the sins of the world,**
> > **grant us peace.**

The invocation may even be repeated several times if the breaking of the bread is prolonged. Only the final time, however, is grant us peace *said.*

KNEEL

We pray in silence and then voice words of humility and hope as our final preparation before meeting Christ in the Eucharist.

Before Communion, the Priest says quietly one of the following prayers:

Lord Jesus Christ, Son of the living God,
who, by the will of the Father
and the work of the Holy Spirit,
through your Death gave life to the world,
free me by this, your most holy Body and Blood,
from all my sins and from every evil;
keep me always faithful to your commandments,
and never let me be parted from you.

—————————— **OR** ——————————

May the receiving of your Body and Blood,
Lord Jesus Christ,
not bring me to judgment and condemnation,
but through your loving mercy
be for me protection in mind and body
and a healing remedy.

27 INVITATION TO COMMUNION*

*The Priest genuflects, takes the host and, holding it
slightly raised above the paten or above the chalice,
while facing the people, says aloud:*

Priest: Behold the Lamb of God,
behold him who takes away the sins of the
world.
Blessed are those called to the supper of
the Lamb.

Priest and **PEOPLE** (once only):

**Lord, I am not worthy
that you should enter under my roof,
but only say the word
and my soul shall be healed.**

*Before reverently consuming the Body of Christ, the Priest
says quietly:*

May the Body of Christ
keep me safe for eternal life.

*Then, before reverently consuming the Blood of Christ, he
takes the chalice and says quietly:*

May the Blood of Christ
keep me safe for eternal life.

* *See Guidelines on pp. 664-665.*

28 COMMUNION

He then gives Communion to the people.

Priest: The Body of Christ. Communicant: **Amen.**
Priest: The Blood of Christ. Communicant: **Amen.**

The Communion Psalm or other appropriate chant is sung while Communion is given to the faithful. If there is no singing, the Communion Antiphon is said.

→ **Turn to Today's Mass**

The vessels are purified by the Priest or Deacon or acolyte. Meanwhile he says quietly:

What has passed our lips as food, O Lord,
may we possess in purity of heart,
that what has been given to us in time
may be our healing for eternity.

After Communion there may be a period of sacred silence, or a canticle of praise or a hymn may be sung.

29 PRAYER AFTER COMMUNION STAND

The Priest prays in our name that we may live the life of faith since we have been strengthened by Christ himself. Our *Amen* makes his prayer our own.

Priest: Let us pray.
Priest and people may pray silently for a while unless silence has just been observed. Then the Priest says the Prayer after Communion.

→ **Turn to Today's Mass**

At the end, **PEOPLE: Amen.**

THE CONCLUDING RITES

We have heard God's Word and eaten the Body of Christ. Now it is time for us to leave, to do good works, to praise and bless the Lord in our daily lives.

30 SOLEMN BLESSING `STAND`

After any brief announcements, the Blessing and Dismissal follow:

Priest: The Lord be with you.

PEOPLE: And with your spirit.

31 FINAL BLESSING

Priest: May almighty God bless you,
the Father, and the Son, ✠ and the Holy Spirit.

PEOPLE: Amen.

On certain days or occasions, this formula of blessing is preceded, in accordance with the rubrics, by another more solemn formula of blessing (pp. 97-105) or by a prayer over the people (pp. 105-110).

32 DISMISSAL

Deacon (or Priest):

A Go forth, the Mass is ended.

B Go and announce the Gospel of the Lord.

C Go in peace, glorifying the Lord by your life.

D Go in peace.

PEOPLE: Thanks be to God.

If any liturgical service follows immediately, the rites of dismissal are omitted.

RITE FOR THE BLESSING
AND SPRINKLING OF WATER

If this rite is celebrated during Mass, it takes the place of the usual Penitential Act at the beginning of Mass.

After the greeting, the Priest stands at his chair and faces the people. With a vessel containing the water to be blessed before him, he calls upon the people to pray in these or similar words:

Dear brethren (brothers and sisters),
let us humbly beseech the Lord our God
to bless this water he has created,
which will be sprinkled on us
as a memorial of our Baptism.
May he help us by his grace
to remain faithful to the Spirit we have received.

And after a brief pause for silence, he continues with hands joined:

Almighty ever-living God,
who willed that through water,
the fountain of life and the source of purification,
even souls should be cleansed
and receive the gift of eternal life;
be pleased, we pray, to ✛ bless this water,
by which we seek protection on this your day, O Lord.
Renew the living spring of your grace within us
and grant that by this water we may be defended
from all ills of spirit and body,
and so approach you with hearts made clean
and worthily receive your salvation.
Through Christ our Lord. ℟. **Amen.**

Or:

Almighty Lord and God,
who are the source and origin of all life,

whether of body or soul,
we ask you to ✠ bless this water,
which we use in confidence
to implore forgiveness for our sins
and to obtain the protection of your grace
against all illness and every snare of the enemy.
Grant, O Lord, in your mercy,
that living waters may always spring up for our
   salvation,
and so may we approach you with a pure heart
and avoid all danger to body and soul.
Through Christ our Lord. ℟. **Amen.**

Or (during Easter Time):

Lord our God,
in your mercy be present to your people's prayers,
and, for us who recall the wondrous work of our creation
and the still greater work of our redemption,
graciously ✠ bless this water.
For you created water to make the fields fruitful
and to refresh and cleanse our bodies.
You also made water the instrument of your mercy:
for through water you freed your people from slavery
and quenched their thirst in the desert;
through water the Prophets proclaimed the new
   covenant
you were to enter upon with the human race;
and last of all,
through water, which Christ made holy in the Jordan,
you have renewed our corrupted nature
in the bath of regeneration.
Therefore, may this water be for us
a memorial of the Baptism we have received,
and grant that we may share
in the gladness of our brothers and sisters
who at Easter have received their Baptism.
Through Christ our Lord. ℟. **Amen.**

Where the circumstances of the place or the custom of the people suggest that the mixing of salt be preserved in the blessing of water, the Priest may bless salt, saying:

We humbly ask you, almighty God:
be pleased in your faithful love to bless ✢ this salt
you have created,
for it was you who commanded the prophet Elisha
to cast salt into water,
that impure water might be purified.
Grant, O Lord, we pray,
that, wherever this mixture of salt and water is sprinkled,
every attack of the enemy may be repulsed
and your Holy Spirit may be present
to keep us safe at all times.
Through Christ our Lord. ℟. **Amen.**

Then he pours the salt into the water, without saying anything.

Afterward, taking the aspergillum, the Priest sprinkles himself and the ministers, then the clergy and people, moving through the church, if appropriate.

Meanwhile, one of the following chants, or another appropriate chant is sung.

Outside Easter Time

ANTIPHON 1 Ps 51 (50):9

Sprinkle me with hyssop, O Lord, and I shall be cleansed; wash me and I shall be whiter than snow.

ANTIPHON 2 Ez 36:25-26

I will pour clean water upon you, and you will be made clean of all your impurities, and I shall give you a new spirit, says the Lord.

HYMN Cf. 1 Pt 1:3-5

Blessed be the God and Father of our Lord Jesus Christ, who in his great mercy has given us new birth into a living hope through the Resurrection of Jesus Christ from the dead, into an inheritance that will not perish, preserved for us in heaven for the salvation to be revealed in the last time!

During Easter Time

ANTIPHON 1 Cf. Ez 47:1-2, 9

I saw water flowing from the Temple, from its right-hand side, alleluia: and all to whom this water came were saved and shall say: Alleluia, alleluia.

ANTIPHON 2 Cf. Zeph 3:8; Ez 36:25

On the day of my resurrection, says the Lord, alleluia, I will gather the nations and assemble the kingdoms and I will pour clean water upon you, alleluia.

ANTIPHON 3 Cf. Dn 3:77, 79

You springs and all that moves in the waters, sing a hymn to God, alleluia.

ANTIPHON 4 1 Pt 2:9

O chosen race, royal priesthood, holy nation, proclaim the mighty works of him who called you out of darkness into his wonderful light, alleluia.

ANTIPHON 5

From your side, O Christ, bursts forth a spring of water, by which the squalor of the world is washed away and life is made new again, alleluia.

When he returns to his chair and the singing is over, the Priest stands facing the people and, with hands joined, says:

May almighty God cleanse us of our sins,
and through the celebration of this Eucharist
make us worthy to share at the table of his Kingdom.
℟. **Amen**.

Then, when it is prescribed, the hymn Gloria in excelsis *(*Glory to God in the highest*) is sung or said.*

PREFACES

PREFACE I OF ADVENT (P 1)

The two comings of Christ

(From the First Sunday of Advent to December 16)

It is truly right and just, our duty and our salvation,
always and everywhere to give you thanks,
Lord, holy Father, almighty and eternal God,
through Christ our Lord.

For he assumed at his first coming
the lowliness of human flesh,
and so fulfilled the design you formed long ago,
and opened for us the way to eternal salvation,
that, when he comes again in glory and majesty
and all is at last made manifest,
we who watch for that day
may inherit the great promise
in which now we dare to hope.

And so, with Angels and Archangels,
with Thrones and Dominions,
and with all the hosts and Powers of heaven,
we sing the hymn of your glory,
as without end we acclaim: ➔ No. 23, p. 23

PREFACE II OF ADVENT (P 2)

The twofold expectation of Christ

(From December 17 to December 24)

It is truly right and just, our duty and our salvation,
always and everywhere to give you thanks,
Lord, holy Father, almighty and eternal God,
through Christ our Lord.

For all the oracles of the prophets foretold him,
the Virgin Mother longed for him
with love beyond all telling,

John the Baptist sang of his coming
and proclaimed his presence when he came.

It is by his gift that already we rejoice
at the mystery of his Nativity,
so that he may find us watchful in prayer
and exultant in his praise.

And so, with Angels and Archangels,
with Thrones and Dominions,
and with all the hosts and Powers of heaven,
we sing the hymn of your glory,
as without end we acclaim: → No. 23, p. 23

PREFACE I OF THE NATIVITY OF THE LORD (P 3)
Christ the Light
(For the Nativity of the Lord, its Octave Day and within the Octave)

It is truly right and just, our duty and our salvation,
always and everywhere to give you thanks,
Lord, holy Father, almighty and eternal God.

For in the mystery of the Word made flesh
a new light of your glory has shone upon the eyes of our
    mind,
so that, as we recognize in him God made visible,
we may be caught up through him in love of things invisible.

And so, with Angels and Archangels,
with Thrones and Dominions,
and with all the hosts and Powers of heaven,
we sing the hymn of your glory,
as without end we acclaim: → No. 23, p. 23

PREFACE II OF THE NATIVITY OF THE LORD (P 4)
The restoration of all things in the Incarnation
(For the Nativity of the Lord, its Octave Day and within the Octave)

It is truly right and just, our duty and our salvation,
always and everywhere to give you thanks,
Lord, holy Father, almighty and eternal God,
through Christ our Lord.

For on the feast of this awe-filled mystery,
though invisible in his own divine nature,

he has appeared visibly in ours;
and begotten before all ages,
he has begun to exist in time;
so that, raising up in himself all that was cast down,
he might restore unity to all creation
and call straying humanity back to the heavenly Kingdom.

And so, with all the Angels, we praise you,
as in joyful celebration we acclaim:　　→ No. 23, p. 23

PREFACE III OF THE NATIVITY OF THE LORD (P 5)

The exchange in the Incarnation of the Word

(For the Nativity of the Lord, its Octave Day and within the Octave)

It is truly right and just, our duty and our salvation,
always and everywhere to give you thanks,
Lord, holy Father, almighty and eternal God,
through Christ our Lord.

For through him the holy exchange that restores our life
has shone forth today in splendor:
when our frailty is assumed by your Word
not only does human mortality receive unending honor
but by this wondrous union we, too, are made eternal.

And so, in company with the choirs of Angels,
we praise you, and with joy we proclaim:　→ No. 23, p. 23

PREFACE I OF LENT (P 8)

The spiritual meaning of Lent

It is truly right and just, our duty and our salvation,
always and everywhere to give you thanks,
Lord, holy Father, almighty and eternal God,
through Christ our Lord.

For by your gracious gift each year
your faithful await the sacred paschal feasts
with the joy of minds made pure,
so that, more eagerly intent on prayer
and on the works of charity,
and participating in the mysteries
by which they have been reborn,

they may be led to the fullness of grace
that you bestow on your sons and daughters.

And so, with Angels and Archangels,
with Thrones and Dominions,
and with all the hosts and Powers of heaven,
we sing the hymn of your glory,
as without end we acclaim: ➜ No. 23, p. 23

PREFACE II OF LENT (P 9)
Spiritual penance

It is truly right and just, our duty and our salvation,
always and everywhere to give you thanks,
Lord, holy Father, almighty and eternal God.

For you have given your children a sacred time
for the renewing and purifying of their hearts,
that, freed from disordered affections,
they may so deal with the things of this passing world
as to hold rather to the things that eternally endure.

And so, with all the Angels and Saints,
we praise you, as without end we acclaim: ➜ No. 23, p. 23

PREFACE I OF EASTER I (P 21)
The Paschal Mystery

(At the Easter Vigil, is said "on this night"; on Easter Sunday and throughout the Octave
of Easter, is said "on this day"; on other days of Easter Time, is said "in this time.")

It is truly right and just, our duty and our salvation,
at all times to acclaim you, O Lord,
but (on this night / on this day / in this time) above all
to laud you yet more gloriously,
when Christ our Passover has been sacrificed.

For he is the true Lamb
who has taken away the sins of the world;
by dying he has destroyed our death,
and by rising, restored our life.

Therefore, overcome with paschal joy,
every land, every people exults in your praise
and even the heavenly Powers, with the angelic hosts,
sing together the unending hymn of your glory,
as they acclaim: ➜ No. 23, p. 23

PREFACE II OF EASTER (P 22)
New life in Christ

It is truly right and just, our duty and our salvation,
at all times to acclaim you, O Lord,
but in this time above all to laud you yet more gloriously,
when Christ our Passover has been sacrificed.

Through him the children of light rise to eternal life
and the halls of the heavenly Kingdom
are thrown open to the faithful;
for his Death is our ransom from death,
and in his rising the life of all has risen.

Therefore, overcome with paschal joy,
every land, every people exults in your praise
and even the heavenly Powers, with the angelic hosts,
sing together the unending hymn of your glory,
as they acclaim: → No. 23, p. 23

PREFACE III OF EASTER (P 23)
Christ living and always interceding for us

It is truly right and just, our duty and our salvation,
at all times to acclaim you, O Lord,
but in this time above all to laud you yet more gloriously,
when Christ our Passover has been sacrificed.

He never ceases to offer himself for us
but defends us and ever pleads our cause before you:
he is the sacrificial Victim who dies no more,
the Lamb, once slain, who lives for ever.

Therefore, overcome with paschal joy,
every land, every people exults in your praise
and even the heavenly Powers, with the angelic hosts,
sing together the unending hymn of your glory,
as they acclaim: → No. 23, p. 23

PREFACE IV OF EASTER (P 24)
*The restoration of the universe through the
Paschal Mystery*

It is truly right and just, our duty and our salvation,
at all times to acclaim you, O Lord,

but in this time above all to laud you yet more gloriously,
when Christ our Passover has been sacrificed.

For, with the old order destroyed,
a universe cast down is renewed,
and integrity of life is restored to us in Christ.

Therefore, overcome with paschal joy,
every land, every people exults in your praise
and even the heavenly Powers, with the angelic hosts,
sing together the unending hymn of your glory,
as they acclaim: ➙ No. 23, p. 23

PREFACE V OF EASTER (P 25)
Christ, Priest and Victim

It is truly right and just, our duty and our salvation,
at all times to acclaim you, O Lord,
but in this time above all to laud you yet more gloriously,
when Christ our Passover has been sacrificed.

By the oblation of his Body,
he brought the sacrifices of old to fulfillment
in the reality of the Cross
and, by commending himself to you for our salvation,
showed himself the Priest, the Altar, and the Lamb of
sacrifice.

Therefore, overcome with paschal joy,
every land, every people exults in your praise
and even the heavenly Powers, with the angelic hosts,
sing together the unending hymn of your glory,
as they acclaim: ➙ No. 23, p. 23

PREFACE I OF THE ASCENSION OF THE LORD (P 26)
The mystery of the Ascension
(Ascension to the Saturday before Pentecost inclusive)

It is truly right and just, our duty and our salvation,
always and everywhere to give you thanks,
Lord, holy Father, almighty and eternal God.

For the Lord Jesus, the King of glory,
conqueror of sin and death,

ascended (today) to the highest heavens,
as the Angels gazed in wonder.

Mediator between God and man,
judge of the world and Lord of hosts,
he ascended, not to distance himself from our lowly state
but that we, his members, might be confident of following
where he, our Head and Founder, has gone before.

Therefore, overcome with paschal joy,
every land, every people exults in your praise
and even the heavenly Powers, with the angelic hosts,
sing together the unending hymn of your glory,
as they acclaim: → No. 23, p. 23

PREFACE II OF THE ASCENSION OF THE LORD (P 27)

The mystery of the Ascension

(Ascension to the Saturday before Pentecost inclusive)

It is truly right and just, our duty and our salvation,
always and everywhere to give you thanks,
Lord, holy Father, almighty and eternal God,
through Christ our Lord.

For after his Resurrection
he plainly appeared to all his disciples
and was taken up to heaven in their sight,
that he might make us sharers in his divinity.

Therefore, overcome with paschal joy,
every land, every people exults in your praise
and even the heavenly Powers, with the angelic hosts,
sing together the unending hymn of your glory,
as they acclaim: → No. 23, p. 23

PREFACE I OF THE SUNDAYS IN ORDINARY TIME (P 29)

The Paschal Mystery and the People of God

It is truly right and just, our duty and our salvation,
always and everywhere to give you thanks,
Lord, holy Father, almighty and eternal God,
through Christ our Lord.

For through his Paschal Mystery,
he accomplished the marvelous deed,

by which he has freed us from the yoke of sin and death,
summoning us to the glory of being now called
a chosen race, a royal priesthood,
a holy nation, a people for your own possession,
to proclaim everywhere your mighty works,
for you have called us out of darkness
into your own wonderful light.

And so, with Angels and Archangels,
with Thrones and Dominions,
and with all the hosts and Powers of heaven,
we sing the hymn of your glory,
as without end we acclaim: ➡ No. 23, p. 23

PREFACE II OF THE SUNDAYS IN ORDINARY TIME (P 30)
The mystery of salvation

It is truly right and just, our duty and our salvation,
always and everywhere to give you thanks,
Lord, holy Father, almighty and eternal God,
through Christ our Lord.

For out of compassion for the waywardness that is ours,
he humbled himself and was born of the Virgin;
by the passion of the Cross he freed us from unending death,
and by rising from the dead he gave us life eternal.

And so, with Angels and Archangels,
with Thrones and Dominions,
and with all the hosts and Powers of heaven,
we sing the hymn of your glory,
as without end we acclaim: ➡ No. 23, p. 23

PREFACE III OF THE SUNDAYS IN ORDINARY TIME (P 31)
The salvation of man by a man

It is truly right and just, our duty and our salvation,
always and everywhere to give you thanks,
Lord, holy Father, almighty and eternal God.

For we know it belongs to your boundless glory,
that you came to the aid of mortal beings with your divinity
and even fashioned for us a remedy out of mortality itself,
that the cause of our downfall

might become the means of our salvation,
through Christ our Lord.

Through him the host of Angels adores your majesty
and rejoices in your presence for ever.
May our voices, we pray, join with theirs
in one chorus of exultant praise, as we acclaim:

➜ No. 23, p. 23

PREFACE IV OF THE SUNDAYS IN ORDINARY TIME (P 32)

The history of salvation

It is truly right and just, our duty and our salvation,
always and everywhere to give you thanks,
Lord, holy Father, almighty and eternal God,
through Christ our Lord.

For by his birth he brought renewal
to humanity's fallen state,
and by his suffering, canceled out our sins;
by his rising from the dead
he has opened the way to eternal life,
and by ascending to you, O Father,
he has unlocked the gates of heaven.

And so, with the company of Angels and Saints,
we sing the hymn of your praise,
as without end we acclaim:

➜ No. 23, p. 23

PREFACE V OF THE SUNDAYS IN ORDINARY TIME (P 33)

Creation

It is truly right and just, our duty and our salvation,
always and everywhere to give you thanks,
Lord, holy Father, almighty and eternal God.

For you laid the foundations of the world
and have arranged the changing of times and seasons;
you formed man in your own image
and set humanity over the whole world in all its wonder,
to rule in your name over all you have made
and for ever praise you in your mighty works,
through Christ our Lord.

And so, with all the Angels, we praise you,
as in joyful celebration we acclaim: ➡ No. 23, p. 23

PREFACE VI OF THE SUNDAYS IN ORDINARY TIME (P 34)

The pledge of the eternal Passover

It is truly right and just, our duty and our salvation,
always and everywhere to give you thanks,
Lord, holy Father, almighty and eternal God.

For in you we live and move and have our being,
and while in this body
we not only experience the daily effects of your care,
but even now possess the pledge of life eternal.

For, having received the first fruits of the Spirit,
through whom you raised up Jesus from the dead,
we hope for an everlasting share in the Paschal Mystery.

And so, with all the Angels, we praise you,
as in joyful celebration we acclaim: ➡ No. 23, p. 23

PREFACE VII OF THE SUNDAYS IN ORDINARY TIME (P 35)

Salvation through the obedience of Christ

It is truly right and just, our duty and our salvation,
always and everywhere to give you thanks,
Lord, holy Father, almighty and eternal God.

For you so loved the world
that in your mercy you sent us the Redeemer,
to live like us in all things but sin,
so that you might love in us what you loved in your Son,
by whose obedience we have been restored to those gifts
    of yours
that, by sinning, we had lost in disobedience.

And so, Lord, with all the Angels and Saints,
we, too, give you thanks, as in exultation we acclaim:
                                              ➡ No. 23, p. 23

PREFACE VIII OF THE SUNDAYS IN ORDINARY TIME (P 36)

The Church united by the unity of the Trinity

It is truly right and just, our duty and our salvation,
always and everywhere to give you thanks,
Lord, holy Father, almighty and eternal God.

For, when your children were scattered afar by sin,
through the Blood of your Son and the power of the Spirit,
you gathered them again to yourself,
that a people, formed as one by the unity of the Trinity,
made the body of Christ and the temple of the Holy Spirit,
might, to the praise of your manifold wisdom,
be manifest as the Church.

And so, in company with the choirs of Angels,
we praise you, and with joy we proclaim: ➔ No. 23, p. 23

PREFACE I OF THE MOST HOLY EUCHARIST (P 47)
The Sacrifice and the Sacrament of Christ

It is truly right and just, our duty and our salvation,
always and everywhere to give you thanks,
Lord, holy Father, almighty and eternal God,
through Christ our Lord.

For he is the true and eternal Priest,
who instituted the pattern of an everlasting sacrifice
and was the first to offer himself as the saving Victim,
commanding us to make this offering as his memorial.
As we eat his flesh that was sacrificed for us,
we are made strong,
and, as we drink his Blood that was poured out for us,
we are washed clean.

And so, with Angels and Archangels,
with Thrones and Dominions,
and with all the hosts and Powers of heaven,
we sing the hymn of your glory,
as without end we acclaim: ➔ No. 23, p. 23

PREFACE II OF THE MOST HOLY EUCHARIST (P 48)
The fruits of the Most Holy Eucharist

It is truly right and just, our duty and our salvation,
always and everywhere to give you thanks,
Lord, holy Father, almighty and eternal God,
through Christ our Lord.

For at the Last Supper with his Apostles,
establishing for the ages to come the saving memorial of
    the Cross,
he offered himself to you as the unblemished Lamb,
the acceptable gift of perfect praise.

Nourishing your faithful by this sacred mystery,
you make them holy, so that the human race,
bounded by one world,
may be enlightened by one faith
and united by one bond of charity.

And so, we approach the table of this wondrous Sacrament,
so that, bathed in the sweetness of your grace,
we may pass over to the heavenly realities here fore-
    shadowed.

Therefore, all creatures of heaven and earth
sing a new song in adoration,
and we, with all the host of Angels,
cry out, and without end we acclaim: ➜ No. 23, p. 23

PREFACE I FOR THE DEAD (P 77)
The hope of resurrection in Christ

It is truly right and just, our duty and our salvation,
always and everywhere to give you thanks,
Lord, holy Father, almighty and eternal God,
through Christ our Lord.

In him the hope of blessed resurrection has dawned,
that those saddened by the certainty of dying
might be consoled by the promise of immortality to come.
Indeed for your faithful, Lord,
life is changed not ended,
and, when this earthly dwelling turns to dust,
an eternal dwelling is made ready for them in heaven.

And so, with Angels and Archangels,
with Thrones and Dominions,
and with all the hosts and Powers of heaven,
we sing the hymn of your glory,
as without end we acclaim: ➜ No. 23, p. 23

PREFACE II FOR THE DEAD (P 78)
Christn died so that we might live

It is truly right and just, our duty and our salvation,
always and everywhere to give you thanks,
Lord, holy Father, almighty and eternal God,
through Christ our Lord.

For as one alone he accepted death,
so that we might all escape from dying;
as one man he chose to die,
so that in your sight we all might live for ever.

And so, in company with the choirs of Angels,
we praise you, and with joy we proclaim: → No. 23, p. 23

PREFACE III FOR THE DEAD (P 79)
Christ, the salvation and the life

It is truly right and just, our duty and our salvation,
always and everywhere to give you thanks,
Lord, holy Father, almighty and eternal God,
through Christ our Lord.

For he is the salvation of the world,
the life of the human race,
the resurrection of the dead.

Through him the host of Angels adores your majesty
and rejoices in your presence for ever.
May our voices, we pray, join with theirs
in one chorus of exultant praise, as we acclaim:
                    → No. 23, p. 23

PREFACE IV FOR THE DEAD (P 80)
From earthly life to heavenly glory

It is truly right and just, our duty and our salvation,
always and everywhere to give you thanks,
Lord, holy Father, almighty and eternal God.

For it is at your summons that we come to birth,
by your will that we are governed,
and at your command that we return,
on account of sin,
to that earth from which we came.

And when you give the sign,
we who have been redeemed by the Death of your Son,
shall be raised up to the glory of his Resurrection.

And so, with the company of Angels and Saints,
we sing the hymn of your praise,
as without end we acclaim: → No. 23, p. 23

PREFACE V FOR THE DEAD (P 81)
Our resurrection through the victory of Christ

It is truly right and just, our duty and our salvation,
always and everywhere to give you thanks,
Lord, holy Father, almighty and eternal God.

For even though by our own fault we perish,
yet by your compassion and your grace,
when seized by death according to our sins,
we are redeemed through Christ's great victory,
and with him called back into life.

And so, with the Powers of heaven,
we worship you constantly on earth,
and before your majesty
without end we acclaim: → No. 23, p. 23

PROPER COMMUNICANTES
AND HANC IGITUR

FOR EUCHARISTIC PRAYER I (THE ROMAN CANON)

Communicantes for the Nativity of the Lord
and throughout the Octave

Celebrating the most sacred night (day)
on which blessed Mary the immaculate Virgin
brought forth the Savior for this world,
and in communion with those whose memory we venerate,
especially the glorious ever-Virgin Mary,
Mother of our God and Lord, Jesus Christ,† etc., p. 25.

Communicantes for the Epiphany of the Lord

Celebrating the most sacred day
on which your Only Begotten Son,
eternal with you in your glory,
appeared in a human body, truly sharing our flesh,

and in communion with those whose memory we venerate,
especially the glorious ever-Virgin Mary,
Mother of our God and Lord, Jesus Christ,† etc., p. 25.

Communicantes for Easter

Celebrating the most sacred night (day)
of the Resurrection of our Lord Jesus Christ in the flesh,
and in communion with those whose memory we venerate,
especially the glorious ever-Virgin Mary,
Mother of our God and Lord, Jesus Christ,† etc., p. 25.

Hanc Igitur for the Easter Vigil
until the Second Sunday of Easter

Therefore, Lord, we pray:
graciously accept this oblation of our service,
that of your whole family,
which we make to you
also for those to whom you have been pleased to give
the new birth of water and the Holy Spirit,
granting them forgiveness of all their sins;
order our days in your peace,
and command that we be delivered from eternal damnation
and counted among the flock of those you have chosen.
(Through Christ our Lord. Amen.)   ➜ *Canon*, p. 25.

Communicantes for the Ascension of the Lord

Celebrating the most sacred day
on which your Only Begotten Son, our Lord,
placed at the right hand of your glory
our weak human nature,
which he had united to himself,
and in communion with those whose memory we venerate,
especially the glorious ever-Virgin Mary,
Mother of our God and Lord, Jesus Christ,† etc., p. 25.

Communicantes for Pentecost Sunday

Celebrating the most sacred day of Pentecost,
on which the Holy Spirit
appeared to the Apostles in tongues of fire,
and in communion with those whose memory we venerate,
especially the glorious ever-Virgin Mary,
Mother of our God and Lord, Jesus Christ,† etc., p. 25.

BLESSINGS AT THE END OF MASS AND PRAYERS OVER THE PEOPLE

SOLEMN BLESSINGS

The following blessings may be used, at the discretion of the Priest, at the end of the celebration of Mass, or of a Liturgy of the Word, or of the Office, or of the Sacraments.

The Deacon or, in his absence, the Priest himself, says the invitation: Bow down for the blessing. *Then the Priest, with hands extended over the people, says the blessing, with all responding:* **Amen**.

I. For Celebrations in the Different Liturgical Times

1. ADVENT

May the almighty and merciful God,
by whose grace you have placed your faith
in the First Coming of his Only Begotten Son
and yearn for his coming again,
sanctify you by the radiance of Christ's Advent
and enrich you with his blessing. ℟. **Amen.**

As you run the race of this present life,
may he make you firm in faith,
joyful in hope and active in charity. ℟. **Amen.**

So that, rejoicing now with devotion
at the Redeemer's coming in the flesh,
you may be endowed with the rich reward of eternal life
when he comes again in majesty. ℟. **Amen.**

And may the blessing of almighty God,
the Father, and the Son, ✠ and the Holy Spirit,
come down on you and remain with you for ever. ℟. **Amen.**

2. THE NATIVITY OF THE LORD

May the God of infinite goodness,
who by the Incarnation of his Son has driven darkness from the world
and by that glorious Birth has illumined this most holy night (day),
drive far from you the darkness of vice
and illumine your hearts with the light of virtue. ℟. **Amen.**

May God, who willed that the great joy
of his Son's saving Birth
be announced to shepherds by the Angel,
fill your minds with the gladness he gives
and make you heralds of his Gospel. ℟. **Amen.**

And may God, who by the Incarnation
brought together the earthly and heavenly realm,
fill you with the gift of his peace and favor
and make you sharers with the Church in heaven. ℟. **Amen.**

And may the blessing of almighty God,
the Father, and the Son, ✠ and the Holy Spirit,
come down on you and remain with you for ever. ℟. **Amen.**

3. THE BEGINNING OF THE YEAR

May God, the source and origin of all blessing,
grant you grace,
pour out his blessing in abundance,
and keep you safe from harm throughout the year. ℟. **Amen.**

May he give you integrity in the faith,
endurance in hope,
and perseverance in charity
with holy patience to the end. ℟. **Amen.**

May he order your days and your deeds in his peace,
grant your prayers in this and in every place,
and lead you happily to eternal life. ℟. **Amen.**

And may the blessing of almighty God,
the Father, and the Son, ✠ and the Holy Spirit,
come down on you and remain with you for ever. ℟. **Amen.**

4. THE EPIPHANY OF THE LORD

May God, who has called you
out of darkness into his wonderful light,
pour out in kindness his blessing upon you
and make your hearts firm
in faith, hope and charity. ℟. **Amen.**

And since in all confidence you follow Christ,
who today appeared in the world
as a light shining in darkness,

may God make you, too,
a light for your brothers and sisters. ℟. **Amen.**

And so when your pilgrimage is ended,
may you come to him
whom the Magi sought as they followed the star
and whom they found with great joy, the Light from Light,
who is Christ the Lord. ℟. **Amen.**

And may the blessing of almighty God,
the Father, and the Son, ✠ and the Holy Spirit,
come down on you and remain with you for ever. ℟. **Amen.**

5. THE PASSION OF THE LORD

May God, the Father of mercies,
who has given you an example of love
in the Passion of his Only Begotten Son,
grant that, by serving God and your neighbor,
you may lay hold of the wondrous gift of his blessing.
℟. **Amen.**

So that you may receive the reward of everlasting life from
him,
through whose earthly Death
you believe that you escape eternal death. ℟. **Amen.**

And by following the example of his self-abasement,
may you possess a share in his Resurrection. ℟. **Amen.**

And may the blessing of almighty God,
the Father, and the Son, ✠ and the Holy Spirit,
come down on you and remain with you for ever. ℟. **Amen.**

6. EASTER TIME

May God, who by the Resurrection of his Only Begotten Son
was pleased to confer on you
the gift of redemption and of adoption,
give you gladness by his blessing. ℟. **Amen.**

May he, by whose redeeming work
you have received the gift of everlasting freedom,
make you heirs to an eternal inheritance. ℟. **Amen.**

And may you, who have already risen with Christ
in Baptism through faith,

by living in a right manner on this earth,
be united with him in the homeland of heaven. ℟. **Amen.**

And may the blessing of almighty God,
the Father, and the Son, ✠ and the Holy Spirit,
come down on you and remain with you for ever. ℟. **Amen.**

7. THE ASCENSION OF THE LORD

May almighty God bless you,
for on this very day his Only Begotten Son
pierced the heights of heaven
and unlocked for you the way
to ascend to where he is. ℟. **Amen.**

May he grant that,
as Christ after his Resurrection
was seen plainly by his disciples,
so when he comes as Judge
he may show himself merciful to you for all eternity.
℟. **Amen.**

And may you, who believe he is seated
with the Father in his majesty,
know with joy the fulfillment of his promise
to stay with you until the end of time. ℟. **Amen.**

And may the blessing of almighty God,
the Father, and the Son, ✠ and the Holy Spirit,
come down on you and remain with you for ever. ℟. **Amen.**

8. THE HOLY SPIRIT

May God, the Father of lights,
who was pleased to enlighten the disciples' minds
by the outpouring of the Spirit, the Paraclete,
grant you gladness by his blessing
and make you always abound with the gifts of the same
Spirit. ℟. **Amen.**

May the wondrous flame that appeared above the disciples,
powerfully cleanse your hearts from every evil
and pervade them with its purifying light. ℟. **Amen.**

And may God, who has been pleased to unite many
tongues

in the profession of one faith,
give you perseverance in that same faith
and, by believing, may you journey from hope to clear
vision. ℞. **Amen.**

And may the blessing of almighty God,
the Father, and the Son, ✠ and the Holy Spirit,
come down on you and remain with you for ever. ℞. **Amen.**

9. ORDINARY TIME I

May the Lord bless you and keep you. ℞. **Amen.**

May he let his face shine upon you
and show you his mercy. ℞. **Amen.**

May he turn his countenance towards you
and give you his peace. ℞. **Amen.**

And may the blessing of almighty God,
the Father, and the Son, ✠ and the Holy Spirit,
come down on you and remain with you for ever. ℞. **Amen.**

10. ORDINARY TIME II

May the peace of God,
which surpasses all understanding,
keep your hearts and minds
in the knowledge and love of God,
and of his Son, our Lord Jesus Christ. ℞. **Amen.**

And may the blessing of almighty God,
the Father, and the Son, ✠ and the Holy Spirit,
come down on you and remain with you for ever. ℞. **Amen.**

11. ORDINARY TIME III

May almighty God bless you in his kindness
and pour out saving wisdom upon you. ℞. **Amen.**

May he nourish you always with the teachings of the faith
and make you persevere in holy deeds. ℞. **Amen.**

May he turn your steps towards himself
and show you the path of charity and peace. ℞. **Amen.**

And may the blessing of almighty God,
the Father, and the Son, ✠ and the Holy Spirit,
come down on you and remain with you for ever. ℟. **Amen.**

12. ORDINARY TIME IV

May the God of all consolation order your days in his peace
and grant you the gifts of his blessing. ℟. **Amen.**

May he free you always from every distress
and confirm your hearts in his love. ℟. **Amen.**

So that on this life's journey
you may be effective in good works,
rich in the gifts of hope, faith and charity,
and may come happily to eternal life. ℟. **Amen.**

And may the blessing of almighty God,
the Father, and the Son, ✠ and the Holy Spirit,
come down on you and remain with you for ever. ℟. **Amen.**

13. ORDINARY TIME V

May almighty God always keep every adversity far from you
and in his kindness pour out upon you the gifts of his
    blessing. ℟. **Amen.**

May God keep your hearts attentive to his words,
that they may be filled with everlasting gladness. ℟. **Amen.**

And so, may you always understand what is good and right,
and be found ever hastening along
in the path of God's commands,
made coheirs with the citizens of heaven. ℟. **Amen.**

And may the blessing of almighty God,
the Father, and the Son, ✠ and the Holy Spirit,
come down on you and remain with you for ever. ℟. **Amen.**

14. ORDINARY TIME VI

May God bless you with every heavenly blessing,
make you always holy and pure in his sight,
pour out in abundance upon you the riches of his glory,
and teach you with the words of truth;
may he instruct you in the Gospel of salvation,
and ever endow you with fraternal charity.
Through Christ our Lord. ℟. **Amen.**

And may the blessing of almighty God,
the Father, and the Son, ✠ and the Holy Spirit,
come down on you and remain with you for ever. ℟. **Amen.**

II. For Celebrations of the Saints

15. THE BLESSED VIRGIN MARY

May God, who through the childbearing of the Blessed
　　Virgin Mary
willed in his great kindness to redeem the human race,
be pleased to enrich you with his blessing. ℟. **Amen.**

May you know always and everywhere the protection of
　　her,
through whom you have been found worthy to receive the
　　author of life. ℟. **Amen.**

May you, who have devoutly gathered on this day,
carry away with you the gifts of spiritual joys and heavenly
　　rewards. ℟. **Amen.**

And may the blessing of almighty God,
the Father, and the Son, ✠ and the Holy Spirit,
come down on you and remain with you for ever. ℟. **Amen.**

16. SAINTS PETER AND PAUL, APOSTLES

May almighty God bless you,
for he has made you steadfast in Saint Peter's saving
　　confession
and through it has set you on the solid rock of the Church's
　　faith. ℟. **Amen.**

And having instructed you
by the tireless preaching of Saint Paul,
may God teach you constantly by his example
to win brothers and sisters for Christ. ℟. **Amen.**

So that by the keys of St. Peter and the words of St. Paul,
and by the support of their intercession,
God may bring us happily to that homeland
that Peter attained on a cross
and Paul by the blade of a sword. ℟. **Amen.**

And may the blessing of almighty God,
the Father, and the Son, ✟ and the Holy Spirit,
come down on you and remain with you for ever. ℟. **Amen.**

17. THE APOSTLES

May God, who has granted you
to stand firm on apostolic foundations,
graciously bless you through the glorious merits
of the holy Apostles *N.* and *N.* (the holy Apostle *N.*). ℟.
    Amen.

And may he, who endowed you
with the teaching and example of the Apostles,
make you, under their protection,
witnesses to the truth before all. ℟. **Amen.**

So that through the intercession of the Apostles,
you may inherit the eternal homeland,
for by their teaching you possess firmness of faith. ℟. **Amen.**

And may the blessing of almighty God,
the Father, and the Son, ✟ and the Holy Spirit,
come down on you and remain with you for ever. ℟. **Amen.**

18. ALL SAINTS

May God, the glory and joy of the Saints,
who has caused you to be strengthened
by means of their outstanding prayers,
bless you with unending blessings. ℟. **Amen.**

Freed through their intercession from present ills
and formed by the example of their holy way of life,
may you be ever devoted
to serving God and your neighbor. ℟. **Amen.**

So that, together with all,
you may possess the joys of the homeland,
where Holy Church rejoices
that her children are admitted in perpetual peace
to the company of the citizens of heaven. ℟. **Amen.**

And may the blessing of almighty God,
the Father, and the Son, ✟ and the Holy Spirit,
come down on you and remain with you for ever. ℟. **Amen.**

III. Other Blessings

19. FOR THE DEDICATION OF A CHURCH

May God, the Lord of heaven and earth,
who has gathered you today for the dedication of this church,
make you abound in heavenly blessings. ℟. **Amen.**

And may he, who has willed that all his scattered children
should be gathered together in his Son,
grant that you may become his temple
and the dwelling place of the Holy Spirit. ℟. **Amen.**

And so, when you are thoroughly cleansed,
may God dwell within you
and grant you to possess with all the Saints
the inheritance of eternal happiness. ℟. **Amen.**

And may the blessing of almighty God,
the Father, ✚ and the Son, ✚ and the Holy ✚ Spirit,
come down on you and remain with you for ever. ℟. **Amen.**

20. IN CELEBRATIONS FOR THE DEAD

May the God of all consolation bless you,
for in his unfathomable goodness he created the human race,
and in the Resurrection of his Only Begotten Son
he has given believers the hope of rising again. ℟. **Amen.**

To us who are alive, may God grant pardon for our sins,
and to all the dead, a place of light and peace. ℟. **Amen.**

So may we all live happily for ever with Christ,
whom we believe truly rose from the dead. ℟. **Amen.**

And may the blessing of almighty God,
the Father, and the Son, ✚ and the Holy Spirit,
come down on you and remain with you for ever. ℟. **Amen.**

PRAYERS OVER THE PEOPLE

The following prayers may be used, at the discretion of the Priest, at the end of the celebration of Mass, or of a Liturgy of the Word, or of the Office, or of the Sacraments.

The Deacon or, in his absence, the Priest himself, says the invitation: Bow down for the blessing. *Then the Priest, with hands outstretched over the people, says the prayer, with all responding:* **Amen**.

After the prayer, the Priest always adds: And may the blessing of almighty God, the Father, and the Son, ✤ and the Holy Spirit, come down on you and remain with you for ever. ℟. **Amen.**

1. Be gracious to your people, O Lord,
   and do not withhold consolation on earth
   from those you call to strive for heaven.
   Through Christ our Lord.

2. Grant, O Lord, we pray,
   that the Christian people
   may understand the truths they profess
   and love the heavenly liturgy
   in which they participate.
   Through Christ our Lord.

3. May your people receive your holy blessing,
   O Lord, we pray,
   and, by that gift,
   spurn all that would harm them
   and obtain what they desire.
   Through Christ our Lord.

4. Turn your people to you with all their heart,
   O Lord, we pray,
   for you protect even those who go astray,
   but when they serve you with undivided heart,
   you sustain them with still greater care.
   Through Christ our Lord.

5. Graciously enlighten your family, O Lord, we pray,
   that by holding fast to what is pleasing to you,
   they may be worthy to accomplish all that is good.
   Through Christ our Lord.

6. Bestow pardon and peace, O Lord, we pray,
   upon your faithful,
   that they may be cleansed from every offense

and serve you with untroubled hearts.
Through Christ our Lord.

7. May your heavenly favor, O Lord, we pray,
   increase in number the people subject to you
   and make them always obedient to your commands.
   Through Christ our Lord.

8. Be propitious to your people, O God,
   that, freed from every evil,
   they may serve you with all their heart
   and ever stand firm under your protection.
   Through Christ our Lord.

9. May your family always rejoice together, O God,
   over the mysteries of redemption they have celebrated,
   and grant its members the perseverance
   to attain the effects that flow from them.
   Through Christ our Lord.

10. Lord God, from the abundance of your mercies
    provide for your servants and ensure their safety,
    so that, strengthened by your blessings,
    they may at all times abound in thanksgiving
    and bless you with unending exultation.
    Through Christ our Lord.

11. Keep your family, we pray, O Lord,
    in your constant care,
    so that, under your protection,
    they may be free from all troubles
    and by good works show dedication to your name.
    Through Christ our Lord.

12. Purify your faithful, both in body and in mind,
    O Lord, we pray,
    so that, feeling the compunction you inspire,
    they may be able to avoid harmful pleasures
    and ever feed upon your delights.
    Through Christ our Lord.

13. May the effects of your sacred blessing, O Lord,
    make themselves felt among your faithful,

to prepare with spiritual sustenance the minds of all,
that they may be strengthened by the power of your
    love
to carry out works of charity.
Through Christ our Lord.

14. The hearts of your faithful submitted to your name,
    entreat your help, O Lord,
    and since without you they can do nothing that is just,
    grant by your abundant mercy
    that they may both know what is right
    and receive all that they need for their good.
    Through Christ our Lord.

15. Hasten to the aid of your faithful people
    who call upon you, O Lord, we pray,
    and graciously give strength in their human weakness,
    so that, being dedicated to you in complete sincerity,
    they may find gladness in your remedies
    both now and in the life to come.
    Through Christ our Lord.

16. Look with favor on your family, O Lord,
    and bestow your endless mercy on those who seek it:
    and just as without your mercy,
    they can do nothing truly worthy of you,
    so through it,
    may they merit to obey your saving commands.
    Through Christ our Lord.

17. Bestow increase of heavenly grace
    on your faithful, O Lord;
    may they praise you with their lips,
    with their souls, with their lives;
    and since it is by your gift that we exist,
    may our whole lives be yours.
    Through Christ our Lord.

18. Direct your people, O Lord, we pray,
    with heavenly instruction,
    that by avoiding every evil
    and pursuing all that is good,
    they may earn not your anger

but your unending mercy.
Through Christ our Lord.

19. Be near to those who call on you, O Lord,
    and graciously grant your protection
    to all who place their hope in your mercy,
    that they may remain faithful in holiness of life
    and, having enough for their needs in this world,
    they may be made full heirs of your promise for eternity.
    Through Christ our Lord.

20. Bestow the grace of your kindness
    upon your supplicant people, O Lord,
    that, formed by you, their creator,
    and restored by you, their sustainer,
    through your constant action they may be saved.
    Through Christ our Lord.

21. May your faithful people, O Lord, we pray,
    always respond to the promptings of your love
    and, moved by wholesome compunction,
    may they do gladly what you command,
    so as to receive the things you promise.
    Through Christ our Lord.

22. May the weakness of your devoted people
    stir your compassion, O Lord, we pray,
    and let their faithful pleading win your mercy,
    that what they do not presume upon by their merits
    they may receive by your generous pardon.
    Through Christ our Lord.

23. In defense of your children, O Lord, we pray,
    stretch forth the right hand of your majesty,
    so that, obeying your fatherly will,
    they may have the unfailing protection
    of your fatherly care.
    Through Christ our Lord.

24. Look, O Lord, on the prayers of your family,
    and grant them the assistance they humbly implore,
    so that, strengthened by the help they need,
    they may persevere in confessing your name.
    Through Christ our Lord.

25. Keep your family safe, O Lord, we pray,
    and grant them the abundance of your mercies,
    that they may find growth
    through the teachings and the gifts of heaven.
    Through Christ our Lord.

26. May your faithful people rejoice, we pray, O Lord,
    to be upheld by your right hand,
    and, progressing in the Christian life,
    may they delight in good things
    both now and in the time to come.
    Through Christ our Lord.

ON FEASTS OF SAINTS

27. May the Christian people exult, O Lord,
    at the glorification of the illustrious members of your
        Son's Body,
    and may they gain a share in the eternal lot
    of the Saints on whose feast day
    they reaffirm their devotion to you,
    rejoicing with them for ever in your glory.
    Through Christ our Lord.

28. Turn the hearts of your people
    always to you, O Lord, we pray,
    and, as you give them the help of such great patrons as
        these,
    grant also the unfailing help of your protection.
    Through Christ our Lord.

"In those days before the flood, they were eating and drinking. . . ."

NOVEMBER 27, 2022

1st SUNDAY OF ADVENT

ENTRANCE ANT. Cf. Ps 25 (24):1-3　　　　　　[Hope]

To you, I lift up my soul, O my God. In you, I have trusted; let me not be put to shame. Nor let my enemies exult over me; and let none who hope in you be put to shame.　　　　　→ No. 2, p. 10 (Omit Gloria)

COLLECT　　　　　　　　　　　　[Meeting Christ]

Grant your faithful, we pray, almighty God,
the resolve to run forth to meet your Christ
with righteous deeds at his coming,
so that, gathered at his right hand,
they may be worthy to possess the heavenly Kingdom.
Through our Lord Jesus Christ, your Son,
who lives and reigns with you in the unity of the Holy
　Spirit,
God, for ever and ever. ℟. **Amen.** ↓

FIRST READING Is 2:1-5   **[The Messianic Time]**

In a vision the prophet sees the promise of salvation being fulfilled. The Word of the Lord is personified; he shall judge. Let us walk in the light of the Lord.

A reading from the Book of the Prophet Isaiah

THIS is what Isaiah, son of Amoz,
   saw concerning Judah and Jerusalem.
   In days to come,
the mountain of the LORD's house
   shall be established as the highest mountain
   and raised above the hills.
All nations shall stream toward it;
   many peoples shall come and say:
"Come, let us climb the LORD's mountain,
   to the house of the God of Jacob,
that he may instruct us in his ways,
   and we may walk in his paths."
For from Zion shall go forth instruction,
   and the word of the LORD from Jerusalem.
He shall judge between the nations,
   and impose terms on many peoples.
They shall beat their swords into plowshares
   and their spears into pruning hooks;
one nation shall not raise the sword against another,
   nor shall they train for war again.
O house of Jacob, come,
   let us walk in the light of the LORD!
The word of the Lord. ℟. **Thanks be to God.** ↓

RESPONSORIAL PSALM Ps 122 [Joy in the Lord's House]

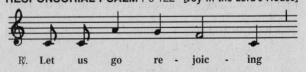

℟. Let   us   go   re - joic - ing

to   the   house   of   the   Lord.

I rejoiced because they said to me,
  "We will go up to the house of the LORD."
And now we have set foot
  within your gates, O Jerusalem.

℟. **Let us go rejoicing to the house of the Lord.**

Jerusalem, built as a city
  with compact unity.
To it the tribes go up,
  the tribes of the LORD.

℟. **Let us go rejoicing to the house of the Lord.**

According to the decree for Israel,
  to give thanks to the name of the LORD.
In it are set up judgment seats,
  seats for the house of David.

℟. **Let us go rejoicing to the house of the Lord.**

Pray for the peace of Jerusalem!
  May those who love you prosper!
May peace be within your walls,
  prosperity in your buildings.

℟. **Let us go rejoicing to the house of the Lord.**

Because of my brothers and friends
  I will say, "Peace be within you!"
Because of the house of the LORD, our God,
  I will pray for your good.

℟. **Let us go rejoicing to the house of the Lord.** ↓

SECOND READING Rom 13:11-14   [Put On the Lord]
  **The Apostle urges us to come out of the darkness of sin
  into the protective light—Jesus is the light.**

A reading from the Letter of Saint Paul to the Romans

BROTHERS and sisters: You know the time; it is the hour now for you to awake from sleep. For our salvation is nearer now than when we first believed; the night is advanced, the day is at hand. Let us then throw off the works of darkness and put on the armor of light; let us conduct ourselves properly as in the day, not in orgies and drunkenness, not in promiscuity and lust, not in rivalry and jealousy. But put on the Lord Jesus Christ, and make no provision for the desires of the flesh.—The word of the Lord. ℟. **Thanks be to God.** ↓

ALLELUIA Cf. Ps 85:8   [Love and Salvation]

℟. **Alleluia, alleluia.**
Show us, Lord, your love;
and grant us your salvation.
℟. **Alleluia, alleluia.** ↓

GOSPEL Mt 24:37-44   [Stay Awake!]

We must always be prepared for the coming of Christ, for no one knows the day or hour. Even though we are prepared, his coming will be unexpected; we must not be caught off guard.

℣. The Lord be with you. ℟. **And with your spirit.**
✝ A reading from the holy Gospel according to Matthew.
℟. **Glory to you, O Lord.**

JESUS said to his disciples: "As it was in the days of Noah, so it will be at the coming of the Son of Man. In those days before the flood, they were eating and drinking, marrying and giving in marriage, up to the day that Noah entered the ark. They did not know until the flood came and carried them all away. So will it be also at the coming of the Son of Man. Two men will be out in the field; one will be taken, and one will be left. Two women will be grinding at the mill; one will be

taken and one will be left. Therefore stay awake! For
you do not know on which day your Lord will come. Be
sure of this: if the master of the house had known the
hour of the night when the thief was coming, he would
have stayed awake and not let his house be broken
into. So too, you also must be prepared, for at an hour
you do not expect, the Son of Man will come."—The
Gospel of the Lord. ℟. **Praise to you, Lord Jesus
Christ.**
                                        ➜ No. 15, p. 18

PRAYER OVER THE OFFERINGS   [Eternal Redemption]

Accept, we pray, O Lord, these offerings we make,
gathered from among your gifts to us,
and may what you grant us to celebrate devoutly here
    below
gain for us the prize of eternal redemption.
Through Christ our Lord.
℟. **Amen.**   ➜ No. 21, p. 22 (Pref. P 1)

COMMUNION ANT. Ps 85 (84):13   [God's Bounty]
**The Lord will bestow his bounty, and our earth shall
yield its increase.** ↓

PRAYER AFTER COMMUNION   [Love for Heaven]

May these mysteries, O Lord,
in which we have participated,
profit us, we pray,
for even now, as we walk amid passing things,
you teach us by them
to love the things of heaven
and hold fast to what endures.
Through Christ our Lord.
℟. **Amen.**   ➜ No. 30, p. 77

Optional Solemn Blessings, p. 97, and Prayers over the People, p. 105

"Repent, for the kingdom of heaven is at hand!"

DECEMBER 4

2nd SUNDAY OF ADVENT

ENTRANCE ANT. Cf. Is 30:19, 30   [Lord of Salvation]

O people of Sion, behold, the Lord will come to save
the nations, and the Lord will make the glory of his
voice heard in the joy of your heart.

→ No. 2, p. 10 (Omit Gloria)

COLLECT   [Heavenly Wisdom]

Almighty and merciful God,
may no earthly undertaking hinder those
who set out in haste to meet your Son,
but may our learning of heavenly wisdom
gain us admittance to his company.
Who lives and reigns with you in the unity of the Holy
   Spirit,
God, for ever and ever. ℟. **Amen.** ↓

FIRST READING Is 11:1-10   [Messiah of Peace]

Jesse, the father of David, is the ancestor of the Messiah.
All nations will turn to him.

A reading from the Book of the Prophet Isaiah

116

O<small>N</small> that day a shoot shall sprout from the stump
      of Jesse,
   and from his roots a bud shall blossom.
The spirit of the L<small>ORD</small> shall rest upon him:
   a spirit of wisdom and of understanding,
a spirit of counsel and of strength,
   a spirit of knowledge and of fear of the L<small>ORD</small>,
   and his delight shall be the fear of the L<small>ORD</small>.
Not by appearance shall he judge,
   nor by hearsay shall he decide,
but he shall judge the poor with justice,
   and decide aright for the land's afflicted.
He shall strike the ruthless with the rod of his mouth,
   and with the breath of his lips he shall slay the
      wicked.
Justice shall be the band around his waist,
   and faithfulness a belt upon his hips.
Then the wolf shall be a guest of the lamb,
   and the leopard shall lie down with the kid;
the calf and the young lion shall browse together,
   with a little child to guide them.
The cow and the bear shall be neighbors,
   together their young shall rest;
   the lion shall eat hay like the ox.
The baby shall play by the cobra's den,
   and the child lay his hand on the adder's lair.
There shall be no harm or ruin on all my holy
      mountain;
   for the earth shall be filled with knowledge of the
      L<small>ORD</small>,
   as water covers the sea.
On that day, the root of Jesse,
   set up as a signal for the nations,
the Gentiles shall seek out,
   for his dwelling shall be glorious.
The word of the Lord. ℟. **Thanks be to God.** ↓

RESPONSORIAL PSALM Ps 72   [Justice and Peace]

℟. Justice shall flourish in his time, and fullness of peace for ev - er.

O God, with your judgment endow the king,
    and with your justice, the king's son;
he shall govern your people with justice
    and your afflicted ones with judgment.

℟. **Justice shall flourish in his time, and fullness of peace for ever.**

Justice shall flower in his days,
    and profound peace, till the moon be no more.
May he rule from sea to sea,
    and from the River to the ends of the earth.

℟. **Justice shall flourish in his time, and fullness of peace for ever.**

For he shall rescue the poor man when he cries out,
    and the afflicted when he has no one to help him.
He shall have pity for the lowly and the poor;
    the lives of the poor he shall save.

℟. **Justice shall flourish in his time, and fullness of peace for ever.**

May his name be blessed forever;
    as long as the sun his name shall remain.
In him shall all the tribes of the earth be blessed;
    all the nations shall proclaim his happiness.

℟. **Justice shall flourish in his time, and fullness of peace for ever.** ↓

SECOND READING Rom 15:4-9   [Instruction from Scripture]
    Remember that the Scriptures are written for our instruction. In Christ the promise of Scripture is fulfilled.

A reading from the Letter of Saint Paul to the Romans

B ROTHERS and sisters: Whatever was written previously was written for our instruction, that by
endurance and by the encouragement of the Scriptures we might have hope. May the God of endurance
and encouragement grant you to think in harmony
with one another, in keeping with Christ Jesus, that
with one accord you may with one voice glorify the
God and Father of our Lord Jesus Christ.

Welcome one another, then, as Christ welcomed you,
for the glory of God. For I say that Christ became a minister of the circumcised to show God's truthfulness, to
confirm the promises to the patriarchs, but so that the
Gentiles might glorify God for his mercy. As it is written:

Therefore, I will praise you among the Gentiles
and sing praises to your name.

The word of the Lord. ℟. **Thanks be to God.** ↓

ALLELUIA Lk 3:4, 6   [Prepare the Way]

℟. **Alleluia, alleluia.**
Prepare the way of the Lord, make straight his paths:
all flesh shall see the salvation of God.
℟. **Alleluia, alleluia.** ↓

GOSPEL Mt 3:1-12   [Prepare for the Lord]

**John the Baptist calls the people to prepare for the Messiah.
He urges a change in lifestyle and calls for repentance.**

℣. The Lord be with you. ℟. **And with your spirit.**
✜ A reading from the holy Gospel according to Matthew.
℟. **Glory to you, O Lord.**

J OHN the Baptist appeared, preaching in the desert
of Judea and saying, "Repent, for the kingdom of
heaven is at hand!" It was of him that the prophet
Isaiah had spoken when he said:

A voice of one crying out in the desert,
Prepare the way of the Lord,
make straight his paths.

John wore clothing made of camel's hair and had a leather belt around his waist. His food was locusts and wild honey. At that time Jerusalem, all Judea, and the whole region around the Jordan were going out to him and were being baptized by him in the Jordan River as they acknowledged their sins.

When he saw many of the Pharisees and Sadducees coming to his baptism, he said to them, "You brood of vipers! Who warned you to flee from the coming wrath? Produce good fruit as evidence of your repentance. And do not presume to say to yourselves, 'We have Abraham as our father.' For I tell you, God can raise up children to Abraham from these stones. Even now the ax lies at the root of the trees. Therefore every tree that does not bear good fruit will be cut down and thrown into the fire. I am baptizing you with water, for repentance, but the one who is coming after me is mightier than I. I am not worthy to carry his sandals. He will baptize you with the Holy Spirit and fire. His winnowing fan is in his hand. He will clear his threshing floor and gather his wheat into his barn, but the chaff he will burn with unquenchable fire."—The Gospel of the Lord. ℞. **Praise to you, Lord Jesus Christ.**

→ No. 15, p. 18

PRAYER OVER THE OFFERINGS [Our Offering]

Be pleased, O Lord, with our humble prayers and
  offerings,
and, since we have no merits to plead our cause,
come, we pray, to our rescue
with the protection of your mercy.
Through Christ our Lord.
℞. **Amen.**

→ No. 21, p. 22 (Pref. P 1)

COMMUNION ANT. Bar 5:5; 4:36 [Coming Joy]

Jerusalem, arise and stand upon the heights, and behold the joy which comes to you from God. ↓

PRAYER AFTER COMMUNION   [Wise Judgment]

Replenished by the food of spiritual nourishment,
we humbly beseech you, O Lord,
that, through our partaking in this mystery,
you may teach us to judge wisely the things of earth
and hold firm to the things of heaven.
Through Christ our Lord.
R̠. **Amen.**   → No. 30, p. 77

Optional Solemn Blessings, p. 97, and Prayers over the People, p. 105

"Hail, full of grace! The Lord is with you."

DECEMBER 8

THE IMMACULATE CONCEPTION
OF THE BLESSED VIRGIN MARY

Patronal Feastday
of the United States of America

Solemnity

ENTRANCE ANT. Is 61:10   [Mary Rejoices in the Lord]

I rejoice heartily in the Lord, in my God is the joy of my
soul; for he has clothed me with a robe of salvation,

and wrapped me in a mantle of justice, like a bride
adorned with her jewels. → No. 2, p. 10

COLLECT [Admitted to God's Presence]

O God, who by the Immaculate Conception of the
    Blessed Virgin
prepared a worthy dwelling for your Son,
grant, we pray,
that, as you preserved her from every stain
by virtue of the Death of your Son, which you foresaw,
so, through her intercession,
we, too, may be cleansed and admitted to your presence.
Through our Lord Jesus Christ, your Son,
who lives and reigns with you in the unity of the Holy
    Spirit,
God, for ever and ever. ℟. **Amen.** ↓

FIRST READING Gn 3:9-15, 20 [Promise of the Redeemer]
In the Garden, humankind enjoys an intimacy with God. It
is disrupted by sin, and the free and happy relationship
between humankind and God is fractured.

A reading from the Book of Genesis

AFTER the man, Adam, had eaten of the tree the
LORD God called to the man and asked him, "Where
are you?" He answered, "I heard you in the garden; but I
was afraid, because I was naked, so I hid myself." Then
he asked, "Who told you that you were naked? You have
eaten, then, from the tree of which I had forbidden you
to eat!" The man replied, "The woman whom you put
here with me—she gave me fruit from the tree, and so I
ate it." The LORD God then asked the woman, "Why did
you do such a thing?" The woman answered, "The serpent tricked me into it, so I ate it."

Then the LORD God said to the serpent:
"Because you have done this, you shall be banned
    from all the animals
    and from all the wild creatures;
on your belly shall you crawl,
    and dirt shall you eat
    all the days of your life.
I will put enmity between you and the woman,
    and between your offspring and hers;
he will strike at your head
    while you strike at his heel."
The man called his wife Eve, because she became
the mother of all the living.—The word of the Lord. ℟.
Thanks be to God. ↓

RESPONSORIAL PSALM Ps 98   [God's Salvation]

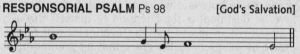

℟. Sing to the Lord a new song, for he has done marvelous deeds.

Sing to the LORD a new song,
    for he has done wondrous deeds;
his right hand has won victory for him,
    his holy arm.

℟. **Sing to the Lord a new song, for he has done marvelous deeds.**

The LORD has made his salvation known:
    in the sight of the nations he has revealed his justice.
He has remembered his kindness and his faithfulness
    toward the house of Israel.

℟. **Sing to the Lord a new song, for he has done marvelous deeds.**

All the ends of the earth have seen
    the salvation by our God.

Sing joyfully to the LORD, all you lands;
  break into song; sing praise.

℟. **Sing to the Lord a new song, for he has done marvelous deeds.** ↓

SECOND READING Eph 1:3-6, 11-12   [God's Saving Plan]
  God is praised for revealing his plan of salvation.
  Whatever God wills he works effectively and surely to
  accomplish. Let us make his will our will.

A reading from the letter of Saint Paul to the Ephesians

BROTHERS and sisters: Blessed be the God and
  Father of our Lord Jesus Christ, who has blessed
us in Christ with every spiritual blessing in the heavens, as he chose us in him, before the foundation of the
world, to be holy and without blemish before him. In
love he destined us for adoption to himself through
Jesus Christ, in accord with the favor of his will, for the
praise of the glory of his grace that he granted us in
the beloved.
  In him we were also chosen, destined in accord with
the purpose of the One who accomplishes all things
according to the intention of his will, so that we might
exist for the praise of his glory, we who first hoped in
Christ.—The word of the Lord. ℟. **Thanks be to God.** ↓

ALLELUIA Cf. Lk 1:28   [Blessed among Women]
℟. **Alleluia, alleluia.**
Hail, Mary, full of grace, the Lord is with you;
blessed are you among women.
℟. **Alleluia, alleluia.** ↓

GOSPEL Lk 1:26-38   [Mary's Great Holiness]
  Mary has received a promise of supreme grace and blessing and accepts it in faith, assenting to God's Word with
  her "Amen."

℣. The Lord be with you. ℟. **And with your spirit.**
✠ A reading from the holy Gospel according to Luke.
℟. **Glory to you, O Lord.**

THE angel Gabriel was sent from God to a town of Galilee called Nazareth, to a virgin betrothed to a man named Joseph, of the house of David, and the virgin's name was Mary. And coming to her, he said, "Hail, full of grace! The Lord is with you." But she was greatly troubled at what was said and pondered what sort of greeting this might be. Then the angel said to her, "Do not be afraid, Mary, for you have found favor with God. Behold, you will conceive in your womb and bear a son, and you shall name him Jesus. He will be great and will be called Son of the Most High, and the Lord God will give him the throne of David his father, and he will rule over the house of Jacob forever, and of his Kingdom there will be no end." But Mary said to the angel, "How can this be, since I have no relations with a man?" And the angel said to her in reply, "The Holy Spirit will come upon you, and the power of the Most High will overshadow you. Therefore the child to be born will be called holy, the Son of God. And behold, Elizabeth, your relative, has also conceived a son in her old age, and this is the sixth month for her who was called barren; for nothing will be impossible for God." Mary said, "Behold, I am the handmaid of the Lord. May it be done to me according to your word." Then the angel departed from her.—The Gospel of the Lord. ℟. **Praise to you, Lord Jesus Christ.**

→ No. 15, p. 18

PRAYER OVER THE OFFERINGS

[Helped by Mary's Intercession]

Graciously accept the saving sacrifice
which we offer you, O Lord,
on the Solemnity of the Immaculate Conception
of the Blessed Virgin Mary,

and grant that, as we profess her,
on account of your prevenient grace,
to be untouched by any stain of sin,
so, through her intercession,
we may be delivered from all our faults.
Through Christ our Lord.
℟. **Amen.** ↓

PREFACE (P 58)   [Mary Our Advocate]

℣. The Lord be with you. ℟. **And with your spirit.**
℣. Lift up your hearts. ℟. **We lift them up to the Lord.**
℣. Let us give thanks to the Lord our God. ℟. **It is right and just.**

It is truly right and just, our duty and our salvation,
always and everywhere to give you thanks,
Lord, holy Father, almighty and eternal God.

For you preserved the most Blessed Virgin Mary
from all stain of original sin,
so that in her, endowed with the rich fullness of your
    grace,
you might prepare a worthy Mother for your Son
and signify the beginning of the Church,
his beautiful Bride without spot or wrinkle.

She, the most pure Virgin, was to bring forth a Son,
the innocent Lamb who would wipe away our offenses;
you placed her above all others
to be for your people an advocate of grace
and a model of holiness.

And so, in company with the choirs of Angels,
we praise you, and with joy we proclaim:

→ No. 23, p. 23

COMMUNION ANT.   [Glorious Things Spoken of Mary]
**Glorious things are spoken of you, O Mary, for from
you arose the sun of justice, Christ our God.** ↓

PRAYER AFTER COMMUNION   [Heal Our Wounds]

May the Sacrament we have received,
O Lord our God,
heal in us the wounds of that fault
from which in a singular way
you preserved Blessed Mary in her Immaculate
    Conception.
Through Christ our Lord.
R̸. **Amen.**   ➔ No. 30, p. 77

Optional Solemn Blessings, p. 97, and Prayers over the People, p. 105

*"[John] heard in prison of the works of the Christ [and] sent
his disciples to Jesus."*

DECEMBER 11

3rd SUNDAY OF ADVENT

ENTRANCE ANT. Phil 4:4-5   [Mounting Joy]

**Rejoice in the Lord always; again I say, rejoice.
Indeed, the Lord is near.** ➔ No. 2, p. 10 (Omit Gloria)

COLLECT   [Joy of Salvation]

O God, who see how your people
faithfully await the feast of the Lord's Nativity,

enable us, we pray,
to attain the joys of so great a salvation
and to celebrate them always
with solemn worship and glad rejoicing.
Through our Lord Jesus Christ, your Son,
who lives and reigns with you in the unity of the Holy
  Spirit,
God, for ever and ever.
℟. **Amen.** ↓

FIRST READING Is 35:1-6, 10   [Here Is Your God]

This vision of the Messiah describes his work—not only in
restoring health and well-being to the infirm, but also in
bringing the mercy and forgiveness of salvation.

A reading from the Book of the Prophet Isaiah

THE desert and the parched land will exult;
  the steppe will rejoice and bloom.
They will bloom with abundant flowers,
  and rejoice with joyful song.
The glory of Lebanon will be given to them,
  the splendor of Carmel and Sharon;
they will see the glory of the LORD,
  the splendor of our God.
Strengthen the hands that are feeble,
  make firm the knees that are weak,
say to those whose hearts are frightened:
  Be strong, fear not!
Here is your God,
  he comes with vindication;
with divine recompense
  he comes to save you.
Then will the eyes of the blind be opened,
  the ears of the deaf be cleared;
then will the lame leap like a stag,
  then the tongue of the mute will sing.

Those whom the Lord has ransomed will return
    and enter Zion singing,
      crowned with everlasting joy;
they will meet with joy and gladness,
    sorrow and mourning will flee.
The word of the Lord. ℟. **Thanks be to God.** ↓

RESPONSORIAL PSALM Ps 146   [The Lord Our Savior]

℟. **Lord, come and save us.**

Or: ℟. **Alleluia.**

The Lord God keeps faith forever,
    secures justice for the oppressed,
    gives food to the hungry.
The Lord sets captives free.

℟. **Lord, come and save us.**

Or: ℟. **Alleluia.**

The Lord gives sight to the blind;
    the Lord raises up those that were bowed down.
The Lord loves the just;
    the Lord protects strangers.

℟. **Lord, come and save us.**

Or: ℟. **Alleluia.**

The fatherless and the widow he sustains,
    but the way of the wicked he thwarts.
The Lord shall reign forever;
    your God, O Zion, through all generations.

℟. **Lord, come and save us.** ↓

Or: ℟. **Alleluia.** ↓

SECOND READING Jas 5:7-10 [The Lord's Coming Is at Hand]
    **Look to the example of prophets and learn patience
    under severe hardships.**

A reading from the Letter of Saint James

BE patient, brothers and sisters, until the coming of the Lord. See how the farmer waits for the precious fruit of the earth, being patient with it until it receives the early and the late rains. You too must be patient. Make your hearts firm, because the coming of the Lord is at hand. Do not complain, brothers and sisters, about one another, that you may not be judged. Behold, the Judge is standing before the gates. Take as an example of hardship and patience, brothers and sisters, the prophets who spoke in the name of the Lord.—The word of the Lord. ℟. **Thanks be to God.** ↓

ALLELUIA Is 61:1 (cited in Lk 4:18)   [Glad Tidings]

℟. **Alleluia, alleluia.**
The Spirit of the Lord is upon me,
because he has anointed me
to bring glad tidings to the poor.
℟. **Alleluia, alleluia.** ↓

GOSPEL Mt 11:2-11   [Effects of the Lord's Coming]

Jesus applies the words of Isaiah to himself. He proclaims the good news of salvation, freedom, and joy.

℣. The Lord be with you. ℟. **And with your spirit.**
✚ A reading from the holy Gospel according to Matthew.
℟. **Glory to you, O Lord.**

WHEN John the Baptist heard in prison of the works of the Christ, he sent his disciples to Jesus with this question, "Are you the one who is to come, or should we look for another?" Jesus said to them in reply, "Go and tell John what you hear and see: the blind regain their sight, the lame walk, lepers are cleansed, the deaf hear, the dead are raised, and the poor have the good news proclaimed to them. And blessed is the one who takes no offense at me."

As they were going off, Jesus began to speak to the crowds about John, "What did you go out to the desert to see? A reed swayed by the wind? Then what did you go out to see? Someone dressed in fine clothing? Those who wear fine clothing are in royal palaces. Then why did you go out? To see a prophet? Yes, I tell you, and more than a prophet. This is the one about whom it is written:

Behold, I am sending my messenger ahead of you;
  he will prepare your way before you.

Amen, I say to you, among those born of women there has been none greater than John the Baptist; yet the least in the kingdom of heaven is greater than he."
—The Gospel of the Lord. ℟. **Praise to you, Lord Jesus Christ.**   ➜ No. 15, p. 18

PRAYER OVER THE OFFERINGS   [Unceasing Sacrifice]

May the sacrifice of our worship, Lord, we pray,
be offered to you unceasingly,
to complete what was begun in sacred mystery
and powerfully accomplish for us your saving work.
Through Christ our Lord.
℟. **Amen.**   ➜ No. 21, p. 22 (Pref. P 1 or 2)

COMMUNION ANT. Cf. Is 35:4   [Trust in God]

Say to the faint of heart: Be strong and do not fear. Behold, our God will come, and he will save us. ↓

PRAYER AFTER COMMUNION   [Preparation for Christ]

We implore your mercy, Lord,
that this divine sustenance may cleanse us of our faults
and prepare us for the coming feasts.
Through Christ our Lord.
℟. **Amen.**   ➜ No. 30, p. 77

Optional Solemn Blessings, p. 97, and Prayers over the People, p. 105

"Joseph . . . took his wife [Mary] into his home."

DECEMBER 18

4th SUNDAY OF ADVENT

ENTRANCE ANT. Cf. Is 45:8   **[The Advent Plea]**

Drop down dew from above, you heavens, and let the clouds rain down the Just One; let the earth be opened and bring forth a Savior. ➙ No. 2, p. 10 (Omit Gloria)

COLLECT   **[From Suffering to Glory]**

Pour forth, we beseech you, O Lord,
your grace into our hearts,
that we, to whom the Incarnation of Christ your Son
was made known by the message of an Angel,
may by his Passion and Cross
be brought to the glory of his Resurrection.
Who lives and reigns with you in the unity of the Holy
    Spirit,
God, for ever and ever. ℟. **Amen.** ↓

FIRST READING Is 7:10-14   **[The Virgin with Child]**

The words of the prophet spoken to the king are applied to the birth of the Savior.

A reading from the Book of the Prophet Isaiah

132

THE LORD spoke to Ahaz, saying: Ask for a sign from the LORD, your God; let it be deep as the netherworld, or high as the sky! But Ahaz answered, "I will not ask! I will not tempt the LORD!" Then Isaiah said: Listen, O house of David! Is it not enough for you to weary people, must you also weary my God? Therefore the Lord himself will give you this sign: the virgin shall conceive, and bear a son, and shall name him Emmanuel.—The word of the Lord. ℟. **Thanks be to God.** ↓

RESPONSORIAL PSALM Ps 24   [The King of Glory]

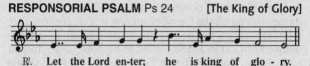

℟.   Let the Lord en-ter;   he   is king of   glo - ry.

The LORD's are the earth and its fullness;
    the world and those who dwell in it.
For he founded it upon the seas
    and established it upon the rivers.

℟. **Let the Lord enter; he is king of glory.**

Who can ascend the mountain of the LORD?
    or who may stand in his holy place?
One whose hands are sinless, whose heart is clean,
    who desires not what is vain.

℟. **Let the Lord enter; he is king of glory.**

He shall receive a blessing from the LORD,
    a reward from God his savior.
Such is the race that seeks for him,
    that seeks the face of the God of Jacob.

℟. **Let the Lord enter; he is king of glory.** ↓

SECOND READING Rom 1:1-7   [Jesus the Savior]

The Messiah is a descendant of David according to the flesh and the Son of God according to the Spirit. His salvation is for all humankind.

A reading from the Letter of Saint Paul to the Romans

PAUL, a slave of Christ Jesus, called to be an apostle and set apart for the gospel of God, which he promised previously through his prophets in the holy Scriptures, the gospel about his Son, descended from David according to the flesh, but established as Son of God in power according to the Spirit of holiness through resurrection from the dead, Jesus Christ our Lord. Through him we have received the grace of apostleship, to bring about the obedience of faith, for the sake of his name, among all the Gentiles, among whom are you also, who are called to belong to Jesus Christ; to all the beloved of God in Rome, called to be holy. Grace to you and peace from God our Father and the Lord Jesus Christ.—The word of the Lord. ℟. **Thanks be to God.** ↓

ALLELUIA Mt 1:23   [Emmanuel]
℟. **Alleluia, alleluia.**
The virgin shall conceive, and bear a son,
and they shall name him Emmanuel.
℟. **Alleluia, alleluia.** ↓

GOSPEL Mt 1:18-24   [God-with-Us]
  Emmanuel means "God is with us." He is conceived by the Holy Spirit and born of the Virgin Mary.

℣. The Lord be with you. ℟. **And with your spirit.**
✚ A reading from the holy Gospel according to Matthew.
℟. **Glory to you, O Lord.**

THIS is how the birth of Jesus Christ came about. When his mother Mary was betrothed to Joseph, but before they lived together, she was found with child through the Holy Spirit. Joseph her husband, since he was a righteous man, yet unwilling to expose her to shame, decided to divorce her quietly. Such was his intention when, behold, the angel of the Lord

appeared to him in a dream and said, "Joseph, son of
David, do not be afraid to take Mary your wife into
your home. For it is through the Holy Spirit that this
child has been conceived in her. She will bear a son
and you are to name him Jesus, because he will save
his people from their sins." All this took place to fulfill
what the Lord had said through the prophet:

Behold, the virgin shall conceive and bear a son,
and they shall name him Emmanuel,

which means "God is with us." When Joseph awoke, he
did as the angel of the Lord had commanded him and
took his wife into his home.—The Gospel of the Lord.
℟. **Praise to you, Lord Jesus Christ.**   ➔ No. 15, p. 18

PRAYER OVER THE OFFERINGS   [Power of the Spirit]

May the Holy Spirit, O Lord,
sanctify these gifts laid upon your altar,
just as he filled with his power the womb of the Blessed
    Virgin Mary.
Through Christ our Lord.
℟. **Amen.**   ➔ No. 21, p. 22 (Pref. P 2)

COMMUNION ANT. Is 7:14   [The Virgin Mother]

**Behold, a Virgin shall conceive and bear a son; and his
name will be called Emmanuel.** ↓

PRAYER AFTER COMMUNION   [Worthy Celebration]

Having received this pledge of eternal redemption,
we pray, almighty God,
that, as the feast day of our salvation draws ever nearer,
so we may press forward all the more eagerly
to the worthy celebration of the mystery of your Son's
    Nativity.
Who lives and reigns for ever and ever.
℟. **Amen.**   ➔ No. 30, p. 77

Optional Solemn Blessings, p. 97, and Prayers over the People, p. 105.

The Word is made flesh.

DECEMBER 25

THE NATIVITY OF THE LORD [CHRISTMAS]

Solemnity

AT THE MASS DURING THE NIGHT

ENTRANCE ANT. Ps 2:7 [Son of God]

The Lord said to me: You are my Son. It is I who have begotten you this day.

OR [True Peace]

Let us all rejoice in the Lord, for our Savior has been born in the world. Today true peace has come down to us from heaven. → No. 2, p. 10

COLLECT [Eternal Gladness]

O God, who have made this most sacred night
radiant with the splendor of the true light,
grant, we pray, that we, who have known the mysteries
    of his light on earth,
may also delight in his gladness in heaven.

Who lives and reigns with you in the unity of the Holy
   Spirit,
God, for ever and ever. ℟. **Amen.** ↓

FIRST READING Is 9:1-6   [The Messiah's Kingdom]
   **The spell of darkness, the shame of sin is broken—the
   Prince of Light is born to us.**

   A reading from the Book of the Prophet Isaiah

T HE people who walked in darkness
   have seen a great light;
upon those who dwelt in the land of gloom
   a light has shone.
You have brought them abundant joy
   and great rejoicing,
as they rejoice before you as at the harvest,
   as people make merry when dividing spoils.
For the yoke that burdened them,
   the pole on their shoulder,
and the rod of their taskmaster
   you have smashed, as on the day of Midian.
For every boot that tramped in battle,
   every cloak rolled in blood,
   will be burned as fuel for flames.
For a child is born to us, a son is given us;
   upon his shoulder dominion rests.
They name him Wonder-Counselor, God-Hero,
   Father-Forever, Prince of Peace.
His dominion is vast
   and forever peaceful,
from David's throne, and over his kingdom,
   which he confirms and sustains
by judgment and justice,
   both now and forever.
The zeal of the LORD of hosts will do this!
The word of the Lord. ℟. **Thanks be to God.** ↓

RESPONSORIAL PSALM Ps 96   [Bless the Lord]

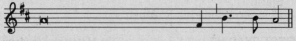

℟. Today is born our Sav - ior, Christ the Lord.

Sing to the LORD a new song;
   sing to the LORD, all you lands.
Sing to the LORD; bless his name.

℟. **Today is born our Savior, Christ the Lord.**

Announce his salvation, day after day.
   Tell his glory among the nations;
   among all peoples, his wondrous deeds.

℟. **Today is born our Savior, Christ the Lord.**

Let the heavens be glad and the earth rejoice;
   let the sea and what fills it resound;
   let the plains be joyful and all that is in them!
Then shall all the trees of the forest exult.

℟. **Today is born our Savior, Christ the Lord.**

They shall exult before the LORD, for he comes;
   for he comes to rule the earth.
He shall rule the world with justice
   and the peoples with his constancy.

℟. **Today is born our Savior, Christ the Lord.** ↓

SECOND READING Ti 2:11-14   [Salvation for All]

**We look to the Second Coming of Christ in glory. Through
his Cross we are freed from the darkness of sin.**

A reading from the Letter of Saint Paul to Titus

B ELOVED: The grace of God has appeared, saving
all and training us to reject godless ways and
worldly desires and to live temperately, justly, and
devoutly in this age, as we await the blessed hope, the
appearance of the glory of our great God and savior
Jesus Christ, who gave himself for us to deliver us

from all lawlessness and to cleanse for himself a people as his own, eager to do what is good.—The word of the Lord. ℟. **Thanks be to God.** ↓

ALLELUIA Lk 2:10-11   [Great Joy]

℟. **Alleluia, alleluia.**
I proclaim to you good news of great joy:
today a Savior is born for us,
Christ the Lord.
℟. **Alleluia, alleluia.** ↓

GOSPEL Lk 2:1-14   [Birth of Christ]

Rejoice in the good news—our Savior is born, and he is revealed to us by the witness of shepherds.

℣. The Lord be with you. ℟. **And with your spirit.**
✛ A reading from the holy Gospel according to Luke.
℟. **Glory to you, O Lord.**

IN those days a decree went out from Caesar Augustus that the whole world should be enrolled. This was the first enrollment, when Quirinius was governor of Syria. So all went to be enrolled, each to his own town. And Joseph too went up from Galilee from the town of Nazareth to Judea, to the city of David that is called Bethlehem, because he was of the house and family of David, to be enrolled with Mary, his betrothed, who was with child. While they were there, the time came for her to have her child, and she gave birth to her firstborn son. She wrapped him in swaddling clothes and laid him in a manger, because there was no room for them in the inn.

Now there were shepherds in that region living in the fields and keeping the night watch over their flock. The angel of the Lord appeared to them and the glory of the Lord shone around them, and they were struck with great fear. The angel said to them, "Do not be afraid; for behold, I proclaim to you good news of great joy that will be for all the people. For today in the city of David a savior has been born for you who is Christ and Lord. And this will be a sign for you: you will find an infant wrapped in swaddling clothes and lying in a manger." And suddenly there was a multitude of the heavenly host with the angel, praising God and saying:

"Glory to God in the highest
and on earth peace to those on whom his favor rests."

The Gospel of the Lord. ℟. **Praise to you, Lord Jesus Christ.**   ➙ No. 15, p. 18

The Creed is said. All kneel at the words and by the Holy Spirit was incarnate.

PRAYER OVER THE OFFERINGS   [Become Like Christ]

May the oblation of this day's feast
be pleasing to you, O Lord, we pray,
that through this most holy exchange
we may be found in the likeness of Christ,
in whom our nature is united to you.
Who lives and reigns for ever and ever.
℟. **Amen.**   ➙ No. 21, p. 22 (Pref. P 3-5)

When the Roman Canon is used, the proper form of the Communicantes *(In communion with those) is said.*

COMMUNION ANT. Jn 1:14   [Glory of Christ]

The Word became flesh, and we have seen his glory. ↓

PRAYER AFTER COMMUNION   [Union with Christ]

Grant us, we pray, O Lord our God,
that we, who are gladdened by participation
in the feast of our Redeemer's Nativity,
may through an honorable way of life become worthy of
union with him.
Who lives and reigns for ever and ever.
℟. **Amen.**   ➙ No. 30, p. 77

Optional Solemn Blessings, p. 97, and Prayers over the People, p. 105

AT THE MASS AT DAWN

ENTRANCE ANT. Cf. Is 9:1, 5; Lk 1:33   [Prince of Peace]

Today a light will shine upon us, for the Lord is born for us; and he will be called Wondrous God, Prince of peace, Father of future ages: and his reign will be without end.   → No. 2, p. 10

COLLECT   [Light of Faith]

Grant, we pray, almighty God,
that, as we are bathed in the new radiance of your
    incarnate Word,
the light of faith, which illumines our minds,
may also shine through in our deeds.
Through our Lord Jesus Christ, your Son,
who lives and reigns with you in the unity of the Holy
    Spirit,
God, for ever and ever.
℟. **Amen.** ↓

FIRST READING Is 62:11-12   [The Savior's Birth]

Our Savior comes. He makes us a holy people and redeems us.

A reading from the Book of the Prophet Isaiah

SEE, the LORD proclaims
    to the ends of the earth:
say to daughter Zion,
    your savior comes!
Here is his reward with him,
    his recompense before him.
They shall be called the holy people,
    the redeemed of the LORD,
and you shall be called "Frequented,"
    a city that is not forsaken.
The word of the Lord. ℟. **Thanks be to God.** ↓

RESPONSORIAL PSALM Ps 97   [Be Glad in the Lord]

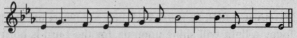

℟. A light will shine on us this day: the Lord is born for us.

The LORD is king; let the earth rejoice;
 let the many isles be glad.
The heavens proclaim his justice,
 and all peoples see his glory.

℟. **A light will shine on us this day: the Lord is born for us.**

Light dawns for the just;
 and gladness, for the upright of heart.
Be glad in the LORD, you just,
 and give thanks to his holy name.

℟. **A light will shine on us this day: the Lord is born for us.** ↓

SECOND READING Ti 3:4-7   [Saved by God's Mercy]

By God's mercy we are saved from sin. Jesus became man
that we might through him receive the Spirit.

A reading from the Letter of Saint Paul to Titus

BELOVED:
 When the kindness and generous love
 of God our savior appeared,
not because of any righteous deeds we had done
 but because of his mercy,
he saved us through the bath of rebirth
 and renewal by the Holy Spirit,
whom he richly poured out on us
 through Jesus Christ our savior,
so that we might be justified by his grace
 and become heirs in hope of eternal life.
The word of the Lord. ℟. **Thanks be to God.** ↓

ALLELUIA Lk 2:14   [Glory to God]

℟. **Alleluia, alleluia.**
Glory to God in the highest,
and on earth peace to those
on whom his favor rests.
℟. **Alleluia, alleluia.** ↓

GOSPEL Lk 2:15-20   [Jesus, the God-Man]

**The wonder of salvation is revealed to the shepherds and
to us. The love of God is manifest because he is with us.**

℣. The Lord be with you. ℟. **And with your spirit.**
✝ A reading from the holy Gospel according to Luke.
℟. **Glory to you, O Lord.**

W HEN the angels went away from them to heaven,
the shepherds said to one another, "Let us go,
then, to Bethlehem to see this thing that has taken
place, which the Lord has made known to us." So they
went in haste and found Mary and Joseph, and the
infant lying in the manger. When they saw this, they
made known the message that had been told them
about this child. All who heard it were amazed by what
had been told them by the shepherds. And Mary kept
all these things, reflecting on them in her heart. Then
the shepherds returned, glorifying and praising God
for all they had heard and seen, just as it had been told
to them. —The Gospel of the Lord. ℟. **Praise to you,
Lord Jesus Christ.**   → No. 15, p. 18

The Creed is said. All kneel at the words and by the Holy Spirit
was incarnate.

PRAYER OVER THE OFFERINGS   [Gift of Divine Life]

May our offerings be worthy, we pray, O Lord,
of the mysteries of the Nativity this day,
that, just as Christ was born a man and also shone forth
    as God,
so these earthly gifts may confer on us what is divine.

Through Christ our Lord.
Ṛ. **Amen.**   → No. 21, p. 22 (Pref. P 3-5)

When the Roman Canon is used, the proper form of the
Communicantes *(In communion with those) is said.*

COMMUNION ANT. Cf. Zec 9:9   [The Holy One]
**Rejoice, O Daughter Sion; lift up praise, Daughter
Jerusalem: Behold, your King will come, the Holy One
and Savior of the world.** ↓

PRAYER AFTER COMMUNION   [Fullness of Faith]

Grant us, Lord, as we honor with joyful devotion
the Nativity of your Son,
that we may come to know with fullness of faith
the hidden depths of this mystery
and to love them ever more and more.
Through Christ our Lord.
Ṛ. **Amen.**   → No. 30, p. 77

Optional Solemn Blessings, p. 97, and Prayers over the People, p. 105

AT THE MASS DURING THE DAY

ENTRANCE ANT. Cf. Is 9:5   [The Gift of God's Son]
**A child is born for us, and a son is given to us; his
scepter of power rests upon his shoulder, and his
name will be called Messenger of great counsel.**
                              → No. 2, p. 10

COLLECT   [Share in Christ's Divinity]

O God, who wonderfully created the dignity of human
   nature
and still more wonderfully restored it,
grant, we pray,
that we may share in the divinity of Christ,
who humbled himself to share in our humanity.

Who lives and reigns with you in the unity of the Holy
   Spirit,
God, for ever and ever. ℞. **Amen.** ↓

FIRST READING Is 52:7-10   [Your God Is King]

**The good news is that the Lord comforts his people by
announcing our salvation.**

A reading from the Book of the Prophet Isaiah

H OW beautiful upon the mountains
   are the feet of him who brings glad tidings,
announcing peace, bearing good news,
   announcing salvation, and saying to Zion,
   "Your God is King!"

Hark! Your sentinels raise a cry,
   together they shout for joy,
for they see directly, before their eyes,
   the Lord restoring Zion.
Break out together in song,
   O ruins of Jerusalem!
For the Lord comforts his people,
   he redeems Jerusalem.
The Lord has bared his holy arm
   in the sight of all the nations;
all the ends of the earth will behold
   the salvation of our God.
The word of the Lord. ℞. **Thanks be to God.** ↓

RESPONSORIAL PSALM Ps 98   [Sing a New Song]

℞. **All the ends of the earth have seen the saving   power of God.**

Sing to the Lord a new song,
   for he has done wondrous deeds;

his right hand has won victory for him,
  his holy arm.

℟. **All the ends of the earth have seen the saving
  power of God.**

The LORD has made his salvation known:
  in the sight of the nations he has revealed his justice.
He has remembered his kindness and his faithfulness
  toward the house of Israel.

℟. **All the ends of the earth have seen the saving
  power of God.**

All the ends of the earth have seen
  the salvation by our God.
Sing joyfully to the LORD, all you lands;
  break into song; sing praise.

℟. **All the ends of the earth have seen the saving
  power of God.**

Sing praise to the LORD with the harp,
  with the harp and melodious song.
With trumpets and the sound of the horn
  sing joyfully before the King, the LORD.

℟. **All the ends of the earth have seen the saving
  power of God.** ↓

SECOND READING Heb 1:1-6 [God Speaks through Jesus]

Now God speaks to us more clearly than ever before. His
Son is with us—God is with us; we are his people.

A reading from the Letter to the Hebrews

BROTHERS and sisters: In times past, God spoke in
partial and various ways to our ancestors through
the prophets; in these last days, he has spoken to us
through the Son, whom he made heir of all things and
through whom he created the universe,
  who is the refulgence of his glory, the very imprint
    of his being,

and who sustains all things by his mighty word.
When he had accomplished purification from sins,
he took his seat at the right hand of the Majesty on
　high,
as far superior to the angels
as the name he has inherited is more excellent than
　theirs.

For to which of the angels did God ever say:
　You are my son; this day I have begotten you?
Or again:
　I will be a father to him, and he shall be a son to me?
And again, when he leads the firstborn into the
　world, he says:
　Let all the angels of God worship him.
The word of the Lord. ℟. **Thanks be to God.** ↓

ALLELUIA　　　　　　　　　　　[Adore the Lord]
℟. **Alleluia, alleluia.**
A holy day has dawned upon us.
Come, you nations, and adore the Lord.
For today a great light has come upon the earth.
℟. **Alleluia, alleluia.** ↓

GOSPEL Jn 1:1-18 or 1:1-5, 9-14　　　[The True Light]
　　**The Word of God is the living Word. The Word became
　　flesh and lives in our midst.**

*[If the "Shorter Form" is used, the indented text in brackets is
omitted.]*

℣. The Lord be with you. ℟. **And with your spirit.**
✠ A reading from the holy Gospel according to John.
℟. **Glory to you, O Lord.**

IN the beginning was the Word,
　and the Word was with God,
　　and the Word was God.
He was in the beginning with God.
All things came to be through him,
　and without him nothing came to be.

What came to be through him was life,
and this life was the light of the human race;
the light shines in the darkness,
and the darkness has not overcome it.

[A man named John was sent from God. He
came for testimony, to testify to the light, so
that all might believe through him. He was not
the light, but came to testify to the light.]

The true light, which enlightens everyone, was coming into the world.

He was in the world,
and the world came to be through him,
but the world did not know him.
He came to what was his own,
but his own people did not accept him.

But to those who did accept him he gave power to become children of God, to those who believe in his name, who were born not by natural generation nor by human choice nor by a man's decision but of God.

And the Word became flesh
and made his dwelling among us,
and we saw his glory,
the glory as of the Father's only Son,
full of grace and truth.

[John testified to him and cried out, saying,
"This was he of whom I said, 'The one who is
coming after me ranks ahead of me because
he existed before me.'" From his fullness we
have all received, grace in place of grace,
because while the law was given through
Moses, grace and truth came through Jesus
Christ. No one has ever seen God. The only
Son, God, who is at the Father's side, has
revealed him.]

The Gospel of the Lord. ℟. **Praise to you, Lord Jesus Christ.**   → No. 15, p. 18

The Creed is said. All kneel at the words and by the Holy Spirit was incarnate.

PRAYER OVER THE OFFERINGS   [Reconciliation]

Make acceptable, O Lord, our oblation on this solemn
   day,
when you manifested the reconciliation
that makes us wholly pleasing in your sight
and inaugurated for us the fullness of divine worship.
Through Christ our Lord.
℟. **Amen.**   → No. 21, p. 22 (Pref. P 3-5)

When the Roman Canon is used, the proper form of the
Communicantes *(*In communion with those*) is said.*

COMMUNION ANT. Cf. Ps 98 (97):3   [Salvation]

**All the ends of the earth have seen the salvation of our
God.** ↓

PRAYER AFTER COMMUNION   [Giver of Immortality]

Grant, O merciful God,
that, just as the Savior of the world, born this day,
is the author of divine generation for us,
so he may be the giver even of immortality.
Who lives and reigns for ever and ever.
℟. **Amen.**   → No. 30, p. 77

Optional Solemn Blessings, p. 97, and Prayers over the People, p. 105

"He was named Jesus. . . ."

JANUARY 1, 2023

SOLEMNITY OF MARY, THE HOLY MOTHER OF GOD

ENTRANCE ANT.   [Hail, Holy Mother]

Hail, Holy Mother, who gave birth to the King who rules heaven and earth for ever.

OR Cf. Is 9:1, 5; Lk 1:33   [Wondrous God]

Today a light will shine upon us, for the Lord is born for us; and he will be called Wondrous God, Prince of peace, Father of future ages: and his reign will be without end.   → No. 2, p. 10

COLLECT   [Mary's Intercession]

O God, who through the fruitful virginity of Blessed
    Mary
bestowed on the human race
the grace of eternal salvation,
grant, we pray,
that we may experience the intercession of her,
through whom we were found worthy
to receive the author of life,

our Lord Jesus Christ, your Son.
Who lives and reigns with you in the unity of the Holy
  Spirit,
God, for ever and ever.
℟. **Amen.** ↓

FIRST READING Nm 6:22-27   [The Aaronic Blessing]
  **Aaron and the Israelites are to pray that God will answer
  their prayers with blessings.**

A reading from the Book of Numbers

T HE LORD said to Moses: "Speak to Aaron and his
   sons and tell them: This is how you shall bless the
Israelites. Say to them:

  The LORD bless you and keep you!
  The LORD let his face shine upon you, and be gracious
    to you!
  The LORD look upon you kindly and give you peace!

So shall they invoke my name upon the Israelites and
I will bless them."—The word of the Lord. ℟. **Thanks
be to God.** ↓

RESPONSORIAL PSALM Ps 67   [God Bless Us]

℟. May   God   bless   us   in   his   mer - cy.

May God have pity on us and bless us;
  may he let his face shine upon us.
So may your way be known upon earth;
  among all nations, your salvation.
℟. **May God bless us in his mercy.**

May the nations be glad and exult
  because you rule the peoples in equity;
  the nations on the earth you guide.
℟. **May God bless us in his mercy.**

May the peoples praise you, O God;
  may all the peoples praise you!
May God bless us,
  and may all the ends of the earth fear him!

℞. **May God bless us in his mercy.** ↓

SECOND READING Gal 4:4-7   [Heirs by God's Design]
God sent Jesus, his Son, born of Mary, to deliver all from the bondage of sin and slavery of the law. By God's choice we are heirs of heaven.

A reading from the Letter of Saint Paul to the Galatians

BROTHERS and sisters: When the fullness of time had come, God sent his Son, born of a woman, born under the law, to ransom those under the law, so that we might receive adoption as sons. As proof that you are sons, God sent the Spirit of his Son into our hearts, crying out, "Abba, Father!" So you are no longer a slave but a son, and if a son then also an heir, through God.—The word of the Lord. ℞. **Thanks be to God.** ↓

ALLELUIA Heb 1:1-2   [God Speaks]
℞. **Alleluia, alleluia.**
In the past God spoke to our ancestors through the
  prophets;
in these last days, he has spoken to us through the Son.
℞. **Alleluia, alleluia.** ↓

GOSPEL Lk 2:16-21   [The Name of Jesus]
When the shepherds came to Bethlehem, they began to understand the message of the angels. Mary prayed about this great event. Jesus received his name according to the Jewish ritual of circumcision.

℣. The Lord be with you. ℞. **And with your spirit.**
✚ A reading from the holy Gospel according to Luke.
℞. **Glory to you, O Lord.**

T HE shepherds went in haste to Bethlehem and found Mary and Joseph, and the infant lying in the manger. When they saw this, they made known the message that had been told them about this child. All who heard it were amazed by what had been told them by the shepherds. And Mary kept all these things, reflecting on them in her heart. Then the shepherds returned, glorifying and praising God for all they had heard and seen, just as it had been told to them.

When eight days were completed for his circumcision, he was named Jesus, the name given him by the angel before he was conceived in the womb.—The Gospel of the Lord. ℟. **Praise to you, Lord Jesus Christ.**   ➜ No. 15, p. 18

PRAYER OVER THE OFFERINGS   [Rejoice in Grace]

O God, who in your kindness begin all good things
and bring them to fulfillment,
grant to us, who find joy in the Solemnity of the holy
    Mother of God,
that, just as we glory in the beginnings of your grace,
so one day we may rejoice in its completion.
Through Christ our Lord.
℟. **Amen.** ↓

PREFACE (P 56)   [Mary, Virgin and Mother]

℣. The Lord be with you. ℟. **And with your spirit.**
℣. Lift up your hearts. ℟. **We lift them up to the Lord.**
℣. Let us give thanks to the Lord our God. ℟. **It is right and just.**

It is truly right and just, our duty and our salvation,
always and everywhere to give you thanks,
Lord, holy Father, almighty and eternal God,
and to praise, bless, and glorify your name
on the Solemnity of the Motherhood
of the Blessed ever-Virgin Mary.

For by the overshadowing of the Holy Spirit
she conceived your Only Begotten Son,
and without losing the glory of virginity,
brought forth into the world the eternal Light,
Jesus Christ our Lord.

Through him the Angels praise your majesty,
Dominions adore and Powers tremble before you.
Heaven and the Virtues of heaven and the blessed
Seraphim
worship together with exultation.
May our voices, we pray, join with theirs
in humble praise, as we acclaim: ➜ No. 23, p. 23

When the Roman Canon is used, the proper form of the
Communicantes *(*In communion with those*) is said.*

COMMUNION ANT. Heb 13:8   [Jesus Forever]
Jesus Christ is the same yesterday, today, and for ever. ↓

PRAYER AFTER COMMUNION   [Mother of the Church]

We have received this heavenly Sacrament with joy,
O Lord:
grant, we pray,
that it may lead us to eternal life,
for we rejoice to proclaim the blessed ever-Virgin Mary
Mother of your Son and Mother of the Church.
Through Christ our Lord.
℟. **Amen.**   ➜ No. 30, p. 77

Optional Solemn Blessings, p. 97, and Prayers over the People, p. 105

"They prostrated themselves and did him homage."

JANUARY 8
THE EPIPHANY OF THE LORD
Solemnity
AT THE VIGIL MASS (January 7)

ENTRANCE ANT. Cf. Bar 5:5   [Arise, Jerusalem]

Arise, Jerusalem, and look to the East and see your children gathered from the rising to the setting of the sun.   ➥ No. 2, p. 10

COLLECT   [Splendor of God's Majesty]

May the splendor of your majesty, O Lord, we pray,
shed its light upon our hearts,
that we may pass through the shadows of this world
and reach the brightness of our eternal home.
Through our Lord Jesus Christ, your Son,
who lives and reigns with you in the unity of the Holy
   Spirit,
God, for ever and ever. ℟. **Amen.** ↓

FIRST READING Is 60:1-6   [Glory of God's Church]

Jerusalem is favored by the Lord. Kings and peoples will come before you. The riches of the earth will be placed at the gates of Jerusalem.

155

A reading from the Book of the Prophet Isaiah

R ISE up in splendor, Jerusalem! Your light has come,
  the glory of the Lord shines upon you.
See, darkness covers the earth,
  and thick clouds cover the peoples;
but upon you the LORD shines,
  and over you appears his glory.
Nations shall walk by your light,
  and kings by your shining radiance.
Raise your eyes and look about;
  they all gather and come to you:
your sons come from afar,
  and your daughters in the arms of their nurses.

Then you shall be radiant at what you see,
  your heart shall throb and overflow,
for the riches of the sea shall be emptied out before you,
  the wealth of nations shall be brought to you.
Caravans of camels shall fill you,
  dromedaries from Midian and Ephah;
all from Sheba shall come
  bearing gold and frankincense,
  and proclaiming the praises of the LORD.
The word of the Lord. ℟. **Thanks be to God.** ↓

RESPONSORIAL PSALM Ps 72   [The Messiah-King]

℟. **Lord, every nation on earth will adore you.**

O God, with your judgment endow the king,
  and with your justice, the king's son;
he shall govern your people with justice
  and your afflicted ones with judgment.
℟. **Lord, every nation on earth will adore you.**

Justice shall flower in his days,
    and profound peace, till the moon be no more.
May he rule from sea to sea,
    and from the River to the ends of the earth.

℟. **Lord, every nation on earth will adore you.**

The kings of Tarshish and the Isles shall offer gifts;
    the kings of Arabia and Seba shall bring tribute.
All kings shall pay him homage,
    all nations shall serve him.

℟. **Lord, every nation on earth will adore you.**

For he shall rescue the poor man when he cries out,
    and the afflicted when he has no one to help him.
He shall have pity for the lowly and the poor;
    the lives of the poor he shall save.

℟. **Lord, every nation on earth will adore you.** ↓

SECOND READING Eph 3:2-3a, 5-6   [Good News for All]
    **Paul admits that God has revealed the divine plan of sal-
    vation to him. Not only the Jews, but also the whole
    Gentile world, will share in the good news.**

A reading from the Letter of Saint Paul to the Ephesians

BROTHERS and sisters: You have heard of the stew-
ardship of God's grace that was given to me for
your benefit, namely, that the mystery was made
known to me by revelation. It was not made known to
people in other generations as it has now been
revealed to his holy apostles and prophets by the
Spirit: that the Gentiles are coheirs, members of the
same body, and copartners in the promise in Christ
Jesus through the gospel.—The word of the Lord.
℟. **Thanks be to God.** ↓

ALLELUIA Mt 2:2   [Leading Star]
℟. **Alleluia, alleluia.**
We saw his star at its rising

and have come to do him homage.
℟. **Alleluia, alleluia.** ↓

GOSPEL Mt 2:1-12   [Magi with Gifts]

King Herod, being jealous of his earthly crown, was threatened by the coming of another king. The magi from the
east followed the star to Bethlehem from which a ruler was
to come.

℣. The Lord be with you. ℟. **And with your spirit.**
✝ A reading from the holy Gospel according to Matthew.
℟. **Glory to you, O Lord.**

WHEN Jesus was born in Bethlehem of Judea, in
the days of King Herod, behold, magi from the
east arrived in Jerusalem, saying, "Where is the new-
born king of the Jews? We saw his star at its rising and
have come to do him homage." When King Herod
heard this, he was greatly troubled, and all Jerusalem
with him. Assembling all the chief priests and the
scribes of the people, he inquired of them where the
Christ was to be born. They said to him, "In Bethlehem
of Judea, for thus it has been written through the
prophet:

And you, Bethlehem, land of Judah,
 are by no means least among the rulers of Judah;
since from you shall come a ruler,
 who is to shepherd my people Israel."

Then Herod called the magi secretly and ascertained
from them the time of the star's appearance. He sent
them to Bethlehem and said, "Go and search diligently
for the child. When you have found him, bring me
word, that I too may go and do him homage." After
their audience with the king they set out. And behold,
the star that they had seen at its rising preceded them,
until it came and stopped over the place where the
child was. They were overjoyed at seeing the star, and
on entering the house they saw the child with Mary his
mother. They prostrated themselves and did him

homage. Then they opened their treasures and offered him gifts of gold, frankincense, and myrrh. And having been warned in a dream not to return to Herod, they departed for their country by another way.—The Gospel of the Lord. ℟. **Praise to you, Lord Jesus Christ.**   ➜ No. 15, p. 18

PRAYER OVER THE OFFERINGS   [Render Praise]

Accept we pray, O Lord, our offerings,
in honor of the appearing of your Only Begotten Son
and the first fruits of the nations,
that to you praise may be rendered
and eternal salvation be ours.
Through Christ our Lord. ℟. **Amen.** ↓

PREFACE (P 6)   [Jesus Revealed to All]

℣. The Lord be with you. ℟. **And with your spirit.**
℣. Lift up your hearts. ℟. **We lift them up to the Lord.**
℣. Let us give thanks to the Lord our God. ℟. **It is right and just.**

It is truly right and just, our duty and our salvation,
always and everywhere to give you thanks,
Lord, holy Father, almighty and eternal God.

For today you have revealed the mystery
of our salvation in Christ
as a light for the nations,
and, when he appeared in our mortal nature,
you made us new by the glory of his immortal nature.

And so, with Angels and Archangels,
with Thrones and Dominions,
and with all the hosts and Powers of heaven,
we sing the hymn of your glory,
as without end we acclaim: ➜ No. 23, p. 23

COMMUNION ANT. Cf. Rev 21:23   [Walking by God's Light]

The brightness of God illumined the holy city Jerusalem, and the nations will walk by its light. ↓

PRAYER AFTER COMMUNION   [True Treasure]

Renewed by sacred nourishment,
we implore your mercy, O Lord,
that the star of your justice
may shine always bright in our minds
and that our true treasure may ever consist in our
    confession of you.
Through Christ our Lord.
℟. **Amen.**   → No. 30, p. 77

Optional Solemn Blessings, p. 97, and Prayers over the People, p. 105

AT THE MASS DURING THE DAY

ENTRANCE ANT. Cf. Mal 3:1; 1 Chr 29:12   [Lord and Ruler]

Behold, the Lord, the Mighty One, has come; and kingship is in his grasp, and power and dominion.

→ No. 2, p. 10

COLLECT   [Behold Glory]

O God, who on this day
revealed your Only Begotten Son to the nations
by the guidance of a star,
grant in your mercy
that we, who know you already by faith,
may be brought to behold the beauty of your sublime
    glory.
Through our Lord Jesus Christ, your Son,
who lives and reigns with you in the unity of the Holy
    Spirit,
God, for ever and ever. ℟. **Amen.** ↓

The readings for this Mass can be found beginning on p. 155.

PRAYER OVER THE OFFERINGS   [Offering of Jesus]

Look with favor, Lord, we pray,
on these gifts of your Church,
in which are offered now not gold or frankincense or
  myrrh,
but he who by them is proclaimed,
sacrificed and received, Jesus Christ.
Who lives and reigns for ever and ever.
℟. **Amen.**   → Pref. P 6, p. 159

When the Roman Canon is used, the proper form of the
Communicantes *(*In communion with those*) is said.*

COMMUNION ANT. Cf. Mt 2:2   [Adore the Lord]

**We have seen his star in the East, and have come with
gifts to adore the Lord.** ↓

PRAYER AFTER COMMUNION   [Heavenly Light]

Go before us with heavenly light, O Lord,
always and everywhere,
that we may perceive with clear sight
and revere with true affection
the mystery in which you have willed us to participate.
Through Christ our Lord.
℟. **Amen.**   → No. 30, p. 77

Optional Solemn Blessings, p. 97, and Prayers over the People, p. 105

*"Behold, the Lamb of God, who takes away
the sin of the world."*

JANUARY 15

2nd SUNDAY IN ORDINARY TIME

ENTRANCE ANT. Ps 66 (65):4   [Proclaim His Glory]

**All the earth shall bow down before you, O God, and
shall sing to you, shall sing to your name, O Most
High!**   ➜ No. 2, p. 10

COLLECT   [Peace on Our Times]

Almighty ever-living God,
who govern all things,
both in heaven and on earth,
mercifully hear the pleading of your people
and bestow your peace on our times.
Through our Lord Jesus Christ, your Son,
who lives and reigns with you in the unity of the Holy
    Spirit,
God, for ever and ever.
R̞. **Amen.** ↓

FIRST READING Is 49:3, 5-6   [God Is My Strength]

> Through Israel the Lord will show forth his glory and
> splendor. Israel is to be a light for all nations whereby sal-
> vation will come to all people.

A reading from the Book of the Prophet Isaiah

THE LORD said to me: You are my servant,
Israel, through whom I show my glory.
Now the LORD has spoken
    who formed me as his servant from the womb,
that Jacob may be brought back to him
    and Israel gathered to him;
and I am made glorious in the sight of the LORD,
    and my God is now my strength!
It is too little, the LORD says, for you to be my servant,
    to raise up the tribes of Jacob,
        and restore the survivors of Israel;
I will make you a light to the nations,
    that my salvation may reach to the ends of the
        earth.

The word of the Lord. ℟. **Thanks be to God.** ↓

RESPONSORIAL PSALM Ps 40   [Doing God's Will]

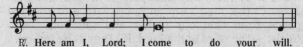

℟. Here am I, Lord; I come to do your will.

I have waited, waited for the LORD,
    and he stooped toward me and heard my cry.
And he put a new song into my mouth,
    a hymn to our God.

℟. **Here am I, Lord; I come to do your will.**

Sacrifice or offering you wished not,
    but ears open to obedience you gave me.
Holocausts or sin-offerings you sought not;
    then said I, "Behold I come."

℟. **Here am I, Lord; I come to do your will.**

"In the written scroll it is prescribed for me,
to do your will, O my God, is my delight,
    and your law is within my heart!"

℟. **Here am I, Lord; I come to do your will.**

I announced your justice in the vast assembly;
    I did not restrain my lips, as you, O LORD, know.

℟. **Here am I, Lord; I come to do your will.**

SECOND READING 1 Cor 1:1-3   [A Holy People]

Paul and Sosthenes greet the people at Corinth. They are
to be a holy people as are all who call upon the name of
Jesus, acknowledging him as Lord.

A reading from the first Letter of Saint Paul
to the Corinthians

PAUL, called to be an apostle of Christ Jesus by the
will of God, and Sosthenes our brother, to the
church of God that is in Corinth, to you who have been
sanctified in Christ Jesus, called to be holy, with all
those everywhere who call upon the name of our Lord
Jesus Christ, their Lord and ours. Grace to you and
peace from God our Father and the Lord Jesus
Christ.—The word of the Lord. ℟. **Thanks be to God.** ↓

ALLELUIA Jn 1:14a, 12a   [Children of God]

℟. **Alleluia, alleluia.**
The Word of God became flesh and dwelt among us.
To those who accepted him,
he gave power to become children of God.
℟. **Alleluia, alleluia.** ↓

*In place of the Alleluia given for each Sunday in Ordinary
Time, another may be selected.*

GOSPEL Jn 1:29-34   [Encountering Christ]

John the Baptist recognized Jesus, the Lamb of God who
takes away the sins of the world. This is God's Chosen
One upon whom the Spirit descended and came to rest.

℣. The Lord be with you. ℟. **And with your spirit.**
✛ A reading from the holy Gospel according to John.
℟. **Glory to you, O Lord.**

JOHN the Baptist saw Jesus coming toward him and
said, "Behold, the Lamb of God, who takes away the
sin of the world. He is the one of whom I said, 'A man
is coming after me who ranks ahead of me because he
existed before me.' I did not know him, but the reason
why I came baptizing with water was that he might be
made known to Israel." John testified further, saying,
"I saw the Spirit come down like a dove from heaven
and remain upon him. I did not know him, but the one
who sent me to baptize with water told me, 'On
whomever you see the Spirit come down and remain,
he is the one who will baptize with the Holy Spirit.'
Now I have seen and testified that he is the Son of
God."—The Gospel of the Lord. ℟. **Praise to you, Lord
Jesus Christ.**   → No. 15, p. 18

PRAYER OVER THE OFFERINGS   [Work of Redemption]

Grant us, O Lord, we pray,
that we may participate worthily in these mysteries,
for whenever the memorial of this sacrifice is celebrated
the work of our redemption is accomplished.
Through Christ our Lord.
℟. **Amen.**   → No. 21, p. 22 (Pref. P 29-36)

COMMUNION ANT. Ps 23 (22):5   [Thirst Quenched]

**You have prepared a table before me, and how pre-
cious is the chalice that quenches my thirst.** ↓

OR 1 Jn 4:16   [God's Love]

**We have come to know and to believe in the love that
God has for us.** ↓

PRAYER AFTER COMMUNION   [One in Heart]

Pour on us, O Lord, the Spirit of your love,
and in your kindness
make those you have nourished
by this one heavenly Bread
one in mind and heart.
Through Christ our Lord.
℟. **Amen.**   → No. 30, p. 77

Optional Solemn Blessings, p. 97, and Prayers over the People, p. 105

"Come after me, and I will make you fishers of men."

JANUARY 22

3rd SUNDAY IN ORDINARY TIME

ENTRANCE ANT. Cf. Ps 96 (95):1, 6   [Sing to the Lord]

**O sing a new song to the Lord; sing to the Lord, all the
earth. In his presence are majesty and splendor,
strength and honor in his holy place.**   → No. 2, p. 10

COLLECT   [Abound in Good Works]

Almighty ever-living God,
direct our actions according to your good pleasure,
that in the name of your beloved Son
we may abound in good works.
Through our Lord Jesus Christ, your Son,
who lives and reigns with you in the unity of the Holy
    Spirit,
God, for ever and ever. ℟. **Amen**. ↓

FIRST READING Is 8:23—9:3   [Joy and Light]

Isaiah tells of the land in the west where there is no gloom,
for the people see a great light. They are to rejoice that the
yoke that bound them is to be smashed.

A reading from the Book of the Prophet Isaiah

FIRST the LORD degraded the land of Zebulun and
the land of Naphtali; but in the end he has glorified
the seaward road, the land west of the Jordan, the
District of the Gentiles.

Anguish has taken wing, dispelled is darkness:
    for there is no gloom where but now there was
        distress.
The people who walked in darkness
    have seen a great light;
upon those who dwelt in the land of gloom
    a light has shone.
You have brought them abundant joy
    and great rejoicing,
as they rejoice before you as at the harvest,
    as people make merry when dividing spoils.
For the yoke that burdened them,
    the pole on their shoulder,
and the rod of their taskmaster
    you have smashed, as on the day of Midian.
The word of the Lord. ℟. **Thanks be to God.** ↓

RESPONSORIAL PSALM Ps 27　　　[Wait with Courage]

℟. The Lord is my light and my sal - va - tion.

The LORD is my light and my salvation;
　whom should I fear?
The LORD is my life's refuge;
　of whom should I be afraid?

℟. **The Lord is my light and my salvation.**

One thing I ask of the LORD;
　this I seek:
to dwell in the house of the LORD
　all the days of my life,
that I may gaze on the loveliness of the LORD
　and contemplate his temple.

℟. **The Lord is my light and my salvation.**

I believe that I shall see the bounty of the LORD
　in the land of the living.
Wait for the LORD with courage;
　be stouthearted, and wait for the LORD.

℟. **The Lord is my light and my salvation.** ↓

SECOND READING 1 Cor 1:10-13, 17　　[Need for Unity]

Paul warns the people of Corinth that there must be unity among the people of God. There is only one Gospel message. Jesus cannot be divided, no matter who preaches about him.

A reading from the first Letter of Saint Paul
to the Corinthians

I URGE you, brothers and sisters, in the name of our
Lord Jesus Christ, that all of you agree in what you say,
and that there be no divisions among you, but that you be
united in the same mind and in the same purpose. For it
has been reported to me about you, my brothers and sisters, by Chloe's people that there are rivalries among

you. I mean that each of you is saying, "I belong to Paul," or "I belong to Apollos," or "I belong to Cephas," or "I belong to Christ." Is Christ divided? Was Paul crucified for you? Or were you baptized in the name of Paul? For Christ did not send me to baptize but to preach the gospel, and not with the wisdom of human eloquence, so that the cross of Christ might not be emptied of its meaning.—The word of the Lord. ℟. **Thanks be to God.** ↓

ALLELUIA Cf. Mt 4:23   [Proclaim the Gospel]
℟. **Alleluia, alleluia.**
Jesus proclaimed the Gospel of the kingdom,
and cured every disease among the people.
℟. **Alleluia, alleluia.** ↓

GOSPEL Mt 4:12-23 or 4:12-17   [Reform Your Lives]
Jesus preached reform. At the Sea of Galilee he called Peter and Andrew, James and John, to become fishers of people. At once, they left their nets to follow him. Jesus taught and worked miracles.

[If the "Shorter Form" is used, the indented text in brackets is omitted.]

℣. The Lord be with you. ℟. **And with your spirit.**
✛ A reading from the holy Gospel according to Matthew.
℟. **Glory to you, O Lord.**

WHEN Jesus heard that John had been arrested, he withdrew to Galilee. He left Nazareth and went to live in Capernaum by the sea, in the region of Zebulun and Naphtali, that what had been said through Isaiah the prophet might be fulfilled:
   Land of Zebulun and land of Naphtali,
       the way to the sea, beyond the Jordan,
       Galilee of the Gentiles,
   the people who sit in darkness
       have seen a great light,
   on those dwelling in a land overshadowed by death,
       light has arisen.

From that time on, Jesus began to preach and say, "Repent for the kingdom of heaven is at hand."

[As he was walking by the Sea of Galilee, he saw two brothers, Simon who is called Peter, and his brother Andrew, casting a net into the sea; they were fishermen. He said to them, "Come after me, and I will make you fishers of men." At once they left their nets and followed him. He walked along from there and saw two other brothers, James, the son of Zebedee, and his brother John. They were in a boat, with their father Zebedee, mending their nets. He called them, and immediately they left their boat and their father and followed him. He went around all of Galilee, teaching in their synagogues, proclaiming the gospel of the kingdom, and curing every disease and illness among the people.]

The Gospel of the Lord. ℟. **Praise to you, Lord Jesus Christ.**   ➜ No. 15, p. 18

PRAYER OVER THE OFFERINGS   [Offerings for Salvation]

Accept our offerings, O Lord, we pray,
and in sanctifying them
grant that they may profit us for salvation.
Through Christ our Lord.
℟. **Amen.**   ➜ No. 21, p. 22 (Pref. P 29-36)

COMMUNION ANT. Cf. Ps 34 (33):6   [Radiance]

Look toward the Lord and be radiant; let your faces not be abashed. ↓

OR Jn 8:12   [Light of Life]

I am the light of the world, says the Lord; whoever follows me will not walk in darkness, but will have the light of life. ↓

PRAYER AFTER COMMUNION   [New Life]

Grant, we pray, almighty God,
that, receiving the grace

by which you bring us to new life,
we may always glory in your gift.
Through Christ our Lord.
℟. **Amen.**   ➜ No. 30, p. 77

Optional Solemn Blessings, p. 97, and Prayers over the People, p. 105

"Your reward will be great in heaven."

JANUARY 29

4th SUNDAY IN ORDINARY TIME

ENTRANCE ANT. Ps 106 (105):47   [Save Us]
**Save us, O Lord our God! And gather us from the
nations, to give thanks to your holy name, and make
it our glory to praise you.**   ➜ No. 2, p. 10

COLLECT   [Christian Love]
Grant us, Lord our God,
that we may honor you with all our mind,
and love everyone in truth of heart.
Through our Lord Jesus Christ, your Son,
who lives and reigns with you in the unity of the Holy
    Spirit,
God, for ever and ever. ℟. **Amen.** ↓

FIRST READING Zep 2:3; 3:12-13   [Seek the Lord]

The Lord is to be found among a people who are humble and lowly. Those who are humble seek after God. They shall find repose in him.

A reading from the Book of the Prophet Zephaniah

Seek the Lord, all you humble of the earth,
who have observed his law;
seek justice, seek humility;
perhaps you may be sheltered
on the day of the Lord's anger.

But I will leave as a remnant in your midst
a people humble and lowly,
who shall take refuge in the name of the Lord:
the remnant of Israel.
They shall do no wrong
and speak no lies;
nor shall there be found in their mouths
a deceitful tongue;
they shall pasture and couch their flocks
with none to disturb them.
The word of the Lord. ℟. **Thanks be to God.** ↓

RESPONSORIAL PSALM Ps 146   [Bounty of the Lord]

℟. Blessed are the poor in spir-it;
the king-dom of heav-en is theirs!

Or: ℟. **Alleluia.**

The Lord keeps faith forever,
secures justice for the oppressed,
gives food to the hungry.
The Lord sets captives free.

℟. **Blessed are the poor in spirit; the kingdom of heaven is theirs!**

The LORD give sight to the blind;
  the LORD raises up those who were bowed down.
The LORD loves the just;
  the LORD protects strangers.

℟. **Blessed are the poor in spirit; the kingdom of heaven is theirs!**

The fatherless and the widow the LORD sustains,
  but the way of the wicked he thwarts.
The LORD shall reign forever;
  your God, O Zion, through all generations. Alleluia.

℟. **Blessed are the poor in spirit; the kingdom of heaven is theirs!** ↓

SECOND READING 1 Cor 1:26-31   [Boast in the Lord]

Contrary to worldly standards, God chooses those who are weak, lowborn and despised. To these God has given his own Son, Jesus, for sanctification and redemption.

A reading from the first Letter of Saint Paul
to the Corinthians

CONSIDER your own calling, brothers and sisters. Not many of you were wise by human standards, not many were powerful, not many were of noble birth. Rather, God chose the foolish of the world to shame the wise, and God chose the weak of the world to shame the strong, and God chose the lowly and despised of the world, those who count for nothing, to reduce to nothing those who are something, so that no human being might boast before God. It is due to him that you are in Christ Jesus, who became for us wisdom from God, as well as righteousness, sanctification, and redemption, so that, as it is written, "Whoever boasts, should boast in the Lord."—The word of the Lord. ℟. **Thanks be to God.** ↓

ALLELUIA Mt 5:12a   [Rejoice and Be Glad]

℟. **Alleluia, alleluia.**
Rejoice and be glad;
your reward will be great in heaven.
℟. **Alleluia, alleluia.** ↓

GOSPEL Mt 5:1-12a   [A New Teaching]

Jesus says that the poor in spirit, the sorrowing, those thirsting for holiness, the merciful, the peacemakers, and those who suffer for holiness' sake are "blessed"—their reward awaits them in heaven.

℣. The Lord be with you. ℟. **And with your spirit.**
✤ A reading from the holy Gospel according to Matthew.
℟. **Glory to you, O Lord.**

WHEN Jesus saw the crowds, he went up the mountain, and after he had sat down, his disciples came to him. He began to teach them, saying:
    "Blessed are the poor in spirit,
        for theirs is the kingdom of heaven.
    Blessed are they who mourn,
        for they will be comforted.
    Blessed are the meek,
        for they will inherit the land.
    Blessed are they who hunger and thirst for
            righteousness,
        for they will be satisfied.
    Blessed are the merciful,
        for they will be shown mercy.
    Blessed are the clean of heart,
        for they will see God.
    Blessed are the peacemakers,
        for they will be called children of God.
    Blessed are they who are persecuted for the sake
            of righteousness,
        for theirs is the kingdom of heaven.

Blessed are you when they insult you and persecute you and utter every kind of slander against you falsely because of me. Rejoice and be glad, for your reward will be great in heaven."—The Gospel of the Lord. ℟. **Praise to you, Lord Jesus Christ.**

➜ No. 15, p. 18

PRAYER OVER THE OFFERINGS [Sacrament of Redemption]

O Lord, we bring to your altar
these offerings of our service:
be pleased to receive them, we pray,
and transform them
into the Sacrament of our redemption.
Through Christ our Lord.
℟. **Amen.**   ➜ No. 21, p. 22 (Pref. P 29-36)

COMMUNION ANT. Cf. Ps 31 (30):17-18   [Save Me]
Let your face shine on your servant. Save me in your merciful love. O Lord, let me never be put to shame, for I call on you. ↓

OR Mt 5:3-4   [Poor in Spirit]
Blessed are the poor in spirit, for theirs is the Kingdom of Heaven. Blessed are the meek, for they shall possess the land. ↓

PRAYER AFTER COMMUNION   [True Faith]

Nourished by these redeeming gifts,
we pray, O Lord,
that through this help to eternal salvation
true faith may ever increase.
Through Christ our Lord.
℟. **Amen.**   ➜ No. 30, p. 77

Optional Solemn Blessings, p. 97, and Prayers over the People, p. 105

"You are the light of the world."

FEBRUARY 5

5th SUNDAY IN ORDINARY TIME

ENTRANCE ANT. Ps 95 (94):6-7   **[Adoration]**

O come, let us worship God and bow low before the God who made us, for he is the Lord our God.

→ No. 2, p. 10

COLLECT   **[God's Protection]**

Keep your family safe, O Lord, with unfailing care,
that, relying solely on the hope of heavenly grace,
they may be defended always by your protection.
Through our Lord Jesus Christ, your Son,
who lives and reigns with you in the unity of the Holy
   Spirit,
God, for ever and ever.
℟. **Amen.** ↓

FIRST READING Is 58:7-10   **[Charity]**

The Lord promises that those who share their food with the hungry and their clothing with the naked shall find true favor with him. A light shall shine for them.

A reading from the Book of the Prophet Isaiah

THUS says the LORD:
  Share your bread with the hungry,
    shelter the oppressed and the homeless;
clothe the naked when you see them,
    and do not turn your back on your own.
Then your light shall break forth like the dawn,
    and your wound shall quickly be healed;
your vindication shall go before you,
    and the glory of the LORD shall be your rear guard.
Then you shall call, and the LORD will answer,
    you shall cry for help, and he will say: Here I am!
If you remove from your midst
    oppression, false accusation and malicious speech;
if you bestow your bread on the hungry
    and satisfy the afflicted;
then light shall rise for you in the darkness,
    and the gloom shall become for you like midday.
The word of the Lord. ℟. **Thanks be to God.** ↓

RESPONSORIAL PSALM Ps 112   [The Just Man]

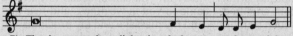

℟. **The just man is a light in dark-ness to the up-right.**

Or: ℟. **Alleluia.**

Light shines through the darkness, for the upright;
  he is gracious and merciful and just.
Well for the man who is gracious and lends,
  who conducts his affairs with justice.

℟. **The just man is a light in darkness to the upright.**
Or: ℟. **Alleluia.**

He shall never be moved;
  the just man shall be in everlasting remembrance.
An evil report he shall not fear;
  his heart is firm, trusting in the LORD.

℟. **The just man is a light in darkness to the upright.**

Or: ℟. **Alleluia.**

His heart is steadfast; he shall not fear.
  Lavishly he gives to the poor;
his justice shall endure forever;
  his horn shall be exalted in glory.

℟. **The just man is a light in darkness to the upright.**

Or: ℟. **Alleluia.** ↓

SECOND READING 1 Cor 2:1-5   [Power of the Spirit]

Paul preached to the Corinthians in weakness and fear. He preached Jesus crucified, but through the working of the Holy Spirit, these people came to be believers.

A reading from the first Letter of Saint Paul
to the Corinthians

WHEN I came to you, brothers and sisters, pro-claiming the mystery of God, I did not come with sublimity of words or of wisdom. For I resolved to know nothing while I was with you except Jesus Christ, and him crucified. I came to you in weakness and fear and much trembling, and my message and my proclamation were not with persuasive words of wisdom, but with a demonstration of Spirit and power, so that your faith might rest not on human wisdom but on the power of God.—The word of the Lord. ℟. **Thanks be to God.** ↓

ALLELUIA Jn 8:12   [Light of Life]

℟. **Alleluia, alleluia.**
I am the light of the world, says the Lord;
whoever follows me will have the light of life.
℟. **Alleluia, alleluia.** ↓

GOSPEL Mt 5:13-16   [Light of the World]

The faithful followers of Jesus are the salt of the earth and a light to the world. Being true Christ-believers, they become an example for others.

℣. The Lord be with you. ℟. **And with your spirit.**
✛ A reading from the holy Gospel according to Matthew.
℟. **Glory to you, O Lord.**

JESUS said to his disciples: "You are the salt of the earth. But if salt loses its taste, with what can it be seasoned? It is no longer good for anything but to be thrown out and trampled underfoot. You are the light of the world. A city set on a mountain cannot be hidden. Nor do they light a lamp and then put it under a bushel basket; it is set on a lampstand, where it gives light to all in the house. Just so, your light must shine before others, that they may see your good deeds and glorify your heavenly Father."—The Gospel of the Lord. ℟. **Praise to you, Lord Jesus Christ.**   ➔ No. 15, p. 18

PRAYER OVER THE OFFERINGS   [Eternal Life]

O Lord our God,
who once established these created things
to sustain us in our frailty,
grant, we pray,
that they may become for us now
the Sacrament of eternal life.
Through Christ our Lord.
℟. **Amen.**   ➔ No. 21, p. 22 (Pref. P 29-36)

COMMUNION ANT. Cf. Ps 107 (106):8-9   [The Lord's Mercy]

Let them thank the Lord for his mercy, his wonders for the children of men, for he satisfies the thirsty soul, and the hungry he fills with good things. ↓

OR Mt 5:5-6   [Those Who Mourn]

Blessed are those who mourn, for they shall be consoled. Blessed are those who hunger and thirst for righteousness, for they shall have their fill. ↓

PRAYER AFTER COMMUNION   [Salvation and Joy]

O God, who have willed that we be partakers
in the one Bread and the one Chalice,

grant us, we pray, so to live
that, made one in Christ,
we may joyfully bear fruit
for the salvation of the world.
Through Christ our Lord.
℟. **Amen.**   ➡ No. 30, p. 77

Optional Solemn Blessings, p. 97, and Prayers over the People, p. 105

"Go first and be reconciled with your brother."

FEBRUARY 12

6th SUNDAY IN ORDINARY TIME

ENTRANCE ANT. Cf. Ps 31 (30):3-4   [Protector]
**Be my protector, O God, a mighty stronghold to save
me. For you are my rock, my stronghold! Lead me,
guide me, for the sake of your name.**   ➡ No. 2, p. 10

COLLECT   [Fashioned by God's Grace]
O God, who teach us that you abide
in hearts that are just and true,
grant that we may be so fashioned by your grace
as to become a dwelling pleasing to you.
Through our Lord Jesus Christ, your Son,

who lives and reigns with you in the unity of the Holy
Spirit,
God, for ever and ever. ℟. **Amen.** ↓

FIRST READING Sir 15:15-20   [Freedom To Do Good]

**God is all-knowing, always aware of everything that we
do. All persons are free to choose to do God's will, for God
uses no force.**

A reading from the Book of Sirach

IF you choose you can keep the commandments, they
will save you;
if you trust in God, you too shall live;
he has set before you fire and water;
to whichever you choose, stretch forth your hand.
Before man are life and death, good and evil,
whichever he chooses shall be given him.
Immense is the wisdom of the Lord;
he is mighty in power, and all-seeing.
The eyes of God are on those who fear him;
he understands man's every deed.
No one does he command to act unjustly,
to none does he give license to sin.
The word of the Lord. ℟. **Thanks be to God.** ↓

RESPONSORIAL PSALM Ps 119   [Following God's Law]

℟. **Blessed are they who follow the law of the Lord!**

Blessed are they whose way is blameless,
who walk in the law of the LORD.
Blessed are they who observe his decrees,
who seek him with all their heart.

℟. **Blessed are they who follow the law of the Lord!**

You have commanded that your precepts
be diligently kept.

Oh, that I might be firm in the ways
  of keeping your statutes!

℟. **Blessed are they who follow the law of the Lord!**

Be good to your servant, that I may live
  and keep your words.
Open my eyes, that I may consider
  the wonders of your law.

℟. **Blessed are they who follow the law of the Lord!**

Instruct me, O LORD, in the way of your statutes,
  that I may exactly observe them.
Give me discernment, that I may observe your law
  and keep it with all my heart.

℟. **Blessed are they who follow the law of the Lord!** ↓

SECOND READING 1 Cor 2:6-10   [God's Wisdom]

**Out of wisdom that is beyond our imagination, God has
revealed the Divinity through the Holy Spirit. The Spirit
knows the inner workings of God.**

A reading from the first Letter of Saint Paul
to the Corinthians

B ROTHERS and sisters: We speak a wisdom to those
  who are mature, not a wisdom of this age, nor of
the rulers of this age who are passing away. Rather, we
speak God's wisdom, mysterious, hidden, which God
predetermined before the ages for our glory, and
which none of the rulers of this age knew; for, if they
had known it, they would not have crucified the Lord
of glory. But as it is written:
  What eye has not seen, and ear has not heard,
    and what has not entered the human heart,
    what God has prepared for those who love him,
    this God has revealed to us through the Spirit.
  For the Spirit scrutinizes everything, even the depths
of God.—The word of the Lord. ℟. **Thanks be to God.** ↓

ALLELUIA Cf. Mt 11:25   [The Kingdom]

℟. **Alleluia, alleluia.**

Blessed are you, Father, Lord of heaven and earth;
you have revealed to little ones the mysteries of the
  kingdom.

℟. **Alleluia, alleluia.** ↓

GOSPEL Mt 5:17-37 or 5:20-22a, 27-28, 33-34a, 37 [Holiness]

God revealed the divine law to the Israelites, and Jesus
came to bring it to perfection. Those who obey God's laws
will become great in the Kingdom of God. Jesus explains
more fully the laws of God.

*[If the "Shorter Form" is used, the indented text in brackets is
omitted.]*

℣. The Lord be with you. ℟. **And with your spirit.**

✛ A reading from the holy Gospel according to Matthew.

℟. **Glory to you, O Lord.**

JESUS said to his disciples:
  ["Do not think that I have come to abolish the law
  or the prophets. I have come not to abolish but to
  fulfill. Amen, I say to you, until heaven and earth
  pass away, not the smallest letter or the smallest
  part of a letter will pass from the law, until all
  things have taken place. Therefore, whoever
  breaks one of the least of these commandments
  and teaches others to do so will be called least in
  the kingdom of heaven. But whoever obeys and
  teaches these commandments will be called greatest in the kingdom of heaven.]

I tell you, unless your righteousness surpasses that of
the scribes and Pharisees, you will not enter the kingdom of heaven.

  "You have heard that it was said to your ancestors,
*You shall not kill; and whoever kills will be liable to
judgment.* But I say to you, whoever is angry with his
brother will be liable to judgment;

[and whoever says to his brother, 'Raqa,' will be answerable to the Sanhedrin; and whoever says, 'You fool,' will be liable to fiery Gehenna. Therefore, if you bring your gift to the altar, and there recall that your brother has anything against you, leave your gift there at the altar, go first and be reconciled with your brother, and then come and offer your gift. Settle with your opponent quickly while on the way to court. Otherwise your opponent will hand you over to the judge, and the judge will hand you over to the guard, and you will be thrown into prison. Amen, I say to you, you will not be released until you have paid the last penny.]

"You have heard that it was said, *You shall not commit adultery*. But I say to you, everyone who looks at a woman with lust has already committed adultery with her in his heart.

[If your right eye causes you to sin, tear it out and throw it away. It is better for you to lose one of your members than to have your whole body thrown into Gehenna. And if your right hand causes you to sin, cut it off and throw it away. It is better for you to lose one of your members than to have your whole body go into Gehenna.

"It was also said, *Whoever divorces his wife must give her a bill of divorce*. But I say to you, whoever divorces his wife—unless the marriage is unlawful—causes her to commit adultery, and whoever marries a divorced woman commits adultery.]

"Again you have heard that it was said to your ancestors, *Do not take a false oath, but make good to the Lord all that you vow*. But I say to you, do not swear at all;

[not by heaven, for it is God's throne; nor by the earth, for it is his footstool; nor by Jerusalem, for it is the city of the great King. Do not swear by your head, for you cannot make a single hair white or black.]

Let your 'Yes' mean 'Yes,' and your 'No' mean 'No.' Anything more is from the evil one." —The Gospel of the Lord. ℟. **Praise to you, Lord Jesus Christ.**

→ No. 15, p. 18

PRAYER OVER THE OFFERINGS   [Renewal]

May this oblation, O Lord, we pray,
cleanse and renew us
and may it become for those who do your will
the source of eternal reward.
Through Christ our Lord.
℟. **Amen.**   → No. 21, p. 22 (Pref. P 29-36)

COMMUNION ANT. Cf. Ps 78 (77):29-30   [God's Food]

They ate and had their fill, and what they craved the Lord gave them; they were not disappointed in what they craved. ↓

OR Jn 3:16   [God's Love]

God so loved the world that he gave his Only Begotten Son, so that all who believe in him may not perish, but may have eternal life. ↓

PRAYER AFTER COMMUNION   [Heavenly Delights]

Having fed upon these heavenly delights,
we pray, O Lord,
that we may always long
for that food by which we truly live.
Through Christ our Lord.
℟. **Amen.**   → No. 30, p. 77

Optional Solemn Blessings, p. 97, and Prayers over the People, p. 105

"If anyone wants to go to law with you over your tunic, hand over your cloak as well."

FEBRUARY 19

7th SUNDAY IN ORDINARY TIME

ENTRANCE ANT. Ps 13 (12):6   [God's Merciful Love]

O Lord, I trust in your merciful love. My heart will rejoice in your salvation. I will sing to the Lord who has been bountiful with me.   ➔ No. 2, p. 10

COLLECT   [Word and Deed]

Grant, we pray, almighty God,
that, always pondering spiritual things,
we may carry out in both word and deed
that which is pleasing to you.
Through our Lord Jesus Christ, your Son,
who lives and reigns with you in the unity of the Holy
    Spirit,
God, for ever and ever. ℟. **Amen.** ↓

FIRST READING Lv 19:1-2, 17-18   [Love of Neighbor]

Our inner attitude before God has a fraternal dimension.
We must be holy because God is holy.

A reading from the Book of Leviticus

THE LORD said to Moses, "Speak to the whole Israelite community and tell them: Be holy, for I, the LORD, your God, am holy.

"You shall not bear hatred for your brother or sister in your heart. Though you may have to reprove your fellow citizen, do not incur sin because of him. Take no revenge and cherish no grudge against any of your people. You shall love your neighbor as yourself. I am the LORD."—The word of the Lord. ℟. **Thanks be to God.** ↓

RESPONSORIAL PSALM Ps 103   [Plea for Pardon]

℟. The Lord is kind and mer - ci - ful.

Bless the LORD, O my soul;
.   and all my being, bless his holy name.
Bless the LORD, O my soul,
    and forget not all his benefits.

℟. **The Lord is kind and merciful.**

He pardons all your iniquities,
    heals all your ills.
He redeems your life from destruction,
    crowns you with kindness and compassion.

℟. **The Lord is kind and merciful.**

Merciful and gracious is the LORD,
    slow to anger and abounding in kindness.
Not according to our sins does he deal with us,
    nor does he requite us according to our crimes.

℟. **The Lord is kind and merciful.**

As far as the east is from the west,
    so far has he put our transgressions from us.

As a father has compassion on his children,
  so the LORD has compassion on those who fear
  him.

℟. **The Lord is kind and merciful.** ↓

SECOND READING 1 Cor 3:16-23   [Temple of God]

The Christian community is the temple of God and so is
each Christian. Hence, respect is owed the community and
each member.

A reading from the first Letter of Saint Paul
to the Corinthians

BROTHERS and sisters: Do you not know that you
are the temple of God, and that the Spirit of God
dwells in you? If anyone destroys God's temple, God
will destroy that person; for the temple of God, which
you are, is holy.

  Let no one deceive himself. If any one among you
considers himself wise in this age, let him become a
fool, so as to become wise. For the wisdom of this
world is foolishness in the eyes of God, for it is written:
  God catches the wise in their own ruses,
and again:
  *The Lord knows the thoughts of the wise, that they
  are vain.*
So let no one boast about human beings, for everything belongs to you, Paul or Apollos or Cephas, or the
world or life or death, or the present or the future: all
belong to you, and you to Christ, and Christ to God.—
The word of the Lord. ℟. **Thanks be to God.** ↓

ALLELUIA 1 Jn 2:5   [Perfected in Love]

℟. **Alleluia, alleluia.**
Whoever keeps the word of Christ,
  the love of God is truly perfected in him.
℟. **Alleluia, alleluia.** ↓

GOSPEL Mt 5:38-48   [Love of Enemies]

We are called not to encourage another's injustice but to
avoid vengeance. We must desire good things for others
in spite of any evil they may do us.

℣. The Lord be with you. ℟. **And with your spirit.**

✛ A reading from the holy Gospel according to Matthew.

℟. **Glory to you, O Lord.**

JESUS said to his disciples: "You have heard that it
was said, *An eye for an eye and a tooth for a tooth.*
But I say to you, offer no resistance to one who is evil.
When someone strikes you on your right cheek, turn
the other one as well. If anyone wants to go to law with
you over your tunic, hand over your cloak as well.
Should anyone press you into service for one mile, go
for two miles. Give to the one who asks of you, and do
not turn your back on one who wants to borrow.

"You have heard that it was said, *You shall love your
neighbor and hate your enemy.* But I say to you, love
your enemies and pray for those who persecute you,
that you may be children of your heavenly Father, for
he makes his sun rise on the bad and the good, and
causes rain to fall on the just and the unjust. For if you
love those who love you, what recompense will you
have? Do not the tax collectors do the same? And if
you greet your brothers only, what is unusual about
that? Do not the pagans do the same? So be perfect,
just as your heavenly Father is perfect."—The Gospel
of the Lord. ℟. **Praise to you, Lord Jesus Christ.**

➔ No. 15, p. 18

PRAYER OVER THE OFFERINGS   [Celebrate Mysteries]

As we celebrate your mysteries, O Lord,
with the observance that is your due,
we humbly ask you,
that what we offer to the honor of your majesty
may profit us for salvation.

Through Christ our Lord.

℟. **Amen.**   ➜ No. 21, p. 22 (Pref. P 29-36)

COMMUNION ANT. Ps 9:2-3   [Joy in God]

I will recount all your wonders, I will rejoice in you and be glad, and sing psalms to your name, O Most High. ↓

OR Jn 11:27   [Belief in Christ]

Lord, I have come to believe that you are the Christ, the Son of the living God, who is coming into this world. ↓

PRAYER AFTER COMMUNION   [Experience Salvation]

Grant, we pray, almighty God,
that we may experience the effects of the salvation
which is pledged to us by these mysteries.
Through Christ our Lord.

℟. **Amen.**   ➜ No. 30, p. 77

Optional Solemn Blessings, p. 97, and Prayers over the People, p. 105

"One does not live on bread alone."

FEBRUARY 26

1st SUNDAY OF LENT

ENTRANCE ANT. Cf. Ps 91 (90):15-16   [Length of Days]

When he calls on me, I will answer him; I will deliver him and give him glory, I will grant him length of days.

➜ No. 2, p. 10 (Omit Gloria)

COLLECT   [Grow in Understanding]

Grant, almighty God,
through the yearly observances of holy Lent,
that we may grow in understanding
of the riches hidden in Christ
and by worthy conduct pursue their effects.
Through our Lord Jesus Christ, your Son,
who lives and reigns with you in the unity of the Holy
    Spirit,
God, for ever and ever.
℟. **Amen.** ↓

FIRST READING Gn 2:7-9; 3:1-7   [Sin of Our First Parents]

God created Adam and Eve and placed them in the luxurious Garden of Eden. They could eat fruit from every tree except one. After being tempted by the devil, Eve—then Adam—disobeyed God's command. Immediately their lives changed.

A reading from the Book of Genesis

THE LORD God formed man out of the clay of the ground and blew into his nostrils the breath of life, and so man became a living being.

Then the LORD God planted a garden in Eden, in the east, and placed there the man whom he had formed. Out of the ground the LORD God made various trees grow that were delightful to look at and good for food, with the tree of life in the middle of the garden and the tree of the knowledge of good and evil.

Now the serpent was the most cunning of all the animals that the LORD God had made. The serpent asked the woman, "Did God really tell you not to eat from any of the trees in the garden?" The woman answered the serpent: "We may eat of the fruit of the trees in the garden; it is only about the fruit of the tree in the middle of the garden that God said, 'You shall not eat it or even touch it, lest you die.'" But the serpent said to the woman: "You certainly will not die! No, God knows well that the moment you eat of it your eyes will be opened and you will be like gods who know what is good and what is evil." The woman saw that the tree was good for food, pleasing to the eyes, and desirable for gaining wisdom. So she took some of its fruit and ate it; and she also gave some to her husband, who was with her, and he ate it. Then the eyes of both of them were opened, and they realized that they were naked; so they sewed fig leaves together and made loincloths for themselves.—The word of the Lord. ℟. **Thanks be to God.** ↓

RESPONSORIAL PSALM Ps 51   [Repentance]

℞. Be   merciful,   O Lord,   for we have sinned.

Have mercy on me, O God, in your goodness;
  in the greatness of your compassion wipe out my
    offense.
Thoroughly wash me from my guilt
  and of my sin cleanse me.

℞. **Be merciful, O Lord, for we have sinned.**

For I acknowledge my offense,
  and my sin is before me always:
"Against you only have I sinned,
  and done what is evil in your sight."

℞. **Be merciful, O Lord, for we have sinned.**

A clean heart create for me, O God,
  and a steadfast spirit renew within me.
Cast me not out from your presence,
  and your Holy Spirit take not from me.

℞. **Be merciful, O Lord, for we have sinned.**

Give me back the joy of your salvation,
  and a willing spirit sustain in me.
O Lord, open my lips,
  and my mouth shall proclaim your praise.

℞. **Be merciful, O Lord, for we have sinned.** ↓

SECOND READING Rom 5:12-19 or 5:12, 17-19
                              [Saved Through Christ]
From the fall of Adam, sin came into the world. God, however, gave the gift of his Son, Jesus. Through him justice
was restored. Through the obedience of Jesus, justice
comes to all.

[If the "Shorter Form" is used, the indented text in brackets is omitted.]

A reading from the Letter of Saint Paul to the Romans

BROTHERS and sisters: Through one man sin entered the world, and through sin, death, and thus death came to all men, inasmuch as all sinned—
[for up to the time of the law, sin was in the world, though sin is not accounted when there is no law. But death reigned from Adam to Moses, even over those who did not sin after the pattern of the trespass of Adam, who is the type of the one who was to come.

But the gift is not like the transgression. For if by the transgression of the one, the many died, how much more did the grace of God and the gracious gift of the one man Jesus Christ overflow for the many. And the gift is not like the result of the one who sinned. For after one sin there was the judgment that brought condemnation; but the gift, after many transgressions, brought acquittal.]
For if, by the transgression of the one, death came to reign through that one, how much more will those who receive the abundance of grace and of the gift of justification come to reign in life through the one Jesus Christ. In conclusion, just as through one transgression condemnation came upon all, so, through one righteous act, acquittal and life came to all. For just as through the disobedience of the one man the many were made sinners, so, through the obedience of the one, the many will be made righteous.—The word of the Lord. ℟. **Thanks be to God.** ↓

VERSE BEFORE THE GOSPEL Mt 4:4b   [Source of Life]

℟. **Praise to you, Lord Jesus Christ, King of endless glory!***

One does not live on bread alone;
but on every word that comes forth from the mouth of God.

℟. **Praise to you, Lord Jesus Christ, King of endless glory!** ↓

GOSPEL Mt 4:1-11   [Temptation]

The devil tempted Adam; he also tempts Jesus three times, making lavish promises. Jesus rebukes Satan, for only God is to be adored.

℣. The Lord be with you. ℟. **And with your spirit.**
✢ A reading from the holy Gospel according to Matthew.
℟. **Glory to you, O Lord.**

AT that time Jesus was led by the Spirit into the desert to be tempted by the devil. He fasted for forty days and forty nights, and afterwards he was hungry. The tempter approached and said to him, "If you are the Son of God, command that these stones become loaves of bread." He said in reply, "It is written:

One does not live on bread alone,
    but on every word that comes forth
    from the mouth of God."

Then the devil took him to the holy city, and made him stand on the parapet of the temple, and said to him, "If you are the Son of God, throw yourself down. For it is written:

He will command his angels concerning you
    and with their hands they will support you,
    lest you dash your foot against a stone."

Jesus answered him, "Again it is written,

You shall not put the Lord, your God, to the test."

---

* See p. 16 for other Gospel Acclamations.

Then the devil took him up to a very high mountain, and showed him all the kingdoms of the world in their magnificence, and he said to him, "All these I shall give to you, if you will prostrate yourself and worship me." At this, Jesus said to him, "Get away, Satan! It is written:

The Lord, your God, shall you worship
   and him alone shall you serve."

Then the devil left him and, behold, angels came and ministered to him.—The Gospel of the Lord. ℟. **Praise to you, Lord Jesus Christ.**   → No. 15, p. 18

PRAYER OVER THE OFFERINGS   [Sacred Time]

Give us the right dispositions, O Lord, we pray,
to make these offerings,
for with them we celebrate the beginning
of this venerable and sacred time.
Through Christ our Lord. ℟. **Amen.** ↓

PREFACE (P 12)   [Christ's Abstinence]

℣. The Lord be with you. ℟. **And with your spirit.**
℣. Lift up your hearts. ℟. **We lift them up to the Lord.**
℣. Let us give thanks to the Lord our God. ℟. **It is right and just.**

It is truly right and just, our duty and our salvation,
always and everywhere to give you thanks,
Lord, holy Father, almighty and eternal God,
through Christ our Lord.

By abstaining forty long days from earthly food,
he consecrated through his fast
the pattern of our Lenten observance
and, by overturning all the snares of the ancient serpent,
taught us to cast out the leaven of malice,
so that, celebrating worthily the Paschal Mystery,
we might pass over at last to the eternal paschal feast.

And so, with the company of Angels and Saints,
we sing the hymn of your praise,
as without end we acclaim: → No. 23, p. 23

COMMUNION ANT. Mt 4:4   [Life-Giving Word]

One does not live by bread alone, but by every word that comes forth from the mouth of God. ↓

OR Cf. Ps 91 (90):4   [Refuge in God]

The Lord will conceal you with his pinions, and under his wings you will trust. ↓

PRAYER AFTER COMMUNION   [Heavenly Bread]

Renewed now with heavenly bread,
by which faith is nourished, hope increased,
and charity strengthened,
we pray, O Lord,
that we may learn to hunger for Christ,
the true and living Bread,
and strive to live by every word
which proceeds from your mouth.
Through Christ our Lord.
℟. **Amen.** ↓

The Deacon or, in his absence, the Priest himself, says the invitation: Bow down for the blessing.

PRAYER OVER THE PEOPLE   [Bountiful Blessing]

May bountiful blessing, O Lord, we pray,
come down upon your people,
that hope may grow in tribulation,
virtue be strengthened in temptation,
and eternal redemption be assured.
Through Christ our Lord.
℟. **Amen.**   → No. 32, p. 77

"Moses and Elijah appeared to them, conversing with him."

MARCH 5

2nd SUNDAY OF LENT

ENTRANCE ANT. Cf. Ps 27 (26):8-9   **[God's Face]**

Of you my heart has spoken: Seek his face. It is your face, O Lord, that I seek; hide not your face from me.

→ No. 2, p. 10 (Omit Gloria)

OR Cf. Ps 25 (24):6, 2, 22   **[God's Merciful Love]**

Remember your compassion, O Lord, and your merciful love, for they are from of old. Let not our enemies exult over us. Redeem us, O God of Israel, from all our distress. → No. 2, p. 10 (Omit Gloria)

COLLECT   **[Nourish Us]**

O God, who have commanded us
to listen to your beloved Son,
be pleased, we pray,
to nourish us inwardly by your word,
that, with spiritual sight made pure,
we may rejoice to behold your glory.
Through our Lord Jesus Christ, your Son,
who lives and reigns with you in the unity of the Holy
   Spirit,

God, for ever and ever.
℟. **Amen.** ↓

FIRST READING Gn 12:1-4a [Mission of Abraham]

**God calls Abraham and promises to make him a leader of
a great nation respected by all.**

A reading from the Book of Genesis

THE LORD said to Abram: "Go forth from the land of
your kinsfolk and from your father's house to a
land that I will show you.

"I will make of you a great nation,
    and I will bless you;
I will make your name great,
    so that you will be a blessing.
I will bless those who bless you
    and curse those who curse you.
All the communities of the earth
    shall find blessing in you."

Abram went as the LORD directed him.—The word of
the Lord. ℟. **Thanks be to God.** ↓

RESPONSORIAL PSALM Ps 33 [Trust in God]

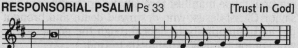

℟. Lord, let your mercy be on us, as we place our trust in you.

Upright is the word of the LORD,
    and all his works are trustworthy.
He loves justice and right;
    of the kindness of the LORD the earth is full.

℟. **Lord, let your mercy be on us, as we place our trust
in you.**

See, the eyes of the LORD are upon those who fear him,
    upon those who hope for his kindness,
to deliver them from death
    and preserve them in spite of famine.

℟. **Lord, let your mercy be on us, as we place our trust in you.**

Our soul waits for the LORD,
   who is our help and our shield.
May your kindness, O LORD, be upon us
   who have put our hope in you.

℟. **Lord, let your mercy be on us, as we place our trust in you.** ↓

SECOND READING 2 Tm 1:8b-10   [Design of God]

God has saved us. He has called us to a holy life. He has brought life to us through the good news of the Gospel.

A reading from the second Letter of Saint Paul
to Timothy

BELOVED: Bear your share of hardship for the gospel with the strength that comes from God.

He saved us and called us to a holy life, not according to our works but according to his own design and the grace bestowed on us in Christ Jesus before time began, but now made manifest through the appearance of our savior Christ Jesus, who destroyed death and brought life and immortality to light through the gospel.—The word of the Lord. ℟. **Thanks be to God.** ↓

VERSE BEFORE THE GOSPEL Cf. Mt. 17:5   [Hear Him]

℟. **Praise and honor to you, Lord Jesus Christ!***

From the shining cloud the Father's voice is heard:
This is my beloved Son, hear him.

℟. **Praise and honor to you, Lord Jesus Christ!** ↓

GOSPEL Mt 17:1-9   [Jesus Transfigured]

Jesus is transfigured before Peter, James, and John. God acknowledges his Son and bids the disciples to listen to

---

* See p. 16 for other Gospel Acclamations.

him. Jesus asks them not to reveal this vision until after
the Resurrection.

℣. The Lord be with you. ℟. **And with your spirit.**
✛ A reading from the holy Gospel according to Matthew.
℟. **Glory to you, O Lord.**

JESUS took Peter, James, and John his brother, and led
them up a high mountain by themselves. And he was
transfigured before them; his face shone like the sun and
his clothes became white as light. And behold, Moses and
Elijah appeared to them, conversing with him. Then Peter
said to Jesus in reply, "Lord, it is good that we are here. If
you wish, I will make three tents here, one for you, one
for Moses, and one for Elijah." While he was still speaking, behold, a bright cloud cast a shadow over them, then
from the cloud came a voice that said, "This is my beloved
Son, with whom I am well pleased; listen to him." When
the disciples heard this, they fell prostrate and were very
much afraid. But Jesus came and touched them, saying,
"Rise, and do not be afraid." And when the disciples
raised their eyes, they saw no one else but Jesus alone.

As they were coming down from the mountain, Jesus
charged them, "Do not tell the vision to anyone until the
Son of Man has been raised from the dead."—The Gospel
of the Lord. ℟. **Praise to you, Lord Jesus Christ.**

→ No. 15, p. 18

PRAYER OVER THE OFFERINGS   [Cleanse Our Faults]

May this sacrifice, O Lord, we pray,
cleanse us of our faults
and sanctify your faithful in body and mind
for the celebration of the paschal festivities.
Through Christ our Lord. ℟. **Amen.** ↓

PREFACE (P 13)   [Jesus in Glory]

℣. The Lord be with you. ℟. **And with your spirit.**
℣. Lift up your hearts. ℟. **We lift them up to the Lord.**

℣. Let us give thanks to the Lord our God. ℟. **It is right and just.**

It is truly right and just, our duty and our salvation,
always and everywhere to give you thanks,
Lord, holy Father, almighty and eternal God,
through Christ our Lord.

For after he had told the disciples of his coming Death,
on the holy mountain he manifested to them his glory,
to show, even by the testimony of the law and the
  prophets,
that the Passion leads to the glory of the Resurrection.

And so, with the Powers of heaven,
we worship you constantly on earth,
and before your majesty
without end we acclaim: ➜ No. 23, p. 23

COMMUNION ANT. Mt 17:5 [Son of God]
**This is my beloved Son, with whom I am well pleased;
listen to him.** ↓

PRAYER AFTER COMMUNION [Things of Heaven]
As we receive these glorious mysteries,
we make thanksgiving to you, O Lord,
for allowing us while still on earth
to be partakers even now of the things of heaven.
Through Christ our Lord. ℟. **Amen.** ↓

*The Deacon or, in his absence, the Priest himself, says the
invitation:* Bow down for the blessing.

PRAYER OVER THE PEOPLE [Faithful to the Gospel]
Bless your faithful, we pray, O Lord,
with a blessing that endures for ever,
and keep them faithful
to the Gospel of your Only Begotten Son,
so that they may always desire and at last attain
that glory whose beauty he showed in his own Body,

to the amazement of his Apostles.
Through Christ our Lord.
℞. **Amen.** _____   → No. 32, p. 77

"I am he [the Messiah], the one speaking with you."

MARCH 12

3rd SUNDAY OF LENT

The alternative prayers given below are for the Ritual Mass for the First Scrutiny assigned to this Sunday in the Rite of Christian Initiation of Adults. (The chants and readings are the same as those for the 3rd Sunday of Lent.)

ENTRANCE ANT. Cf. Ps 25 (24):15-16   [Eyes on God]
My eyes are always on the Lord, for he rescues my feet from the snare. Turn to me and have mercy on me, for I am alone and poor. → No. 2, p. 10 (Omit Gloria)

OR Ez 36:23-26   [A New Spirit]
[Also for First Scrutiny]
When I prove my holiness among you, I will gather you from all the foreign lands; and I will pour clean water upon you and cleanse you from all your impurities, and I will give you a new spirit, says the Lord.
→ No. 2, p. 10 (Omit Gloria)

Or Entrance Ant. for First Scrutiny Cf. Is 55:1

[Drink Joyfully]

Come to the waters, you who are thirsty, says the Lord; you who have no money, come and drink joyfully. ➜ No. 2, p. 10 (Omit Gloria)

COLLECT [Fasting, Prayer, Almsgiving]

O God, author of every mercy and of all goodness,
who in fasting, prayer and almsgiving
have shown us a remedy for sin,
look graciously on this confession of our lowliness,
that we, who are bowed down by our conscience,
may always be lifted up by your mercy.
Through our Lord Jesus Christ, your Son,
who lives and reigns with you in the unity of the Holy
    Spirit,
God, for ever and ever. ℟. **Amen.** ↓

Collect for First Scrutiny [Fashioned Anew]

Grant, we pray, O Lord,
that these chosen ones may come worthily and wisely
to the confession of your praise,
so that in accordance with that first dignity
which they lost by original sin
they may be fashioned anew through your glory.
Through our Lord Jesus Christ, your Son,
who lives and reigns with you in the unity of the Holy
    Spirit,
God, for ever and ever. ℟. **Amen.** ↓

FIRST READING Ex 17:3-7 [Water from Rock]

The Israelites murmured against God in their thirst. God directs Moses to strike a rock with his staff, and water issues forth.

A reading from the Book of Exodus

IN those days, in their thirst for water, the people grumbled against Moses, saying, "Why did you ever make us leave Egypt? Was it just to have us die here of thirst with our children and our livestock?" So Moses cried out to the LORD, "What shall I do with this people? A little more and they will stone me!"The LORD answered Moses, "Go over there in front of the people, along with some of the elders of Israel, holding in your hand, as you go, the staff with which you struck the river. I will be standing there in front of you on the rock in Horeb. Strike the rock, and the water will flow from it for the people to drink." This Moses did, in the presence of the elders of Israel. The place was called Massah and Meribah, because the Israelites quarreled there and tested the LORD, saying, "Is the LORD in our midst or not?"— The word of the Lord. ℞. **Thanks be to God.** ↓

RESPONSORIAL PSALM Ps 95   [The Lord Our Rock]

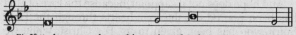

℞. If today you hear his voice, harden not your hearts.

Come, let us sing joyfully to the LORD;
  let us acclaim the Rock of our salvation.
Let us come into his presence with thanksgiving;
  let us joyfully sing psalms to him.

℞. **If today you hear his voice, harden not your hearts.**

Come, let us bow down in worship;
  let us kneel before the LORD who made us.
For he is our God,
    and we are the people he shepherds, the flock he
      guides.

℞. **If today you hear his voice, harden not your hearts.**

Oh, that today you would hear his voice:
"Harden not your hearts as at Meribah,
as in the day of Massah in the desert,
where your fathers tempted me;
they tested me though they had seen my works."

℟. **If today you hear his voice, harden not your hearts.** ↓

SECOND READING Rom 5:1-2, 5-8   [God's Love for Us]

Through Jesus we have received the grace of faith. The love of God has been poured upon us. Jesus laid down his life for us while we were still sinners.

A reading from the Letter of Saint Paul
to the Romans

BROTHERS and sisters: Since we have been justified by faith, we have peace with God through our Lord Jesus Christ, through whom we have gained access by faith to this grace in which we stand, and we boast in hope of the glory of God.

And hope does not disappoint, because the love of God has been poured out into our hearts through the Holy Spirit who has been given to us. For Christ, while we were still helpless, died at the appointed time for the ungodly. Indeed, only with difficulty does one die for a just person, though perhaps for a good person one might even find courage to die. But God proves his love for us in that while we were still sinners Christ died for us.— The word of the Lord. ℟. **Thanks be to God.** ↓

VERSE BEFORE THE GOSPEL Cf. Jn 4:42, 15 [Living Water]

℟. **Glory and praise to you, Lord Jesus Christ!***
Lord, you are truly the Savior of the world;
give me living water, that I may never thirst again.
℟. **Glory and praise to you, Lord Jesus Christ!** ↓

---

* See p. 16 for other Gospel Acclamations.

GOSPEL Jn 4:5-42 or 4:5-15, 19b-26, 39a, 40-42 [Samaritan Woman]

Jesus speaks to the Samaritan woman at the well. He searches her soul, and she recognizes him as a prophet. Jesus speaks of the water of eternal life. He also notes the fields are ready for harvest.

[If the "Shorter Form" is used, the indented text in brackets is omitted.]

℣. The Lord be with you. ℟. **And with your spirit.**
✤ A reading from the holy Gospel according to John.
℟. **Glory to you, O Lord.**

JESUS came to a town of Samaria called Sychar, near the plot of land that Jacob had given to his son Joseph. Jacob's well was there. Jesus, tired from his journey, sat down there at the well. It was about noon. A woman of Samaria came to draw water. Jesus said to her, "Give me a drink." His disciples had gone into the town to buy food. The Samaritan woman said to him, "How can you, a Jew, ask me, a Samaritan woman, for a drink?"—For Jews use nothing in common with Samaritans.—Jesus answered and said to her, "If you knew the gift of God and who is saying to you, 'Give me a drink,' you would have asked him and he would have given you living water." The woman said to him, "Sir, you do not even have a bucket and the cistern is deep; where then can you get this living water? Are you greater than our father Jacob, who gave us this cistern and drank from it himself with his children and his flocks?" Jesus answered and said to her, "Everyone who drinks this water will be thirsty again; but whoever drinks the water I shall give will never thirst; the water I shall give will become in him a spring of water welling up to eternal life." The woman said to him, "Sir, give me this water, so that I may not be thirsty or have to keep coming here to draw water."

[Jesus said to her, "Go call your husband and come back." The woman answered and said to him, "I do not have a husband." Jesus answered her, "You are right in saying, 'I do not have a husband.' For you have had five husbands, and the one you have now is not your husband. What you have said is true."]

[The woman said to him,] "[Sir,] I can see that you are a prophet. Our ancestors worshiped on this mountain; but you people say that the place to worship is in Jerusalem." Jesus said to her, "Believe me, woman, the hour is coming when you will worship the Father neither on this mountain nor in Jerusalem. You people worship what you do not understand; we worship what we understand, because salvation is from the Jews. But the hour is coming, and is now here, when true worshippers will worship the Father in Spirit and truth; and indeed the Father seeks such people to worship him. God is Spirit, and those who worship him must worship in Spirit and truth." The woman said to him, "I know that the Messiah is coming, the one called the Christ; when he comes, he will tell us everything." Jesus said to her, "I am he, the one* speaking with you."

[At that moment his disciples returned, and were amazed that he was talking with a woman, but still no one said, "What are you looking for?" or "Why are you talking with her?" The woman left her water jar and went into the town and said to the people, "Come see a man who told me everything I have done. Could he possibly be the Christ?" They went out of the town and came to him. Meanwhile, the disciples urged him, "Rabbi, eat." But he said to them, "I have food to eat of which you do not know." So the disciples said to

* *Shorter Form reads: the one who is.*

one another, "Could someone have brought him something to eat?" Jesus said to them, "My food is to do the will of the one who sent me and to finish his work. Do you not say, 'In four months the harvest will be here'? I tell you, look up and see the fields ripe for the harvest. The reaper is already receiving payment and gathering crops for eternal life, so that the sower and reaper can rejoice together. For here the saying is verified that 'One sows and another reaps.' I sent you to reap what you have not worked for; others have done the work, and you are sharing the fruits of their work."]

Many of the Samaritans of that town began to believe in him [because of the word of the woman who testified, "He told me everything I have done."]** When the Samaritans came to him, they invited him to stay with them; and he stayed there two days. Many more began to believe in him because of his word, and they said to the woman, "We no longer believe because of your word; for we have heard for ourselves, and we know that this is truly the savior of the world."—The Gospel of the Lord. ℟. **Praise to you, Lord Jesus Christ.**
→ No. 15, p. 18

PRAYER OVER THE OFFERINGS   [Pardon]

Be pleased, O Lord, with these sacrificial offerings,
and grant that we who beseech pardon for our own sins,
may take care to forgive our neighbor.
Through Christ our Lord.
℟. **Amen.** ↓

** *Appears only in Longer Form.*

Prayer over the Offerings for First Scrutiny
[Merciful Grace]

May your merciful grace prepare your servants,
   O Lord,
for the worthy celebration of these mysteries
and lead them to it by a devout way of life.
Through Christ our Lord. ℟. **Amen.** ↓

PREFACE (P 14)   [Gift of Faith]

℣. The Lord be with you. ℟. **And with your spirit.**
℣. Lift up your hearts. ℟. **We lift them up to the Lord.**
℣. Let us give thanks to the Lord our God. ℟. **It is right
and just.**

It is truly right and just, our duty and our salvation,
always and everywhere to give you thanks,
Lord, holy Father, almighty and eternal God,
through Christ our Lord.

For when he asked the Samaritan woman for water to
   drink,
he had already created the gift of faith within her
and so ardently did he thirst for her faith,
that he kindled in her the fire of divine love.

And so we, too, give you thanks
and with the Angels
praise your mighty deeds, as we acclaim: ➔ No. 23, p. 23

When the Roman Canon is used, in the section Memento,
Domine *(*Remember, Lord, your servants*) there is a com-
memoration of the godparents, and the proper form of the*
Hanc igitur *(*Therefore, Lord, we pray*), is said.*

Remember, Lord, your servants
who are to present your chosen ones
for the holy grace of your Baptism,

Here the names of the godparents are read out.

and all gathered here,
whose faith and devotion are known to you ... (p. 24)

Therefore, Lord, we pray:
graciously accept this oblation
which we make to you for your servants,
whom you have been pleased
to enroll, choose and call for eternal life
and for the blessed gift of your grace.
(Through Christ our Lord. Amen.)

The rest follows the Roman Canon, pp. 25-29.

When Eucharistic Prayer II is used, after the words and all
the clergy, *the following is added:*

Remember also, Lord, your servants
who are to present these chosen ones
at the font of rebirth.

When Eucharistic Prayer III is used, after the words the
entire people you have gained for your own, *the following
is added:*

Assist your servants with your grace,
O Lord, we pray,
that they may lead these chosen ones by word and
    example
to new life in Christ, our Lord.

COMMUNION ANT. Jn 4:14   [Water of Eternal Life]
**For anyone who drinks it, says the Lord, the water I
shall give will become in him a spring welling up to
eternal life.** ↓

PRAYER AFTER COMMUNION   [Nourishment from Heaven]

As we receive the pledge
of things yet hidden in heaven
and are nourished while still on earth
with the Bread that comes from on high,
we humbly entreat you, O Lord,
that what is being brought about in us in mystery
may come to true completion.
Through Christ our Lord. ℟. **Amen.** ↓

Prayer after Communion for First Scrutiny

[God's Protection]

Give help, O Lord, we pray,
by the grace of your redemption
and be pleased to protect and prepare
those you are to initiate
through the Sacraments of eternal life.
Through Christ our Lord.
℟. **Amen.**   → No. 30, p. 77

Optional Solemn Blessings, p. 97, and Prayers over the People, p. 105

The Deacon or, in his absence, the Priest himself, says the invitation: Bow down for the blessing.

PRAYER OVER THE PEOPLE   [Love of God and Neighbor]

Direct, O Lord, we pray, the hearts of your faithful,
and in your kindness grant your servants this grace:
that, abiding in the love of you and their neighbor,
they may fulfill the whole of your commands.
Through Christ our Lord.
℟. **Amen.**   _____ → No. 32, p. 77

"I am the light of the world."

MARCH 19

4th SUNDAY OF LENT

The alternative chants and prayers given below are for the Ritual Mass for the Second Scrutiny assigned to this Sunday in the Rite of Christian Initiation of Adults. (The readings are the same as those for the 4th Sunday of Lent.)

ENTRANCE ANT. Cf. Is 66:10-11 [Rejoice]

Rejoice, Jerusalem, and all who love her. Be joyful, all who were in mourning; exult and be satisfied at her consoling breast. ➙ No. 2, p. 10 (Omit Gloria)

Entrance Ant. for Second Scrutiny

Cf. Ps 25 (24):15-16 [Have Mercy]

My eyes are always on the Lord, for he rescues my feet from the snare. Turn to me and have mercy on me, for I am alone and poor.

➙ No. 2, p. 10 (Omit Gloria)

COLLECT　　　　　　　　　　[Devotion and Faith]

O God, who through your Word
reconcile the human race to yourself in a wonderful way,
grant, we pray,
that with prompt devotion and eager faith
the Christian people may hasten
toward the solemn celebrations to come.
Through our Lord Jesus Christ, your Son,
who lives and reigns with you in the unity of the Holy
　　Spirit,
God, for ever and ever. ℟. **Amen.** ↓

Collect for Second Scrutiny　　　　　[Spiritual Joy]

Almighty ever-living God,
give to your Church an increase in spiritual joy,
so that those once born of earth
may be reborn as citizens of heaven.
Through our Lord Jesus Christ, your Son,
who lives and reigns with you in the unity of the Holy
　　Spirit,
God, for ever and ever. ℟. **Amen.** ↓

FIRST READING 1 Sm 16:1b, 6-7, 10-13a
　　　　　　　　　　　　　　　[The Lord's Anointed]

**God directs Samuel to anoint David king. God looks into
the heart of each person.**

　　　A reading from the first Book of Samuel

THE LORD said to Samuel: "Fill your horn with oil,
and be on your way. I am sending you to Jesse of
Bethlehem, for I have chosen my king from among his
sons."
　　As Jesse and his sons came to the sacrifice, Samuel
looked at Eliab and thought, "Surely the LORD's anointed is here before him." But the LORD said to Samuel:
"Do not judge from his appearance or from his lofty
stature, because I have rejected him. Not as man sees

does God see, because man sees the appearance but
the LORD looks into the heart." In the same way Jesse
presented seven sons before Samuel, but Samuel said
to Jesse, "The LORD has not chosen any one of these."
Then Samuel asked Jesse, "Are these all the sons you
have?" Jesse replied, "There is still the youngest, who is
tending the sheep." Samuel said to Jesse, "Send for him;
we will not begin the sacrificial banquet until he
arrives here." Jesse sent and had the young man
brought to them. He was ruddy, a youth handsome to
behold and making a splendid appearance. The LORD
said, "There—anoint him, for this is the one!" Then
Samuel, with the horn of oil in hand, anointed him in
the presence of his brothers; and from that day on, the
spirit of the LORD rushed upon David.—The word of the
Lord. ℟. **Thanks be to God.** ↓

RESPONSORIAL PSALM Ps 23   [The Lord's Protection]

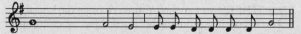

℟. The Lord is my shep-herd, there is noth-ing I shall want.

The LORD is my shepherd, I shall not want.
    In verdant pastures he gives me repose;
beside restful waters he leads me;
    he refreshes my soul.
℟. **The Lord is my shepherd, there is nothing I shall
    want.**
He guides me in right paths
    for his name's sake.
Even though I walk in the dark valley
    I fear no evil; for you are at my side
with your rod and your staff
    that give me courage.
℟. **The Lord is my shepherd, there is nothing I shall
    want.**

You spread the table before me
   in the sight of my foes;
you anoint my head with oil;
   my cup overflows.

℟. **The Lord is my shepherd, there is nothing I shall
want.**

Only goodness and kindness follow me
   all the days of my life;
and I shall dwell in the house of the LORD
   for years to come.

℟. **The Lord is my shepherd, there is nothing I shall
want. ↓**

SECOND READING Eph 5:8-14   [Children of Light]

   **We are to walk in the light that shows goodness, justice,
and truth. Christ gives this light whereby we live.**

A reading from the Letter of Saint Paul to the Ephesians

BROTHERS and sisters: You were once darkness, but
now you are light in the Lord. Live as children of
light, for light produces every kind of goodness and
righteousness and truth. Try to learn what is pleasing to
the Lord. Take no part in the fruitless works of darkness;
rather expose them, for it is shameful even to mention
the things done by them in secret; but everything
exposed by the light becomes visible, for everything that
becomes visible is light. Therefore, it says:
   "Awake, O sleeper,
   and arise from the dead,
   and Christ will give you light."
The word of the Lord. ℟. **Thanks be to God. ↓**

VERSE BEFORE THE GOSPEL Jn 8:12   [Light of Life]
℟. **Glory to you, Word of God, Lord Jesus Christ!***
I am the light of the world, says the Lord;

---
* *See p. 16 for other Gospel Acclamations.*

whoever follows me will have the light of life.

℞. **Glory to you, Word of God, Lord Jesus Christ!** ↓

GOSPEL Jn 9:1-41 or 9:1, 6-9, 13-17, 34-38 [Cure of Blind Man]
> **Jesus is the light. He cures a man born blind. Jesus identifies himself as the Son of Man.**

[If the "Shorter Form" is used, the indented text in brackets is omitted.]

℣. The Lord be with you. ℞. **And with your spirit.**

✠ A reading from the holy Gospel according to John.

℞. **Glory to you, O Lord.**

AS Jesus passed by he saw a man blind from birth. [His disciples asked him, "Rabbi, who sinned, this man or his parents, that he was born blind?" Jesus answered, "Neither he nor his parents sinned; it is so that the works of God might be made visible through him. We have to do the works of the one who sent me while it is day. Night is coming when no one can work. While I am in the world, I am the light of the world." When he had said this,] he spat on the ground and made clay with the saliva, and smeared the clay on his eyes, and said to him, "Go wash in the Pool of Siloam"—which means Sent—. So he went and washed, and came back able to see.

His neighbors and those who had seen him earlier as a beggar said, "Isn't this the one who used to sit and beg?" Some said, "It is," but others said, "No, he just looks like him." He said, "I am."

[So they said to him, "How were your eyes opened?" He replied, "The man called Jesus made clay and anointed my eyes and told me, 'Go to Siloam and wash.' So I went there and washed and was able to see." And they said to him, "Where is he?" He said, "I don't know."]

They brought the one who was once blind to the Pharisees. Now Jesus had made clay and opened his eyes on a sabbath. So then the Pharisees also asked him how he was able to see. He said to them, "He put clay on my eyes, and I washed, and now I can see." So some of the Pharisees said, "This man is not from God, because he does not keep the sabbath." But others said, "How can a sinful man do such signs?" And there was a division among them. So they said to the blind man again, "What do you have to say about him, since he opened your eyes?" He said, "He is a prophet."

[Now the Jews did not believe that he had been blind and gained his sight until they summoned the parents of the one who had gained his sight. They asked them, "Is this your son, who you say was born blind? How does he now see?" His parents answered and said, "We know that this is our son and that he was born blind. We do not know how he sees now, nor do we know who opened his eyes. Ask him, he is of age; he can speak for himself." His parents said this because they were afraid of the Jews, for the Jews had already agreed that if anyone acknowledged him as the Christ, he would be expelled from the synagogue. For this reason his parents said, "He is of age; question him."

So a second time they called the man who had been blind and said to him, "Give God the praise! We know that this man is a sinner." He replied, "If he is a sinner, I do not know. One thing I do know is that I was blind and now I see." So they said to him, "What did he do to you? How did he open your eyes?" He answered them, "I told you already and you did not listen. Why do you want to hear it again? Do you want to become his disciples, too?" They ridiculed him and said, "You are that man's disciple; we are disciples of Moses! We know that God spoke to Moses, but we do not know where this one is from."The man answered and said to them, "This is what is so amazing, that you do not know where he is from, yet he opened my eyes. We know that God does not listen to sinners, but if one is devout and does his will, he listens to him. It is unheard of that anyone ever opened the eyes of a person born blind. If this man were not from God, he would not be able to do anything."]

They answered and said to him, "You were born totally in sin, and are you trying to teach us?" Then they threw him out.

When Jesus heard that they had thrown him out, he found him and said, "Do you believe in the Son of Man?" He answered and said, "Who is he, sir, that I may believe in him?" Jesus said to him, "You have seen him, and the one speaking with you is he." He said, "I do believe, Lord," and he worshiped him.

[Then Jesus said, "I came into this world for judgment, so that those who do not see might see, and those who do see might become blind."

Some of the Pharisees who were with him heard this and said to him, "Surely we are not also blind, are we?" Jesus said to them, "If you were blind, you would have no sin; but now you are saying, 'We see,' so your sin remains."]

The Gospel of the Lord. ℟. **Praise to you, Lord Jesus Christ.**   ➜ No. 15, p. 18

PRAYER OVER THE OFFERINGS   [Eternal Remedy]

We place before you with joy these offerings,
which bring eternal remedy, O Lord,
praying that we may both faithfully revere them
and present them to you, as is fitting,
for the salvation of all the world.
Through Christ our Lord.
℟. **Amen.** ↓

Prayer over the Offerings for Second Scrutiny
[Seeking Salvation]

We place before you with joy these offerings,
which bring eternal remedy, O Lord,
praying that we may both faithfully revere them
and present them to you, as is fitting,
for those who seek salvation.
Through Christ our Lord.
℟. **Amen.** ↓

PREFACE (P 15)   [From Darkness to Radiance]
℣. The Lord be with you. ℟. **And with your spirit.**
℣. Lift up your hearts. ℟. **We lift them up to the Lord.**
℣. Let us give thanks to the Lord our God. ℟. **It is right
and just.**

It is truly right and just, our duty and our salvation,
always and everywhere to give you thanks,
Lord, holy Father, almighty and eternal God,
through Christ our Lord.

By the mystery of the Incarnation,
he has led the human race that walked in darkness
into the radiance of the faith
and has brought those born in slavery to ancient sin
through the waters of regeneration
to make them your adopted children.

Therefore, all creatures of heaven and earth
sing a new song in adoration,
and we, with all the host of Angels,
cry out, and without end acclaim: ➜ No. 23, p. 23

When the Roman Canon is used, in the section Memento, Domine *(*Remember, Lord, your servants*) there is a commemoration of the godparents, and the proper form of the* Hanc igitur *(*Therefore, Lord, we pray*) is said.*

Remember, Lord, your servants
who are to present your chosen ones
for the holy grace of your Baptism,

Here the names of the godparents are read out.

and all gathered here,
whose faith and devotion are known to you . . . (p. 24).

Therefore, Lord, we pray:
graciously accept this oblation
which we make to you for your servants,
whom you have been pleased
to enroll, choose and call for eternal life
and for the blessed gift of your grace.
(Through Christ our Lord. Amen.)

The rest follows the Roman Canon, pp. 25-29.

[For commemoration of the godparents in Eucharistic Prayers II and III, see p. 211.]

COMMUNION ANT. Cf. Jn 9:11, 38   [Spiritual Sight]
The Lord anointed my eyes: I went, I washed, I saw and I believed in God. ↓

PRAYER AFTER COMMUNION   [Illuminate Our Hearts]
O God, who enlighten everyone who comes into this
    world,
illuminate our hearts, we pray,
with the splendor of your grace,
that we may always ponder
what is worthy and pleasing to your majesty
and love you in all sincerity.

Through Christ our Lord.
℟. **Amen.** ↓

Prayer after Communion for Second Scrutiny
[God's Kindness]

Sustain your family always in your kindness,
O Lord, we pray,
correct them, set them in order,
graciously protect them under your rule,
and in your unfailing goodness
direct them along the way of salvation.
Through Christ our Lord.
℟. **Amen.**   → No. 30, p. 77

Optional Solemn Blessings, p. 97, and Prayers over the People, p. 105

---

*The Deacon or, in his absence, the Priest himself, says the
invitation:* Bow down for the blessing.

PRAYER OVER THE PEOPLE   [Life-Giving Light]

Look upon those who call to you, O Lord,
and sustain the weak;
give life by your unfailing light
to those who walk in the shadow of death,
and bring those rescued by your mercy from every evil
to reach the highest good.
Through Christ our Lord.
℟. **Amen.**   → No. 32, p. 77

"The dead man came out, tied hand and foot."

MARCH 26

5th SUNDAY OF LENT

The alternative chants and prayers given below are for the Ritual Mass for the Third Scrutiny assigned to this Sunday in the Rite of Christian Initiation of Adults. (The readings are the same as those for the 5th Sunday of Lent.)

ENTRANCE ANT. Cf. Ps 43 (42):1-2   [Rescue Me]

Give me justice, O God, and plead my cause against a nation that is faithless. From the deceitful and cunning rescue me, for you, O God, are my strength.

→ No. 2, p. 10 (Omit Gloria)

Entrance Ant. for Third Scrutiny

Cf. Ps 18 (17):5-7 [The Lord Hears Me]

The waves of death rose about me; the pains of the netherworld surrounded me. In my anguish I called to the Lord; and from his holy temple he heard my voice. → No. 2, p. 10 (Omit Gloria)

COLLECT [Walk in Charity]

By your help, we beseech you, Lord our God,
may we walk eagerly in that same charity
with which, out of love for the world,
your Son handed himself over to death.
Through our Lord Jesus Christ, your Son,
who lives and reigns with you in the unity of the Holy
    Spirit,
God, for ever and ever. ℟. **Amen.** ↓

Collect for Third Scrutiny [Chosen Ones]

Grant, O Lord, to these chosen ones
that, instructed in the holy mysteries,
they may receive new life at the font of Baptism
and be numbered among the members of your
    Church.
Through our Lord Jesus Christ, your Son,
who lives and reigns with you in the unity of the Holy
    Spirit,
God, for ever and ever. ℟. **Amen.** ↓

FIRST READING Ez 37:12-14 [The Lord's Promise]

**The Lord promises to bring his people back to their home-
land. He will be with them and they will know him.**

A reading from the Book of the Prophet Ezekiel

THUS says the Lord GOD: O my people, I will open
your graves and have you rise from them, and
bring you back to the land of Israel. Then you shall
know that I am the LORD, when I open your graves and
have you rise from them, O my people! I will put my
spirit in you that you may live, and I will settle you
upon your land; thus you shall know that I am the
LORD. I have promised, and I will do it, says the LORD.—
The word of the Lord. ℟. **Thanks be to God.** ↓

RESPONSORIAL PSALM Ps 130   [Mercy and Redemption]

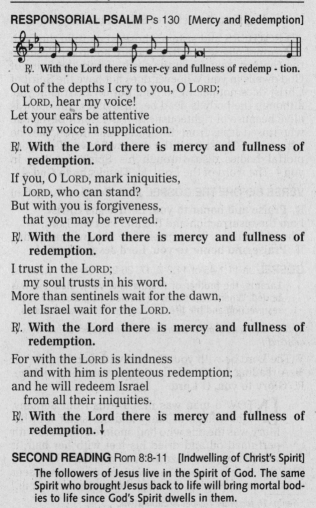

℟. With the Lord there is mer-cy and fullness of redemp - tion.

Out of the depths I cry to you, O LORD;
　　LORD, hear my voice!
Let your ears be attentive
　　to my voice in supplication.

℟. **With the Lord there is mercy and fullness of redemption.**

If you, O LORD, mark iniquities,
　　LORD, who can stand?
But with you is forgiveness,
　　that you may be revered.

℟. **With the Lord there is mercy and fullness of redemption.**

I trust in the LORD;
　　my soul trusts in his word.
More than sentinels wait for the dawn,
　　let Israel wait for the LORD.

℟. **With the Lord there is mercy and fullness of redemption.**

For with the LORD is kindness
　　and with him is plenteous redemption;
and he will redeem Israel
　　from all their iniquities.

℟. **With the Lord there is mercy and fullness of redemption.** ↓

SECOND READING Rom 8:8-11   [Indwelling of Christ's Spirit]
　　The followers of Jesus live in the Spirit of God. The same
　　Spirit who brought Jesus back to life will bring mortal bod-
　　ies to life since God's Spirit dwells in them.

A reading from the Letter of Saint Paul to the Romans

BROTHERS and sisters: Those who are in the flesh cannot please God. But you are not in the flesh; on the contrary, you are in the spirit, if only the Spirit of God dwells in you. Whoever does not have the Spirit of Christ does not belong to him. But if Christ is in you, although the body is dead because of sin, the spirit is alive because of righteousness. If the Spirit of the one who raised Jesus from the dead dwells in you, the one who raised Christ from the dead will give life to your mortal bodies also, through his Spirit dwelling in you.—The word of the Lord. ℟. **Thanks be to God.** ↓

VERSE BEFORE THE GOSPEL Jn 11:25a, 26   [Resurrection]

℟. **Praise and honor to you, Lord Jesus Christ!***
I am the resurrection and the life, says the Lord;
whoever believes in me, even if he dies, will never die.
℟. **Praise and honor to you, Lord Jesus Christ!** ↓

GOSPEL Jn 11:1-45 or 11:3-7, 17, 20-27, 33b-45   [Lazarus]

Lazarus, the brother of Martha and Mary, died and was buried. When Jesus came, he assured them that he was the resurrection and the life. Jesus gave life back to Lazarus.

[If the "Shorter Form" is used, the indented text in brackets is omitted.]

℣. The Lord be with you. ℟. **And with your spirit.**
✝ A reading from the holy Gospel according to John.
℟. **Glory to you, O Lord.**

NOW a man was ill, Lazarus from Bethany, the village of Mary and her sister Martha. Mary was the one who had anointed the Lord with perfumed oil and dried his feet with her hair; it was her brother Lazarus who was ill.]
[So] the sisters [*only in Shorter Form:* of Lazarus] sent word to Jesus, saying, "Master, the one you love is ill."

* See p. 16 for other Gospel Acclamations.

When Jesus heard this he said,"This illness is not to end in death, but is for the glory of God, that the Son of God may be glorified through it." Now Jesus loved Martha and her sister and Lazarus. So when he heard that he was ill, he remained for two days in the place where he was. Then after this he said to his disciples, "Let us go back to Judea."

[The disciples said to him, "Rabbi, the Jews were just trying to stone you, and you want to go back there?" Jesus answered, "Are there not twelve hours in a day? If one walks during the day, he does not stumble, because he sees the light of this world. But if one walks at night, he stumbles, because the light is not in him." He said this, and then told them, "Our friend Lazarus is asleep, but I am going to awaken him." So the disciples said to him, "Master, if he is asleep, he will be saved." But Jesus was talking about his death, while they thought that he meant ordinary sleep. So then Jesus said to them clearly, "Lazarus has died. And I am glad for you that I was not there, that you may believe. Let us go to him." So Thomas, called Didymus, said to his fellow disciples, "Let us also go to die with him."]

When Jesus arrived, he found that Lazarus had already been in the tomb for four days.

[Now Bethany was near Jerusalem, only about two miles away. And many of the Jews had come to Martha and Mary to comfort them about their brother.]

When Martha heard that Jesus was coming, she went to meet him; but Mary sat at home. Martha said to Jesus, "Lord, if you had been here, my brother would not have died. But even now I know that whatever you ask of God, God will give you." Jesus said to her, "Your brother will rise." Martha said to him, "I know he will rise, in the resurrection on the last day." Jesus told her, "I am the resurrection and the life; whoever believes in me, even if he dies, will live, and everyone who lives and believes in me will never die. Do you believe this?" She said to him, "Yes, Lord. I have come to believe that you are the Christ, the Son of God, the one who is coming into the world."

[When she had said this, she went and called her sister Mary secretly, saying, "The teacher is here and is asking for you." As soon as she heard this, she rose quickly and went to him. For Jesus had not yet come into the village, but was still where Martha had met him. So when the Jews who were with her in the house comforting her saw Mary get up quickly and go out, they followed her, presuming that she was going to the tomb to weep there. When Mary came to where Jesus was and saw him, she fell at his feet and said to him, "Lord, if you had been here, my brother would not have died." When Jesus saw her weeping and the Jews who had come with her weeping,]
he became perturbed and deeply troubled, and said, "Where have you laid him?" They said to him, "Sir, come and see." And Jesus wept. So the Jews said, "See how he loved him." But some of them said, "Could not the one who opened the eyes of the blind man have done something so that this man would not have died?"

So Jesus, perturbed again, came to the tomb. It was a cave, and a stone lay across it. Jesus said, "Take away the stone." Martha, the dead man's sister, said to him, "Lord, by now there will be a stench; he has been dead for four days." Jesus said to her, "Did I not tell you that if you believe you will see the glory of God?" So they took away the stone. And Jesus raised his eyes and said, "Father, I thank you for hearing me. I know that

you always hear me; but because of the crowd here I
have said this, that they may believe that you sent me."
And when he had said this, he cried out in a loud voice,
"Lazarus, come out!" The dead man came out, tied
hand and foot with burial bands, and his face was
wrapped in a cloth. So Jesus said to them, "Untie him
and let him go."

   Now many of the Jews who had come to Mary and
seen what he had done began to believe in him.—The
Gospel of the Lord. ℟. **Praise to you, Lord Jesus
Christ.**   ➙ No. 15, p. 18

PRAYER OVER THE OFFERINGS   [Hear Us]

Hear us, almighty God,
and, having instilled in your servants
the teachings of the Christian faith,
graciously purify them
by the working of this sacrifice.
Through Christ our Lord.
℟. **Amen.** ↓

Prayer over the Offerings for Third Scrutiny   [Hear Us]
Hear us, almighty God,
and, having instilled in your servants
the first fruits of the Christian faith,
graciously purify them by the working of this
   sacrifice.
Through Christ our Lord. ℟. **Amen.** ↓

PREFACE (P 16)   [Christ Raised Lazarus]
℣. The Lord be with you. ℟. **And with your spirit.**
℣. Lift up your hearts. ℟. **We lift them up to the Lord.**
℣. Let us give thanks to the Lord our God. ℟. **It is right
and just.**

It is truly right and just, our duty and our salvation,
always and everywhere to give you thanks,

Lord, holy Father, almighty and eternal God,
through Christ our Lord.

For as true man he wept for Lazarus his friend
and as eternal God raised him from the tomb,
just as, taking pity on the human race,
he leads us by sacred mysteries to new life.

Through him the host of Angels adores your majesty
and rejoices in your presence for ever.
May our voices, we pray, join with theirs
in one chorus of exultant praise, as we acclaim:

➜ No. 23, p. 23

When the Roman Canon is used, in the section Memento,
Domine *(*Remember, Lord, your servants*) there is a com-
memoration of the godparents, and the proper form of the*
Hanc igitur *(*Therefore, Lord, we pray*) is said.*

Remember, Lord, your servants
who are to present your chosen ones
for the holy grace of your Baptism,

Here the names of the godparents are read out.

and all gathered here,
whose faith and devotion are known to you . . . (p. 24).

Therefore, Lord, we pray:
graciously accept this oblation
which we make to you for your servants,
whom you have been pleased
to enroll, choose and call for eternal life
and for the blessed gift of your grace.
(Through Christ our Lord: Amen.)

The rest follows the Roman Canon, pp. 25-29.

*[For commemoration of the godparents in Eucharistic
Prayers II and III, see p. 211.]*

COMMUNION ANT. Cf. Jn 11:26   [Eternal Life]

Everyone who lives and believes in me will not die for ever, says the Lord. ↓

PRAYER AFTER COMMUNION   [Union with Jesus]

We pray, almighty God,
that we may always be counted among the members of
   Christ,
in whose Body and Blood we have communion.
Who lives and reigns for ever and ever.
℟. **Amen.** ↓

Prayer after Communion for Third Scrutiny
                                        [God's Children]

May your people be as one, O Lord, we pray,
and in wholehearted submission to you
may they obtain this grace:
that, safe from all distress,
they may readily live out their joy at being saved
and remember in loving prayer those to be reborn.
Through Christ our Lord.
℟. **Amen.**   ➙ No. 30, p. 77

Optional Solemn Blessings, p. 97, and Prayers over the People, p. 105

The Deacon or, in his absence, the Priest himself, says the invitation: Bow down for the blessing.

PRAYER OVER THE PEOPLE   [Gift of Mercy]

Bless, O Lord, your people,
who long for the gift of your mercy,
and grant that what, at your prompting, they desire
they may receive by your generous gift.
Through Christ our Lord.
℟. **Amen.**   ➙ No. 32, p. 77

*"Blessed are you, who have come
in your abundant mercy!"*

APRIL 2

PALM SUNDAY OF THE PASSION
OF THE LORD

On this day the Church recalls the entrance of Christ the Lord into Jerusalem to accomplish his Paschal Mystery. Accordingly, the memorial of this entrance of the Lord takes place at all Masses, by means of the Procession or the Solemn Entrance before the principal Mass or the Simple Entrance before other Masses. The Solemn Entrance, but not the Procession, may be repeated before other Masses that are usually celebrated with a large gathering of people.

It is desirable that, where neither the Procession nor the Solemn Entrance can take place, there be a sacred celebration of the Word of God on the messianic entrance and on the Passion of the Lord, either on Saturday evening or on Sunday at a convenient time.

The Commemoration of the Lord's Entrance
into Jerusalem

FIRST FORM: THE PROCESSION

At an appropriate hour, a gathering takes place at a smaller church or other suitable place other than inside the church to which the procession will go. The faithful hold branches in their hands.

Meanwhile, the following antiphon or another appropriate chant is sung.

ANTIPHON Mt 21:9   [Hosanna]

Hosanna to the Son of David;
blessed is he who comes
in the name of the Lord,
the King of Israel.
Hosanna in the highest.

After this, the Priest and people sign themselves, while the Priest says: In the name of the Father, and of the Son, and of the Holy Spirit. *Then he greets the people in the usual way. A brief address is given, in which the faithful are invited to participate actively and consciously in the celebration of this day, in these or similar words:*

Dear brethren (brothers and sisters),
since the beginning of Lent until now
we have prepared our hearts by penance and charitable
    works.
Today we gather together to herald with the whole
    Church
the beginning of the celebration
of our Lord's Paschal Mystery,
that is to say, of his Passion and Resurrection.
For it was to accomplish this mystery
that he entered his own city of Jerusalem.
Therefore, with all faith and devotion,
let us commemorate
the Lord's entry into the city for our salvation,
following in his footsteps,
so that, being made by his grace partakers of the Cross,
we may have a share also in his Resurrection and in his
    life.

After the address, the Priest says one of the following prayers with hands extended.

PRAYER   [Following Christ]

Let us pray.
Almighty ever-living God,
sanctify ✠ these branches with your blessing,
that we, who follow Christ the King in exultation,
may reach the eternal Jerusalem through him.
Who lives and reigns for ever and ever. ℟. **Amen.** ↓

OR   [Christ in Triumph]

Increase the faith of those who place their hope in you,
    O God,
and graciously hear the prayers of those who call on you,
that we, who today hold high these branches
to hail Christ in his triumph,
may bear fruit for you by good works accomplished in
    him.
Who lives and reigns for ever and ever.
℟. **Amen.** ↓

The Priest sprinkles the branches with holy water without say-ing anything.

Then a Deacon or, if there is no Deacon, a Priest, proclaims in the usual way the Gospel concerning the Lord's entrance according to one of the four Gospels.

GOSPEL Mt 21:1-11   [Jesus' Triumphal Entry]

In triumphant glory Jesus comes into Jerusalem. The peo-ple spread their cloaks on the ground for him, wave palm branches, and call him blessed.

℣. The Lord be with you. ℟. **And with your spirit.**
✠ A reading from the holy Gospel according to Matthew.
℟. **Glory to you, O Lord.**

WHEN Jesus and the disciples drew near Jeru-salem and came to Bethphage on the Mount of Olives, Jesus sent two disciples, saying to them, "Go into the village opposite you, and immediately you will find an ass tethered, and a colt with her. Untie them and bring them here to me. And if anyone should say anything to you, reply, 'The master has need of them.' Then he will send them at once." This happened so that what had been spoken through the prophet might be fulfilled:

Say to daughter Zion,
"Behold, your king comes to you,
meek and riding on an ass,
and on a colt, the foal of a beast of burden."

The disciples went and did as Jesus had ordered them. They brought the ass and the colt and laid their cloaks over them, and he sat upon them. The very large crowd spread their cloaks on the road, while others cut branches from the trees and strewed them on the road. The crowds preceding him and those following kept crying out and saying:

"Hosanna to the Son of David;
blessed is he who comes in the name of the Lord;
hosanna in the highest."

And when he entered Jerusalem the whole city was shaken and asked, "Who is this?" And the crowds replied, "This is Jesus the prophet, from Nazareth in Galilee."—The Gospel of the Lord. ℟. **Praise to you, Lord Jesus Christ.**

After the Gospel, a brief homily may be given. Then, to begin the Procession, an invitation may be given by a Priest or a Deacon or a lay minister, in these or similar words:

Dear brethren (brothers and sisters),
like the crowds who acclaimed Jesus in Jerusalem,
let us go forth in peace.

OR

Let us go forth in peace.
℟. **In the name of Christ. Amen.**

The Procession to the church where Mass will be celebrated then sets off in the usual way. If incense is used, the thurifer goes first, carrying a thurible with burning incense, then an acolyte or another minister, carrying a cross decorated with palm branches according to local custom, between two ministers with lighted candles. Then follow the Deacon carrying the Book of the Gospels, the Priest with the ministers, and, after them, all the faithful carrying branches.

As the Procession moves forward, the following or other suitable chants in honor of Christ the King are sung by the choir and people.

ANTIPHON 1   [Hosanna]

**The children of the Hebrews, carrying olive branches,
went to meet the Lord, crying out and saying:
Hosanna in the highest.**

If appropriate, this antiphon is repeated between the strophes (verses) of the following Psalm.

PSALM 24 (23)   [The King of Glory]

**The LORD's is the earth and its fullness,
the world, and those who dwell in it.
It is he who set it on the seas;
on the rivers he made it firm.**   *(The antiphon is repeated.)*

**Who shall climb the mountain of the LORD?
Who shall stand in his holy place?
The clean of hands and pure of heart,
whose soul is not set on vain things,
who has not sworn deceitful words.**
(The antiphon is repeated.)

**Blessings from the LORD shall he receive,
and right reward from the God who saves him.
Such are the people who seek him,
who seek the face of the God of Jacob.**
(The antiphon is repeated.)

**O gates, lift high your heads;
grow higher, ancient doors.
Let him enter, the king of glory!**
(The antiphon is repeated.)

Who is this king of glory?
The LORD, the mighty, the valiant;
the LORD, the valiant in war.   *(The antiphon is repeated.)*

O gates, lift high your heads;
grow higher, ancient doors.
Let him enter, the king of glory!

(The antiphon is repeated.)

Who is this king of glory?
He, the LORD of hosts,
he is the king of glory.   *(The antiphon is repeated.)*

ANTIPHON 2   [Hosanna]

The children of the Hebrews spread their garments on
    the road,
crying out and saying: Hosanna to the Son of David;
blesssed is he who comes in the name of the Lord.

*If appropriate, this antiphon is repeated between the
strophes (verses) of the following Psalm.*

PSALM 47 (46)   [The Great King]

All peoples, clap your hands.
Cry to God with shouts of joy!
For the LORD, the Most High, is awesome,
the great king over all the earth.

(The antiphon is repeated.)

He humbles peoples under us
and nations under our feet.
Our heritage he chose for us,
the pride of Jacob whom he loves.

(The antiphon is repeated.)

God has gone up with shouts of joy.
The LORD goes up with trumpet blast.
Sing praise for God; sing praise!
Sing praise to our king; sing praise!

(The antiphon is repeated.)

For God is king of all the earth.
Sing praise with a hymn.

God is reigning over nations.
God sits upon his holy throne.   *(The antiphon is repeated.)*

The princes of the peoples are assembled
with the people of the God of Abraham.
The rulers of the earth belong to God,
who is greatly exalted.   *(The antiphon is repeated.)*

Hymn to Christ the King

Chorus:
Glory and honor and praise be to you, Christ, King and
   Redeemer,
to whom young children cried out loving Hosannas with
   joy.

All repeat: Glory and honor ...

Chorus:
Israel's King are you, King David's magnificent off-
   spring;
you are the ruler who come blest in the name of the
   Lord.

All repeat: Glory and honor ...

Chorus:
Heavenly hosts on high unite in singing your praises;
men and women on earth and all creation join in.

All repeat: Glory and honor ...

Chorus:
Bearing branches of palm, Hebrews came crowding to
   greet you;
see how with prayers and hymns we come to pay you
   our vows.

All repeat: Glory and honor ...

Chorus:
They offered gifts of praise to you, so near to your
   Passion;
see how we sing this song now to you reigning on high.

All repeat: Glory and honor ...

Chorus:
**Those you were pleased to accept; now accept our gifts
of devotion,
good and merciful King, lover of all that is good.**

All repeat: **Glory and honor . . .**

As the procession enters the church, there is sung the following responsory or another chant, which should speak of the Lord's entrance.

RESPONSORY   [Hosanna]

℟. **As the Lord entered the holy city, the children of the Hebrews proclaimed the resurrection of life. Waving their branches of palm, they cried: Hosanna in the Highest.**

℣. **When the people heard that Jesus was coming to Jerusalem, they went out to meet him. Waving their branches of palm, they cried: Hosanna in the Highest.**

When the Priest arrives at the altar, he venerates it and, if appropriate, incenses it. Then he goes to the chair, where he puts aside the cope, if he has worn one, and puts on the chasuble. Omitting the other Introductory Rites of the Mass and, if appropriate, the Kyrie *(Lord, have mercy), he says the Collect of the Mass, and then continues the Mass in the usual way.*

SECOND FORM: THE SOLEMN ENTRANCE

When a procession outside the church cannot take place, the entrance of the Lord is celebrated inside the church by means of a Solemn Entrance before the principal Mass.

Holding branches in their hands, the faithful gather either outside, in front of the church door, or inside the church itself. The Priest and ministers and a representative group of the faithful go to a suitable place in the church outside the sanctuary, where at least the greater part of the faithful can see the rite.

While the Priest approaches the appointed place, the antiphon Hosanna *or another appropriate chant is sung. Then the blessing of branches and the proclamation of the Gospel of the Lord's entrance into Jerusalem take place as above (pp. 234-235). After the Gospel, the Priest processes solemnly with the ministers and the representative group of the faithful through the church to the sanctuary, while the responsory* As the Lord entered *(p. 239) or another appropriate chant is sung.*

Arriving at the altar, the Priest venerates it. He then goes to the chair and, omitting the Introductory Rites of the Mass and, if appropriate, the Kyrie *(Lord, have mercy), he says the Collect of the Mass, and then continues the Mass in the usual way.*

THIRD FORM: THE SIMPLE ENTRANCE

At all other Masses of this Sunday at which the Solemn Entrance is not held, the memorial of the Lord's entrance into Jerusalem takes place by means of a Simple Entrance.

While the Priest proceeds to the altar, the Entrance Antiphon with its Psalm (below) or another chant on the same theme is sung. Arriving at the altar, the Priest venerates it and goes to the chair. After the Sign of the Cross, he greets the people and continues the Mass in the usual way.

At other Masses, in which singing at the entrance cannot take place, the Priest, as soon as he has arrived at the altar and venerated it, greets the people, reads the Entrance Antiphon, and continues the Mass in the usual way.

ENTRANCE ANT. Cf. Jn 12:1, 12-13; Ps 24 (23): 9-10
[Hosanna in the Highest]

Six days before the Passover, when the Lord came into the city of Jerusalem, the children ran to meet him; in their hands they carried palm branches and with a loud voice cried out: Hosanna in the highest! Blessed are you, who have come in your abundant mercy!

O gates, lift high your heads; grow higher, ancient doors. Let him enter, the king of glory! Who is this king of glory? He, the Lord of hosts, he is the king of glory. Hosanna in the highest! Blessed are you, who have come in your abundant mercy!

AT THE MASS

After the Procession or Solemn Entrance the Priest begins the Mass with the Collect.

COLLECT   [Patient Suffering]

Almighty ever-living God,
who as an example of humility for the human race to
    follow
caused our Savior to take flesh and submit to the Cross,
graciously grant that we may heed his lesson of patient
    suffering
and so merit a share in his Resurrection.
Who lives and reigns with you in the unity of the Holy
    Spirit,
God, for ever and ever. ℟. **Amen.** ↓

FIRST READING Is 50:4-7   [Christ's Suffering]

**The servant was persecuted and struck by his own people;
he was spit upon and beaten. He proclaims the true faith
and suffers to atone for the sins of his people. Here we see
a foreshadowing of the true Servant of God.**

A reading from the Book of the Prophet Isaiah

THE Lord GOD has given me
    a well-trained tongue,
that I might know how to speak to the weary
    a word that will rouse them.
Morning after morning
    he opens my ear that I may hear;
and I have not rebelled,
    have not turned back.
I gave my back to those who beat me,
    my cheeks to those who plucked my beard;
my face I did not shield
    from buffets and spitting.

The Lord GOD is my help,
    therefore I am not disgraced;

I have set my face like flint,
    knowing that I shall not be put to shame.
The word of the Lord. ℟. **Thanks be to God.** ↓

RESPONSORIAL PSALM Ps 22   [Christ's Abandonment]

℟. **My God, my God, why have you a-ban-doned me?**

All who see me scoff at me;
    they mock me with parted lips, they wag their
        heads:
"He relied on the LORD; let him deliver him,
    let him rescue him, if he loves him."

℟. **My God, my God, why have you abandoned me?**

Indeed, many dogs surround me,
    a pack of evildoers closes in upon me;
they have pierced my hands and my feet;
    I can count all my bones.

℟. **My God, my God, why have you abandoned me?**

They divide my garments among them,
    and for my vesture they cast lots.
But you, O LORD, be not far from me;
    O my help, hasten to aid me.

℟. **My God, my God, why have you abandoned me?**

I will proclaim your name to my brethren;
    in the midst of the assembly I will praise you:
"You who fear the LORD, praise him;
    all you descendants of Jacob, give glory to him,
    revere him, all you descendants of Israel."

℟. **My God, my God, why have you abandoned me?** ↓

SECOND READING Phil 2:6-11   [Humility]

Paul urges us to humility by which we are made like Christ
our Lord. He put off the majesty of his divinity and became
man and humbled himself in obedience to the ignominious
Death on the Cross.

A reading from the Letter of Saint Paul to the Philippians

CHRIST Jesus, though he was in the form of God,
did not regard equality with God
  something to be grasped.
Rather, he emptied himself,
  taking the form of a slave,
  coming in human likeness;
  and found human in appearance,
  he humbled himself,
  becoming obedient to the point of death,
  even death on a cross.
Because of this, God greatly exalted him
  and bestowed on him the name
  which is above every name,
  that at the name of Jesus
  every knee should bend,
  of those in heaven and on earth and under the earth,
  and every tongue confess that
  Jesus Christ is Lord,
  to the glory of God the Father.
The word of the Lord. ℟. **Thanks be to God.** ↓

VERSE BEFORE THE GOSPEL Phil 2:8-9 [Obedient to Death]

℟. **Praise to you, Lord Jesus Christ, King of endless
  glory!***
Christ became obedient to the point of death,
even death on a cross.
Because of this, God greatly exalted him
and bestowed on him the name which is above every
  name.
℟. **Praise to you, Lord Jesus Christ, King of endless
  glory!** ↓

---

* *See p. 16 for other Gospel Acclamations.*

GOSPEL Mt 26:14—27:66 or 27:11-54   [Christ's Passion]

Matthew portrays the Passion and Death of Jesus. Jesus gives his disciples his Body and Blood. Judas betrays him. Jesus is condemned to die on the Cross.

When the Shorter Form is read, the Passion begins at no. 9 below and ends after no. 13, pp. 249-252.

The fourteen subheadings introduced into the reading enable those who so desire to meditate on this text while making the Stations of the Cross.

The Passion may be read by lay readers, with the part of Christ, if possible, read by a Priest. The Narrator is noted by N, the words of Jesus by a ✠ and the words of others by V (Voice) and C (Crowd). The part of the Crowd (C) printed in boldface type may be recited by the people.

We participate in the passion narrative in several ways: by reading it and reflecting on it during the week ahead; by listening with faith as it is proclaimed; by respectful posture during the narrative; by reverent silence after the passage about Christ's Death. We do not hold the palms during the reading on Palm Sunday.

The message of the liturgy in proclaiming the passion narratives in full is to enable the assembly to see vividly the love of Christ for each person, despite their sins, a love that even death could not vanquish. The crimes during the Passion of Christ cannot be attributed indiscriminately to all Jews of that time, nor to Jews today. The Jewish people should not be referred to as though rejected or cursed, as if this view followed from Scripture. The Church ever keeps in mind that Jesus, his mother Mary, and the Apostles were Jewish. As the Church has always held, Christ freely suffered his Passion and Death because of the sins of all, that all might be saved.

This week we are challenged by the Passion narrative to reflect on the way we are living up to our baptismal promises of dying with Christ to sin and living with him for God.

N. THE Passion of our Lord Jesus Christ according to Matthew.

1. THE BETRAYER

N. ONE of the Twelve, who was called Judas Iscariot, went to the chief priests and said, **V.** "What are you willing to give me if I hand him over to you?" **N.** They paid him thirty pieces of silver, and from that time on he looked for an opportunity to hand him over.

On the first day of the Feast of Unleavened Bread, the disciples approached Jesus and said, **V.** "Where do you want us to prepare for you to eat the Passover?" **N.** He said, ✤ "Go into the city to a certain man and tell him, 'The teacher says, "My appointed time draws near; in your house I shall celebrate the Passover with my disciples."'" **N.** The disciples then did as Jesus had ordered, and prepared the Passover.

When it was evening, he reclined at table with the Twelve. And while they were eating, he said, ✤ "Amen, I say to you, one of you will betray me." **N.** Deeply distressed at this, they began to say to him one after another, **V.** "Surely it is not I, Lord?" **N.** He said in reply, ✤ "He who has dipped his hand into the dish with me is the one who will betray me. The Son of Man indeed goes, as it is written of him, but woe to that man by whom the Son of Man is betrayed. It would be better for that man if he had never been born." **N.** Then Judas, his betrayer, said in reply, **V.** "Surely it is not I, Rabbi?" **N.** He answered, ✤ "You have said so."

2. THE LORD'S SUPPER

N. WHILE they were eating, Jesus took bread, said the blessing, broke it, and giving it to his disciples said, ✤ "Take and eat; this is my body." **N.** Then he took a cup, gave thanks, and gave it to them, saying, ✤ "Drink from it, all of you, for this is my blood of the covenant, which will be shed on behalf of many for the forgiveness of sins. I tell you, from now on I shall not drink this fruit of the vine until the day when I drink it with you new in the kingdom of my Father." **N.** Then, after singing a hymn, they went out to the Mount of Olives.

3. PETER'S DENIAL FORETOLD

N. THEN Jesus said to them, ✠ "This night all of you will have your faith in me shaken, for it is written:
I will strike the shepherd,
    and the sheep of the flock will be dispersed;
but after I have been raised up, I shall go before you to Galilee." **N.** Peter said to him in reply, **V.** "Though all may have their faith in you shaken, mine will never be." **N.** Jesus said to him, ✠ "Amen, I say to you, this very night before the cock crows, you will deny me three times." **N.** Peter said to him, **V.** "Even though I should have to die with you, I will not deny you." **N.** And all the disciples spoke likewise.

4. THE AGONY IN THE GARDEN

N. THEN Jesus came with them to a place called Gethsemane, and he said to his disciples, ✠ "Sit here while I go over there and pray." **N.** He took along Peter and the two sons of Zebedee, and began to feel sorrow and distress. Then he said to them, ✠ "My soul is sorrowful even to death. Remain here and keep watch with me." **N.** He advanced a little and fell prostrate in prayer, saying, ✠ "My Father, if it is possible, let this cup pass from me; yet, not as I will, but as you will." **N.** When he returned to his disciples he found them asleep. He said to Peter, ✠ "So you could not keep watch with me for one hour? Watch and pray that you may not undergo the test. The spirit is willing, but the flesh is weak." **N.** Withdrawing a second time, he prayed again, ✠ "My Father, if it is not possible that this cup pass without my drinking it, your will be done!" **N.** Then he returned once more and found them asleep, for they could not keep their eyes open. He left them and withdrew again and prayed a third time, saying the same thing again. Then he returned to his disciples and said to them, ✠ "Are you still sleeping and taking your rest? Behold, the hour is at hand when the Son of Man is to be handed over to sinners. Get up, let us go. Look, my betrayer is at hand."

5. THE BETRAYAL AND ARREST OF JESUS

N. **W**HILE he was still speaking, Judas, one of the Twelve, arrived, accompanied by a large crowd, with swords and clubs, who had come from the chief priests and the elders of the people. His betrayer had arranged a sign with them, saying, **V.** "The man I shall kiss is the one; arrest him." **N.** Immediately he went over to Jesus and said, **V.** "Hail, Rabbi!" **N.** and he kissed him. Jesus answered him, ✠ "Friend, do what you have come for." **N.** Then stepping forward they laid hands on Jesus and arrested him. And behold, one of those who accompanied Jesus put his hand to his sword, drew it, and struck the high priest's servant, cutting off his ear. Then Jesus said to him, ✠ "Put your sword back into its sheath, for all who take the sword will perish by the sword. Do you think that I cannot call upon my Father and he will not provide me at this moment with more than twelve legions of angels? But then how would the Scriptures be fulfilled which say that it must come to pass in this way?" **N.** At that hour Jesus said to the crowds, ✠ "Have you come out as against a robber, with swords and clubs to seize me? Day after day I sat teaching in the temple area, yet you did not arrest me. But all this has come to pass that the writings of the prophets may be fulfilled." **N.** Then all the disciples left him and fled.

6. JESUS BEFORE THE SANHEDRIN

N. **T**HOSE who had arrested Jesus led him away to Caiaphas the high priest, where the scribes and the elders were assembled. Peter was following him at a distance as far as the high priest's courtyard, and going inside he sat down with the servants to see the outcome. The chief priests and the entire Sanhedrin kept trying to obtain false testimony against Jesus in order to put him to death, but they found none, though many false witnesses came forward. Finally two came forward who stated, **C. "This man said, 'I can destroy the temple of God and within three days rebuild it.' "** **N.** The high priest rose and addressed him, **V.** "Have you no answer? What are these men testifying against you?" **N.** But Jesus was silent. Then the high priest said to him, **V.** "I order you to tell us under oath before the living God whether you are the Christ, the Son of God." **N.** Jesus said to him in reply, ✠ "You have said so. But I tell you:

From now on you will see 'the Son of Man
     seated at the right hand of the Power'
     and 'coming on the clouds of heaven.' "

N. Then the high priest tore his robes and said, **V.** "He has blasphemed! What further need have we of witnesses? You have now heard the blasphemy; what is your opinion?" **N.** They said in reply, **C. "He deserves to die!"** **N.** Then they spat in his face and struck him, while some slapped him, saying, **C. "Prophesy for us, Christ: who is it that struck you?"** *[7. PETER'S DENIAL]* **N.** Now Peter was sitting outside in the courtyard. One of the maids came over to him and said, **C. "You too were with Jesus the Galilean."** **N.** But he denied it in front of everyone, saying, **V.** "I do not know what you are talking about!" **N.** As he went out to the gate, another girl saw him and said to those who were there, **C. "This man was with Jesus the Nazorean."** **N.** Again he denied it with an oath, **V.** "I do not know the man!" **N.** A little later the bystanders came over and said to Peter, **C. "Surely you too are one of them; even your speech gives you away."** **N.** At that he began to curse and to swear, **V.** "I do not know the man." **N.** And immediately a cock crowed. Then Peter remembered the word that Jesus had spoken: "Before the cock crows you will deny me three times." He went out and began to weep bitterly.

8. JESUS HANDED OVER TO PILATE

N. **W**HEN it was morning, all the chief priests and the elders of the people took counsel against Jesus to put him to death. They bound him, led him away, and handed him over to Pilate, the governor.

Then Judas, his betrayer, seeing that Jesus had been condemned, deeply regretted what he had done. He returned the thirty pieces of silver to the chief priests and elders, saying, **V.** "I have sinned in betraying innocent blood." **N.** They said, **C.** **"What is that to us? Look to it yourself."** **N.** Flinging the money into the temple, he departed and went off and hanged himself. The chief priests gathered up the money, but said, **C.** **"It is not lawful to deposit this in the temple treasury, for it is the price of blood."** **N.** After consultation, they used it to buy the potter's field as a burial place for foreigners. That is why that field even today is called the Field of Blood. Then was fulfilled what had been said through Jeremiah the prophet, *And they took the thirty pieces of silver, the value of a man with a price on his head, a price set by some of the Israelites, and they paid it out for the potter's field just as the Lord had commanded me.*

[Beginning of Shorter Form]

9. JESUS BEFORE PILATE

N. **[N**OW**]** Jesus stood before the governor, and he questioned him, **V.** "Are you the king of the Jews?" **N.** Jesus said, ✚ "You say so." **N.** And when he was accused by the chief priests and elders, he made no answer. Then Pilate said to him, **V.** "Do you not hear how many things they are testifying against you?" **N.** But he did not answer him one word, so that the governor was greatly amazed.

Now on the occasion of the feast the governor was accustomed to release to the crowd one prisoner whom they wished. And at that time they had a notorious prisoner called Barabbas. So when they had assembled, Pilate said to them, **V.** "Which one do you want me to release to you, Barabbas, or Jesus called Christ?" **N.** For he knew that it was out of envy that they had handed him over. While he was still seated on the bench, his wife sent him a message, "Have nothing to do with that righteous man. I suffered much in a dream today because of him." The chief priests and the elders persuaded the crowds to ask for Barabbas but to destroy Jesus. The governor said to them in reply, **V.** "Which of the two do you want me to release to you?" **N.** They answered, **C.** **"Barabbas!"** **N.** Pilate said to them, **V.** "Then what shall I do with Jesus called Christ?" **N.** They all said, **C.** **"Let him be crucified!"** **N.** But he said, **V.** "Why? What evil has he done?" **N.** They only shouted the louder, **C.** **"Let him be crucified!"** **N.** When Pilate saw that he was not succeeding at all, but that a riot was breaking out instead, he took water and washed his hands in the sight of the crowd, saying, **V.** "I am innocent of this man's blood. Look to it yourselves." **N.** And the whole people said in reply, **C.** **"His blood be upon us and upon our children."** **N.** Then he released Barabbas to them, but after he had Jesus scourged, he handed him over to be crucified.

10. THE CROWNING WITH THORNS

N. **T**HEN the soldiers of the governor took Jesus inside the praetorium and gathered the whole cohort around him. They stripped off his clothes and threw a scarlet military cloak about him. Weaving a crown out of thorns, they placed it on his head, and a reed in his right hand. And kneeling before him, they mocked him, saying, **C. "Hail, King of the Jews!"** They spat upon him and took the reed and kept striking him on the head. And when they had mocked him, they stripped him of the cloak, dressed him in his own clothes, and led him off to crucify him.

11. THE WAY OF THE CROSS

N. **A**S they were going out, they met a Cyrenian named Simon; this man they pressed into service to carry his cross.

And when they came to a place called Golgotha—which means Place of the Skull—, they gave Jesus wine to drink mixed with gall. But when he had tasted it, he refused to drink. *[12. THE CRUCIFIXION]* **N.** After they had crucified him, they divided his garments by casting lots; then they sat down and kept watch over him there. And they placed over his head the written charge against him: This is Jesus, the King of the Jews. Two revolutionaries were crucified with him, one on his right and the other on his left. Those passing by reviled him, shaking their heads and saying, **C. "You who would destroy the temple and rebuild it in three days, save yourself, if you are the Son of God, and come down from the cross!"** **N.** Likewise the chief priests with the scribes and elders mocked him and said, **C. "He saved others; he cannot save himself. So he is the king of Israel! Let him come down from the cross now, and we will believe in him. He trusted in God; let him deliver him now if he wants him. For he said, 'I am the Son of God.' "** **N.** The revolutionaries who were crucified with him also kept abusing him in the same way.

13. THE DEATH OF JESUS

N. **F**ROM noon onward, darkness came over the whole land until three in the afternoon. And about three o'clock Jesus cried out in a loud voice, ✚ *"Eli, Eli, lema sabachthani?"* **N.** which means, ✚ "My God, my God, why have you forsaken me?" **N.** Some of the bystanders who heard it said, **C. "This one is calling for Elijah."** **N.** Immediately one of them ran to get a sponge; he soaked it in wine, and putting it on a reed, gave it to him to drink. But the rest said, **C. "Wait, let us see if Elijah comes to save him."** **N.** But Jesus cried out again in a loud voice, and gave up his spirit.

Here all kneel and pause for a short time.

And behold, the veil of the sanctuary was torn in two from top to bottom. The earth quaked, rocks were split, tombs were opened, and the bodies of many saints who had fallen asleep were raised. And coming forth from their tombs after his resurrection, they entered the holy city and appeared to many. The centurion and the men with him who were keeping watch over Jesus feared greatly when they saw the earthquake and all that was happening, and they said, **C. "Truly, this was the Son of God!"**

[End of Shorter Form]

N. There were many women there, looking on from a distance, who had followed Jesus from Galilee, ministering to him. Among them were Mary Magdalene and Mary the mother of James and Joseph, and the mother of the sons of Zebedee.

14. THE BURIAL

N. WHEN it was evening, there came a rich man from Arimathea named Joseph, who was himself a disciple of Jesus. He went to Pilate and asked for the body of Jesus; then Pilate ordered it to be handed over. Taking the body, Joseph wrapped it in clean linen and laid it in his new tomb that he had hewn in the rock. Then he rolled a huge stone across the entrance to the tomb and departed. But Mary

Magdalene and the other Mary remained sitting there, facing the tomb.

The next day, the one following the day of preparation, the chief priests and the Pharisees gathered before Pilate and said, **C. "Sir, we remember that this impostor while still alive said, 'After three days I will be raised up.' Give orders, then, that the grave be secured until the third day, lest his disciples come and steal him and say to the people, 'He has been raised from the dead.' This last imposture would be worse than the first." N.** Pilate said to them, **V.** "The guard is yours; go, secure it as best you can." **N.** So they went and secured the tomb by fixing a seal to the stone and setting the guard.—The Gospel of the Lord. ℟. **Praise to you, Lord Jesus Christ.**   ➙ No. 15, p. 18

After the narrative of the Passion, a brief homily should take place, if appropriate. A period of silence may also be observed.

PRAYER OVER THE OFFERINGS   [Reconciled with God]

Through the Passion of your Only Begotten Son, O Lord,
may our reconciliation with you be near at hand,
so that, though we do not merit it by our own deeds,
yet by this sacrifice made once for all,
we may feel already the effects of your mercy.
Through Christ our Lord. ℟. **Amen.** ↓

PREFACE (P 19)   [Purchased Our Justification]

℣. The Lord be with you. ℟. **And with your spirit.**
℣. Lift up your hearts. ℟. **We lift them up to the Lord.**
℣. Let us give thanks to the Lord our God. ℟. **It is right and just.**

It is truly right and just, our duty and our salvation,
always and everywhere to give you thanks,
Lord, holy Father, almighty and eternal God,
through Christ our Lord.

For, though innocent, he suffered willingly for sinners
and accepted unjust condemnation to save the guilty.
His Death has washed away our sins,
and his Resurrection has purchased our justification.

And so, with all the Angels,
we praise you, as in joyful celebration we acclaim:

➜ No. 23, p. 23

COMMUNION ANT. Mt 26:42   [God's Will]
**Father, if this chalice cannot pass without my drinking
it, your will be done.** ↓

PRAYER AFTER COMMUNION   [Nourishing Gifts]

Nourished with these sacred gifts,
we humbly beseech you, O Lord,
that, just as through the death of your Son
you have brought us to hope for what we believe,
so by his Resurrection
you may lead us to where you call.
Through Christ our Lord.
℟. **Amen.** ↓

*The Deacon or, in his absence, the Priest himself, says the
invitation:* Bow down for the blessing.

PRAYER OVER THE PEOPLE   [God's Family]

Look, we pray, O Lord, on this your family,
for whom our Lord Jesus Christ
did not hesitate to be delivered into the hands of the
    wicked
and submit to the agony of the Cross.
Who lives and reigns for ever and ever.
℟. **Amen.**   ————   ➜ No. 32, p. 77

"The Spirit of the Lord is upon me."

APRIL 6

THURSDAY OF HOLY WEEK
[HOLY THURSDAY]

THE CHRISM MASS

This Mass, which the Bishop concelebrates with his presbyter-ate, should be, as it were, a manifestation of the Priests' com-munion with their Bishop. Accordingly it is desirable that all the Priests participate in it, insofar as is possible, and during it receive Communion even under both kinds. To signify the unity of the presbyterate of the diocese, the Priests who concelebrate with the Bishop should be from different regions of the diocese.

In accord with traditional practice, the blessing of the Oil of the Sick takes place before the end of the Eucharistic Prayer, but the bless-ing of the Oil of Catechumens and the consecration of the Chrism take place after Communion. Nevertheless, for pastoral reasons, it is permitted for the entire rite of blessing to take place after the Liturgy of the Word.

ENTRANCE ANT. Rev 1:6   [Kingdom of Priests]
Jesus Christ has made us into a kingdom, priests for his God and Father. To him be glory and power for ever and ever. Amen.   ➜ No. 2, p. 10

255

The Gloria *is said.*

COLLECT [Faithful Witnesses]

O God, who anointed your Only Begotten Son with the
   Holy Spirit
and made him Christ and Lord,
graciously grant
that, being made sharers in his consecration,
we may bear witness to your Redemption in the world.
Through our Lord Jesus Christ, your Son,
who lives and reigns with you in the unity of the Holy
   Spirit,
God, for ever and ever.
℟. **Amen.** ↓

FIRST READING Is 61:1-3ab, 6a, 8b-9 [The Lord's Anointed]

**The prophet, anointed by God to bring good news to the
poor, proclaims a message filled with hope. It is one that
replaces mourning with gladness.**

A reading from the Book of the Prophet Isaiah

The Spirit of the Lord GOD is upon me,
      because the LORD has anointed me;
He has sent me to bring glad tidings to the lowly,
      to heal the brokenhearted,
To proclaim liberty to the captives
      and release to the prisoners,
To announce a year of favor from the LORD
      and a day of vindication by our God,
      to comfort all who mourn;
To place on those who mourn in Zion
      a diadem instead of ashes,
To give them oil of gladness in place of mourning,
      a glorious mantle instead of a listless spirit.

You yourselves shall be named priests of the LORD,
      ministers of our God you shall be called.

I will give them their recompense faithfully,
    a lasting covenant I will make with them.
Their descendants shall be renowned among the
    · nations,
    and their offspring among the peoples;
All who see them shall acknowledge them
    as a race the LORD has blessed.
The word of the Lord. ℟. **Thanks be to God.** ↓

RESPONSORIAL PSALM Ps 89   [God the Savior]

    ℟. For ev - er I will sing the good-ness of the Lord.

"I have found David, my servant;
    with my holy oil I have anointed him,
that my hand may be always with him,
    and that my arm may make him strong."

℟. **For ever I will sing the goodness of the Lord.**

"My faithfulness and my kindness shall be with him,
    and through my name shall his horn be exalted.
He shall cry to me, 'You are my father,
    my God, the Rock my savior.' "

℟. **For ever I will sing the goodness of the Lord.** ↓

SECOND READING Rv 1:5-8   [The Alpha and the Omega]

**God says, "I am the Alpha and the Omega, the one who is
and who was and who is to come, the Almighty!" All shall
see God as he comes amid the clouds.**

A reading from the Book of Revelation

[G]RACE to you and peace] from Jesus Christ, who is
    the faithful witness, the firstborn of the dead and
ruler of the kings of the earth. To him who loves us and
has freed us from our sins by his Blood, who has made
us into a Kingdom, priests for his God and Father, to
him be glory and power forever and ever! Amen.

Behold, he is coming amid the clouds,
    and every eye will see him,
    even of those who pierced him.
All the peoples of the earth will lament him.   ·
    Yes. Amen.
"I am the Alpha and the Omega," says the Lord God, "the one who is and who was and who is to come, the Almighty!"—The word of the Lord. ℟. **Thanks be to God.** ↓

VERSE BEFORE THE GOSPEL Is 61:1 (cited in Lk 4:18)

[Glad Tidings]

℟. **Glory to you, Word of God, Lord Jesus Christ!***
The Spirit of the LORD is upon me
for he sent me to bring glad tidings to the poor.
℟. **Glory to you, Word of God, Lord Jesus Christ!** ↓

GOSPEL Lk 4:16-21   [Christ the Messiah]

Jesus reads in the synagogue at Nazareth the words of Isaiah quoted in the First Reading. Jesus is the Anointed One. He tells the people that today Isaiah's prophecy is fulfilled.

℣. The Lord be with you. ℟. **And with your spirit.**
✢ A reading from the holy Gospel according to Luke.
℟. **Glory to you, O Lord.**

JESUS came to Nazareth, where he had grown up, and went according to his custom into the synagogue on the sabbath day. He stood up to read and was handed a scroll of the prophet Isaiah. He unrolled the scroll and found the passage where it was written:
    The Spirit of the Lord is upon me,
    because he has anointed me
        to bring glad tidings to the poor.
    He has sent me to proclaim liberty to captives
        and recovery of sight to the blind,
        to let the oppressed go free,
    and to proclaim a year acceptable to the Lord.

* *See p. 16 for other Gospel Acclamations.*

Rolling up the scroll, he handed it back to the attendant and sat down, and the eyes of all in the synagogue looked intently at him. He said to them, "Today this Scripture passage is fulfilled in your hearing."— The Gospel of the Lord. ℟. **Praise to you, Lord Jesus Christ.**

After the reading of the Gospel, the Bishop preaches the Homily in which, taking his starting point from the text of the readings proclaimed in the Liturgy of the Word, he speaks to the people and to his Priests about priestly anointing, urging the Priests to be faithful in their office and calling on them to renew publicly their priestly promises.

Renewal of Priestly Promises

After the Homily, the Bishop speaks with the Priests in these or similar words.

Beloved sons,
on the anniversary of that day
when Christ our Lord conferred his priesthood
on his Apostles and on us,
are you resolved to renew,
in the presence of your Bishop and God's holy people,
the promises you once made?
Priests: I am.

Bishop:
Are you resolved to be more united with the Lord Jesus
and more closely conformed to him,
denying yourselves and confirming those promises
about sacred duties towards Christ's Church
which, prompted by love of him,
you willingly and joyfully pledged
on the day of your priestly ordination?
Priests: I am.

Bishop:
Are you resolved to be faithful stewards of the mysteries
   of God

in the Holy Eucharist and the other liturgical rites
and to discharge faithfully the sacred office of teaching,
following Christ the Head and Shepherd,
not seeking any gain,
but moved only by zeal for souls?

Priests: I am.

Then, turned towards the people, the Bishop continues:

As for you, dearest sons and daughters,
pray for your Priests,
that the Lord may pour out his gifts abundantly upon
   them,
and keep them faithful as ministers of Christ, the High
   Priest,
so that they may lead you to him,
who is the source of salvation.

People: Christ, hear us. Christ, graciously hear us.

Bishop:
And pray also for me,
that I may be faithful to the apostolic office
entrusted to me in my lowliness
and that in your midst I may be made day by day
a living and more perfect image of Christ,
the Priest, the Good Shepherd,
the Teacher and the Servant of all.

People: Christ, hear us. Christ, graciously hear us.

Bishop:
May the Lord keep us all in his charity
and lead all of us,
shepherds and flock,
to eternal life.

All: Amen.

The Creed is not said.   → No. 17, p. 20

PRAYER OVER THE OFFERINGS   [New Life]
May the power of this sacrifice, O Lord, we pray,
mercifully wipe away what is old in us

and increase in us grace of salvation and newness of life.
Through Christ our Lord.
℟. **Amen.** ↓

PREFACE (P 20)   [Continuation of Christ's Priesthood]

℣. The Lord be with you. ℟. **And with your spirit.**
℣. Lift up your hearts. ℟. **We lift them up to the Lord.**
℣. Let us give thanks to the Lord our God. ℟. **It is right and just.**

It is truly right and just, our duty and our salvation,
always and everywhere to give you thanks,
Lord, holy Father, almighty and eternal God.

For by the anointing of the Holy Spirit
you made your Only Begotten Son
High Priest of the new and eternal covenant,
and by your wondrous design were pleased to decree
that his one Priesthood should continue in the Church.

For Christ not only adorns with a royal priesthood
the people he has made his own,
but with a brother's kindness he also chooses men
to become sharers in his sacred ministry
through the laying on of hands.

They are to renew in his name
the sacrifice of human redemption,
to set before your children the paschal banquet,
to lead your holy people in charity,
to nourish them with the word
and strengthen them with the Sacraments.

As they give up their lives for you
and for the salvation of their brothers and sisters,
they strive to be conformed to the image of Christ himself
and offer you a constant witness of faith and love.

And so, Lord, with all the Angels and Saints,
we, too, give you thanks, as in exultation we acclaim:

➟ No. 23, p. 23

COMMUNION ANT. Ps 89 (88):2   [The Lord's Fidelity]

I will sing for ever of your mercies, O Lord; through all
ages my mouth will proclaim your fidelity. ↓

PRAYER AFTER COMMUNION   [Renewed in Christ]

We beseech you, almighty God,
that those you renew by your Sacraments
may merit to become the pleasing fragrance of Christ.
Who lives and reigns for ever and ever.
℟. **Amen.**   → No. 30, p. 77

Optional Solemn Blessings, p. 97, and Prayers over the People, p. 105

"Do this in remembrance of me."

THE SACRED PASCHAL TRIDUUM
APRIL 6

THURSDAY OF THE LORD'S SUPPER
[HOLY THURSDAY]

AT THE EVENING MASS

The Evening Mass of the Lord's Supper commemorates the institution of the Holy Eucharist and the sacrament of Holy Orders. It was
at this Mass that Jesus changed bread and wine into his Body and
Blood. He then directed his disciples to carry out this same ritual:
"Do this in remembrance of me."

ENTRANCE ANT. Cf. Gal 6:14   [Glory in the Cross]
We should glory in the Cross of our Lord Jesus Christ, in whom is our salvation, life and resurrection, through whom we are saved and delivered.

➡ No. 2, p. 10

The Gloria in excelsis *(Glory to God in the highest) is said. While the hymn is being sung, bells are rung, and when it is finished, they remain silent until the* Gloria in excelsis *of the Easter Vigil, unless, if appropriate, the Diocesan Bishop has decided otherwise. Likewise, during this same period, the organ and other musical instruments may be used only so as to support the singing.*

COLLECT   [Fullness of Charity]

O God, who have called us to participate
in this most sacred Supper,
in which your Only Begotten Son,
when about to hand himself over to death,
entrusted to the Church a sacrifice new for all eternity,
the banquet of his love,
grant, we pray,
that we may draw from so great a mystery,
the fullness of charity and of life.
Through our Lord Jesus Christ, your Son,
who lives and reigns with you in the unity of the Holy
    Spirit,
God, for ever and ever.
℞. **Amen.** ↓

FIRST READING Ex 12:1-8, 11-14   [The First Passover]
For the protection of the Jewish people, strict religious and dietary instructions are given to Moses by God. The law of the Passover meal requires that the doorposts and lintels of each house be marked with the blood of the sacrificial animal so that the Lord can "go through Egypt, striking down every firstborn of the land, both man and beast."

A reading from the Book of Exodus

THE LORD said to Moses and Aaron in the land of Egypt, "This month shall stand at the head of your calendar; you shall reckon it the first month of the year. Tell the whole community of Israel: On the tenth of this month every one of your families must procure for itself a lamb, one apiece for each household. If a family is too small for a whole lamb, it shall join the nearest household in procuring one and shall share in the lamb in proportion to the number of persons who partake of it. The lamb must be a year-old male and without blemish. You may take it from either the sheep or the goats. You shall keep it until the fourteenth day of this month, and then, with the whole assembly of Israel present, it shall be slaughtered during the evening twilight. They shall take some of its blood and apply it to the two doorposts and the lintel of every house in which they partake of the lamb. That same night they shall eat its roasted flesh with unleavened bread and bitter herbs.

"This is how you are to eat it: with your loins girt, sandals on your feet and your staff in hand, you shall eat like those who are in flight. It is the Passover of the LORD. For on this same night I will go through Egypt, striking down every firstborn of the land, both man and beast, and executing judgment on all the gods of Egypt—I, the LORD! But the blood will mark the houses where you are. Seeing the blood, I will pass over you; thus, when I strike the land of Egypt, no destructive blow will come upon you.

"This day shall be a memorial feast for you, which all your generations shall celebrate with pilgrimage to the LORD, as a perpetual institution."—The word of the Lord. ℟. **Thanks be to God.** ↓

RESPONSORIAL PSALM Ps 116   [Thanksgiving]

℞. **Our blessing-cup is a communion with the Blood of Christ.**

How shall I make a return to the LORD
   for all the good he has done for me?
The cup of salvation I will take up,
   and I will call upon the name of the LORD.

℞. **Our blessing-cup is a communion with the Blood of Christ.**

Precious in the eyes of the LORD
   is the death of his faithful ones.
I am your servant, the son of your handmaid;
   you have loosed my bonds.

℞. **Our blessing-cup is a communion with the Blood of Christ.**

To you will I offer sacrifice of thanksgiving,
   and I will call upon the name of the LORD.
My vows to the LORD I will pay
   in the presence of all his people.

℞. **Our blessing-cup is a communion with the Blood of Christ.** ↓

SECOND READING 1 Cor 11:23-26   [The Lord's Supper]
   Paul recounts the events of the Last Supper that were
   handed down to him. The changing of bread and wine into
   the Body and Blood of the Lord proclaimed again his
   Death. It was to be a sacrificial meal.

A reading from the first Letter of Saint Paul
          to the Corinthians

BROTHERS and sisters: I received from the Lord what I also handed on to you, that the Lord Jesus, on the night he was handed over, took bread, and, after he had given thanks, broke it and said, "This is my body that is for you. Do this in remembrance of me." In the same way also the cup, after supper, saying, "This cup is the new covenant in my blood. Do this, as often as you drink it, in remembrance of me." For as often as you eat this bread and drink the cup, you proclaim the death of the Lord until he comes.—The word of the Lord. ℟. **Thanks be to God.** ↓

VERSE BEFORE THE GOSPEL Jn 13:34 **[Love One Another]**

℟. **Praise to you, Lord Jesus Christ, King of endless glory!***

I give you a new commandment, says the Lord:
love one another as I have loved you.

℟. **Praise to you, Lord Jesus Christ, King of endless glory!** ↓

GOSPEL Jn 13:1-15   **[Love and Service]**

Jesus washes the feet of his disciples to prove to them his sincere love and great humility, which they should imitate. He teaches them that, although free from sin and not unworthy to receive his Most Holy Body and Blood, they should be purified of all evil inclinations.

℣. The Lord be with you. ℟. **And with your spirit.**
✣ A reading from the holy Gospel according to John.
℟. **Glory to you, O Lord.**

BEFORE the feast of Passover, Jesus knew that his hour had come to pass from this world to the Father. He loved his own in the world and he loved them to the end. The devil had already induced Judas, son of Simon the Iscariot, to hand him over. So, during supper, fully aware that the Father had put everything

---

* *See p. 16 for other Gospel Acclamations.*

into his power and that he had come from God and was returning to God, he rose from supper and took off his outer garments. He took a towel and tied it around his waist. Then he poured water into a basin and began to wash the disciples' feet and dry them with the towel around his waist. He came to Simon Peter, who said to him, "Master, are you going to wash my feet?" Jesus answered and said to him, "What I am doing, you do not understand now, but you will understand later." Peter said to him, "You will never wash my feet." Jesus answered him, "Unless I wash you, you will have no inheritance with me." Simon Peter said to him, "Master, then not only my feet, but my hands and head as well." Jesus said to him, "Whoever has bathed has no need except to have his feet washed, for he is clean all over; so you are clean, but not all." For he knew who would betray him; for this reason, he said, "Not all of you are clean."

So when he had washed their feet and put his garments back on and reclined at table again, he said to them, "Do you realize what I have done for you? You call me 'teacher' and 'master,' and rightly so, for indeed I am. If I, therefore, the master and teacher, have washed your feet, you ought to wash one another's feet. I have given you a model to follow, so that as I have done for you, you should also do."—The Gospel of the Lord. ℟. **Praise to you, Lord Jesus Christ.**

After the proclamation of the Gospel, the Priest gives a homily in which light is shed on the principal mysteries that are commemorated in this Mass, namely, the institution of the Holy Eucharist and of the priestly Order, and the commandment of the Lord concerning fraternal charity.

The Washing of Feet

After the Homily, where a pastoral reason suggests it, the Washing of Feet follows.

Those who are chosen from among the people of God are led by the ministers to seats prepared in a suitable place. Then the Priest (removing his chasuble if necessary) goes to each one, and, with the help of the ministers, pours water over each one's feet and then dries them.

Meanwhile some of the following antiphons or other appropriate chants are sung.

ANTIPHON 1 Cf. Jn 13:4, 5, 15   [Jesus' Example]

**After the Lord had risen from supper,
he poured water into a basin
and began to wash the feet of his disciples:
he left them this example.**

ANTIPHON 2 Cf. Jn 13:12, 13, 15   [Do Likewise]

**The Lord Jesus, after eating supper with his disciples,
washed their feet and said to them:
Do you know what I, your Lord and Master, have done
   for you?
I have given you an example, that you should do likewise.**

ANTIPHON 3 Jn 13:6, 7, 8   [Peter's Understanding]

**Lord, are you to wash my feet? Jesus said to him in
   answer:
If I do not wash your feet, you will have no share with
   me.**

℣. **So he came to Simon Peter and Peter said to him:**
—**Lord.**

℣. **What I am doing, you do not know for now,
but later you will come to know.**
—**Lord.**

ANTIPHON 4 Cf. Jn 13:14   [Service]

**If I, your Lord and Master, have washed your feet,
how much more should you wash each other's feet?**

ANTIPHON 5 Jn 13:35   [Identified by Love]

This is how all will know that you are my disciples:
if you have love for one another.

℣. Jesus said to his disciples:
—This is how.

ANTIPHON 6 Jn 13:34   [New Commandment]

I give you a new commandment,
that you love one another
as I have loved you, says the Lord.

ANTIPHON 7 1 Cor 13:13   [Greatest Is Charity]

Let faith, hope and charity, these three, remain among
    you,
but the greatest of these is charity.

℣. Now faith, hope and charity, these three, remain;
but the greatest of these is charity.
—Let.

*After the Washing of Feet, the Priest washes and dries his
hands, puts the chasuble back on, and returns to the chair,
and from there he directs the Universal Prayer.*

The Creed is not said.

The Liturgy of the Eucharist

*At the beginning of the Liturgy of the Eucharist, there may be a
procession of the faithful in which gifts for the poor may be presented with the bread and wine.*

Meanwhile the following, or another appropriate chant, is sung.

[Christ's Love]

Ant. **Where true charity is dwelling, God is present there.**

℣. By the love of Christ we have been brought to-
    gether:
℣. let us find in him our gladness and our pleasure;
℣. may we love him and revere him, God the living,
℣. and in love respect each other with sincere hearts.

Ant. **Where true charity is dwelling, God is present there.**

℣. **So when we as one are gathered all together,**
℣. **let us strive to keep our minds free of division;**
℣. **may there be an end to malice, strife and quarrels,**
℣. **and let Christ our God be dwelling here among us.**

Ant. **Where true charity is dwelling, God is present there.**

℣. **May your face thus be our vision, bright in glory,**
℣. **Christ our God, with all the blessed Saints in heaven:**
℣. **such delight is pure and faultless, joy unbounded,**
℣. **which endures through countless ages world without end. Amen.**   ➙ No. 17, p. 20

PRAYER OVER THE OFFERINGS   [Work of Redemption]

Grant us, O Lord, we pray,
that we may participate worthily in these mysteries,
for whenever the memorial of this sacrifice is celebrated
the work of our redemption is accomplished.
Through Christ our Lord.
℟. **Amen.**   ➙ No. 21, p. 22 (Pref. P 47)

*When the Roman Canon is used, this special form of it is said,
with proper formulas for the* Communicantes *(In communion
with those),* Hanc igitur *(Therefore, Lord, we pray), and* Qui
pridie *(On the day before he was to suffer).*

To you, therefore, most merciful Father,
we make humble prayer and petition
through Jesus Christ, your Son, our Lord:
that you accept
and bless ✚ these gifts, these offerings,
these holy and unblemished sacrifices,
which we offer you firstly
for your holy catholic Church.
Be pleased to grant her peace,
to guard, unite and govern her

throughout the whole world,
together with your servant *N.* our Pope
and *N.* our Bishop,
and all those who, holding to the truth,
hand on the catholic and apostolic faith.

Remember, Lord, your servants *N.* and *N.*
and all gathered here,
whose faith and devotion are known to you.
For them we offer you this sacrifice of praise
or they offer it for themselves
and all who are dear to them:
for the redemption of their souls,
in hope of health and well-being,
and paying their homage to you,
the eternal God, living and true.

Celebrating the most sacred day
on which our Lord Jesus Christ
was handed over for our sake,
and in communion with those whose memory we
    venerate,
especially the glorious ever-Virgin Mary,
Mother of our God and Lord, Jesus Christ,
and † blessed Joseph, her Spouse,
your blessed Apostles and Martyrs
Peter and Paul, Andrew,
(James, John,
Thomas, James, Philip,
Bartholomew, Matthew, Simon and Jude;
Linus, Cletus, Clement, Sixtus,
Cornelius, Cyprian,
Lawrence, Chrysogonus,
John and Paul,
Cosmas and Damian)
and all your Saints;
we ask that through their merits and prayers,
in all things we may be defended

by your protecting help.
(Through Christ our Lord. Amen.)

Therefore, Lord, we pray:
graciously accept this oblation of our service,
that of your whole family,
which we make to you
as we observe the day
on which our Lord Jesus Christ
handed on the mysteries of his Body and Blood
for his disciples to celebrate;
order our days in your peace,
and command that we be delivered from eternal
   damnation
and counted among the flock of those you have chosen.
(Through Christ our Lord. Amen.)

Be pleased, O God, we pray,
to bless, acknowledge,
and approve this offering in every respect;
make it spiritual and acceptable,
so that it may become for us
the Body and Blood of your most beloved Son,
our Lord Jesus Christ.

On the day before he was to suffer
for our salvation and the salvation of all,
that is today,
he took bread in his holy and venerable hands,
and with eyes raised to heaven
to you, O God, his almighty Father,
giving you thanks, he said the blessing,
broke the bread
and gave it to his disciples, saying:

Take this, all of you, and eat of it,
for this is my Body,
which will be given up for you.

In a similar way, when supper was ended,
he took this precious chalice
in his holy and venerable hands,
and once more giving you thanks, he said the blessing
and gave the chalice to his disciples, saying:

Take this, all of you, and drink from it,
for this is the chalice of my Blood,
the Blood of the new and eternal covenant,
which will be poured out for you and for many
for the forgiveness of sins.

Do this in memory of me.

The rest follows the Roman Canon, pp. 26-29.

COMMUNION ANT. 1 Cor 11:24-25   [In Memory of Christ]

This is the Body that will be given up for you; this is the Chalice of the new covenant in my Blood, says the Lord; do this, whenever you receive it, in memory of me. ↓

After the distribution of Communion, a ciborium with hosts for Communion on the following day is left on the altar. The Priest, standing at the chair, says the Prayer after Communion.

PRAYER AFTER COMMUNION   [Renewed]

Grant, almighty God,
that, just as we are renewed
by the Supper of your Son in this present age,
so we may enjoy his banquet for all eternity.
Who lives and reigns for ever and ever.
℞. **Amen.**

The Transfer of the Most Blessed Sacrament

After the Prayer after Communion, the Priest puts incense in the thurible while standing, blesses it and then, kneeling, incenses the Blessed Sacrament three times. Then, having put on a white humeral veil, he rises, takes the ciborium, and covers it with the ends of the veil.

A procession is formed in which the Blessed Sacrament, accompanied by torches and incense, is carried through the church to a place of repose prepared in a part of the church or in a chapel suitably decorated. A lay minister with a cross, standing between two other ministers with lighted candles leads off. Others carrying lighted candles follow. Before the Priest carrying the Blessed Sacrament comes the thurifer with a smoking thurible. Meanwhile, the hymn Pange, lingua *(exclusive of the last two stanzas) or another eucharistic chant is sung.*

PANGE LINGUA   [Adoring the Lord]

Sing my tongue, the Savior's glory,
Of his flesh the mystery sing;
Of his blood all price exceeding,
Shed by our immortal king,
Destined for the world's redemption,
From a noble womb to spring.

Of a pure and spotless Virgin
Born for us on earth below,
He, as man with man conversing,
Stayed the seeds of truth to sow;
Then he closed in solemn order
Wondrously his life of woe.

On the night of that Last Supper,
Seated with his chosen band,
He, the paschal victim eating,
First fulfills the law's command;
Then as food to all his brethren
Gives himself with his own hand.

Word made Flesh, the bread of nature,
By his word to flesh he turns;
Wine into his blood he changes:
What though sense no change discerns,
Only be the heart in earnest,
Faith her lesson quickly learns.

When the procession reaches the place of repose, the Priest, with the help of the Deacon if necessary, places the ciborium in the tabernacle, the door of which remains open. Then he puts incense in the thurible and, kneeling, incenses the Blessed Sacrament, while Tantum ergo Sacramentum *or another eucharistic chant is sung. Then the Deacon or the Priest himself places the Sacrament in the tabernacle and closes the door.*

Down in adoration falling,
Lo! the sacred host we hail,
Lo! o'er ancient forms departing
Newer rites of grace prevail;
Faith for all defects supplying,
Where the feeble senses fail.

To the everlasting Father,
And the Son who reigns on high
With the Holy Spirit proceeding
Forth from each eternally,
Be salvation, honor, blessing,
Might and endless majesty.
Amen.

After a period of adoration in silence, the Priest and ministers genuflect and return to the sacristy.

At an appropriate time, the altar is stripped and, if possible, the crosses are removed from the church. It is expedient that any crosses which remain in the church be veiled.

The faithful are invited to continue adoration before the Blessed Sacrament for a suitable length of time during the night, according to local circumstances, but after midnight the adoration should take place without solemnity.

"And bowing his head, [Jesus] handed over the spirit."

APRIL 7

FRIDAY OF THE PASSION OF THE LORD [GOOD FRIDAY]

THE CELEBRATION OF THE PASSION OF THE LORD

The liturgy of Good Friday recalls graphically the Passion and Death of Jesus. The reading of the Passion describes the suffering and Death of Jesus. Today we show great reverence for the crucifix, the sign of our redemption.

On this and the following day, by a most ancient tradition, the Church does not celebrate the Sacraments at all, except for Penance and the Anointing of the Sick. On the afternoon of this day, about three o'clock (unless a later hour is chosen for a pastoral reason), there takes place the celebration of the Lord's Passion.

The Priest and the Deacon, if a Deacon is present, wearing red vestments as for Mass, go to the altar in silence and, after making a reverence to the altar, prostrate themselves or, if appropriate, kneel and pray in silence for a while. All others kneel. Then the Priest, with the ministers, goes to the chair where, facing the people, who are standing, he says, with hands extended, one of the following prayers, omitting the invitation Let us pray.

PRAYER   [Sanctify Your Servants]
Remember your mercies, O Lord,
and with your eternal protection sanctify your servants,
for whom Christ your Son,
by the shedding of his Blood,
established the Paschal Mystery.
Who lives and reigns for ever and ever. ℟. **Amen.** ↓

OR   [Image of Christ]
O God, who by the Passion of Christ your Son, our Lord,
abolished the death inherited from ancient sin
by every succeeding generation,
grant that just as, being conformed to him,
we have borne by the law of nature
the image of the man of earth,
so by the sanctification of grace
we may bear the image of the Man of heaven.
Through Christ our Lord. ℟. **Amen.** ↓

FIRST PART: THE LITURGY OF THE WORD

FIRST READING Is 52:13—53:12   [Suffering and Glory]
**The Suffering Servant shall be raised up and exalted. The
Servant remains one with all people in sorrow and yet dis-
tinct from each of them in innocence of life and total service to God. The doctrine of expiatory suffering finds
supreme expression in these words.**

A reading from the Book of the Prophet Isaiah

S EE, my servant shall prosper,
he shall be raised high and greatly exalted.
Even as many were amazed at him—
    so marred was his look beyond human semblance
    and his appearance beyond that of the sons of
        man—
so shall he startle many nations,
    because of him kings shall stand speechless;
for those who have not been told shall see,
    those who have not heard shall ponder it.

Who would believe what we have heard?
　To whom has the arm of the Lord been revealed?
He grew up like a sapling before him,
　like a shoot from the parched earth;
there was in him no stately bearing to make us look
　　at him,
　nor appearance that would attract us to him.
He was spurned and avoided by people,
　a man of suffering, accustomed to infirmity,
one of those from whom people hide their faces,
　spurned, and we held him in no esteem.

Yet it was our infirmities that he bore,
　our sufferings that he endured,
while we thought of him as stricken,
　as one smitten by God and afflicted.
But he was pierced for our offenses,
　crushed for our sins;
upon him was the chastisement that makes us whole,
　by his stripes we were healed.
We had all gone astray like sheep,
　each following his own way;
but the Lord laid upon him
　the guilt of us all.

Though he was harshly treated, he submitted
　and opened not his mouth;
like a lamb led to the slaughter
　or a sheep before the shearers,
　he was silent and opened not his mouth.
Oppressed and condemned, he was taken away,
　　and who would have thought any more of his
　　　destiny?
When he was cut off from the land of the living,
　and smitten for the sin of his people,
a grave was assigned him among the wicked
　and a burial place with evildoers,
though he had done no wrong
　nor spoken any falsehood.

But the LORD was pleased
   to crush him in infirmity.
If he gives his life as an offering for sin,
   he shall see his descendants in a long life,
      and the will of the LORD shall be accomplished
         through him.
Because of his affliction
   he shall see the light in fullness of days;
through his suffering, my servant shall justify many,
   and their guilt he shall bear.
Therefore I will give him his portion among the great,
   and he shall divide the spoils with the mighty,
because he surrendered himself to death
   and was counted among the wicked;
and he shall take away the sins of many,
   and win pardon for their offenses.
The word of the Lord. ℟. **Thanks be to God.** ↓

RESPONSORIAL PSALM Ps 31   [Trust in God]

℟. Fa - ther, in -to your hands I com - mend my spir - it.

In you, O LORD, I take refuge;
   let me never be put to shame.
In your justice rescue me.
Into your hands I commend my spirit;
   you will redeem me, O LORD, O faithful God.

℟. **Father, into your hands I commend my spirit.**

For all my foes I am an object of reproach,
   a laughingstock to my neighbors, and a dread to my
      friends;
   they who see me abroad flee from me.
I am forgotten like the unremembered dead;
   I am like a dish that is broken.

℞. **Father, into your hands I commend my spirit.**

But my trust is in you, O LORD;
    I say, "You are my God."
In your hands is my destiny; rescue me
    from the clutches of my enemies and my persecutors.

℞. **Father, into your hands I commend my spirit.**

Let your face shine upon your servant;
    save me in your kindness.
Take courage and be stouthearted,
    all you who hope in the LORD.

℞. **Father, into your hands I commend my spirit.** ↓

SECOND READING Heb 4:14-16; 5:7-9   [Access to Christ]

> The theme of the compassionate high priest appears again
> in this passage. In him the Christian can approach God
> confidently and without fear. Christ learned obedience
> from his sufferings, whereby he became the source of eter-
> nal life for all.

A reading from the Letter to the Hebrews

BROTHERS and sisters: Since we have a great high
priest who has passed through the heavens, Jesus,
the Son of God, let us hold fast to our confession. For
we do not have a high priest who is unable to sympa-
thize with our weaknesses, but one who has similarly
been tested in every way, yet without sin. So let us confidently approach the throne of grace to receive mercy
and to find grace for timely help.

In the days when Christ was in the flesh, he offered
prayers and supplications with loud cries and tears to
the one who was able to save him from death, and he
was heard because of his reverence. Son though he
was, he learned obedience from what he suffered; and
when he was made perfect, he became the source of

eternal salvation for all who obey him.—The word of the Lord. ℟. **Thanks be to God.** ↓

VERSE BEFORE THE GOSPEL Phil 2:8-9   [Obedient for Us]

℟. **Praise and honor to you, Lord Jesus Christ!***
Christ became obedient to the point of death,
even death on a cross.
Because of this, God greatly exalted him
and bestowed on him the name which is above every
    other name.
℟. **Praise and honor to you, Lord Jesus Christ!** ↓

GOSPEL Jn 18:1—19:42   [Christ's Passion]

Finally the Passion is read in the same way as on the preceding Sunday. The narrator is noted by N, the words of Jesus by a ✠ and the words of others by V (Voice) and C (Crowd). The parts of the Crowd (C) printed in boldface type may be recited by the people.

It is important for us to understand the meaning of Christ's sufferings today. See the note on p. 244.

> The beginning scene is Christ's Agony in the Garden. Our Lord knows what is to happen. The Scriptures recount the betrayal, the trial, the condemnation, and the Crucifixion of Jesus.

N. **T**HE Passion of our Lord Jesus Christ according to John.

1. JESUS IS ARRESTED

N. **J**ESUS went out with his disciples across the Kidron valley to where there was a garden, into which he and his disciples entered. Judas his betrayer also knew the place, because Jesus had often met there with his disciples. So Judas got a band of soldiers and guards from the chief priests and the Pharisees and went there with lanterns, torches, and weapons. Jesus, knowing everything that was going to happen to him, went out and said to them, ✠ "Whom are you looking for?" N. They answered him, C. **"Jesus**

---

* *See p. 16 for other Gospel Acclamations.*

the Nazorean." **N.** He said to them, ✠ "I AM." **N.**
Judas his betrayer was also with them. When he said
to them, "I AM," they turned away and fell to the
ground. So he again asked them, ✠ "Whom are you
looking for?" **N.** They said, **C.** **"Jesus the Nazorean." N.**
Jesus answered, ✠ "I told you that I AM. So if you are
looking for me, let these men go." **N.** This was to fulfill
what he had said, "I have not lost any of those you gave
me." Then Simon Peter, who had a sword, drew it,
struck the high priest's slave, and cut off his right ear.
The slave's name was Malchus. Jesus said to Peter, ✠
"Put your sword into its scabbard. Shall I not drink the
cup that the Father gave me?"

    N. So the band of soldiers, the tribune, and the
Jewish guards seized Jesus, bound him, and brought
him to Annas first. He was the father-in-law of
Caiaphas, who was high priest that year. It was
Caiaphas who had counseled the Jews that it was bet-
ter that one man should die rather than the people.

2. PETER'S FIRST DENIAL

N. **S**IMON Peter and another disciple followed
Jesus. Now the other disciple was known to the
high priest, and he entered the courtyard of the high
priest with Jesus. But Peter stood at the gate outside.
So the other disciple, the acquaintance of the high
priest, went out and spoke to the gatekeeper and
brought Peter in. Then the maid who was the gatekeeper said to Peter, **C.** **"You are not one of this man's disciples, are you?"** **N.** He said, **V.** "I am not." **N.** Now the
slaves and the guards were standing around a char-
coal fire that they had made, because it was cold, and
were warming themselves. Peter was also standing
there keeping warm.

3. THE INQUIRY BEFORE ANNAS

N. **T**HE high priest questioned Jesus about his disciples and about his doctrine. Jesus answered

him, ✠ "I have spoken publicly to the world. I have always taught in a synagogue or in the temple area where all the Jews gather, and in secret I have said nothing. Why ask me? Ask those who heard me what I said to them. They know what I said." **N.** When he had said this, one of the temple guards standing there struck Jesus and said, **V.** "Is this the way you answer the high priest?" **N.** Jesus answered him, ✠ "If I have spoken wrongly, testify to the wrong; but if I have spoken rightly, why do you strike me?" **N.** Then Annas sent him bound to Caiaphas the high priest.

4. THE FURTHER DENIALS

N. **N**OW Simon Peter was standing there keeping warm. And they said to him, **C. "You are not one of his disciples, are you?"** **N.** He denied it and said, **V.** "I am not." **N.** One of the slaves of the high priest, a relative of the one whose ear Peter had cut off, said, **C. "Didn't I see you in the garden with him?"** **N.** Again Peter denied it. And immediately the cock crowed.

5. JESUS BROUGHT BEFORE PILATE

N. **T**HEN they brought Jesus from Caiaphas to the praetorium. It was morning. And they themselves did not enter the praetorium, in order not to be defiled so that they could eat the Passover. So Pilate came out to them and said, **V.** "What charge do you bring against this man?" **N.** They answered and said to him, **C. "If he were not a criminal, we would not have handed him over to you."** **N.** At this, Pilate said to them, **V.** "Take him yourselves, and judge him according to your law." **N.** The Jews answered him, **C. "We do not have the right to execute anyone,"** **N.** in order that the word of Jesus might be fulfilled that he said indicating the kind of death he would die.

[6. JESUS QUESTIONED BY PILATE]

N. So Pilate went back into the praetorium and summoned Jesus and said to him, **V.** "Are you the King of the Jews?" **N.** Jesus answered, ✠ "Do you say this on your own or have others told you about me?" **N.** Pilate answered, **V.** "I am not a Jew, am I? Your own nation and the chief priests handed you over to me. What have you done?" **N.** Jesus answered, ✠ "My kingdom does not belong to this world. If my kingdom did belong to this world, my attendants would be fighting to keep me from being handed over to the Jews. But as it is, my kingdom is not here." **N.** So Pilate said to him, **V.** "Then you are a king?" **N.** Jesus answered, ✠ "You say I am a king. For this I was born and for this I came into the world, to testify to the truth. Everyone who belongs to the truth listens to my voice." **N.** Pilate said to him, **V.** "What is truth?"

7. BARABBAS CHOSEN OVER JESUS

N. **W**HEN he had said this, he again went out to the Jews and said to them, **V.** "I find no guilt in him. But you have a custom that I release one prisoner to you at Passover. Do you want me to release to you the King of the Jews?" **N.** They cried out again, **C.** **"Not this one but Barabbas!"** **N.** Now Barabbas was a revolutionary.

8. JESUS IS SCOURGED

N. **T**HEN Pilate took Jesus and had him scourged. And the soldiers wove a crown out of thorns and placed it on his head, and clothed him in a purple cloak, and they came to him and said, **C.** **"Hail, King of the Jews!"** **N.** And they struck him repeatedly.

[9. JESUS IS PRESENTED TO THE CROWD]

Once more Pilate went out and said to them, **V.** "Look, I am bringing him out to you, so that you may know that I find no guilt in him." **N.** So Jesus came out, wearing the crown of thorns and the purple cloak. And Pilate said to them, **V.** "Behold, the man!" **N.** When the chief priests and the guards saw him they cried out, **C. "Crucify him, crucify him!"** **N.** Pilate said to them, **V.** "Take him yourselves and crucify him. I find no guilt in him." **N.** The Jews answered, **C. "We have a law, and according to that law he ought to die, because he made himself the Son of God."**

[*10. JESUS AGAIN QUESTIONED BY PILATE*]

N. Now when Pilate heard this statement, he became even more afraid, and went back into the praetorium and said to Jesus, **V.** "Where are you from?" **N.** Jesus did not answer him. So Pilate said to him, **V.** "Do you not speak to me? Do you not know that I have power to release you and I have power to crucify you?" **N.** Jesus answered him, ✠ "You would have no power over me if it had not been given to you from above. For this reason the one who handed me over to you has the greater sin."

[*11. JESUS SENTENCED TO BE CRUCIFIED*]

N. Consequently, Pilate tried to release him; but the Jews cried out, **C. "If you release him, you are not a Friend of Caesar. Everyone who makes himself a king opposes Caesar."**

N. When Pilate heard these words he brought Jesus out and seated him on the judge's bench in the place called Stone Pavement, in Hebrew, Gabbatha. It was preparation day for Passover, and it was about noon. And he said to the Jews, **V.** "Behold, your king!" **N.** They cried out, **C. "Take him away, take him away! Crucify him!"** **N.** Pilate said to them, **V.** "Shall I crucify your king?" **N.** The chief priests answered, **C. "We have no king but Caesar."** **N.** Then he handed him over to them to be crucified.

12. CRUCIFIXION AND DEATH

N. **S**O they took Jesus, and, carrying the cross himself, he went out to what is called the Place of the Skull, in Hebrew, Golgotha. There they crucified him, and with him two others, one on either side, with Jesus in the middle. Pilate also had an inscription written and put on the cross. It read, "Jesus the Nazorean, the King of the Jews." Now many of the Jews read this inscription, because the place where Jesus was crucified was near the city; and it was written in Hebrew, Latin, and Greek. So the chief priests of the Jews said to Pilate, **C.** **"Do not write 'The King of the Jews,' but that he said, 'I am the King of the Jews.' "** **N.** Pilate answered, **V.** "What I have written, I have written."

N. When the soldiers had crucified Jesus, they took his clothes and divided them into four shares, a share for each soldier. They also took his tunic, but the tunic was seamless, woven in one piece from the top down. So they said to one another, **C.** **"Let's not tear it, but cast lots for it to see whose it will be,"** **N.** in order that the passage of Scripture might be fulfilled that says:

They divided my garments among them,
and for my vesture they cast lots.

This is what the soldiers did. Standing by the cross of Jesus were his mother and his mother's sister, Mary the wife of Clopas, and Mary of Magdala. When Jesus saw his mother and the disciple there whom he loved he said to his mother, ✠ "Woman, behold, your son." **N.** Then he said to the disciple, ✠ "Behold, your mother." **N.** And from that hour the disciple took her into his home.

After this, aware that everything was now finished, in order that the Scripture might be fulfilled, Jesus said, ✠ "I thirst." **N.** There was a vessel filled with common wine. So they put a sponge soaked in wine on a sprig of hyssop and put it up to his mouth. When Jesus had taken the wine, he said, ✠ "It is finished." **N.** And bowing his head, he handed over the spirit.

Here all kneel and pause for a short time.

13. THE BLOOD AND WATER

N. NOW since it was preparation day, in order that the bodies might not remain on the cross on the sabbath, for the sabbath day of that week was a solemn one, the Jews asked Pilate that their legs be broken and that they be taken down. So the soldiers came and broke the legs of the first and then of the other one who was crucified with Jesus. But when they came to Jesus and saw that he was already dead, they did not break his legs, but one soldier thrust his lance into his side, and immediately blood and water flowed out. An eyewitness has testified, and his testimony is true; he knows that he is speaking the truth, so that you also may come to believe. For this happened so that the Scripture passage might be fulfilled:

Not a bone of it will be broken.

And again another passage says:

They will look upon him whom they have pierced.

14. BURIAL OF JESUS

N. AFTER this, Joseph of Arimathea, secretly a disciple of Jesus for fear of the Jews, asked Pilate if he could remove the body of Jesus. And Pilate permitted it. So he came and took his body. Nicodemus, the one who had first come to him at night, also came bringing a mixture of myrrh and aloes weighing about one hundred pounds. They took the body of Jesus and bound it with burial cloths along with the spices, according to the Jewish burial custom. Now in the place where he had been crucified there was a garden, and in the garden a new tomb, in which no one had yet been buried. So they laid Jesus there because of the Jewish preparation day; for the tomb was close by.

—The Gospel of the Lord. ℞. **Praise to you, Lord Jesus Christ.**

THE SOLEMN INTERCESSIONS

The Liturgy of the Word concludes with the Solemn Intercessions, which take place in this way: the Deacon, if a Deacon is present, or if he is not, a lay minister, stands at the ambo, and sings or says the invitation in which the intention is expressed. Then all pray in silence for a while, and afterwards the Priest, standing at the chair or, if appropriate, at the altar, with hands extended, sings or says the prayer.

The faithful may remain either kneeling or standing throughout the entire period of the prayers.

Before the Priest's prayer, in accord with tradition, it is permissible to use the Deacon's invitations Let us kneel—Let us stand, *with all kneeling for silent prayer.*

I. For Holy Church

Let us pray, dearly beloved, for the holy Church of God,
that our God and Lord be pleased to give her peace,
to guard her and to unite her throughout the whole
    world
and grant that, leading our life in tranquility and quiet,
we may glorify God the Father almighty.

Prayer in silence. Then the Priest says:

Almighty ever-living God,
who in Christ revealed your glory to all the nations,
watch over the works of your mercy,
that your Church, spread throughout all the world,
may persevere with steadfast faith in confessing your
    name.
Through Christ our Lord. ℞. **Amen.** ↓

II. For the Pope

Let us pray also for our most Holy Father Pope *N.*,
that our God and Lord,
who chose him for the Order of Bishops,

may keep him safe and unharmed for the Lord's holy
    Church,
to govern the holy People of God.

Prayer in silence. Then the Priest says:

Almighty ever-living God,
by whose decree all things are founded,
look with favor on our prayers
and in your kindness protect the Pope chosen for us,
that, under him, the Christian people,
governed by you their maker,
may grow in merit by reason of their faith.
Through Christ our Lord. ℟. **Amen.** ↓

III. For all orders and degrees of the faithful

Let us pray also for our Bishop *N.*,
for all Bishops, Priests, and Deacons of the Church
and for the whole of the faithful people.

Prayer in silence. Then the Priest says:

Almighty ever-living God,
by whose Spirit the whole body of the Church
is sanctified and governed,
hear our humble prayer for your ministers,
that, by the gift of your grace,
all may serve you faithfully.
Through Christ our Lord. ℟. **Amen.** ↓

IV. For catechumens

Let us pray also for (our) catechumens,
that our God and Lord
may open wide the ears of their inmost hearts
and unlock the gates of his mercy,
that, having received forgiveness of all their sins
through the waters of rebirth,
they, too, may be one with Christ Jesus our Lord.

Prayer in silence. Then the Priest says:

Almighty ever-living God,
who make your Church ever fruitful with new offspring,
increase the faith and understanding of (our) cate-
    chumens,
that, reborn in the font of Baptism,
they may be added to the number of your adopted
    children.
Through Christ our Lord. ℟. **Amen.** ↓

V. For the unity of Christians

Let us pray also for all our brothers and sisters who
    believe in Christ,
that our God and Lord may be pleased,
as they live the truth,
to gather them together and keep them in his one Church.

Prayer in silence. Then the Priest says:

Almighty ever-living God,
who gather what is scattered
and keep together what you have gathered,
look kindly on the flock of your Son,
that those whom one Baptism has consecrated
may be joined together by integrity of faith
and united in the bond of charity.
Through Christ our Lord. ℟. **Amen.** ↓

VI. For the Jewish people

Let us pray also for the Jewish people,
to whom the Lord our God spoke first,
that he may grant them to advance in love of his name
and in faithfulness to his covenant.

Prayer in silence. Then the Priest says:

Almighty ever-living God,
who bestowed your promises on Abraham and his
    descendants,

graciously hear the prayers of your Church,
that the people you first made your own
may attain the fullness of redemption.
Through Christ our Lord. ℟. **Amen.** ↓

VII. For those who do not believe in Christ

Let us pray also for those who do not believe in Christ,
that, enlightened by the Holy Spirit,
they, too, may enter on the way of salvation.

Prayer in silence. Then the Priest says:

Almighty ever-living God,
grant to those who do not confess Christ
that, by walking before you with a sincere heart,
they may find the truth
and that we ourselves, being constant in mutual love
and striving to understand more fully the mystery of
    your life,
may be made more perfect witnesses to your love in the
    world.
Through Christ our Lord.
℟. **Amen.** ↓

VIII. For those who do not believe in God

Let us pray also for those who do not acknowledge God,
that, following what is right in sincerity of heart,
they may find the way to God himself.

Prayer in silence. Then the Priest says:

Almighty ever-living God,
who created all people
to seek you always by desiring you
and, by finding you, come to rest,
grant, we pray,
that, despite every harmful obstacle,
all may recognize the signs of your fatherly love
and the witness of the good works

done by those who believe in you,
and so in gladness confess you,
the one true God and Father of our human race.
Through Christ our Lord. ℟. **Amen.** ↓

IX. For those in public office

Let us pray also for those in public office,
that our God and Lord
may direct their minds and hearts according to his will
for the true peace and freedom of all.

Prayer in silence. Then the Priest says:

Almighty ever-living God,
in whose hand lies every human heart
and the rights of peoples,
look with favor, we pray,
on those who govern with authority over us,
that throughout the whole world,
the prosperity of peoples,
the assurance of peace,
and freedom of religion
may through your gift be made secure.
Through Christ our Lord. ℟. **Amen.** ↓

X. For those in tribulation

Let us pray, dearly beloved,
to God the Father almighty,
that he may cleanse the world of all errors,
banish disease, drive out hunger,
unlock prisons, loosen fetters,
granting to travelers safety, to pilgrims return,
health to the sick, and salvation to the dying.

Prayer in silence. Then the Priest says:

Almighty ever-living God,
comfort of mourners, strength of all who toil,
may the prayers of those who cry out in any tribulation

come before you,
that all may rejoice,
because in their hour of need
your mercy was at hand.
Through Christ our Lord. ℞. **Amen.** ↓

SECOND PART: THE ADORATION OF THE HOLY CROSS

After the Solemn Intercessions, the solemn Adoration of the Holy Cross takes place. Of the two forms of the showing of the Cross presented here, the more appropriate one, according to pastoral needs, should be chosen.

The Showing of the Holy Cross: First Form

The Deacon accompanied by ministers, or another suitable minister, goes to the sacristy, from which, in procession, accompanied by two ministers with lighted candles, he carries the Cross, covered with a violet veil, through the church to the middle of the sanctuary.

The Priest, standing before the altar and facing the people, receives the Cross, uncovers a little of its upper part and elevates it while beginning the Ecce lignum Crucis *(Behold the wood of the Cross). He is assisted in singing by the Deacon or, if need be, by the choir. All respond,* Come, let us adore. *At the end of the singing, all kneel and for a brief moment adore in silence, while the Priest stands and holds the Cross raised.*

℣. Behold the wood of the Cross,
on which hung the salvation of the world.

℞. **Come, let us adore.**

Then the Priest uncovers the right arm of the Cross and again, raising up the Cross, begins, Behold the wood of the Cross *and everything takes place as above.*

Finally, he uncovers the Cross entirely and, raising it up, he begins the invitation Behold the wood of the Cross *a third time and everything takes place like the first time.*

The Showing of the Holy Cross: Second Form

The Priest or the Deacon accompanied by ministers, or another suitable minister, goes to the door of the church, where he receives the unveiled Cross, and the ministers take lighted candles; then the procession sets off through the church to the sanctuary. Near the door, in the middle of the church and before the entrance of the sanctuary, the one who carries the Cross elevates it, singing, Behold the wood of the Cross, *to which all respond,* Come, let us adore. *After each response all kneel and for a brief moment adore in silence, as above.*

The Adoration of the Holy Cross

Then, accompanied by two ministers with lighted candles, the Priest or the Deacon carries the Cross to the entrance of the sanctuary or to another suitable place and there puts it down or hands it over to the ministers to hold. Candles are placed on the right and left sides of the Cross.

For the Adoration of the Cross, first the Priest Celebrant alone approaches, with the chasuble and his shoes removed, if appropriate. Then the clergy, the lay ministers, and the faithful approach, moving as if in procession, and showing reverence to the Cross by a simple genuflection or by some other sign appropriate to the usage of the region, for example, by kissing the Cross.

Only one Cross should be offered for adoration. If, because of the large number of people, it is not possible for all to approach individually, the Priest, after some of the clergy and faithful have adored, takes the Cross and, standing in the middle before the altar, invites the people in a few words to adore the Holy Cross and afterwards holds the Cross elevated higher for a brief time, for the faithful to adore it in silence.

While the adoration of the Holy Cross is taking place, the antiphon Crucem tuam adoramus *(We adore your Cross, O Lord), the Reproaches, the hymn* Crux fidelis *(Faithful Cross) or other suitable chants are sung, during which all who have already adored the Cross remain seated.*

Chants to Be Sung during the Adoration of the Holy Cross

ANTIPHON   [Holy Cross]

We adore your Cross, O Lord,
we praise and glorify your holy Resurrection,

for behold, because of the wood of a tree
joy has come to the whole world.

May God have mercy on us and bless us;
may he let his face shed its light upon us
and have mercy on us.   Cf. Ps 67 (66):2

And the antiphon is repeated: **We adore . . .**

THE REPROACHES

Parts assigned to one of the two choirs separately are indicated by the numbers 1 *(first choir) and* 2 *(second choir); parts sung by both choirs together are marked:* 1 and 2. *Some of the verses may also be sung by two cantors.*

I

1 and 2: **My people, what have I done to you?
    Or how have I grieved you? Answer me!**
1: **Because I led you out of the land of Egypt,
    you have prepared a Cross for your Savior.**
1: **Hagios o Theos,**
2: **Holy is God,**
1: **Hagios Ischyros,**
2: **Holy and Mighty,**
1: **Hagios Athanatos, eleison himas.**
2: **Holy and Immortal One, have mercy on us.**

1 and 2: **Because I led you out through the desert forty
    years
    and fed you with manna and brought you into
     a land of plenty,
    you have prepared a Cross for your Savior.**
1: **Hagios o Theos,**
2: **Holy is God,**
1: **Hagios Ischyros,**
2: **Holy and Mighty,**
1: **Hagios Athanatos, eleison himas.**
2: **Holy and Immortal One, have mercy on us.**

1 and 2: **What more should I have done for you and
  have not done?
  Indeed, I planted you as my most beautiful chosen
    vine
  and you have turned very bitter for me,
  for in my thirst you gave me vinegar to drink
  and with a lance you pierced your Savior's side.**

1: **Hagios o Theos,**
2: **Holy is God,**
1: **Hagios Ischyros,**
2: **Holy and Mighty,**
1: **Hagios Athanatos, eleison himas.**
2: **Holy and Immortal One, have mercy on us.**

II

Cantors:

**I scourged Egypt for your sake with its firstborn sons,
and you scourged me and handed me over.**

1 and 2 repeat:

**My people, what have I done to you?
Or how have I grieved you? Answer me!**

Cantors:

**I led you out from Egypt as Pharaoh lay sunk in the
  Red Sea,
and you handed me over to the chief priests.**

1 and 2 repeat:

My people . . .

Cantors:

**I opened up the sea before you,
and you opened my side with a lance.**

1 and 2 repeat:

My people . . .

Cantors:

**I went before you in a pillar of cloud,
and you led me into Pilate's palace.**

1 and 2 repeat:

My people ...

Cantors:

**I fed you with manna in the desert,
and on me you rained blows and lashes.**

1 and 2 repeat:

My people ...

Cantors:

**I gave you saving water from the rock to drink,
and for drink you gave me gall and vinegar.**

1 and 2 repeat:

My people ...

Cantors:

**I struck down for you the kings of the Canaanites,
and you struck my head with a reed.**

1 and 2 repeat:

My people ...

Cantors:

**I put in your hand a royal scepter,
and you put on my head a crown of thorns.**

1 and 2 repeat:

My people ...

Cantors:

**I exalted you with great power,
and you hung me on the scaffold of the Cross.**

1 and 2 repeat:

My people ...

HYMN   [Faithful Cross]

All:
Faithful Cross the Saints rely on,
Noble tree beyond compare!
Never was there such a scion,
Never leaf or flower so rare.
Sweet the timber, sweet the iron,
Sweet the burden that they bear!

Cantors:
Sing, my tongue, in exultation
Of our banner and device!
Make a solemn proclamation
Of a triumph and its price:
How the Savior of creation
Conquered by his sacrifice!

All:
Faithful Cross the Saints rely on,
Noble tree beyond compare!
Never was there such a scion,
Never leaf or flower so rare.

Cantors:
For, when Adam first offended,
Eating that forbidden fruit,
Not all hopes of glory ended
With the serpent at the root:
Broken nature would be mended
By a second tree and shoot.

All:
Sweet the timber, sweet the iron,
Sweet the burden that they bear!

Cantors:
Thus the tempter was outwitted
By a wisdom deeper still:
Remedy and ailment fitted,
Means to cure and means to kill;

That the world might be acquit-
        ted,
Christ would do his Father's will.

All:
Faithful Cross the Saints rely on,
Noble tree beyond compare!
Never was there such a scion,
Never leaf or flower so rare.

Cantors:
So the Father, out of pity
For our self-inflicted doom,
Sent him from the heavenly city
When the holy time had come:
He, the Son and the Almighty,
Took our flesh in Mary's womb.

All:
Sweet the timber, sweet the iron,
Sweet the burden that they bear!

Cantors:
Hear a tiny baby crying,
Founder of the seas and strands;
See his virgin Mother tying
Cloth around his feet and hands;
Find him in a manger lying
Tightly wrapped in swaddling-
        bands!

All:
Faithful Cross the Saints rely on,
Noble tree beyond compare!
Never was there such a scion,
Never leaf or flower so rare.

Cantors:
So he came, the long-expected,
Not in glory, not to reign;
Only born to be rejected,

Choosing hunger, toil and pain,
Till the scaffold was erected
And the Paschal Lamb was slain.

All:

Sweet the timber, sweet the iron,
Sweet the burden that they bear!

Cantors:

No disgrace was too abhorrent:
Nailed and mocked and parched
    he died;
Blood and water, double war-
    rant,
Issue from his wounded side,
Washing in a mighty torrent
Earth and stars and oceantide.

All:

Faithful Cross the Saints rely on,
Noble tree beyond compare!
Never was there such a scion,
Never leaf or flower so rare.

Cantors:

Lofty timber, smooth your rough-
    ness,
Flex your boughs for blossom-
    ing;
Let your fibers lose their tough-
    ness,
Gently let your tendrils cling;

Lay aside your native gruffness,
Clasp the body of your King!

All:

Sweet the timber, sweet the iron,
Sweet the burden that they bear!

Cantors:

Noblest tree of all created,
Richly jeweled and embossed:
Post by Lamb's blood conse-
    crated;
Spar that saves the tempest-
    tossed;
Scaffold-beam which, elevated,
Carries what the world has cost!

All:

Faithful Cross the Saints rely on,
Noble tree beyond compare!
Never was there such a scion,
Never leaf or flower so rare.

*The following conclusion is never
to be omitted:*

All:

Wisdom, power, and adoration
To the blessed Trinity
For redemption and salvation
Through the Paschal Mystery,
Now, in every generation,
And for all eternity. Amen.

*In accordance with local circumstances or popular traditions
and if it is pastorally appropriate, the* Stabat Mater *may be
sung, as found in the* Graduale Romanum, *or another suitable
chant in memory of the compassion of the Blessed Virgin Mary.*

*When the adoration has been concluded, the Cross is carried
by the Deacon or a minister to its place at the altar. Lighted
candles are placed around or on the altar or near the Cross.*

THIRD PART: HOLY COMMUNION

A cloth is spread on the altar, and a corporal and the Missal put in place. Meanwhile the Deacon or, if there is no Deacon, the Priest himself, putting on a humeral veil, brings the Blessed Sacrament back from the place of repose to the altar by a shorter route, while all stand in silence. Two ministers with lighted candles accompany the Blessed Sacrament and place their candlesticks around or upon the altar.

When the Deacon, if a Deacon is present, has placed the Blessed Sacrament upon the altar and uncovered the ciborium, the Priest goes to the altar and genuflects.

Then the Priest, with hands joined, says aloud:

At the Savior's command
and formed by divine teaching,
we dare to say:

The Priest, with hands extended says, and all present continue:

Our Father . . .

With hands extended, the Priest continues alone:

Deliver us, Lord, we pray, from every evil,
graciously grant peace in our days,
that, by the help of your mercy,
we may be always free from sin
and safe from all distress,
as we await the blessed hope
and the coming of our Savior, Jesus Christ.

The people conclude the prayer, acclaiming:

**For the kingdom,
the power and the glory are yours
now and for ever.**

Then the Priest, with hands joined, says quietly:

May the receiving of your Body and Blood,
Lord Jesus Christ,
not bring me to judgment and condemnation,

but through your loving mercy
be for me protection in mind and body
and a healing remedy.

*The Priest then genuflects, takes a particle, and, holding it
slightly raised over the ciborium, while facing the people, says
aloud:*

Behold the Lamb of God,
behold him who takes away the sins of the world.
Blessed are those called to the supper of the Lamb.

And together with the people he adds once:

**Lord, I am not worthy
that you should enter under my roof,
but only say the word
and my soul shall be healed.**

*And facing the altar, he reverently consumes the Body of
Christ, saying quietly:* May the Body of Christ keep me safe for
eternal life.

*He then proceeds to distribute Communion to the faithful.
During Communion, Psalm 22 (21) or another appropriate
chant may be sung.*

*When the distribution of Communion has been completed, the
ciborium is taken by the Deacon or another suitable
minister to a place prepared outside the church or, if circumstances so require, it is placed in the tabernacle.*

Then the Priest says: Let us pray. *and, after a period of sacred
silence, if circumstances so suggest, has been observed, he
says the Prayer after Communion.*

Almighty ever-living God,   **[Devoted to God]**
who have restored us to life
by the blessed Death and Resurrection of your Christ,
preserve in us the work of your mercy,
that, by partaking of this mystery,
we may have a life unceasingly devoted to you.
Through Christ our Lord.
℟. **Amen.** ↓

For the Dismissal the Deacon or, if there is no Deacon, the Priest himself, may say the invitation Bow down for the blessing.

Then the Priest, standing facing the people and extending his hands over them, says this:

PRAYER OVER THE PEOPLE   [Redemption Secured]

May abundant blessing, O Lord, we pray,
descend upon your people,
who have honored the Death of your Son
in the hope of their resurrection:
may pardon come,
comfort be given,
holy faith increase,
and everlasting redemption be made secure.
Through Christ our Lord.
℟. **Amen.** ↓

And all, after genuflecting to the Cross, depart in silence.

After the celebration, the altar is stripped, but the Cross remains on the altar with two or four candlesticks.

APRIL 8
HOLY SATURDAY

On Holy Saturday the Church waits at the Lord's tomb in prayer and fasting, meditating on his Passion and Death and on his Descent into Hell, and awaiting his Resurrection.

The Church abstains from the Sacrifice of the Mass, with the sacred table left bare, until after the solemn Vigil, that is, the anticipation by night of the Resurrection, when the time comes for paschal joys, the abundance of which overflows to occupy fifty days.

"He is not here, for he has been raised."

APRIL 8

THE EASTER VIGIL
IN THE HOLY NIGHT

By most ancient tradition, this is the night of keeping vigil for the Lord (Ex 12:42), in which, following the Gospel admonition (Lk 12:35-37), the faithful, carrying lighted lamps in their hands, should be like those looking for the Lord when he returns, so that at his coming he may find them awake and have them sit at his table.

Of this night's Vigil, which is the greatest and most noble of all solemnities, there is to be only one celebration in each church. It is arranged, moreover, in such a way that after the Lucernarium and Easter Proclamation (which constitutes the first part of this Vigil), Holy Church meditates on the wonders the Lord God has done for his people from the beginning, trusting in his word and promise (the second part, that is, the Liturgy of the Word) until, as day approaches, with new members reborn in Baptism (the third part), the Church is called to the table the Lord has prepared for his people, the memorial of his Death and Resurrection until he comes again (the fourth part).

Candles should be prepared for all who participate in the Vigil. The lights of the church are extinguished.

FIRST PART:
THE SOLEMN BEGINNING OF THE VIGIL
OR LUCERNARIUM

The Blessing of the Fire and Preparation of the Candle

A blazing fire is prepared in a suitable place outside the church. When the people are gathered there, the Priest approaches with the ministers, one of whom carries the paschal candle. The processional cross and candles are not carried.

Where, however, a fire cannot be lit outside the church, the rite is carried out as below, p. 306.

The Priest and faithful sign themselves while the Priest says:
In the name of the Father, and of the Son, and of the Holy Spirit, *and then he greets the assembled people in the usual way and briefly instructs them about the night vigil in these or similar words:*

[Keeping the Lord's Paschal Solemnity]

Dear brethren (brothers and sisters),
on this most sacred night,
in which our Lord Jesus Christ
passed over from death to life,
the Church calls upon her sons and daughters,
scattered throughout the world,
to come together to watch and pray.
If we keep the memorial
of the Lord's paschal solemnity in this way,
listening to his word and celebrating his mysteries,
then we shall have the sure hope
of sharing his triumph over death
and living with him in God.

Then the Priest blesses the fire, saying with hands extended:

Let us pray.   [Fire of God's Glory]

O God, who through your Son
bestowed upon the faithful the fire of your glory,
sanctify ✠ this new fire, we pray,

and grant that,
by these paschal celebrations,
we may be so inflamed with heavenly desires,
that with minds made pure
we may attain festivities of unending splendor.
Through Christ our Lord. R̸. **Amen.** ↓

*After the blessing of the new fire, one of the ministers brings
the paschal candle to the Priest, who cuts a cross into the candle with a stylus. Then he makes the Greek letter Alpha above
the cross, the letter Omega below, and the four numerals of the
current year between the arms of the cross, saying meanwhile:*

1. Christ yesterday and today *(he cuts a vertical line);*
2. the Beginning and the End *(he cuts a horizontal
   line);*
3. the Alpha *(he cuts the letter Alpha above the vertical line);*
4. and the Omega *(he cuts the letter Omega below
   the vertical line).*
5. All time belongs to him *(he cuts the first numeral of
   the current year in the upper left corner of the
   cross);*
6. and all the ages *(he cuts the second numeral of the
   current year in the upper right corner of the cross).*
7. To him be glory and power *(he cuts the
   third numeral of the current year in the
   lower left corner of the cross);*
8. through every age and for ever. Amen *(he
   cuts the fourth numeral of the current year
   in the lower right corner of the cross).*

```
      A
   2  |  0
   ───┼───
   2  |  3
      |
      Ω
```

*When the cutting of the cross and of the other signs has been
completed, the Priest may insert five grains of incense into the
candle in the form of a cross, meanwhile saying:*

1. By his holy   1
2. and glorious wounds,   4 2 5
3. may Christ the Lord   3
4. guard us
5. and protect us. Amen.

Where, because of difficulties that may occur, a fire is not lit, the blessing of fire is adapted to the circumstances. When the people are gathered in the church as on other occasions, the Priest comes to the door of the church, along with the ministers carrying the paschal candle. The people, insofar as is possible, turn to face the Priest.

The greeting and address take place as above, p. 304; then the fire is blessed and the candle is prepared, as above, pp. 304-306.

The Priest lights the paschal candle from the new fire, saying:

May the light of Christ rising in glory
dispel the darkness of our hearts and minds.

Procession

When the candle has been lit, one of the ministers takes burning coals from the fire and places them in the thurible, and the Priest puts incense into it in the usual way. The Deacon or, if there is no Deacon, another suitable minister, takes the paschal candle and a procession forms. The thurifer with the smoking thurible precedes the Deacon or other minister who carries the paschal candle. After them follows the Priest with the ministers and the people, all holding in their hands unlit candles.

At the door of the church the Deacon, standing and raising up the candle, sings:

The Light of Christ.

And all reply:

Thanks be to God.

The Priest lights his candle from the flame of the paschal candle.

Then the Deacon moves forward to the middle of the church and, standing and raising up the candle, sings a second time:

The Light of Christ.

And all reply:

Thanks be to God.

All light their candles from the flame of the paschal candle and continue in procession.

When the Deacon arrives before the altar, he stands facing the people, raises up the candle and sings a third time:

The Light of Christ.

And all reply:

Thanks be to God.

Then the Deacon places the paschal candle on a large candle-stand prepared next to the ambo or in the middle of the sanctuary.

And lights are lit throughout the church, except for the altar candles.

The Easter Proclamation (Exsultet)

Arriving at the altar, the Priest goes to his chair, gives his candle to a minister, puts incense into the thurible and blesses the incense as at the Gospel at Mass. The Deacon goes to the Priest and saying, Your blessing, Father, *asks for and receives a blessing from the Priest, who says in a low voice:*

May the Lord be in your heart and on your lips,
that you may proclaim his paschal praise worthily and
   well,
in the name of the Father and of the Son, ✠ and of the
   Holy Spirit.

The Deacon replies: Amen. ↓

This blessing is omitted if the Proclamation is made by someone who is not a Deacon.

The Deacon, after incensing the book and the candle, proclaims the Easter Proclamation (Exsultet) at the ambo or at a lectern, with all standing and holding lighted candles in their hands.

The Easter Proclamation may be made, in the absence of a Deacon, by the Priest himself or by another concelebrating Priest. If, however, because of necessity, a lay cantor sings the Proclamation, the words Therefore, dearest friends *up to the end of the invitation are omitted, along with the greeting* The Lord be with you.

[When the Shorter Form is used, omit the italicized parts.]

Exult, let them exult, the hosts of heaven,
exult, let Angel ministers of God exult,
let the trumpet of salvation
sound aloud our mighty King's triumph!
Be glad, let earth be glad, as glory floods her,
ablaze with light from her eternal King,
let all corners of the earth be glad,
knowing an end to gloom and darkness.
Rejoice, let Mother Church also rejoice,
arrayed with the lightning of his glory,
let this holy building shake with joy,
filled with the mighty voices of the peoples.
(Therefore, dearest friends,
standing in the awesome glory of this holy light,
invoke with me, I ask you,
the mercy of God almighty,
that he, who has been pleased to number me,
though unworthy, among the Levites,
may pour into me his light unshadowed,
that I may sing this candle's perfect praises).

(℣. The Lord be with you. ℟. **And with your spirit.**)
℣. Lift up your hearts. ℟. **We lift them up to the Lord.**
℣. Let us give thanks to the Lord our God. ℟. **It is right and just.**

It is truly right and just,
with ardent love of mind and heart
and with devoted service of our voice,
to acclaim our God invisible, the almighty Father,
and Jesus Christ, our Lord, his Son, his Only Begotten.

Who for our sake paid Adam's debt to the eternal Father,
and, pouring out his own dear Blood,
wiped clean the record of our ancient sinfulness.

These then are the feasts of Passover,
in which is slain the Lamb, the one true Lamb,
whose Blood anoints the doorposts of believers.

This is the night,
when once you led our forebears, Israel's children,
from slavery in Egypt
and made them pass dry-shod through the Red Sea.

This is the night
that with a pillar of fire
banished the darkness of sin.

This is the night
that even now, throughout the world,
sets Christian believers apart from worldly vices
and from the gloom of sin,
leading them to grace
and joining them to his holy ones.

This is the night,
when Christ broke the prison-bars of death
and rose victorious from the underworld.

Our birth would have been no gain,
had we not been redeemed.
O wonder of your humble care for us!
O love, O charity beyond all telling,
to ransom a slave you gave away your Son!

O truly necessary sin of Adam,
destroyed completely by the Death of Christ!

O happy fault
that earned so great, so glorious a Redeemer!

O truly blessed night,
worthy alone to know the time and hour
when Christ rose from the underworld!

This is the night
of which it is written:
The night shall be as bright as day,
dazzling is the night for me,
and full of gladness.

The sanctifying power of this night
dispels wickedness, washes faults away,
restores innocence to the fallen, and joy to mourners,
drives out hatred, fosters concord, and brings down the
    mighty.

On this, your night of grace, O holy Father,
accept this candle, a solemn offering,
the work of bees and of your servants' hands,
an evening sacrifice of praise,
this gift from your most holy Church.

But now we know the praises of this pillar,
which glowing fire ignites for God's honor,
a fire into many flames divided,
yet never dimmed by sharing of its light,
for it is fed by melting wax,
drawn out by mother bees
to build a torch so precious.

O truly blessed night,
when things of heaven are wed to those of earth,
and divine to the human.

> *Shorter Form only:*
> On this, your night of grace, O holy Father,
> accept this candle, a solemn offering,
> the work of bees and of your servants' hands,
> an evening sacrifice of praise,
> this gift from your most holy Church.

Therefore, O Lord,
we pray you that this candle,

hallowed to the honor of your name,
may persevere undimmed,
to overcome the darkness of this night.
Receive it as a pleasing fragrance,
and let it mingle with the lights of heaven.
May this flame be found still burning
by the Morning Star:
the one Morning Star who never sets,
Christ your Son,
who, coming back from death's domain,
has shed his peaceful light on humanity,
and lives and reigns for ever and ever.
℟. **Amen.** ↓

SECOND PART:
THE LITURGY OF THE WORD

*In this Vigil, the mother of all Vigils, nine readings are provid-
ed, namely seven from the Old Testament and two from the New
(the Epistle and Gospel), all of which should be read whenever
this can be done, so that the character of the Vigil, which
demands an extended period of time, may be preserved.*

*Nevertheless, where more serious pastoral circumstances
demand it, the number of readings from the Old Testament
may be reduced, always bearing in mind that the reading of
the Word of God is a fundamental part of this Easter Vigil. At
least three readings should be read from the Old Testament,
both from the Law and from the Prophets, and their respective
Responsorial Psalms should be sung. Never, moreover, should
the reading of chapter 14 of Exodus with its canticle be omitted.*

*After setting aside their candles, all sit. Before the readings
begin, the Priest instructs the people in these or similar words:*

[Listen with Quiet Hearts]

Dear brethren (brothers and sisters),
now that we have begun our solemn Vigil,
let us listen with quiet hearts to the Word of God.

Let us meditate on how God in times past saved his
   people
and in these, the last days, has sent us his Son as our
   Redeemer.
Let us pray that our God may complete this paschal
   work of salvation
by the fullness of redemption.

*Then the readings follow. A reader goes to the ambo and pro-
claims the reading. Afterwards a psalmist or a cantor sings or
says the Psalm with the people making the response. Then all
rise, the Priest says,* Let us pray *and, after all have prayed for
a while in silence, he says the prayer corresponding to the
reading. In place of the Responsorial Psalm a period of sacred
silence may be observed, in which case the pause after* Let us
pray *is omitted.*

FIRST READING Gn 1:1—2:2 or 1:1, 26-31a   [God Our Creator]

**God created the world and all that is in it. He saw that it
was good. This reading from the first book of the Bible
shows that God loved all that he made.**

*[If the "Shorter Form" is used, the indented text in brackets is
omitted.]*

A reading from the Book of Genesis

IN the beginning, when God created the heavens and
the earth,

[the earth was a formless wasteland, and darkness
covered the abyss, while a mighty wind swept over
the waters.

   Then God said, "Let there be light," and there
was light. God saw how good the light was. God
then separated the light from the darkness. God
called the light "day," and the darkness he called
"night." Thus evening came, and morning followed—the first day.

   Then God said, "Let there be a dome in the
middle of the waters, to separate one body of
water from the other." And so it happened: God

made the dome, and it separated the water above the dome from the water below it. God called the dome "the sky." Evening came; and morning followed—the second day.

Then God said, "Let the water under the sky be gathered into a single basin, so that the dry land may appear." And so it happened: the water under the sky was gathered into its basin, and the dry land appeared. God called the dry land "the earth," and the basin of the water he called "the sea." God saw how good it was. Then God said, "Let the earth bring forth vegetation: every kind of plant that bears seed and every kind of fruit tree on earth that bears fruit with its seed in it." And so it happened: the earth brought forth every kind of plant that bears seed and every kind of fruit tree on earth that bears fruit with its seed in it. God saw how good it was. Evening came, and morning followed—the third day.

Then God said: "Let there be lights in the dome of the sky, to separate day from night. Let them mark the fixed times, the days and the years, and serve as luminaries in the dome of the sky, to shed light upon the earth." And so it happened: God made the two great lights, the greater one to govern the day, and the lesser one to govern the night; and he made the stars. God set them in the dome of the sky, to shed light upon the earth, to govern the day and the night, and to separate the light from the darkness. God saw how good it was. Evening came, and morning followed—the fourth day.

Then God said, "Let the water teem with an abundance of living creatures, and on the earth let birds fly beneath the dome of the sky." And so it happened: God created the great sea monsters and all kinds of swimming creatures with which the water teems, and all kinds of winged birds. God saw how good it was, and God blessed them, saying, "Be fertile, multiply, and fill the water of the seas; and let the birds multiply on the earth." Evening came, and morning followed—the fifth day.

Then God said, "Let the earth bring forth all kinds of living creatures: cattle, creeping things, and wild animals of all kinds." And so it happened: God made all kinds of wild animals, all kinds of cattle, and all kinds of creeping things of the earth. God saw how good it was. Then]
God said: "Let us make man in our image, after our likeness. Let them have dominion over the fish of the sea, the birds of the air, and the cattle, and over all the wild animals and all the creatures that crawl on the ground."

God created man in his image;
    in the divine image he created him;
    male and female he created them.

God blessed them, saying: "Be fertile and multiply; fill the earth and subdue it. Have dominion over the fish of the sea, the birds of the air, and all the living things that move on the earth." God also said: "See, I give you every seed-bearing plant all over the earth and every tree that has seed-bearing fruit on it to be your food; and to all the animals of the land, all the birds of the air, and all the living creatures that crawl on the ground, I give all the green plants for food." And so it happened. God looked at everything he had made, and he found it very good.

[Evening came, and morning followed—the sixth day.

Thus the heavens and the earth and all their array were completed. Since on the seventh day God was finished with the work he had been doing, he rested on the seventh day from all the work he had undertaken.]

The word of the Lord. ℟. **Thanks be to God.** ↓

RESPONSORIAL PSALM Ps 104   [Come, Holy Spirit]

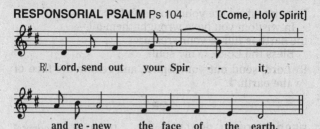

℟. Lord, send out your Spir - it,

and re - new the face of the earth.

Bless the LORD, O my soul!
   O LORD, my God, you are great indeed!
You are clothed with majesty and glory,
   robed in light as with a cloak.

℟. **Lord, send out your Spirit, and renew the face of
   the earth.**

You fixed the earth upon its foundation,
   not to be moved forever;
with the ocean, as with a garment, you covered it;
   above the mountains the waters stood.

℟. **Lord, send out your Spirit, and renew the face of
   the earth.**

You send forth springs into the watercourses
   that wind among the mountains.
Beside them the birds of heaven dwell;
   from among the branches they send forth their song.

℟. **Lord, send out your Spirit, and renew the face of
   the earth.**

You water the mountains from your palace;
   the earth is replete with the fruit of your works.
You raise grass for the cattle,
   and vegetation for men's use,
producing bread from the earth.

℟. **Lord, send out your Spirit, and renew the face of
   the earth.**

How manifold are your works, O LORD!
  In wisdom you have wrought them all—
the earth is full of your creatures.
  Bless the LORD, O my soul!

℟. **Lord, send out your Spirit, and renew the face of
  the earth.** ↓

OR

RESPONSORIAL PSALM Ps 33   [The Lord's Goodness]

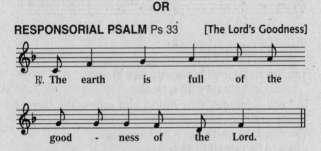

℟. The earth is full of the good-ness of the Lord.

Upright is the word of the LORD,
  and all his works are trustworthy.
He loves justice and right;
  of the kindness of the LORD the earth is full.

℟. **The earth is full of the goodness of the Lord.**

By the word of the LORD the heavens were made;
  by the breath of his mouth all their host.
He gathers the waters of the sea as in a flask;
  in cellars he confines the deep.

℟. **The earth is full of the goodness of the Lord.**

Blessed the nation whose God is the LORD,
  the people he has chosen for his own inheritance.
From heaven the LORD looks down;
  he sees all mankind.

℟. **The earth is full of the goodness of the Lord.**

Our soul waits for the LORD,
  who is our help and our shield.

May your kindness, O LORD, be upon us
  who have put our hope in you.

℟. **The earth is full of the goodness of the Lord.** ↓

PRAYER   [Creation in the Beginning]
Let us pray.

Almighty ever-living God,
who are wonderful in the ordering of all your works,
may those you have redeemed understand
that there exists nothing more marvelous
than the world's creation in the beginning
except that, at the end of the ages,
Christ our Passover has been sacrificed.
Who lives and reigns for ever and ever. ℟. **Amen.** ↓

OR

PRAYER (On the creation of man)   [Eternal Joys]

O God, who wonderfully created human nature
and still more wonderfully redeemed it,
grant us, we pray,
to set our minds against the enticements of sin,
that we may merit to attain eternal joys.
Through Christ our Lord. ℟. **Amen.** ↓

SECOND READING Gn 22:1-18 or 22:1-2, 9a, 10-13, 15-18
                [Obedience to God]
  **Abraham is obedient to the will of God. Because God asks
  him, without hesitation he prepares to sacrifice his son
  Isaac. In the new order, God sends his Son to redeem man
  by his Death on the Cross.**

*[If the "Shorter Form" is used, the indented text in brackets is
omitted.]*

A reading from the Book of Genesis

GOD put Abraham to the test. He called to him,
"Abraham!" "Here I am," he replied. Then God
said: "Take your son Isaac, your only one, whom you

love, and go to the land of Moriah. There you shall offer him up as a holocaust on a height that I will point out to you."

[Early the next morning Abraham saddled his donkey, took with him his son Isaac, and two of his servants as well, and with the wood that he had cut for the holocaust, set out for the place of which God had told him.

On the third day Abraham got sight of the place from afar. Then he said to his servants: "Both of you stay here with the donkey, while the boy and I go on over yonder. We will worship and then come back to you." Thereupon Abraham took the wood for the holocaust and laid it on his son Isaac's shoulders, while he himself carried the fire and the knife. As the two walked on together, Isaac spoke to his father Abraham. "Father!" Isaac said. "Yes, son," he replied. Isaac continued, "Here are the fire and the wood, but where is the sheep for the holocaust?" "Son," Abraham answered, "God himself will provide the sheep for the holocaust." Then the two continued going forward.]

When they came to the place of which God had told him, Abraham built an altar there and arranged the wood on it.

[Next he tied up his son Isaac, and put him on top of the wood on the altar.]

Then he reached out and took the knife to slaughter his son. But the LORD's messenger called to him from heaven, "Abraham, Abraham!" "Here I am," he answered. "Do not lay your hand on the boy," said the messenger. "Do not do the least thing to him. I know now how devoted you are to God, since you did not withhold from me your own beloved son." As Abraham looked about, he spied a ram caught by its horns in the thicket. So he went and took the ram and offered it up as a holocaust in place of his son.

[Abraham named the site Yahweh-yireh; hence people now say, "On the mountain the Lord will see."]

Again the Lord's messenger called to Abraham from heaven and said: "I swear by myself, declares the Lord, that because you acted as you did in not withholding from me your beloved son, I will bless you abundantly and make your descendants as countless as the stars of the sky and the sands of the seashore; your descendants shall take possession of the gates of their enemies, and in your descendants all the nations of the earth shall find blessing—all this because you obeyed my command."—The word of the Lord.
℟. **Thanks be to God.** ↓

RESPONSORIAL PSALM Ps 16   [God Our Hope]

℟. You are my in - her - i -tance, O Lord.

O Lord, my allotted portion and my cup,
    you it is who hold fast my lot.
I set the Lord ever before me;
    with him at my right I shall not be disturbed.

℟. **You are my inheritance, O Lord.**

Therefore my heart is glad and my soul rejoices,
    my body, too, abides in confidence;
because you will not abandon my soul to the netherworld,
    nor will you suffer your faithful one to undergo corruption.

℟. **You are my inheritance, O Lord.**

You will show me the path to life,
    fullness of joys in your presence,
    the delights at your right hand forever.

℟. **You are my inheritance, O Lord.** ↓

PRAYER   [Entering into Grace]

Let us pray.

O God, supreme Father of the faithful,
who increase the children of your promise
by pouring out the grace of adoption
throughout the whole world
and who through the Paschal Mystery
make your servant Abraham father of nations,
as once you swore,
grant, we pray,
that your peoples may enter worthily
into the grace to which you call them.
Through Christ our Lord. ℟. **Amen.** ↓

THIRD READING Ex 14:15—15:1   [Exodus]

Moses leads the Israelites out of Egypt. He opens a path of
escape through the Red Sea. God protects his people.
Through the waters of Baptism, human beings are freed
from sin.

A reading from the Book of Exodus

THE LORD said to Moses, "Why are you crying out to
me? Tell the Israelites to go forward. And you, lift
up your staff and, with hand outstretched over the sea,
split the sea in two, that the Israelites may pass
through it on dry land. But I will make the Egyptians
so obstinate that they will go in after them. Then I will
receive glory through Pharaoh and all his army, his
chariots and charioteers. The Egyptians shall know
that I am the LORD, when I receive glory through
Pharaoh and his chariots and charioteers."

The angel of God, who had been leading Israel's
camp, now moved and went around behind them. The
column of cloud also, leaving the front, took up its
place behind them, so that it came between the camp
of the Egyptians and that of Israel. But the cloud now
became dark, and thus the night passed without the

rival camps coming any closer together all night long. Then Moses stretched out his hand over the sea, and the LORD swept the sea with a strong east wind throughout the night and so turned it into dry land. When the water was thus divided, the Israelites marched into the midst of the sea on dry land, with the water like a wall to their right and to their left.

The Egyptians followed in pursuit; all Pharaoh's horses and chariots and charioteers went after them right into the midst of the sea. In the night watch just before dawn the LORD cast through the column of the fiery cloud upon the Egyptian force a glance that threw it into a panic; and he so clogged their chariot wheels that they could hardly drive. With that the Egyptians sounded the retreat before Israel, because the LORD was fighting for them against the Egyptians.

Then the LORD told Moses, "Stretch out your hand over the sea, that the water may flow back upon the Egyptians, upon their chariots and their charioteers." So Moses stretched out his hand over the sea, and at dawn the sea flowed back to its normal depth. The Egyptians were fleeing head on toward the sea, when the LORD hurled them into its midst. As the water flowed back, it covered the chariots and the charioteers of Pharaoh's whole army which had followed the Israelites into the sea. Not a single one of them escaped. But the Israelites had marched on dry land through the midst of the sea, with the water like a wall to their right and to their left. Thus the LORD saved Israel on that day from the power of the Egyptians. When Israel saw the Egyptians lying dead on the seashore and beheld the great power that the LORD had shown against the Egyptians, they feared the LORD and believed in him and in his servant Moses.

Then Moses and the Israelites sang this song to the LORD:

I will sing to the L��rd, for he is gloriously triumphant;
  horse and chariot he has cast into the sea.
The word of the Lord. R̶⟩. **Thanks be to God.** ↓

RESPONSORIAL PSALM Ex 15   [God the Savior]

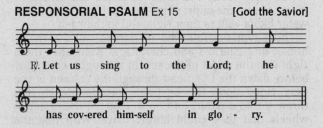

R̶⟩. Let us sing to the Lord; he has cov-ered him-self in glo - ry.

I will sing to the L��rd, for he is gloriously triumphant;
  horse and chariot he has cast into the sea.
My strength and my courage is the L��rd,
  and he has been my savior.
He is my God, I praise him;
  the God of my father, I extol him.

R̶⟩. **Let us sing to the Lord; he has covered himself in glory.**

The L��rd is a warrior,
  L��rd is his name!
Pharaoh's chariots and army he hurled into the sea;
  the elite of his officers were submerged into the Red
    Sea.

R̶⟩. **Let us sing to the Lord; he has covered himself in glory.**

The flood waters covered them,
  they sank into the depths like a stone.
Your right hand, O L��rd, magnificent in power,
  your right hand, O L��rd, has shattered the enemy.

R̶⟩. **Let us sing to the Lord; he has covered himself in glory.**

You brought in the people you redeemed
  and planted them on the mountain of your inheri-
    tance—
the place where you made your seat, O LORD,
  the sanctuary, O LORD, which your hands estab-
    lished.
The LORD shall reign forever and ever.

℟. **Let us sing to the Lord; he has covered himself in
glory.** ↓

PRAYER   [Children of Abraham]

Let us pray.

O God, whose ancient wonders
remain undimmed in splendor even in our day,
for what you once bestowed on a single people,
freeing them from Pharaoh's persecution
by the power of your right hand,
now you bring about as the salvation of the nations
through the waters of rebirth,
grant, we pray, that the whole world
may become children of Abraham
and inherit the dignity of Israel's birthright.
Through Christ our Lord. ℟. **Amen.** ↓

OR

PRAYER   [Reborn]

O God, who by the light of the New Testament
have unlocked the meaning
of wonders worked in former times,
so that the Red Sea prefigures the sacred font
and the nation delivered from slavery
foreshadows the Christian people,
grant, we pray, that all nations,
obtaining the privilege of Israel by merit of faith,
may be reborn by partaking of your Spirit.
Through Christ our Lord. ℟. **Amen.** ↓

FOURTH READING Is 54:5-14   [God's Love]

For a time, God hid from his people, but his love for them is everlasting. He takes pity on them and promises them prosperity.

A reading from the Book of the Prophet Isaiah

THE One who has become your husband is your
    Maker;
    his name is the LORD of hosts;
your redeemer is the Holy One of Israel,
    called God of all the earth.
The LORD calls you back,
    like a wife forsaken and grieved in spirit,
    a wife married in youth and then cast off,
    says your God.
For a brief moment I abandoned you,
    but with great tenderness I will take you back.
In an outburst of wrath, for a moment
    I hid my face from you;
but with enduring love I take pity on you,
    says the LORD, your redeemer.
This is for me like the days of Noah,
    when I swore that the waters of Noah
    should never again deluge the earth;
so I have sworn not to be angry with you,
    or to rebuke you.
Though the mountains leave their place
    and the hills be shaken,
my love shall never leave you
    nor my covenant of peace be shaken,
    says the LORD, who has mercy on you.
O afflicted one, storm-battered and unconsoled,
    I lay your pavements in carnelians,
    and your foundations in sapphires;
I will make your battlements of rubies,
    your gates of carbuncles,
    and all your walls of precious stones.

All your children shall be taught by the Lord,
  and great shall be the peace of your children.
In justice shall you be established,
  far from the fear of oppression,
  where destruction cannot come near you.
The word of the Lord. ℟. **Thanks be to God.** ↓

RESPONSORIAL PSALM Ps 30   [God Our Help]

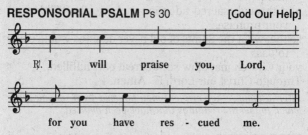

℟. I   will   praise   you,   Lord,
for   you   have   res - cued   me.

I will extol you, O Lord, for you drew me clear
  and did not let my enemies rejoice over me.
O Lord, you brought me up from the netherworld;
  you preserved me from among those going down
    into the pit.

℟. **I will praise you, Lord, for you have rescued me.**

Sing praise to the Lord, you his faithful ones,
  and give thanks to his holy name.
For his anger lasts but a moment;
  a lifetime, his good will.
At nightfall, weeping enters in,
  but with the dawn, rejoicing.

℟. **I will praise you, Lord, for you have rescued me.**

Hear, O Lord, and have pity on me;
  O Lord, be my helper.
You changed my mourning into dancing;
  O Lord, my God, forever will I give you thanks.

℟. **I will praise you, Lord, for you have rescued me.**

PRAYER [Fulfillment of God's Promise]

Let us pray.

Almighty ever-living God,
surpass, for the honor of your name,
what you pledged to the Patriarchs by reason of their
  faith,
and through sacred adoption increase the children of
  your promise,
so that what the Saints of old never doubted would come
  to pass
your Church may now see in great part fulfilled.
Through Christ our Lord. ℟. **Amen.** ↓

*Alternatively, other prayers may be used from among those
which follow the readings that have been omitted.*

FIFTH READING Is 55:1-11 [God of Forgiveness]

**God is a loving Father and he calls his people back. He
promises an everlasting covenant with them. God is merciful, generous, and forgiving.**

A reading from the Book of the Prophet Isaiah

THUS says the LORD:
All you who are thirsty,
  come to the water!
You who have no money,
  come, receive grain and eat;
come, without paying and without cost,
  drink wine and milk!
Why spend your money for what is not bread;
  your wages for what fails to satisfy?
Heed me, and you shall eat well,
  you shall delight in rich fare.
Come to me heedfully,
  listen, that you may have life.

I will renew with you the everlasting covenant,
  the benefits assured to David.
As I made him a witness to the peoples,
  a leader and commander of nations,
so shall you summon a nation you knew not,
  and nations that knew you not shall run to you,
because of the LORD, your God,
  the Holy One of Israel, who has glorified you.

Seek the LORD while he may be found,
  call him while he is near.
Let the scoundrel forsake his way,
  and the wicked man his thoughts;
let him turn to the LORD for mercy;
  to our God, who is generous in forgiving.
For my thoughts are not your thoughts,
  nor are your ways my ways, says the LORD.
As high as the heavens are above the earth,
  so high are my ways above your ways,
  and my thoughts above your thoughts.

For just as from the heavens
  the rain and snow come down
and do not return there
  till they have watered the earth,
  making it fertile and fruitful,
giving seed to the one who sows
  and bread to the one who eats,
so shall my word be
  that goes forth from my mouth;
my word shall not return to me void,
  but shall do my will,
  achieving the end for which I sent it.
The word of the Lord. ℟. **Thanks be to God.** ↓

RESPONSORIAL PSALM Is 12 [Make Known God's Deeds]

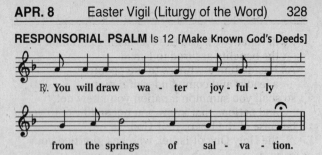

℟. You will draw wa - ter joy - ful - ly
from the springs of sal - va - tion.

God indeed is my savior;
  I am confident and unafraid.
My strength and my courage is the LORD,
  and he has been my savior.
With joy you will draw water
  at the fountain of salvation.

℟. **You will draw water joyfully from the springs of salvation.**

Give thanks to the LORD, acclaim his name;
  among the nations make known his deeds,
  proclaim how exalted is his name.

℟. **You will draw water joyfully from the springs of salvation.**

Sing praise to the LORD for his glorious achievement;
  let this be known throughout all the earth.
Shout with exultation, O city of Zion,
  for great in your midst
  is the Holy One of Israel!

℟. **You will draw water joyfully from the springs of salvation.** ↓

PRAYER   [Progress in Virtue]

Let us pray.
Almighty ever-living God,
sole hope of the world,
who by the preaching of your Prophets

unveiled the mysteries of this present age,
graciously increase the longing of your people,
for only at the prompting of your grace
do the faithful progress in any kind of virtue.
Through Christ our Lord. ℞. **Amen.** ↓

SIXTH READING Bar 3:9-15, 32—4:4 [Walk in God's Ways]
Baruch tells the people of Israel to walk in the ways of God. They have to learn prudence, wisdom, and understanding. Then they will have peace forever.

A reading from the Book of the Prophet Baruch

HEAR, O Israel, the commandments of life:
listen, and know prudence!
How is it, Israel,
    that you are in the land of your foes,
    grown old in a foreign land,
defiled with the dead,
    accounted with those destined for the netherworld?
You have forsaken the fountain of wisdom!
    Had you walked in the way of God,
    you would have dwelt in enduring peace.
Learn where prudence is,
    where strength, where understanding;
that you may know also
    where are length of days, and life,
    where light of the eyes, and peace.
Who has found the place of wisdom,
    who has entered into her treasuries?

The One who knows all things knows her;
    he has probed her by his knowledge—
the One who established the earth for all time,
    and filled it with four-footed beasts;
he who dismisses the light, and it departs,
    calls it, and it obeys him trembling;
before whom the stars at their posts
    shine and rejoice;

when he calls them, they answer, "Here we are!"
　　shining with joy for their Maker.
Such is our God;
　　no other is to be compared to him:
he has traced out all the way of understanding,
　　and has given her to Jacob, his servant,
　　to Israel, his beloved son.

Since then she has appeared on earth,
　　and moved among people.
She is the book of the precepts of God,
　　the law that endures forever;
all who cling to her will live,
　　but those will die who forsake her.
Turn, O Jacob, and receive her:
　　walk by her light toward splendor.
Give not your glory to another,
　　your privileges to an alien race.
Blessed are we, O Israel;
　　for what pleases God is known to us!
The word of the Lord. ℟. **Thanks be to God.** ↓

RESPONSORIAL PSALM Ps 19   [Words of Eternal Life]

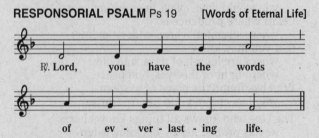

℟. **Lord, you have the words of everlasting life.**

The law of the LORD is perfect,
　　refreshing the soul;
the decree of the LORD is trustworthy,
　　giving wisdom to the simple.
℟. **Lord, you have the words of everlasting life.**

The precepts of the LORD are right,
    rejoicing the heart;
the command of the LORD is clear,
    enlightening the eye.

℟. **Lord, you have the words of everlasting life.**

The fear of the LORD is pure,
    enduring forever;
the ordinances of the LORD are true,
    all of them just.

℟. **Lord, you have the words of everlasting life.**

They are more precious than gold,
    than a heap of purest gold;
sweeter also than syrup
    or honey from the comb.

℟. **Lord, you have the words of everlasting life.** ↓

PRAYER   [Unfailing Protection]

Let us pray.

O God, who constantly increase your Church
by your call to the nations,
graciously grant
to those you wash clean in the waters of Baptism
the assurance of your unfailing protection.
Through Christ our Lord. ℟. **Amen.** ↓

SEVENTH READING Ez 36:16-17a,18-28   [God's People]

Ezekiel, as God's prophet, speaks for God who is to keep
his name holy among his people. All shall know the holiness of God. He will cleanse his people from idol worship
and make them his own again. This promise is again fulfilled in Baptism in the restored order of redemption.

A reading from the Book of the Prophet Ezekiel

THE word of the LORD came to me, saying: Son of
man, when the house of Israel lived in their land,
they defiled it by their conduct and deeds. Therefore I
poured out my fury upon them because of the blood

that they poured out on the ground, and because they defiled it with idols. I scattered them among the nations, dispersing them over foreign lands; according to their conduct and deeds I judged them. But when they came among the nations wherever they came, they served to profane my holy name, because it was said of them: "These are the people of the LORD, yet they had to leave their land." So I have relented because of my holy name which the house of Israel profaned among the nations where they came. Therefore say to the house of Israel: Thus says the Lord GOD: Not for your sakes do I act, house of Israel, but for the sake of my holy name, which you profaned among the nations to which you came. I will prove the holiness of my great name, profaned among the nations, in whose midst you have profaned it. Thus the nations shall know that I am the LORD, says the Lord GOD, when in their sight I prove my holiness through you. For I will take you away from among the nations, gather you from all the foreign lands, and bring you back to your own land. I will sprinkle clean water upon you to cleanse you from all your impurities, and from all your idols I will cleanse you. I will give you a new heart and place a new spirit within you, taking from your bodies your stony hearts and giving you natural hearts. I will put my spirit within you and make you live by my statutes, careful to observe my decrees. You shall live in the land I gave your fathers; you shall be my people, and I will be your God.—The word of the Lord. ℟. **Thanks be to God.** ↓

When Baptism is celebrated, Responsorial Psalm 42 is used; when Baptism is not celebrated, Is 12 or Ps 51 is used.

RESPONSORIAL PSALM Ps 42   [Longing for God]

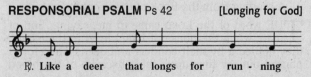

℟. Like a deer that longs for run - ning

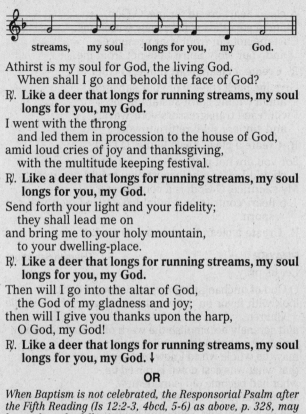

streams,   my soul   longs for you,   my   God.

Athirst is my soul for God, the living God.
  When shall I go and behold the face of God?

℟. **Like a deer that longs for running streams, my soul
   longs for you, my God.**

I went with the throng
  and led them in procession to the house of God,
amid loud cries of joy and thanksgiving,
  with the multitude keeping festival.

℟. **Like a deer that longs for running streams, my soul
   longs for you, my God.**

Send forth your light and your fidelity;
  they shall lead me on
and bring me to your holy mountain,
  to your dwelling-place.

℟. **Like a deer that longs for running streams, my soul
   longs for you, my God.**

Then will I go into the altar of God,
  the God of my gladness and joy;
then will I give you thanks upon the harp,
  O God, my God!

℟. **Like a deer that longs for running streams, my soul
   longs for you, my God.** ↓

OR

*When Baptism is not celebrated, the Responsorial Psalm after
the Fifth Reading (Is 12:2-3, 4bcd, 5-6) as above, p. 328, may
be used; or the following:*

RESPONSORIAL PSALM Ps 51   [A Clean Heart]

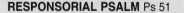

℟. Cre - ate   a   clean heart   in   me,   O   God.

A clean heart create for me, O God,
  and a steadfast spirit renew within me.
Cast me not out from your presence,
  and your Holy Spirit take not from me.

R̸. **Create a clean heart in me, O God.**

Give me back the joy of your salvation,
  and a willing spirit sustain in me.
I will teach transgressors your ways,
  and sinners shall return to you.

R̸. **Create a clean heart in me, O God.**

For you are not pleased with sacrifices;
  should I offer a holocaust, you would not accept it.
My sacrifice, O God, is a contrite spirit;
  a heart contrite and humbled, O God, you will not
    spurn.

R̸. **Create a clean heart in me, O God.** ↓

PRAYER   [Human Salvation]
Let us pray.

O God of unchanging power and eternal light,
look with favor on the wondrous mystery of the whole
    Church
and serenely accomplish the work of human salvation,
which you planned from all eternity;
may the whole world know and see
that what was cast down is raised up,
what had become old is made new,
and all things are restored to integrity through Christ,
just as by him they came into being.
Who lives and reigns for ever and ever. R̸. **Amen.** ↓

OR

PRAYER   [Confirm Our Hope]
O God, who by the pages of both Testaments
instruct and prepare us to celebrate the Paschal Mystery,

grant that we may comprehend your mercy,
so that the gifts we receive from you this night
may confirm our hope of the gifts to come.
Through Christ our Lord. ℟. **Amen.** ↓

*After the last reading from the Old Testament with its
Responsorial Psalm and its prayer, the altar candles are lit,
and the Priest intones the hymn* Gloria in excelsis Deo *(Glory
to God in the highest), which is taken up by all, while bells are
rung, according to local custom.*

*When the hymn is concluded, the Priest says the Collect in the
usual way.*

COLLECT   [Renewed in Body and Mind]
Let us pray.

O God, who make this most sacred night radiant
with the glory of the Lord's Resurrection,
stir up in your Church a spirit of adoption,
so that, renewed in body and mind,
we may render you undivided service.
Through our Lord Jesus Christ, your Son,
who lives and reigns with you in the unity of the Holy
    Spirit,
God, for ever and ever. ℟. **Amen.** ↓

Then the reader proclaims the reading from the Apostle.

EPISTLE Rom 6:3-11   [Alive in Christ]

**By Baptism the Christian is not merely identified with the
dying Christ, who has won a victory over sin, but is introduced into the very act by which Christ died to sin.**

A reading from the Letter of Saint Paul to the Romans

BROTHERS and sisters: Are you unaware that we
who were baptized into Christ Jesus were baptized
into his death? We were indeed buried with him
through baptism into death, so that, just as Christ was
raised from the dead by the glory of the Father, we too
might live in newness of life.

For if we have grown into union with him through a death like his, we shall also be united with him in the resurrection. We know that our old self was crucified with him, so that our sinful body might be done away with, that we might no longer be in slavery to sin. For a dead person has been absolved from sin. If, then, we have died with Christ, we believe that we shall also live with him. We know that Christ, raised from the dead, dies no more; death no longer has power over him. As to his death, he died to sin once and for all; as to his life, he lives for God. Consequently, you too must think of yourselves as being dead to sin and living for God in Christ Jesus.—The word of the Lord. ℟. **Thanks be to God.** ↓

After the Epistle has been read, all rise, then the Priest solemnly intones the Alleluia *three times, raising his voice by a step each time, with all repeating it. If necessary, the psalmist intones the* Alleluia.

RESPONSORIAL PSALM Ps 118   [God's Mercy]

℟. Al -le -lu -ia.   Al - le-lu -ia.   Al - le -lu - ia.

Give thanks to the LORD, for he is good,
　　for his mercy endures forever.
Let the house of Israel say,
　　"His mercy endures forever."

℟. **Alleluia. Alleluia. Alleluia.**

The right hand of the LORD has struck with power;
　　the right hand of the LORD is exalted.
I shall not die, but live,
　　and declare the works of the LORD.

℟. **Alleluia. Alleluia. Alleluia.**

The stone which the builders rejected
　　has become the cornerstone.

By the Lord has this been done;
  it is wonderful in our eyes.

℟. **Alleluia. Alleluia. Alleluia.** ↓

The Priest, in the usual way, puts incense in the thurible and blesses the Deacon. At the Gospel lights are not carried, but only incense.

GOSPEL Mt 28:1-10   [The Resurrection]

Jesus has risen; he is not here. The Cross has yielded to the empty tomb. The Easter message is first announced to the faithful, devoted women who followed Jesus.

℣. The Lord be with you. ℟. **And with your spirit.**

✛ A reading from the holy Gospel according to Matthew.
℟. **Glory to you, O Lord.**

AFTER the sabbath, as the first day of the week was dawning, Mary Magdalene and the other Mary came to see the tomb. And behold, there was a great earthquake; for an angel of the Lord descended from heaven, approached, rolled back the stone, and sat upon it. His appearance was like lightning and his clothing was white as snow. The guards were shaken with fear of him and became like dead men. Then the angel said to the women in reply, "Do not be afraid! I know that you are seeking Jesus the crucified. He is not here, for he has been raised just as he said. Come and see the place where he lay. Then go quickly and tell his disciples, 'He has been raised from the dead, and he is going before you to Galilee; there you will see him.' Behold, I have told you." Then they went away quickly from the tomb, fearful yet overjoyed, and ran to announce this to his disciples. And behold, Jesus met them on their way and greeted them. They approached, embraced his feet, and did him homage. Then Jesus said to them, "Do not be afraid. Go tell my brothers to go to Galilee, and there they will see me."— The Gospel of the Lord. ℟. **Praise to you, Lord Jesus Christ.**

After the Gospel, the Homily, even if brief, is not to be omitted. Then the Celebration of the Sacraments of Initiation begins.

THIRD PART:
CELEBRATION OF THE SACRAMENTS OF INITIATION

The following is adapted from the Rite of Christian Initiation of Adults.

Celebration of Baptism

PRESENTATION OF THE CANDIDATES

An assisting Deacon or other minister calls the candidates for Baptism forward and their godparents present them. The Invitation to Prayer and the Litany of the Saints follow.

INVITATION TO PRAYER   [Supportive Prayer]

The Priest addresses the following or a similar invitation for the assembly to join in prayer for the candidates for Baptism.

Dearly beloved,
with one heart and one soul, let us by our prayers
come to the aid of these our brothers and sisters in their
   blessed hope,
so that, as they approach the font of rebirth,
the almighty Father may bestow on them
all his merciful help.

LITANY OF THE SAINTS   [Petitioning the Saints]

The singing of the Litany of the Saints is led by cantors and may include, at the proper place, the names of some Saints, especially the Titular Saint of the church and the Patron Saints of the place and of those to be baptized.

Lord, have mercy.
Lord, have mercy.

Christ, have mercy.
Christ, have mercy.

Lord, have mercy.
Lord, have mercy.

Holy Mary, Mother of God,
   pray for us.

Saint Michael, **pray for us.**

Holy Angels of God, **pray for us.**

Saint John the Baptist, **pray for us.**

Saint Joseph, **pray for us.**

Saint Peter and Saint Paul, **pray for us.**

Saint Andrew, **pray for us.**

Saint John, **pray for us.**

Saint Mary Magdalene, **pray for us.**

Saint Stephen, **pray for us.**

Saint Ignatius of Antioch, **pray for us.**

Saint Lawrence, **pray for us.**

Saint Perpetua and Saint Felicity, **pray for us.**

Saint Agnes, **pray for us.**

Saint Gregory, **pray for us.**

Saint Augustine, **pray for us.**

Saint Athanasius, **pray for us.**

Saint Basil, **pray for us.**

Saint Martin, **pray for us.**

Saint Benedict, **pray for us.**

Saint Francis and Saint Dominic, **pray for us.**

Saint Francis Xavier, **pray for us.**

Saint John Vianney, **pray for us.**

Saint Catherine of Siena, **pray for us.**

Saint Teresa of Jesus, **pray for us.**

All holy men and women, Saints of God, **pray for us.**

Lord, be merciful, **Lord, deliver us, we pray.**

From all evil, **Lord, deliver us, we pray.**

From every sin, **Lord, deliver us, we pray.**

From everlasting death, **Lord, deliver us, we pray.**

By your Incarnation, **Lord, deliver us, we pray.**

By your Death and Resurrection, **Lord, deliver us, we pray.**

By the outpouring of the Holy Spirit, **Lord, deliver us, we pray.**

Be merciful to us sinners, **Lord, we ask you, hear our prayer.**

Bring these chosen ones to new birth through the grace of Baptism, **Lord, we ask you, hear our prayer.**

Jesus, Son of the living God, **Lord, we ask you, hear our prayer.**

Christ, hear us.
Christ, hear us.

Christ, graciously hear us.
Christ, graciously hear us.

BLESSING OF BAPTISMAL WATER [Grace-Filled Water]

The Priest then blesses the baptismal water, saying the following prayer with hands extended:

O God, who by invisible power
accomplish a wondrous effect
through sacramental signs
and who in many ways have prepared water, your
 creation,
to show forth the grace of Baptism;

O God, whose Spirit
in the first moments of the world's creation
hovered over the waters,
so that the very substance of water
would even then take to itself the power to sanctify;

O God, who by the outpouring of the flood
foreshadowed regeneration,
so that from the mystery of one and the same element of
 water
would come an end to vice and a beginning of virtue;

O God, who caused the children of Abraham
to pass dry-shod through the Red Sea,
so that the chosen people,
set free from slavery to Pharaoh,
would prefigure the people of the baptized;

O God, whose Son,
baptized by John in the waters of the Jordan,
was anointed with the Holy Spirit,
and, as he hung upon the Cross,
gave forth water from his side along with blood,
and after his Resurrection, commanded his disciples:
"Go forth, teach all nations, baptizing them
in the name of the Father and of the Son and of the Holy
 Spirit,"
look now, we pray, upon the face of your Church
and graciously unseal for her the fountain of Baptism.

May this water receive by the Holy Spirit
the grace of your Only Begotten Son,
so that human nature, created in your image
and washed clean through the Sacrament of Baptism
from all the squalor of the life of old,
may be found worthy to rise to the life of newborn
    children
through water and the Holy Spirit.

*And, if appropriate, lowering the paschal candle into the
water either once or three times, he continues:*

May the power of the Holy Spirit,
O Lord, we pray,
come down through your Son
into the fullness of this font,

and, holding the candle in the water, he continues:

so that all who have been buried with Christ
by Baptism into death
may rise again to life with him.
Who lives and reigns with you in the unity of the Holy
    Spirit,
God, for ever and ever. ℟. **Amen.**

*Then the candle is lifted out of the water, as the people
acclaim:*

**Springs of water, bless the Lord;
praise and exalt him above all for ever.**

THE BLESSING OF WATER   [Memorial of Baptism]

*If no one present is to be baptized and the font is not to be
blessed, the Priest introduces the faithful to the blessing of
water, saying:*

Dear brothers and sisters,
let us humbly beseech the Lord our God
to bless this water he has created,
which will be sprinkled upon us
as a memorial of our Baptism.

May he graciously renew us,
that we may remain faithful to the Spirit
whom we have received.

And after a brief pause in silence, he proclaims the following prayer, with hands extended:

Lord our God,
in your mercy be present to your people
who keep vigil on this most sacred night,
and, for us who recall the wondrous work of our creation
and the still greater work of our redemption,
graciously bless this water.
For you created water to make the fields fruitful
and to refresh and cleanse our bodies.
You also made water the instrument of your mercy:
for through water you freed your people from slavery
and quenched their thirst in the desert;
through water the Prophets proclaimed the new
    covenant
you were to enter upon with the human race;
and last of all,
through water, which Christ made holy in the Jordan,
you have renewed our corrupted nature
in the bath of regeneration.

Therefore, may this water be for us
a memorial of the Baptism we have received,
and grant that we may share
in the gladness of our brothers and sisters,
who at Easter have received their Baptism.
Through Christ our Lord.
℟. **Amen.**

RENUNCIATION OF SIN AND PROFESSION OF FAITH
[Witnessing to Our Faith]

*If there are baptismal candidates, the Priest, in a series of questions to which the candidates reply, **I do**, asks the candidates to renounce sin and profess their faith.*

BAPTISM   [Children of God]

The Priest baptizes each candidate either by immersion or by the pouring of water.

N., I baptize you in the name of the Father, and of the Son, and of the Holy Spirit.

EXPLANATORY RITES

The celebration of Baptism continues with the explanatory rites, after which the celebration of Confirmation normally follows.

ANOINTING AFTER BAPTISM   [Chrism of Salvation]

If the Confirmation of those baptized is separated from their Baptism, the Priest anoints them with Chrism immediately after Baptism.

The God of power and Father of our Lord Jesus Christ
has freed you from sin
and brought you to new life
through water and the Holy Spirit.

He now anoints you with the chrism of salvation,
so that, united with his people,
you may remain for ever a member of Christ
who is Priest, Prophet, and King.

Newly baptized: **Amen.**

In silence each of the newly baptized is anointed with Chrism on the crown of the head.

CLOTHING WITH A BAPTISMAL GARMENT
                                        [Clothed in Christ]

The garment used in this Rite may be white or of a color that conforms to local custom. If circumstances suggest, this Rite may be omitted.

N. and N., you have become a new creation
and have clothed yourselves in Christ.

Receive this baptismal garment
and bring it unstained to the judgment seat of our Lord
  Jesus Christ,
so that you may have everlasting life.

Newly baptized: **Amen.**

PRESENTATION OF A LIGHTED CANDLE [Light of Christ]

*The Priest takes the Easter candle in his hands or touches it,
saying:*

Godparents, please come forward to give to the newly
baptized the light of Christ.

*A godparent of each of the newly baptized goes to the Priest,
lights a candle from the Easter candle, then presents it to the
newly baptized.*

You have been enlightened by Christ.
Walk always as children of the light
and keep the flame of faith alive in your hearts.
When the Lord comes, may you go out to meet him
with all the saints in the heavenly kingdom.

Newly baptized: **Amen.**

The Renewal of Baptismal Promises

INVITATION   [Call to Renewal]

*After the celebration of Baptism, the Priest addresses the com-
munity, in order to invite those present to the renewal of their
baptismal promises; the candidates for reception into full communion join the rest of the community in this renunciation of sin
and profession of faith. All stand and hold lighted candles.*

The Priest addresses the faithful in these or similar words:

Dear brethren (brothers and sisters), through the
  Paschal Mystery
we have been buried with Christ in Baptism,
so that we may walk with him in newness of life.
And so, now that our Lenten observance is concluded,
let us renew the promises of Holy Baptism,

by which we once renounced Satan and his works
and promised to serve God in the holy catholic Church.
And so I ask you:

A   [Reject Evil]

Priest: Do you renounce Satan?
All: **I do.**

Priest: And all his works?
All: **I do.**

Priest: And all his empty show?
All: **I do.**

B

Priest: Do you renounce sin,
   so as to live in the freedom of the children of God?
All: **I do.**

Priest: Do you renounce the lure of evil,
   so that sin may have no mastery over you?
All: **I do.**

Priest: Do you renounce Satan,
   the author and prince of sin?
All: **I do.**

PROFESSION OF FAITH   [I Believe]

Then the Priest continues:

Priest: Do you believe in God,
      the Father almighty,
         Creator of heaven and earth?

All: **I do.**

Priest: Do you believe in Jesus Christ, his only Son, our
         Lord,
      who was born of the Virgin Mary,
      suffered death and was buried,
      rose again from the dead
      and is seated at the right hand of the Father?
All: **I do.**

Priest: Do you believe in the Holy Spirit,
the holy catholic Church,
the communion of saints,
the forgiveness of sins,
the resurrection of the body,
and life everlasting?
All: **I do.**

And the Priest concludes:
And may almighty God, the Father of our Lord Jesus
  Christ,
who has given us new birth by water and the Holy Spirit
and bestowed on us forgiveness of our sins,
keep us by his grace,
in Christ Jesus our Lord,
for eternal life.
All: **Amen.**

SPRINKLING WITH BAPTISMAL WATER   [Water of Life]

*The Priest sprinkles all the people with the blessed baptismal
water, while all sing the following song or any other that is
baptismal in character.*

ANTIPHON

**I saw water flowing from the Temple,
from its right-hand side, alleluia;
and all to whom this water came were saved
and shall say: Alleluia, alleluia.**

Celebration of Reception

INVITATION   [Call To Come Forward]

*If Baptism has been celebrated at the font, the Priest, the
assisting ministers, and the newly baptized with their godparents proceed to the sanctuary. As they do so the assembly may
sing a suitable song.*

*Then in the following or similar words the Priest invites the
candidates for reception, along with their sponsors, to come
into the sanctuary and before the community to make a profession of faith.*

N. and N., of your own free will you have asked to be received into the full communion of the Catholic Church. You have made your decision after careful thought under the guidance of the Holy Spirit. I now invite you to come forward with your sponsors and in the presence of this community to profess the Catholic faith. In this faith you will be one with us for the first time at the eucharistic table of the Lord Jesus, the sign of the Church's unity.

PROFESSION BY THE CANDIDATES   [Belief in Church]

When the candidates for reception and their sponsors have taken their places in the sanctuary, the Priest asks the candidates to make the following profession of faith. The candidates say:

I believe and profess all that the holy Catholic Church believes, teaches, and proclaims to be revealed by God.

ACT OF RECEPTION   [Full Communion]

Then the candidates with their sponsors go individually to the Priest, who says to each candidate (laying his right hand on the head of any candidate who is not to receive Confirmation):

N., the Lord receives you into the Catholic Church.
His loving kindness has led you here,
so that in the unity of the Holy Spirit
you may have full communion with us
in the faith that you have professed in the presence of
his family.

Celebration of Confirmation

INVITATION   [Strength in the Spirit]

The newly baptized with their godparents and, if they have not received the Sacrament of Confirmation, the newly received with their sponsors, stand before the Priest. He first speaks briefly to the newly baptized and the newly received in these or similar words.

My dear candidates for Confirmation, by your Baptism you have been born again in Christ and you have become members of Christ and of his priestly people. Now you are to share in the outpouring of the Holy Spirit among us, the Spirit sent by the Lord upon his apostles at Pentecost and given by them and their successors to the baptized.

The promised strength of the Holy Spirit, which you are to receive, will make you more like Christ and help you to be witnesses to his suffering, death, and resurrection. It will strengthen you to be active members of the Church and to build up the Body of Christ in faith and love.

My dear friends, let us pray to God our Father, that he will pour out the Holy Spirit on these candidates for Confirmation to strengthen them with his gifts and anoint them to be more like Christ, the Son of God.

All pray briefly in silence.

LAYING ON OF HANDS   [Gifts of the Spirit]

The Priest holds his hands outstretched over the entire group of those to be confirmed and says the following prayer.

Almighty God, Father of our Lord Jesus Christ,
who brought these your servants to new birth
by water and the Holy Spirit,
freeing them from sin:
send upon them, O Lord, the Holy Spirit, the Paraclete;
give them the spirit of wisdom and understanding,
the spirit of counsel and fortitude,
the spirit of knowledge and piety;

fill them with the spirit of the fear of the Lord.
Through Christ our Lord.
℟. **Amen.**

ANOINTING WITH CHRISM   [Sealed in the Spirit]

*Either or both godparents and sponsors place the right hand
on the shoulder of the candidate; and a godparent or a spon-
sor of the candidate gives the candidate's name to the minister of the Sacrament. During the conferral of the Sacrament
an appropriate song may be sung.*

*The minister of the Sacrament dips his right thumb in the
Chrism and makes the Sign of the Cross on the forehead of the
one to be confirmed as he says:*

N., be sealed with the Gift of the Holy Spirit.
Newly confirmed: **Amen.**
Minister: Peace be with you.
Newly confirmed: **And with your spirit.**

*After all have received the Sacrament, the newly confirmed as
well as the godparents and sponsors are led to their places in
the assembly.*

*[Since the Profession of Faith is not said, the Universal Prayer
(no. 16, p. 19) begins immediately and for the first time the
neophytes take part in it.]*

FOURTH PART:
THE LITURGY OF THE EUCHARIST

*The Priest goes to the altar and begins the Liturgy of the
Eucharist in the usual way.*

*It is desirable that the bread and wine be brought forward by
the newly baptized or, if they are children, by their parents or
godparents.*

PRAYER OVER THE OFFERINGS   [God's Saving Work]

Accept, we ask, O Lord,
the prayers of your people

with the sacrificial offerings,
that what has begun in the paschal mysteries
may, by the working of your power,
bring us to the healing of eternity.
Through Christ our Lord.
℞. **Amen.**

> ➜ No. 21, p. 22 (Pref P 21: on this night above all)

In the Eucharistic Prayer, a commemoration is made of the baptized and their godparents in accord with the formulas which are found in the Roman Missal and Roman Ritual for each of the Eucharistic Prayers.

COMMUNION ANT. 1 Cor 5:7-8   [Purity and Truth]

Christ our Passover has been sacrificed; therefore let us keep the feast with the unleavened bread of purity and truth, alleluia. ↓

Psalm 118 (117) may appropriately be sung.

PRAYER AFTER COMMUNION   [One in Mind and Heart]

Pour out on us, O Lord, the Spirit of your love,
and in your kindness make those you have nourished
by this paschal Sacrament
one in mind and heart.
Through Christ our Lord. ℞. **Amen.**

SOLEMN BLESSING   [God's Blessings]

May almighty God bless you
through today's Easter Solemnity
and, in his compassion,
defend you from every assault of sin. ℞. **Amen.**

And may he, who restores you to eternal life
in the Resurrection of his Only Begotten,
endow you with the prize of immortality. ℞. **Amen.**

Now that the days of the Lord's Passion have drawn to a
   close,
may you who celebrate the gladness of the Paschal Feast
come with Christ's help, and exulting in spirit,
to those feasts that are celebrated in eternal joy.
℟. **Amen.**

And may the blessing of almighty God,
the Father, and the Son, ✠ and the Holy Spirit,
come down on you and remain with you for ever.
℟. **Amen.** ↓

*The final blessing formula from the Rite of Baptism of Adults
or of Children may also be used, according to circumstances.*

*To dismiss the people the Deacon or, if there is no Deacon, the
Priest himself sings or says:*

Go forth, the Mass is ended, alleluia, alleluia.

Or:

Go in peace, alleluia, alleluia.

℟. **Thanks be to God, alleluia, alleluia.**

This practice is observed throughout the Octave of Easter.

"I have risen, and I am with you still."

APRIL 9

EASTER SUNDAY

ENTRANCE ANT. Cf. Ps 139 (138):18, 5-6

[Christ's Resurrection]

I have risen, and I am with you still, alleluia. You have laid your hand upon me, alleluia. Too wonderful for me, this knowledge, alleluia, alleluia. → No. 2, p. 10

OR Lk 24:34; cf. Rev 1:6 [Glory and Power]

The Lord is truly risen, alleluia. To him be glory and power for all the ages of eternity, alleluia, alleluia.

→ No. 2, p. 10

COLLECT [Renewal]

O God, who on this day,
through your Only Begotten Son,
have conquered death
and unlocked for us the path to eternity,
grant, we pray, that we who keep
the solemnity of the Lord's Resurrection
may, through the renewal by your Spirit,
rise up in the light of life.
Through our Lord Jesus Christ, your Son,

who lives and reigns with you in the unity of the Holy
   Spirit,
God, for ever and ever. ℟. **Amen.** ↓

FIRST READING Acts 10:34a, 37-43   [Salvation in Christ]

**In his sermon Peter sums up the good news, the Gospel.
Salvation comes through Christ, the beloved Son of the
Father, the anointed of the Holy Spirit.**

A reading from the Acts of the Apostles

PETER proceeded to speak and said: "You know
   what has happened all over Judea, beginning in
Galilee after the baptism that John preached, how God
anointed Jesus of Nazareth with the Holy Spirit and
power. He went about doing good and healing all those
oppressed by the devil, for God was with him. We are
witnesses of all that he did both in the country of the
Jews and in Jerusalem. They put him to death by hang-
ing him on a tree. This man God raised on the third day
and granted that he be visible, not to all the people, but
to us, the witnesses chosen by God in advance, who ate
and drank with him after he rose from the dead. He
commissioned us to preach to the people and testify
that he is the one appointed by God as judge of the living and the dead. To him all the prophets bear witness,
that everyone who believes in him will receive forgiveness of sins through his name."—The word of the Lord.
℟. **Thanks be to God.** ↓

RESPONSORIAL PSALM Ps 118   [The Day of the Lord]

℟. This is the day the Lord has made;
let us re - joice and be glad.

Or: ℟. **Alleluia**.

Give thanks to the LORD, for he is good,
   for his mercy endures forever.
Let the house of Israel say,
   "His mercy endures forever."

℟. **This is the day the Lord has made; let us rejoice and be glad.**

Or: ℟. **Alleluia.**

"The right hand of the LORD has struck with power;
   the right hand of the LORD is exalted.
I shall not die, but live,
   and declare the works of the LORD."

℟. **This is the day the Lord has made; let us rejoice and be glad.**

Or: ℟. **Alleluia.**

The stone which the builders rejected
   has become the cornerstone.
By the LORD has this been done;
   it is wonderful in our eyes.

℟. **This is the day the Lord has made; let us rejoice and be glad.**

Or: ℟. **Alleluia.** ↓

One of the following texts may be chosen as the Second Reading.

SECOND READING Col 3:1-4   [Seek Heavenly Things]

Look to the glory of Christ in which we share because our lives are hidden in him (through Baptism) and we are destined to share in the glory.

A reading from the Letter of Saint Paul to the Colossians

BROTHERS and sisters: If then you were raised with Christ, seek what is above, where Christ is seated at the right hand of God. Think of what is above, not of what is on earth. For you have died, and your life is hidden with Christ in God. When Christ your life

appears, then you too will appear with him in glory.—
The word of the Lord. ℟. **Thanks be to God.** ↓

OR

SECOND READING 1 Cor 5:6b-8   [Change of Heart]

Turn away from your old ways, from sin. Have a change of
heart; be virtuous.

A reading from the first Letter of Saint Paul
to the Corinthians

BROTHERS and sisters: Do you not know that a little yeast leavens all the dough? Clear out the old
yeast, so that you may become a fresh batch of dough,
inasmuch as you are unleavened. For our paschal
lamb, Christ, has been sacrificed. Therefore, let us celebrate the feast, not with the old yeast, the yeast of
malice and wickedness, but with the unleavened bread
of sincerity and truth.—The word of the Lord. ℟.
Thanks be to God. ↓

SEQUENCE (*Victimae paschali laudes*)   [Hymn to the Victor]

Christians, to the Paschal Victim
  Offer your thankful praises!
A Lamb the sheep redeems;
  Christ, who only is sinless,
  Reconciles sinners to the Father.
Death and life have contended in that combat stupendous:
  The Prince of life, who died, reigns immortal.
Speak, Mary, declaring
  What you saw, wayfaring.
"The tomb of Christ, who is living,
  The glory of Jesus' resurrection;
Bright angels attesting,
  The shroud and napkin resting.
Yes, Christ my hope is arisen;
  To Galilee he goes before you."

Christ indeed from death is risen, our new life ob-
   taining.
   Have mercy, victor King, ever reigning!
   Amen. Alleluia. ↓

ALLELUIA Cf. 1 Cor 5:7b-8a   [Joy in the Lord]
℟. **Alleluia, alleluia.**
Christ, our paschal lamb, has been sacrificed;
let us then feast with joy in the Lord.
℟. **Alleluia, alleluia.** ↓

(For Morning Mass)

GOSPEL Jn 20:1-9   [Renewed Faith]
   Let us discover the empty tomb and ponder this mystery, and
   like Christ's first followers be strengthened in our faith.

℣. The Lord be with you. ℟. **And with your spirit.**
✝ A reading from the holy Gospel according to John.
℟. **Glory to you, O Lord.**

ON the first day of the week, Mary of Magdala came
to the tomb early in the morning, while it was still
dark, and saw the stone removed from the tomb. So she
ran and went to Simon Peter and to the other disciple
whom Jesus loved, and told them, "They have taken the
Lord from the tomb, and we don't know where they put
him." So Peter and the other disciple went out and came
to the tomb. They both ran, but the other disciple ran
faster than Peter and arrived at the tomb first; he bent
down and saw the burial cloths there, but did not go in.
When Simon Peter arrived after him, he went into the
tomb and saw the burial cloths there, and the cloth that
had covered his head, not with the burial cloths but
rolled up in a separate place. Then the other disciple
also went in, the one who had arrived at the tomb first,
and he saw and believed. For they did not yet understand the Scripture that he had to rise from the dead.

—The Gospel of the Lord. ℟. **Praise to you, Lord Jesus Christ.**   → No. 15, p. 18

However, in Easter Sunday Masses which are celebrated with a congregation, the rite of the renewal of baptismal promises may take place after the Homily, according to the text used at the Easter Vigil (p. 344). In that case the Creed is omitted.

OR

GOSPEL Mt 28:1-10 ·   [The Resurrection]
See p. 337.   _____

(For an Afternoon or Evening Mass)

GOSPEL Lk 24:13-35   [The Messiah's Need To Suffer]
Let us accept the testimony of these two witnesses that our hearts may burn with the fire of faith.

℣. The Lord be with you. ℟. **And with your spirit.**
✤ A reading from the holy Gospel according to Luke.
℟. **Glory to you, O Lord.**

THAT very day, the first day of the week, two of Jesus' disciples were going to a village seven miles from Jerusalem called Emmaus, and they were conversing about all the things that had occurred. And it happened that while they were conversing and debating, Jesus himself drew near and walked with them, but their eyes were prevented from recognizing him. He asked them, "What are you discussing as you walk along?" They stopped, looking downcast. One of them, named Cleopas, said to him in reply, "Are you the only visitor to Jerusalem who does not know of the things that have taken place there in these days?" And he replied to them, "What sort of things?" They said to him, "The things that happened to Jesus the Nazarene, who was a prophet mighty in deed and word before God and all the people, how our chief priests and rulers both handed him over to a sentence of death and crucified him. But we were hoping that he would be the one to redeem Israel; and besides all this, it is now the third day since this took place. Some women from our group, however, have astounded us: they were at the tomb early in the morning and did not find his body; they came back and reported that they had indeed seen a vision of angels who announced that he was alive. Then some of those with us went to the tomb and found things just as the women had described, but him they did not see." And he said to them, "Oh, how foolish you are! How slow of heart to believe all that the prophets spoke! Was is not necessary that the Christ should suffer these things and enter into his glory?" Then beginning with Moses and all the prophets, he interpreted to them what referred to him in all the Scriptures. As they approached the village to which they were going, he gave the impression that he was going on farther. But they urged him, "Stay with us, for it is nearly evening and the day is almost over." So he went in to stay with them. And it happened that, while he was with them at table, he took bread, said the blessing, broke it, and gave it to them. With that their eyes were opened and they recognized him, but he vanished from their sight. They said to each other, "Were not our hearts burning within us while he spoke to us on the way and opened the Scriptures to us?" So they set out at once and returned to Jerusalem where they found gathered together the eleven and those with them who were saying, "The Lord has truly been raised and has appeared to Simon!" Then the two recounted what had taken place on the way and how he was made known to them in the breaking of bread.—The Gospel of the Lord. ℟. **Praise to you, Lord Jesus Christ.** ➜ No. 15, p. 18

However, in Easter Sunday Masses which are celebrated with a congregation, the rite of the renewal of baptismal promises may take place after the Homily, according to the text used at the Easter Vigil (p. 344). In that case the Creed is omitted.

PRAYER OVER THE OFFERINGS   [Reborn and Nourished]

Exultant with paschal gladness, O Lord,
we offer the sacrifice
by which your Church
is wondrously reborn and nourished.
Through Christ our Lord. R̶. **Amen.**

→ No. 21, p. 22 (Pref. P 21: on this day above all)

When the Roman Canon is used, the proper forms of the Communicantes *(In communion with those) and* Hanc igitur *(Therefore, Lord, we pray) are said.*

COMMUNION ANT. 1 Cor 5:7-8   [Purity and Truth]

Christ our Passover has been sacrificed, alleluia; therefore let us keep the feast with the unleavened bread of purity and truth, alleluia, alleluia. ↓

PRAYER AFTER COMMUNION   [Glory of Resurrection]

Look upon your Church, O God,
with unfailing love and favor,
so that, renewed by the paschal mysteries,
she may come to the glory of the resurrection.
Through Christ our Lord.

R̶. **Amen.**   → No. 30, p. 77

To impart the blessing at the end of Mass, the Priest may appropriately use the formula of Solemn Blessing for the Mass of the Easter Vigil, p. 350.

For the dismissal of the people, there is sung or said:

Go forth, the Mass is ended, alleluia, alleluia.

Or:

Go in peace, alleluia, alleluia.

R̶. **Thanks be to God, alleluia, alleluia.**

"Thomas . . . said to him, 'My Lord and my God!' "

APRIL 16

2nd SUNDAY OF EASTER
(or of Divine Mercy)

ENTRANCE ANT. 1 Pt 2:2   **[Long for Spiritual Milk]**

Like newborn infants, you must long for the pure, spiritual milk, that in him you may grow to salvation, alleluia.   ➜ No. 2, p. 10

OR 4 Esdr 2:36-37   **[Give Thanks]**

Receive the joy of your glory, giving thanks to God, who has called you into the heavenly Kingdom, alleluia.   ➜ No. 2, p. 10

COLLECT   **[Kindle Faith]**

God of everlasting mercy,
who in the very recurrence of the paschal feast
kindle the faith of the people you have made your own,
increase, we pray, the grace you have bestowed,
that all may grasp and rightly understand
in what font they have been washed,
by whose Spirit they have been reborn,

by whose Blood they have been redeemed.
Through our Lord Jesus Christ, your Son,
who lives and reigns with you in the unity of the Holy
  Spirit,
God, for ever and ever. ℟. **Amen.** ↓

FIRST READING Acts 2:42-47   [True Christian Fellowship]

**The faithful lived a common life, sharing all their goods.
The Apostles worked many miracles. They prayed together and broke bread. Their numbers increased daily.**

A reading from the Acts of the Apostles

THEY devoted themselves to the teaching of the
apostles and to the communal life, to the breaking
of bread and to the prayers. Awe came upon everyone,
and many wonders and signs were done through the
apostles. All who believed were together and had all
things in common; they would sell their property and
possessions and divide them among all according to
each one's need. Every day they devoted themselves to
meeting together in the temple area and to breaking
bread in their homes. They ate their meals with exultation and sincerity of heart, praising God and enjoying
favor with all the people. And every day the Lord
added to their number those who were being saved.—
The word of the Lord. ℟. **Thanks be to God.** ↓

RESPONSORIAL PSALM Ps 118   [The Lord's Goodness]

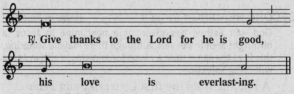

℟. Give thanks to the Lord for he is good,

his love is everlast-ing.

Or: ℟. **Alleluia.**

Let the house of Israel say,
  "His mercy endures forever."

Let the house of Aaron say,
"His mercy endures forever."
Let those who fear the LORD say,
"His mercy endures forever."

℟. **Give thanks to the Lord for he is good, his love is everlasting.**

Or: ℟. **Alleluia.**

I was hard pressed and was falling,
but the LORD helped me.
My strength and my courage is the LORD,
and he has been my savior.
The joyful shout of victory
in the tents of the just:

℟. **Give thanks to the Lord for he is good, his love is everlasting.**

Or: ℟. **Alleluia.**

The stone which the builders rejected
has become the cornerstone.
By the LORD has this been done;
it is wonderful in our eyes.
This is the day the LORD has made;
let us be glad and rejoice in it.

℟. **Give thanks to the Lord for he is good, his love is everlasting.**

Or: ℟. **Alleluia.** ↓

SECOND READING 1 Pt 1:3-9   [Love in Practice]

God, our Father, has given us a new hope in Jesus, a birthright kept in heaven. Although there may be suffering, this is at the same time a cause for rejoicing. Faith in Jesus will bring salvation.

A reading from the first Letter of Saint Peter

B LESSED be the God and Father of our Lord Jesus Christ, who in his great mercy gave us a new birth to a living hope through the resurrection of Jesus

Christ from the dead, to an inheritance that is imperishable, undefiled, and unfading, kept in heaven for you who by the power of God are safeguarded through faith, to a salvation that is ready to be revealed in the final time. In this you rejoice, although now for a little while you may have to suffer through various trials, so that the genuineness of your faith, more precious than gold that is perishable even though tested by fire, may prove to be for praise, glory, and honor at the revelation of Jesus Christ. Although you have not seen him you love him; even though you do not see him now yet believe in him, you rejoice with an indescribable and glorious joy, as you attain the goal of your faith, the salvation of your souls.—The word of the Lord. ℟. **Thanks be to God.** ↓

ALLELUIA Jn 20:29   [Blind Faith]

℟. **Alleluia, alleluia.**

You believe in me, Thomas, because you have seen me, says the Lord;

blessed are they who have not seen me, but still believe!

℟. **Alleluia, alleluia.** ↓

GOSPEL Jn 20:19-31   [Living Faith]

Jesus appears to the disciples, coming through locked doors. He shows them his hands and side. He greets them in peace and gives them the power to forgive sins. A week later, Jesus appears again directly to Thomas who now professes his belief.

℣. The Lord be with you. ℟. **And with your spirit.**

✛ A reading from the holy Gospel according to John.

℟. **Glory to you, O Lord.**

ON the evening of that first day of the week, when the doors were locked, where the disciples were, for fear of the Jews, Jesus came and stood in their midst and said to them, "Peace be with you." When he had said this, he showed them his hands and his side. The disciples rejoiced when they saw the Lord. Jesus said to them again, "Peace be with you. As the Father has sent me, so I send you." And when he had said this, he breathed on them and said to them, "Receive the Holy Spirit. Whose sins you forgive are forgiven them, and whose sins you retain are retained."

Thomas, called Didymus, one of the Twelve, was not with them when Jesus came. So the other disciples said to him, "We have seen the Lord." But he said to them, "Unless I see the mark of the nails in his hands and put my finger into the nailmarks and put my hand into his side, I will not believe."

Now a week later his disciples were again inside and Thomas was with them. Jesus came, although the doors were locked, and stood in their midst and said, "Peace be with you." Then he said to Thomas, "Put your finger here and see my hands, and bring your hand and put it into my side, and do not be unbelieving, but believe." Thomas answered and said to him, "My Lord and my God!" Jesus said to him, "Have you come to believe because you have seen me? Blessed are those who have not seen and have believed."

Now, Jesus did many other signs in the presence of his disciples that are not written in this book. But these are written that you may come to believe that Jesus is the Christ, the Son of God, and that through this belief you may have life in his name.—The Gospel of the Lord. ℟. **Praise to you, Lord Jesus Christ.**   ➜ No. 15, p. 18

PRAYER OVER THE OFFERINGS   [Unending Happiness]

Accept, O Lord, we pray,
the oblations of your people
(and of those you have brought to new birth),
that, renewed by confession of your name and by
    Baptism,

they may attain unending happiness.
Through Christ our Lord. ℟. **Amen.**

        → No. 21, p. 22 (Pref. P 21: on this day above all)

When the Roman Canon is used, the proper forms of the Communicantes *(In communion with those) and* Hanc igitur *(Therefore, Lord, we pray) are said.*

COMMUNION ANT. Cf. Jn 20:27   [Believe]

Bring your hand and feel the place of the nails, and do not be unbelieving but believing, alleluia. ↓

PRAYER AFTER COMMUNION   [Devout Reception]

Grant, we pray, almighty God,
that our reception of this paschal Sacrament
may have a continuing effect
in our minds and hearts.
Through Christ our Lord.
℟. **Amen.**   → No. 30, p. 77

Optional Solemn Blessings, p. 97, and Prayers over the People, p. 105

For the dismissal of the people, there is sung or said: Go forth, the Mass is ended, alleluia, alleluia. *Or:* Go in peace, alleluia, alleluia. *The people respond:* **Thanks be to God, alleluia, alleluia.**

"Their eyes were opened and they recognized him."

APRIL 23

3rd SUNDAY OF EASTER

ENTRANCE ANT. Cf. Ps 66 (65):1-2   [Praise the Lord]

Cry out with joy to God, all the earth; O sing to the glory of his name. O render him glorious praise, alleluia.
→ No. 2, p. 10

COLLECT   [Hope of Resurrection]

May your people exult for ever, O God,
in renewed youthfulness of spirit,
so that, rejoicing now in the restored glory of our
   adoption,
we may look forward in confident hope
to the rejoicing of the day of resurrection.
Through our Lord Jesus Christ, your Son,
who lives and reigns with you in the unity of the Holy
   Spirit,
God, for ever and ever. ℞. **Amen.** ↓

FIRST READING Acts 2:14, 22-33   [Reform Your Lives]

Peter proposes in short summary the name, work, Death, and Resurrection of our Lord. The Church teaches that although some of the authorities of Christ's time bear responsibility for carrying out his execution, this charge must not be laid

against all the Jewish people of Jesus' day or of our own. We all are responsible for sin and for our Lord's suffering.

A reading from the Acts of the Apostles

THEN Peter stood up with the Eleven, raised his voice, and proclaimed: "You who are Jews, indeed all of you staying in Jerusalem. Let this be known to you, and listen to my words. You who are Israelites, hear these words. Jesus the Nazorean was a man commended to you by God with mighty deeds, wonders, and signs, which God worked through him in your midst, as you yourselves know. This man, delivered up by the set plan and foreknowledge of God, you killed, using lawless men to crucify him. But God raised him up, releasing him from the throes of death, because it was impossible for him to be held by it. For David says of him:

I saw the Lord ever before me,
     with him at my right hand I shall not be disturbed.
Therefore my heart has been glad and my tongue
          has exulted;
     my flesh, too, will dwell in hope,
because you will not abandon my soul to the nether-
          world,
     nor will you suffer your holy one to see corrup-
          tion.
You have made known to me the paths of life;
     you will fill me with joy in your presence.

"My brothers, one can confidently say to you about the patriarch David that he died and was buried, and his tomb is in our midst to this day. But since he was a prophet and knew that God had sworn an oath to him that he would set one of his descendants upon his throne, he foresaw and spoke of the resurrection of the Christ, that neither was he abandoned to the nether-world nor did his flesh see corruption. God raised this Jesus; of this we are all witnesses. Exalted at the right hand of God, he received the promise of the Holy Spirit from the Father and poured him forth, as you see and hear."—The word of the Lord. ℟. **Thanks be to God.** ↓

RESPONSORIAL PSALM Ps 16   [Divine Security]

℟. **Lord, you will show us the path of life.**

Or: ℟. **Alleluia.**

Keep me, O God, for in you I take refuge;
    I say to the LORD, "My Lord are you."
O LORD, my allotted portion and my cup,
    you it is who hold fast my lot.

℟. **Lord, you will show us the path of life.**

Or: ℟. **Alleluia.**

I bless the LORD who counsels me;
    even in the night my heart exhorts me.
I set the LORD ever before me;
    with him at my right hand I shall not be disturbed.

℟. **Lord, you will show us the path of life.**

Or: ℟. **Alleluia.**

Therefore my heart is glad and my soul rejoices,
    my body, too, abides in confidence;
because you will not abandon my soul to the netherworld,
    nor will you suffer your faithful one to undergo corruption.

℟. **Lord, you will show us the path of life.**

Or: ℟. **Alleluia.**

You will show me the path to life,
    abounding joy in your presence,
    the delights at your right hand forever.

℟. **Lord, you will show us the path of life.**

Or: ℟. **Alleluia.** ↓

SECOND READING 1 Pt 1:17-21

[Conduct Yourselves Reverently]

As followers of Jesus, we have been ransomed by his Blood. Through him, we are believers in God who raised Jesus from the dead. Our faith and hope are in him.

A reading from the first Letter of Saint Peter

BELOVED: If you invoke as Father him who judges impartially according to each one's works, conduct yourselves with reverence during the time of your sojourning, realizing that you were ransomed from your futile conduct, handed on by your ancestors, not with perishable things like silver or gold but with the precious blood of Christ as of a spotless unblemished lamb. He was known before the foundation of the world but revealed in the final time for you, who through him believe in God who raised him from the dead and gave him glory, so that your faith and hope are in God.—The word of the Lord. ℟. **Thanks be to God.** ↓

ALLELUIA Cf. Lk 24:32   [Ardent Word]
℟. **Alleluia, alleluia.**
Lord Jesus, open the Scriptures to us;
make our hearts burn while you speak to us.
℟. **Alleluia, alleluia.** ↓

GOSPEL Lk 24:13-35   [Christ Is Lord]

Two disciples who do not recognize Jesus walk with him. Cleopas tells about Jesus—his miracles, Passion, Death, and Resurrection, and the hope Israel had in him. Finally, in the breaking of bread they see that Jesus is with them, truly risen.

℣. The Lord be with you. ℟. **And with your spirit.**
✠ A reading from the holy Gospel according to Luke.
℟. **Glory to you, O Lord.**

THAT very day, the first day of the week, two of Jesus' disciples were going to a village seven miles from Jerusalem called Emmaus, and they were conversing about all the things that had occurred. And it happened that while they were conversing and debating, Jesus himself drew near and walked with them, but their eyes were prevented from recognizing him. He asked them, "What are you discussing as you walk along?" They stopped, looking downcast. One of them, named Cleopas, said to him in reply,"Are you the only visitor to Jerusalem who does not know of the things that have taken place there in these days?" And he replied to them, "What sort of things?" They said to him,"The things that happened to Jesus the Nazarene, who was a prophet mighty in deed and word before God and all the people, how our chief priests and rulers both handed him over to a sentence of death and crucified him. But we were hoping that he would be the one to redeem Israel; and besides all this, it is now the third day since this took place. Some women from our group, however, have astounded us: they were at the tomb early in the morning and did not find his body; they came back and reported that they had indeed seen a vision of angels who announced that he was alive. Then some of those with us went to the tomb and found things just as the women had described, but him they did not see." And he said to them, "Oh, how foolish you are! How slow of heart to believe all that the prophets spoke! Was it not necessary that the Christ should suffer these things and enter into his glory?" Then beginning with Moses and all the prophets, he interpreted to them what referred to him in all the Scriptures. As they approached the village to which they were going, he gave the impression that he was going on farther. But they urged him,"Stay with us, for it is nearly evening and the day is almost over." So he went in to stay with them. And it happened that, while he was with them at table, he took bread, said the blessing, broke it, and gave it to them. With that their eyes were opened and they recognized him, but he vanished from their sight. Then they said to each other,"Were not our hearts burning within us while he spoke to us on the way and opened the Scriptures to us?" So they set out at once and returned to Jerusalem where they found gathered together the eleven and those with them who were saying, "The Lord has truly been raised and has appeared to Simon!" Then the two recounted what had taken place on the way and how he was made known to them in the breaking of bread.—The Gospel of the Lord. ℟. **Praise to you, Lord Jesus Christ.**   ➜ No. 15, p. 18

PRAYER OVER THE OFFERINGS   [Exultant Church]

Receive, O Lord, we pray,
these offerings of your exultant Church,
and, as you have given her cause for such great
    gladness,
grant also that the gifts we bring
may bear fruit in perpetual happiness.
Through Christ our Lord.
℟. **Amen.**   ➜ No. 21, p. 22 (Pref. P 21-25)

COMMUNION ANT. Cf. Lk 24:35   [Christ's Presence]

The disciples recognized the Lord Jesus in the breaking of the bread, alleluia. ↓

PRAYER AFTER COMMUNION   [The Lord's Kindness]

Look with kindness upon your people, O Lord,
and grant, we pray,
that those you were pleased to renew by eternal
    mysteries
may attain in their flesh
the incorruptible glory of the resurrection.
Through Christ our Lord.
℟. **Amen.**   ➜ No. 30, p. 77

Optional Solemn Blessings, p. 97, and Prayers over the People, p. 105

"The sheep follow him, because they recognize his voice."

APRIL 30

4th SUNDAY OF EASTER

ENTRANCE ANT. Cf. Ps 33 (32):5-6   [God the Creator]

The merciful love of the Lord fills the earth; by the word of the Lord the heavens were made, alleluia.

→ No. 2, p. 10

COLLECT   [Joys of Heaven]

Almighty ever-living God,
lead us to a share in the joys of heaven,
so that the humble flock may reach
where the brave Shepherd has gone before.
Who lives and reigns with you in the unity of the Holy
   Spirit,
God, for ever and ever.
℟. **Amen.** ↓

FIRST READING Acts 2:14a, 36-41   [Salvation in Jesus]

Peter states that Jesus is the Messiah who was crucified. Peter admonishes the people to reform and be baptized to receive the Holy Spirit. (See introduction to First Reading on p. 366.)

A reading from the Acts of the Apostles

THEN Peter stood up with the Eleven, raised his voice, and proclaimed: "Let the whole house of Israel know for certain that God has made both Lord and Christ, this Jesus whom you crucified."

Now when they heard this, they were cut to the heart, and they asked Peter and the other apostles, "What are we to do, my brothers?" Peter said to them, "Repent and be baptized, every one of you, in the name of Jesus Christ for the forgiveness of your sins; and you will receive the gift of the Holy Spirit. For the promise is made to you and to your children and to all those far off, whomever the Lord our God will call." He testified with many other arguments, and was exhorting them, "Save yourselves from this corrupt generation." Those who accepted his message were baptized, and about three thousand persons were added that day.—The word of the Lord. ℟. **Thanks be to God.** ↓

RESPONSORIAL PSALM Ps 23   [Refuge in God]

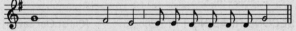

℟. **The Lord is my shep-herd; there is noth-ing I shall want.**

Or: ℟. **Alleluia.**

The LORD is my shepherd; I shall not want.
    In verdant pastures he gives me repose;
beside restful waters he leads me;
    he refreshes my soul.

℟. **The Lord is my shepherd; there is nothing I shall want.**

Or: ℟. **Alleluia.**

He guides me in right paths
    for his name's sake.
Even though I walk in the dark valley
    I fear no evil; for you are at my side

with your rod and your staff
    that give me courage.

℟. **The Lord is my shepherd; there is nothing I shall want.**

Or: ℟. **Alleluia.**

You spread the table before me
    in the sight of my foes;
you anoint my head with oil;
    my cup overflows.

℟. **The Lord is my shepherd; there is nothing I shall want.**

Or: ℟. **Alleluia.**

Only goodness and kindness follow me
    all the days of my life;
and I shall dwell in the house of the LORD
    for years to come.

℟. **The Lord is my shepherd; there is nothing I shall want.**

Or: ℟. **Alleluia.** ↓

SECOND READING 1 Pt 2:20b-25   [Christ Our Savior]

Jesus gave an example. He suffered for us. He did no wrong; he did not answer with insults or threats. He died for our sins. By his wounds we are healed.

A reading from the first Letter of Saint Peter

BELOVED: If you are patient when you suffer for doing what is good, this is a grace before God. For to this you have been called, because Christ also suffered for you, leaving you an example that you should follow in his footsteps.

He committed no sin, and no deceit was found in his mouth.

When he was insulted, he returned no insult; when he suffered, he did not threaten; instead, he handed himself over to the one who judges justly. He himself bore our sins in his body upon the cross, so that, free from sin, we might live for righteousness. By his wounds you have been healed. For you had gone astray like sheep, but you have now returned to the shepherd and guardian of your souls.—The word of the Lord. ℟. **Thanks be to God.** ↓

ALLELUIA Jn 10:14   [God's Sheep]

℟. **Alleluia, alleluia.**
I am the good shepherd, says the Lord;
I know my sheep, and mine know me.
℟. **Alleluia, alleluia.** ↓

GOSPEL Jn 10:1-10   [The Good Shepherd]

> Jesus is the "Good Shepherd." He knows his sheep and they know him. Whoever enters his sheepfold will be safe.

℣. The Lord be with you. ℟. **And with your spirit.**
✠ A reading from the holy Gospel according to John.
℟. **Glory to you, O Lord.**

JESUS said: "Amen, amen, I say to you, whoever does not enter a sheepfold through the gate but climbs over elsewhere is a thief and a robber. But whoever enters through the gate is the shepherd of the sheep. The gatekeeper opens it for him, and the sheep hear his voice, as the shepherd calls his own sheep by name and leads them out. When he has driven out all his own, he walks ahead of them, and the sheep follow him, because they recognize his voice. But they will not follow a stranger; they will run away from him, because they do not recognize the voice of strangers." Although Jesus used this figure of speech, the Pharisees did not realize what he was trying to tell them.

So Jesus said again, "Amen, amen, I say to you, I am the gate for the sheep. All who came before me are

thieves and robbers, but the sheep did not listen to
them. I am the gate. Whoever enters through me will
be saved, and will come in and go out and find pasture.
A thief comes only to steal and slaughter and destroy;
I came so that they might have life and have it more
abundantly."—The Gospel of the Lord. ℟. **Praise to
you, Lord Jesus Christ.**   ➜ No. 15, p. 18

PRAYER OVER THE OFFERINGS   [Unending Joy]

Grant, we pray, O Lord,
that we may always find delight in these paschal
    mysteries,
so that the renewal constantly at work within us
may be the cause of our unending joy.
Through Christ our Lord.
℟. **Amen.**   ➜ No. 21, p. 22 (Pref. P 21-25)

COMMUNION ANT.   [The Risen Shepherd]

**The Good Shepherd has risen, who laid down his life for
his sheep and willingly died for his flock, alleluia.** ↓

PRAYER AFTER COMMUNION   [Kind Shepherd]

Look upon your flock, kind Shepherd,
and be pleased to settle in eternal pastures
the sheep you have redeemed
by the Precious Blood of your Son.
Who lives and reigns for ever and ever.
℟. **Amen.**   ➜ No. 30, p. 77

Optional Solemn Blessings, p. 97, and Prayers over the People, p. 105

"In my Father's house there are many dwelling places."

MAY 7

5th SUNDAY OF EASTER

ENTRANCE ANT. Cf. Ps 98 (97):1-2   [Wonders of the Lord]

O sing a new song to the Lord, for he has worked wonders; in the sight of the nations he has shown his deliverance, alleluia.   → No. 2, p. 10

COLLECT   [Much Fruit]

Almighty ever-living God,
constantly accomplish the Paschal Mystery within us,
that those you were pleased to make new in Holy
    Baptism
may, under your protective care, bear much fruit
and come to the joys of life eternal.
Through our Lord Jesus Christ, your Son,
who lives and reigns with you in the unity of the Holy
    Spirit,
God, for ever and ever. ℟. **Amen.** ↓

FIRST READING Acts 6:1-7   [Spiritual and Material Tasks]

Since the number of faithful was growing, seven men were proposed as ministers to help in the work of the Church.

377

The Apostles prayed over them and imposed hands on them.

A reading from the Acts of the Apostles

AS the number of disciples continued to grow, the Hellenists complained against the Hebrews because their widows were being neglected in the daily distribution. So the Twelve called together the community of the disciples and said, "It is not right for us to neglect the word of God to serve at table. Brothers, select from among you seven reputable men, filled with the Spirit and wisdom, whom we shall appoint to this task, whereas we shall devote ourselves to prayer and to the ministry of the word." The proposal was acceptable to the whole community, so they chose Stephen, a man filled with faith and the Holy Spirit, also Philip, Prochorus, Nicanor, Timon, Parmenas, and Nicholas of Antioch, a convert to Judaism. They presented these men to the apostles who prayed and laid hands on them. The word of God continued to spread, and the number of the disciples in Jerusalem increased greatly; even a large group of priests were becoming obedient to the faith.—The word of the Lord. ℟. **Thanks be to God.** ↓

RESPONSORIAL PSALM Ps 33   [Exult in the Lord]

℟. Lord, let your mercy be   on us,   as we place our trust in you.

Or: ℟. **Alleluia.**

Exult, you just, in the LORD;
   praise from the upright is fitting.
Give thanks to the LORD on the harp;
   with the ten-stringed lyre chant his praises.

℟. **Lord, let your mercy be on us, as we place our trust in you.**

Or: ℟. **Alleluia.**

Upright is the word of the LORD,
  and all his works are trustworthy.
He loves justice and right;
  of the kindness of the LORD the earth is full.

℟. **Lord, let your mercy be on us, as we place our trust in you.**

Or: ℟. **Alleluia.**

See, the eyes of the LORD are upon those who fear him,
  upon those who hope for his kindness,
to deliver them from death
  and preserve them in spite of famine.

℟. **Lord, let your mercy be on us, as we place our trust in you.**

Or: ℟. **Alleluia.** ↓

SECOND READING 1 Pt 2:4-9   [A Royal Priesthood]

Jesus is the cornerstone of the Church. The People of God are living stones. We are a royal priesthood, a consecrated nation, a people set apart to proclaim Jesus' good works.

A reading from the first Letter of Saint Peter

BELOVED: Come to him, a living stone, rejected by human beings but chosen and precious in the sight of God, and, like living stones, let yourselves be built into a spiritual house to be a holy priesthood to offer spiritual sacrifices acceptable to God through Jesus Christ. For it says in Scripture:

  Behold, I am laying a stone in Zion,
  a cornerstone, chosen and precious,
  and whoever believes in it shall not be put to shame.
Therefore, its value is for you who have faith, but for those without faith:

*The stone that the builders rejected
has become the cornerstone,*

and

*A stone that will make people stumble,
and a rock that will make them fall.*

They stumble by disobeying the word, as is their destiny.

You are "a chosen race, a royal priesthood, a holy nation, a people of his own, so that you may announce the praises" of him who called you out of darkness into his wonderful light.—The word of the Lord. ℟. **Thanks be to God.** ↓

ALLELUIA Jn 14:6   [Christ the Way]

℟. **Alleluia, alleluia.**
I am the way, the truth and the life, says the Lord;
no one comes to the Father, except through me.
℟. **Alleluia, alleluia.** ↓

GOSPEL Jn 14:1-12   [Faith in God]

Jesus assures his Apostles that he is the way, the truth, and the life. The Father lives in him and he in the Father. Whoever has faith in Jesus will do the works of God.

℣. The Lord be with you. ℟. **And with your spirit.**
✛ A reading from the holy Gospel according to John.
℟. **Glory to you, O Lord.**

JESUS said to his disciples: "Do not let your hearts be troubled. You have faith in God; have faith also in me. In my Father's house there are many dwelling places. If there were not, would I have told you that I am going to prepare a place for you? And if I go and prepare a place for you, I will come back again and take you to myself, so that where I am you also may be. Where I am going you know the way." Thomas said to him, "Master, we do not know where you are going; how can we know the way?" Jesus said to him, "I am the way and the truth and the life. No one comes to the Father except through me. If you know me, then you will also know my Father. From now on you do know him and have seen him." Philip said to him, "Master, show us the Father, and that will be enough for us." Jesus said to him, "Have I been with you for so long a time and you still do not know me, Philip? Whoever has seen me has seen the Father. How can you say, 'Show us the Father'? Do you not believe that I am in the Father and the Father is in me? The words that I speak to you I do not speak on my own. The Father who dwells in me is doing his works. Believe me that I am in the Father and the Father is in me, or else, believe because of the works themselves. Amen, amen, I say to you, whoever believes in me will do the works that I do, and will do greater ones than these, because I am going to the Father."—The Gospel of the Lord. ℟. **Praise to you, Lord Jesus Christ.**   ➔ No. 15, p. 18

PRAYER OVER THE OFFERINGS [Guided by God's Truth]

O God, who by the wonderful exchange effected in this
    sacrifice
have made us partakers of the one supreme Godhead,
grant, we pray,
that, as we have come to know your truth,
we may make it ours by a worthy way of life.
Through Christ our Lord.
℟. **Amen.**   ➔ No. 21, p. 22 (Pref. P 21-25)

COMMUNION ANT. Cf. Jn 15:1, 5   [Union with Christ]

I am the true vine and you are the branches, says the Lord. Whoever remains in me, and I in him, bears fruit in plenty, alleluia. ↓

PRAYER AFTER COMMUNION   [New Life]

Graciously be present to your people, we pray, O Lord, and lead those you have imbued with heavenly mysteries to pass from former ways to newness of life.
Through Christ our Lord.
℟. **Amen.**   ➔ No. 30, p. 77

Optional Solemn Blessings, p. 97, and Prayers over the People, p. 105

"I will ask the Father, and he will give you another Advocate."

MAY 14

6th SUNDAY OF EASTER

ENTRANCE ANT. Cf. Is 48:20   [Spiritual Freedom]

Proclaim a joyful sound and let it be heard; proclaim to the ends of the earth: The Lord has freed his people, alleluia.   ➔ No. 2, p. 10

COLLECT   [Heartfelt Devotion]

Grant, almighty God,
that we may celebrate with heartfelt devotion these
   days of joy,
which we keep in honor of the risen Lord,
and that what we relive in remembrance
we may always hold to in what we do.
Through our Lord Jesus Christ, your Son,
who lives and reigns with you in the unity of the Holy
   Spirit,
God, for ever and ever. ℞. **Amen.** ↓

FIRST READING Acts 8:5-8, 14-17 [Reception of Holy Spirit]

> Philip carried the good news to Samaria. He performed many miracles. Peter and John laid hands on these people in Samaria and they received the Holy Spirit.

A reading from the Acts of the Apostles

PHILIP went down to the city of Samaria and proclaimed the Christ to them. With one accord, the crowds paid attention to what was said by Philip when they heard it and saw the signs he was doing. For unclean spirits, crying out in a loud voice, came out of many possessed people, and many paralyzed or crippled people were cured. There was great joy in that city.

Now when the apostles in Jerusalem heard that Samaria had accepted the word of God, they sent them Peter and John, who went down and prayed for them, that they might receive the Holy Spirit, for it had not yet fallen upon any of them; they had only been baptized in the name of the Lord Jesus. Then they laid hands on them and they received the Holy Spirit.—The word of the Lord. ℟. **Thanks be to God.** ↓

RESPONSORIAL PSALM Ps 66   [Glorious Deeds]

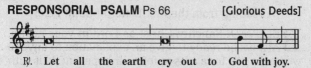

℟. Let all the earth cry out to God with joy.

Or: ℟. **Alleluia.**

Shout joyfully to God, all the earth,
    sing praise to the glory of his name;
    proclaim his glorious praise.
Say to God, "How tremendous are your deeds!

℟. **Let all the earth cry out to God with joy.**

Or: ℟. **Alleluia.**

Let all on earth worship and sing praise to you,
    sing praise to your name!"
Come and see the works of God,
    his tremendous deeds among the children of Adam.

℟. **Let all the earth cry out to God with joy.**

Or: ℟. **Alleluia.**

He has changed the sea into dry land;
   through the river they passed on foot;
   therefore let us rejoice in him.
He rules by his might forever.

℞. **Let all the earth cry out to God with joy.**

Or: ℞. **Alleluia.**

Hear now, all you who fear God, while I declare
   what he has done for me.
Blessed be God who refused me not
   my prayer or his kindness!

℞. **Let all the earth cry out to God with joy.**

Or: ℞. **Alleluia.** ↓

SECOND READING 1 Pt 3:15-18   [Life in the Spirit]

**Always worship God in your hearts. Jesus died for sins just
once for all who are sinners to lead us to God.**

A reading from the first Letter of Saint Peter

BELOVED: Sanctify Christ as Lord in your hearts.
Always be ready to give an explanation to anyone
who asks you for a reason for your hope, but do it with
gentleness and reverence, keeping your conscience
clear, so that, when you are maligned, those who
defame your good conduct in Christ may themselves
be put to shame. For it is better to suffer for doing
good, if that be the will of God, than for doing evil. For
Christ also suffered for sins once, the righteous for the
sake of the unrighteous, that he might lead you to God.
Put to death in the flesh, he was brought to life in the
Spirit.—The word of the Lord. ℞. **Thanks be to God.** ↓

ALLELUIA Jn 14:23   [Divine Love]

℞. **Alleluia, alleluia.**
Whoever loves me will keep my word, says the Lord,
and my Father will love him and we will come to him.
℞. **Alleluia, alleluia.** ↓

GOSPEL Jn 14:15-21　　　　　　　　[Eternal Presence]

> Jesus promises to ask for a Paraclete for those who love him. The world will not accept or understand the Paraclete. All who obey the commandments show their love for God and will be loved in return.

℣. The Lord be with you. ℟. **And with your spirit.**

✢ A reading from the holy Gospel according to John.
℟. **Glory to you, O Lord.**

JESUS said to his disciples: "If you love me, you will keep my commandments. And I will ask the Father, and he will give you another Advocate to be with you always, the Spirit of truth, whom the world cannot accept, because it neither sees nor knows him. But you know him, because he remains with you, and will be in you. I will not leave you orphans; I will come to you. In a little while the world will no longer see me, but you will see me, because I live and you will live. On that day you will realize that I am in my Father and you are in me and I in you. Whoever has my commandments and observes them is the one who loves me. And whoever loves me will be loved by my Father, and I will love him and reveal myself to him."—The Gospel of the Lord. ℟. **Praise to you, Lord Jesus Christ.**　　　　　→ No. 15, p. 18

PRAYER OVER THE OFFERINGS　　[God's Mighty Love]

May our prayers rise up to you, O Lord,
together with the sacrificial offerings,
so that, purified by your graciousness,
we may be conformed to the mysteries of your mighty
　　love.
Through Christ our Lord.
℟. **Amen.**　　　　　→ No. 21, p. 22 (Pref. P 21-25)

COMMUNION ANT. Jn 14:15-16　　[Role of the Paraclete]

If you love me, keep my commandments, says the Lord, and I will ask the Father and he will send you another Paraclete, to abide with you for ever, alleluia. ↓

PRAYER AFTER COMMUNION [Eucharistic Strength]

Almighty ever-living God,
who restore us to eternal life in the Resurrection of Christ,
increase in us, we pray, the fruits of this paschal
    Sacrament
and pour into our hearts the strength of this saving food.
Through Christ our Lord.
℟. **Amen.** ➙ No. 30, p. 77

Optional Solemn Blessings, p. 97; and Prayers over the People, p. 105

"Go, therefore, and make disciples of all nations."

*In those dioceses in which the Ascension is celebrated on
Sunday, the Mass of the Ascension (Vigil Mass, below, or Mass
during the Day, p. 391) is celebrated in place of the Mass of
the 7th Sunday of Easter that appears on p. 393.*

MAY 18

THE ASCENSION OF THE LORD

Solemnity

AT THE VIGIL MASS (May 17)

ENTRANCE ANT. Ps 68 (67): 33, 35 [Praise the Lord]
You kingdoms of the earth, sing to God; praise the Lord,
who ascends above the highest heavens; his majesty and
might are in the skies, alleluia. ➙ No. 2, p. 10

COLLECT   [Jesus' Promise]

O God, whose Son today ascended to the heavens
as the Apostles looked on,
grant, we pray, that, in accordance with his promise,
we may be worthy for him to live with us always on
    earth,
and we with him in heaven.
Who lives and reigns with you in the unity of the Holy
    Spirit,
God, for ever and ever. ℟. **Amen.** ↓

FIRST READING Acts 1:1-11   [Christ's Ascension]

Christ is divine! He will come again! Our faith affirms this
for us. We live in the era of the Holy Spirit.

A reading from the the Acts of the Apostles

IN the first book, Theophilus, I dealt with all that
Jesus did and taught until the day he was taken up,
after giving instructions through the Holy Spirit to the
apostles whom he had chosen. He presented himself
alive to them by many proofs after he had suffered,
appearing to them during forty days and speaking
about the kingdom of God. While meeting with them,
he enjoined them not to depart from Jerusalem, but to
wait for "the promise of the Father about which you
have heard me speak; for John baptized with water,
but in a few days you will be baptized with the Holy
Spirit."

When they had gathered together they asked him,
"Lord, are you at this time going to restore the kingdom to Israel?" He answered them, "It is not for you to
know the times or seasons that the Father has established by his own authority. But you will receive power
when the Holy Spirit comes upon you, and you will be
my witnesses in Jerusalem, throughout Judea and
Samaria, and to the ends of the earth." When he had
said this, as they were looking on, he was lifted up, and

a cloud took him from their sight. While they were looking intently at the sky as he was going, suddenly two men dressed in white garments stood beside them. They said, "Men of Galilee, why are you standing there looking at the sky? This Jesus who has been taken up from you into heaven will return in the same way as you have seen him going into heaven."—The word of the Lord. ℟. **Thanks be to God.** ↓

RESPONSORIAL PSALM Ps 47   [Praise to the Lord]

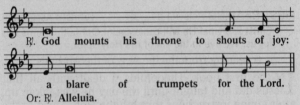

℟. God mounts his throne to shouts of joy: a blare of trumpets for the Lord.

Or: ℟. **Alleluia.**

All you peoples, clap your hands,
  shout to God with cries of gladness.
For the LORD, the Most High, the awesome,
  is the great king over all the earth.

℟. **God mounts his throne to shouts of joy: a blare of trumpets for the Lord.** ↓

Or: ℟. **Alleluia.**

God mounts his throne amid shouts of joy;
  the LORD, amid trumpet blasts.
Sing praise to God, sing praise;
  sing praise to our king, sing praise.

℟. **God mounts his throne to shouts of joy: a blare of trumpets for the Lord.** ↓

Or: ℟. **Alleluia.**

For king of all the earth is God;
  sing hymns of praise.

God reigns over the nations,
  God sits upon his holy throne.

℟. **God mounts his throne to shouts of joy: a blare of trumpets for the Lord.** ↓

Or: ℟. **Alleluia.** ↓

SECOND READING Eph 1:17-23   [Glorification of Jesus]
  Our hope is in God. He is our strength. With Christ our head, we his people will receive the gifts of wisdom and insight.

A reading from the Letter of Saint Paul to the Ephesians

BROTHERS and sisters: May the God of our Lord Jesus Christ, the Father of glory, give you a Spirit of wisdom and revelation resulting in knowledge of him. May the eyes of your hearts be enlightened, that you may know what is the hope that belongs to his call, what are the riches of glory in his inheritance among the holy ones, and what is the surpassing greatness of his power for us who believe, in accord with the exercise of his great might, which he worked in Christ, raising him from the dead and seating him at his right hand in the heavens, far above every principality, authority, power, and dominion, and every name that is named not only in this age but also in the one to come. And he put all things beneath his feet and gave him as head over all things to the church, which is his body, the fullness of the one who fills all things in every way.—The word of the Lord. ℟. **Thanks be to God.** ↓

ALLELUIA Mt 28:19a, 20b   [Christ's Abiding Presence]
℟. **Alleluia, alleluia.**
Go and teach all nations, says the Lord;
I am with you always, until the end of the world.
℟. **Alleluia, alleluia.** ↓

GOSPEL Mt 28:16-20   [Commission of the Apostles]

Jesus speaks to the Eleven, admitting his full authority. He commissions them to make disciples of all people and to baptize them. Jesus also promises to be with them to the end of the world.

℣. The Lord be with you. ℟. **And with your spirit.**

✣ A reading from the holy Gospel according to Matthew.
℟. **Glory to you, O Lord.**

THE eleven disciples went to Galilee, to the mountain to which Jesus had ordered them. When they saw him, they worshiped, but they doubted. Then Jesus approached and said to them, "All power in heaven and on earth has been given to me. Go, therefore, and make disciples of all nations, baptizing them in the name of the Father, and of the Son, and of the Holy Spirit, teaching them to observe all that I have commanded you. And behold, I am with you always, until the end of the age."—The Gospel of the Lord. ℟. **Praise to you, Lord Jesus Christ.**   ➙ No. 15, p. 18

PRAYER OVER THE OFFERINGS   [Obtain Mercy]

O God, whose Only Begotten Son, our High Priest,
is seated ever-living at your right hand to intercede for
    us,
grant that we may approach with confidence the
    throne of grace
and there obtain your mercy.
Through Christ our Lord.
℟. **Amen.**   ➙ No. 21, p. 22 (Pref. P. 26-27)

When the Roman Canon is used, the proper form of the Communicantes *(In communion with those) is said.*

COMMUNION ANT. Cf. Heb 10:12
                              [Christ at God's Right Hand]

Christ, offering a single sacrifice for sins, is seated for ever at God's right hand, alleluia. ↓

PRAYER AFTER COMMUNION   [Longing for Heaven]

May the gifts we have received from your altar, Lord,
kindle in our hearts a longing for the heavenly homeland
and cause us to press forward, following in the Savior's
    footsteps,
to the place where for our sake he entered before us.
Who lives and reigns for ever and ever.
℟. **Amen.**   ➙ No. 30, p. 77

Optional Solemn Blessings, p. 97, and Prayers over the People, p. 105

AT THE MASS DURING THE DAY

ENTRANCE ANT. Acts 1:11   [The Lord Will Return]
**Men of Galilee, why gaze in wonder at the heavens?
This Jesus whom you saw ascending into heaven will
return as you saw him go, alleluia.**   ➙ No. 2, p. 10

COLLECT   [Thankful for the Ascension]

Gladden us with holy joys, almighty God,
and make us rejoice with devout thanksgiving,
for the Ascension of Christ your Son
is our exaltation,
and, where the Head has gone before in glory,
the Body is called to follow in hope.
Through our Lord Jesus Christ, your Son,
who lives and reigns with you in the unity of the Holy
    Spirit,
God, for ever and ever. ℟. **Amen.** ↓

OR   [Belief in the Ascension]

Grant, we pray, almighty God,
that we, who believe that your Only Begotten Son, our
    Redeemer,
ascended this day to the heavens,
may in spirit dwell already in heavenly realms.

Who lives and reigns with you in the unity of the Holy
 Spirit,
God, for ever and ever. ℟. **Amen.** ↓

The readings for this Mass can be found beginning on p. 387.

PRAYER OVER THE OFFERINGS
[Rise to Heavenly Realms]

We offer sacrifice now in supplication, O Lord,
to honor the wondrous Ascension of your Son:
grant, we pray,
that through this most holy exchange
we, too, may rise up to the heavenly realms.
Through Christ our Lord.
℟. **Amen.** → No. 21, p. 22 (Pref. P 26-27)

When the Roman Canon is used, the proper form of the
Communicantes *(In communion with those) is said.*

COMMUNION ANT. Mt 28:20
[Christ's Presence]
**Behold, I am with you always, even to the end of the
age, alleluia.** ↓

PRAYER AFTER COMMUNION
[United with Christ]
Almighty ever-living God,
who allow those on earth to celebrate divine mysteries,
grant, we pray,
that Christian hope may draw us onward
to where our nature is united with you.
Through Christ our Lord.
℟. **Amen.** → No. 30, p. 77

Optional Solemn Blessings, p. 97, and Prayers over the People, p. 105

"Father, the hour has come. Give glory to your Son."

In those dioceses in which the Ascension is celebrated on Sunday, the Mass of the Ascension (Vigil Mass, p. 386, or Mass during the Day, p. 391) is celebrated in place of the Mass of the 7th Sunday of Easter that appears below.

MAY 21

7th SUNDAY OF EASTER

ENTRANCE ANT. Cf. Ps 27 (26):7-9   [Seek the Lord]

O Lord, hear my voice, for I have called to you; of you my heart has spoken: Seek his face; hide not your face from me, alleluia.   ➡ No. 2, p. 10

COLLECT   [Experience Christ among Us]

Graciously hear our supplications, O Lord,
so that we, who believe that the Savior of the human race
is with you in your glory,
may experience, as he promised,
until the end of the world,
his abiding presence among us.
Who lives and reigns with you in the unity of the Holy
    Spirit,
God, for ever and ever. ℟. **Amen.** ↓

FIRST READING Acts 1:12-14   [Constant Prayer]

After the Ascension, the Apostles returned to pray in the upper room at Jerusalem. Mary and some other women were with them. They prayed continuously for nine days.

A reading from the Acts of the Apostles

AFTER Jesus had been taken up to heaven the apostles returned to Jerusalem from the mount called Olivet, which is near Jerusalem, a sabbath day's journey away.

When they entered the city they went to the upper room where they were staying, Peter and John and James and Andrew, Philip and Thomas, Bartholomew and Matthew, James son of Alphaeus, Simon the Zealot, and Judas son of James. All these devoted themselves with one accord to prayer, together with some women, and Mary the mother of Jesus, and his brothers.—The word of the Lord. ℟. **Thanks be to God.** ↓

RESPONSORIAL PSALM Ps 27   [The House of the Lord]

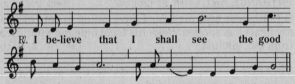

℟. I be-lieve that I shall see the good things of the Lord in the land- of the liv-ing.

Or: ℟. **Alleluia.**

The LORD is my light and my salvation;
  whom should I fear?
The LORD is my life's refuge;
  of whom should I be afraid?

℟. **I believe that I shall see the good things of the Lord in the land of the living.**

Or: ℟. **Alleluia.**

One thing I ask of the L<small>ORD</small>;
  this I seek;
to dwell in the house of the L<small>ORD</small>
  all the days of my life,
that I may gaze on the loveliness of the L<small>ORD</small>
  and contemplate his temple.

R̂. **I believe that I shall see the good things of the Lord
  in the land of the living.**

Or: R̂. **Alleluia.**

Hear, O L<small>ORD</small>, the sound of my call;
  have pity on me, and answer me.
Of you my heart speaks; you my glance seeks.

R̂. **I believe that I shall see the good things of the Lord
  in the land of the living.** ↓

Or: R̂. **Alleluia.** ↓

SECOND READING 1 Pt 4:13-16   [Joy in Suffering]

**We should rejoice in sharing in the suffering of Jesus; for
this we should not be ashamed. Beware, however, not to
violate the rights of others.**

A reading from the first Letter of Saint Peter

B<small>ELOVED</small>: Rejoice to the extent that you share in the
sufferings of Christ, so that when his glory is revealed
you may also rejoice exultantly. If you are insulted for the
name of Christ, blessed are you, for the Spirit of glory
and of God rests upon you. But let no one among you be
made to suffer as a murderer, a thief, an evildoer, or as an
intriguer. But whoever is made to suffer as a Christian
should not be ashamed but glorify God because of the
name.—The word of the Lord. R̂. **Thanks be to God.** ↓

ALLELUIA Cf. Jn 14:18   [Joyous Return]

R̂. **Alleluia, alleluia.**
I will not leave you orphans, says the Lord.
I will come back to you, and your hearts will rejoice.
R̂. **Alleluia, alleluia.** ↓

GOSPEL Jn 17:1-11a   [Eternal Life]

> Jesus prays to his Father, noting that the work given him is
> finished. The Father is known on earth. Jesus prays for his
> Apostles to whom he entrusted the good news of salvation.

℣. The Lord be with you. ℟. **And with your spirit.**

✠ A reading from the holy Gospel according to John.
℟. **Glory to you, O Lord.**

JESUS raised his eyes to heaven and said, "Father,
the hour has come. Give glory to your son, so that
your son may glorify you, just as you gave him authority over all people, so that your son may give eternal
life to all you gave him. Now this is eternal life, that
they should know you, the only true God, and the one
whom you sent, Jesus Christ. I glorified you on earth
by accomplishing the work you gave me to do. Now
glorify me, Father, with you, with the glory that I had
with you before the world began.

"I revealed your name to those whom you gave me
out of the world. They belonged to you, and you gave
them to me, and they have kept your word. Now they
know that everything you gave me is from you, because
the words you gave to me I have given to them, and they
accepted them and truly understood that I came from
you, and they have believed that you sent me. I pray for
them. I do not pray for the world but for the ones you
have given me, because they are yours, and everything
of mine is yours and everything of yours is mine, and I
have been glorified in them. And now I will no longer be
in the world, but they are in the world, while I am coming to you."—The Gospel of the Lord. ℟. **Praise to you,
Lord Jesus Christ.**   → No. 15, p. 18

PRAYER OVER THE OFFERINGS   [Glory of Heaven]

Accept, O Lord, the prayers of your faithful
with the sacrificial offerings,
that through these acts of devotedness

we may pass over to the glory of heaven.
Through Christ our Lord.
℟. **Amen.**   ➙   No. 21, p. 22 (Pref. P 21-25 or P 26-27)

COMMUNION ANT. Jn 17:22   [Christian Unity]
**Father, I pray that they may be one as we also are one,
alleluia.** ↓

PRAYER AFTER COMMUNION   [Grant Us Confidence]
Hear us, O God our Savior,
and grant us confidence,
that through these sacred mysteries
there will be accomplished in the body of the whole
   Church
what has already come to pass in Christ her Head.
Who lives and reigns for ever and ever.
℟. **Amen.**   ➙   No. 30, p. 77

Optional Solemn Blessings, p. 97, and Prayers over the People, p. 105

"They were all filled with the Holy Spirit."

MAY 28

PENTECOST SUNDAY

Solemnity

AT THE VIGIL MASS (May 27) (Simple Form)

ENTRANCE ANT. Rom 5:5; cf. 8:11   [Love-Imparting Spirit]

The love of God has been poured into our hearts through the Spirit of God dwelling within us, alleluia.

→ No. 2, p. 10

COLLECT   [Heavenly Grace]

Almighty ever-living God,
who willed the Paschal Mystery
to be encompassed as a sign in fifty days,
grant that from out of the scattered nations
the confusion of many tongues
may be gathered by heavenly grace
into one great confession of your name.
Through our Lord Jesus Christ, your Son,
who lives and reigns with you in the unity of the Holy
    Spirit,
God, for ever and ever. ℟. **Amen.** ↓

OR   [New Birth in the Spirit]

Grant, we pray, almighty God,
that the splendor of your glory
may shine forth upon us
and that, by the bright rays of the Holy Spirit,
the light of your light may confirm the hearts
of those born again by your grace.
Through our Lord Jesus Christ, your Son,
who lives and reigns with you in the unity of the Holy
    Spirit;
God, for ever and ever. ℟. **Amen.** ↓

FIRST READING

A Gn 11:1-9   [Dangers of Human Pride]

Those who put their trust in pride and human ability are bound to fail.

A reading from the Book of Genesis

THE whole world spoke the same language, using the same words. While the people were migrating in the east, they came upon a valley in the land of Shinar and settled there. They said to one another, "Come, let us mold bricks and harden them with fire." They used bricks for stone, and bitumen for mortar. Then they said, "Come, let us build ourselves a city and a tower with its top in the sky, and so make a name for ourselves; otherwise we shall be scattered all over the earth."

The LORD came down to see the city and the tower that the people had built. Then the LORD said: "If now, while they are one people, all speaking the same language, they have started to do this, nothing will later stop them from doing whatever they presume to do. Let us then go down there and confuse their language, so that one will not understand what another says." Thus the LORD scattered them from there all over the earth, and they stopped building the city. That is why it was called Babel, because there the LORD confused the speech of all the world. It was from that place that he scattered them all over the earth.—The word of the Lord. ℟. **Thanks be to God.** ↓

OR

B Ex 19:3-8a, 16-20b   [The Lord on Mount Sinai]

The Lord God covenants with the Israelites—they are to be a holy nation, a priestly kingdom.

A reading from the Book of Exodus

MOSES went up the mountain to God. Then the LORD called to him and said, "Thus shall you say to the house of Jacob; tell the Israelites: You have seen for yourselves how I treated the Egyptians and how I bore you up on eagle wings and brought you here to myself. Therefore, if you hearken to my voice and keep my covenant, you shall be my special possession, dearer to me than all other people, though all the earth is mine. You shall be to me a kingdom of priests, a holy nation. That is what you must tell the Israelites." So Moses went and summoned the elders of the people. When he set before them all that the LORD had ordered him to tell them, the people all answered together, "Everything the LORD has said, we will do."

On the morning of the third day there were peals of thunder and lightning, and a heavy cloud over the mountain, and a very loud trumpet blast, so that all the people in the camp trembled. But Moses led the people out of the camp to meet God, and they stationed themselves at the foot of the mountain. Mount Sinai was all wrapped in smoke, for the LORD came down upon it in fire. The smoke rose from it as though from a furnace, and the whole mountain trembled violently. The trumpet blast grew louder and louder, while Moses was speaking and God answering him with thunder.

When the LORD came down to the top of Mount Sinai, he summoned Moses to the top of the mountain.—The word of the Lord. ℟. **Thanks be to God.** ↓

OR

C Ez 37:1-14 [Life-Giving Spirit]

The prophet, in a vision, sees the power of God—the band of the living and the dead, as he describes the resurrection of the dead.

A reading from the Book of the Prophet Ezekiel

THE hand of the LORD came upon me, and he led me out in the spirit of the LORD and set me in the center of the plain, which was now filled with bones. He made me walk among the bones in every direction so that I saw how many they were on the surface of the plain. How dry they were! He asked me: Son of man, can these bones come to life? I answered, "Lord GOD, you alone know that." Then he said to me: Prophesy over these bones, and say to them: Dry bones, hear the word of the LORD! Thus says the Lord GOD to these bones: See! I will bring spirit into you, that you may come to life. I will put sinews upon you, make flesh grow over you, cover you with skin, and put spirit in you so that you may come to life and know that I am the LORD. I, Ezekiel, prophesied as I had been told, and even as I was prophesying I heard a noise; it was a rattling as the bones came together, bone joining bone. I saw the sinews and the flesh come upon them, and the skin cover them, but there was no spirit in them. Then the LORD said to me: Prophesy to the spirit, prophesy, son of man, and say to the spirit: Thus says the Lord GOD: From the four winds come, O spirit, and breathe into these slain that they may come to life. I prophesied as he told me, and the spirit came into them; they came alive and stood upright, a vast army. Then he said to me: Son of man, these bones are the whole house of Israel. They have been saying, "Our bones are dried up, our hope is lost, and we are cut off." Therefore, prophesy and say to them: Thus says the Lord GOD: O my people, I will open

your graves and have you rise from them, and bring you
back to the land of Israel. Then you shall know that I am
the LORD, when I open your graves and have you rise
from them, O my people! I will put my spirit in you that
you may live, and I will settle you upon your land; thus
you shall know that I am the LORD. I have promised, and
I will do it, says the LORD.—The word of the Lord. ℟.
Thanks be to God. ↓

OR

D Jl 3:1-5   [Signs of the Spirit]

**At the end of time, the Day of the Lord, Judgment Day,
those who persevere in faith will be saved.**

A reading from the Book of the Prophet Joel

THUS says the LORD:
  I will pour out my spirit upon all flesh.
Your sons and daughters shall prophesy,
    your old men shall dream dreams,
    your young men shall see visions;
even upon the servants and the handmaids,
    in those days, I will pour out my spirit.
And I will work wonders in the heavens and on the
      earth,
    blood, fire, and columns of smoke;
the sun will be turned to darkness,
    and the moon to blood,
at the coming of the day of the LORD,
    the great and terrible day.
Then everyone shall be rescued
    who calls on the name of the LORD;
for on Mount Zion there shall be a remnant,
    as the LORD has said,
and in Jerusalem survivors
    whom the LORD shall call.
The word of the Lord. ℟. **Thanks be to God.** ↓

RESPONSORIAL PSALM Ps 104   [Send Out Your Spirit]

℟. Lord, send out your Spir - it, and re-new the face of the earth.

Or: ℟. **Alleluia.**

Bless the LORD, O my soul!
  O LORD, my God, you are great indeed!
You are clothed with majesty and glory,
  robed in light as with a cloak.

℟. **Lord, send out your Spirit, and renew the face of the earth.**

Or: ℟. **Alleluia.**

How manifold are your works, O LORD!
  In wisdom you have wrought them all—
the earth is full of your creatures;
  bless the LORD, O my soul! Alleluia.

℟. **Lord, send out your Spirit, and renew the face of the earth.**

Or: ℟. **Alleluia.**

Creatures all look to you
  to give them food in due time.
When you give it to them, they gather it;
  when you open your hand, they are filled with good
    things.

℟. **Lord, send out your Spirit, and renew the face of the earth.**

Or: ℟. **Alleluia.**

If you take away their breath, they perish
  and return to their dust.
When you send forth your spirit, they are created,
  and you renew the face of the earth.

℟. **Lord, send out your Spirit, and renew the face of the earth.**

Or: ℟. **Alleluia.** ↓

SECOND READING Rom 8:22-27   [The Spirit Our Helper]

Be patient and have hope. The Spirit intercedes for us.

A reading from the Letter of Saint Paul to the Romans

B ROTHERS and sisters: We know that all creation is groaning in labor pains even until now; and not only that, but we ourselves, who have the firstfruits of the Spirit, we also groan within ourselves as we wait for adoption, the redemption of our bodies. For in hope we were saved. Now hope that sees is not hope. For who hopes for what one sees? But if we hope for what we do not see, we wait with endurance.

In the same way, the Spirit too comes to the aid of our weakness; for we do not know how to pray as we ought, but the Spirit himself intercedes with inexpressible groanings. And the one who searches hearts knows what is the intention of the Spirit, because he intercedes for the holy ones according to God's will.— The word of the Lord. ℟. **Thanks be to God.** ↓

ALLELUIA   [Fire of God's Love]

℟. **Alleluia, alleluia.**
Come, Holy Spirit, fill the hearts of your faithful
and kindle in them the fire of your love.
℟. **Alleluia, alleluia.** ↓

GOSPEL Jn 7:37-39   [Prediction of the Spirit]

The Spirit is the source of life for those who believe.

℣. The Lord be with you. ℟. **And with your spirit.**
✣ A reading from the holy Gospel according to John.
℟. **Glory to you, O Lord.**

O N the last and greatest day of the feast, Jesus stood up and exclaimed, "Let anyone who thirsts come to me and drink. As scripture says:
Rivers of living water will flow from within him who believes in me."

He said this in reference to the Spirit that those who came to believe in him were to receive. There was, of course, no Spirit yet, because Jesus had not yet been glorified.—The Gospel of the Lord. ℟. **Praise to you, Lord Jesus Christ.** → No. 15, p. 18

PRAYER OVER THE OFFERINGS [Manifestation of Salvation]

Pour out upon these gifts the blessing of your Spirit, we pray, O Lord,
so that through them your Church may be imbued with such love
that the truth of your saving mystery
may shine forth for the whole world.
Through Christ our Lord.
℟. **Amen.** → Pref. P 28, p. 416

When the Roman Canon is used, the proper form of the Communicantes *(In communion with those) is said.*

COMMUNION ANT. Jn 7:37   [Thirst for the Spirit]

On the last day of the festival, Jesus stood and cried out: If anyone is thirsty, let him come to me and drink, alleluia. ↓

PRAYER AFTER COMMUNION   [Aflame with the Spirit]

May these gifts we have consumed
benefit us, O Lord,
that we may always be aflame with the same Spirit,
whom you wondrously poured out on your Apostles.
Through Christ our Lord.
℟. **Amen.** → No. 30, p. 77

Optional Solemn Blessings, p. 97, and Prayers over the People, p. 105

(At the end of the Dismissal the people respond: **"Thanks be to God, alleluia, alleluia."**)

AT THE VIGIL MASS (May 27) (Extended Form)

ENTRANCE ANT. Rom 5:5; cf. 8:11   [Love-Imparting Spirit]

The love of God has been poured into our hearts through the Spirit of God dwelling within us, alleluia.

➙ No. 2, p. 10

Grant, we pray, almighty God,
that the splendor of your glory
may shine forth upon us
and that, by the bright rays of the Holy Spirit,
the light of your light may confirm the hearts
of those born again by your grace.
Through our Lord Jesus Christ, your Son,
who lives and reigns with you in the unity of the Holy
    Spirit,
God, for ever and ever. ℟. **Amen.** ↓

Then the Priest may address the people in these or similar words:

Dear brethren (brothers and sisters), [God's Great Deeds]
we have now begun our Pentecost Vigil,
after the example of the Apostles and disciples,
who with Mary, the Mother of Jesus, persevered in
    prayer,
awaiting the Spirit promised by the Lord;
like them, let us, too, listen with quiet hearts to the
    Word of God.
Let us meditate on how many great deeds
God in times past did for his people
and let us pray that the Holy Spirit,
whom the Father sent as the first fruits for those who
    believe,
may bring to perfection his work in the world.

FIRST READING

See p. 399, A. ↓

RESPONSORIAL PSALM Ps 33   [God's People]

R/. **Blessed the people the Lord has chosen to be his own.**

The LORD brings to nought the plans of nations;
    he foils the designs of peoples.
But the plan of the LORD stands forever;
    the design of his heart, through all generations.—R/.

Blessed the nation whose God is the LORD,
    the people he has chosen for his own inheritance.
From heaven the LORD looks down;
    he sees all mankind.—R/.

From his fixed throne he beholds
    all who dwell on the earth,
He who fashioned the heart of each,
    he who knows all their works.—R/. ↓

All rise.

PRAYER   [Church Formed as One]
Let us pray.

Grant, we pray, almighty God,
that your Church may always remain that holy people,
formed as one by the unity of Father, Son and Holy
    Spirit,
which manifests to the world
the Sacrament of your holiness and unity
and leads it to the perfection of your charity.
Through Christ our Lord.
R/. **Amen.** ↓

SECOND READING
See p. 400, B. ↓

RESPONSORIAL PSALM Dn 3   [Praiseworthy and Exalted]

R/. **Glory and praise for ever!**

"Blessed are you, O Lord, the God of our fathers,
    praiseworthy and exalted above all forever;

And blessed is your holy and glorious name,
   praiseworthy and exalted above all for all ages."—R̷.

"Blessed are you in the temple of your holy glory,
   praiseworthy and glorious above all forever."—R̷.

"Blessed are you on the throne of your Kingdom,
   praiseworthy and exalted above all forever."—R̷.

"Blessed are you who look into the depths
   from your throne upon the cherubim,
   praiseworthy and exalted above all forever."—R̷.

"Blessed are you in the firmament of heaven,
   praiseworthy and glorious forever."—R̷. ↓

OR

Ps 19   [The Lord's Words]

R̷. **Lord, you have the words of everlasting life.**

The law of the LORD is perfect,
   refreshing the soul;
The decree of the LORD is trustworthy,
   giving wisdom to the simple.—R̷.

The precepts of the LORD are right,
   rejoicing the heart;
The command of the LORD is clear,
   enlightening the eye.—R̷.

The fear of the LORD is pure,
   enduring forever;
The ordinances of the LORD are true,
   all of them just.—R̷.

They are more precious than gold,
   than a heap of purest gold;
Sweeter also than syrup
   or honey from the comb.—R̷.

All rise.

PRAYER   [Fire of the Spirit]

Let us pray.

O God, who in fire and lightning
gave the ancient Law to Moses on Mount Sinai
and on this day manifested the new covenant
in the fire of the Spirit,
grant, we pray,
that we may always be aflame with that same Spirit
whom you wondrously poured out on your Apostles,
and that the new Israel,
gathered from every people,
may receive with rejoicing
the eternal commandment of your love.
Through Christ our Lord.

℟. **Amen.** ↓

THIRD READING

See p. 401, C. ↓

RESPONSORIAL PSALM Ps 107   [God's Love]

℟. **Give thanks to the Lord; his love is everlasting.**

Or: ℟. **Alleluia.**

Let the redeemed of the LORD say,
      those whom he has redeemed from the hand of the
            foe
And gathered from the lands,
      from the east and the west, from the north and the
            south.—℟.

They went astray in the desert wilderness;
      the way to an inhabited city they did not find.
Hungry and thirsty,
      their life was wasting away within them.—℟.

They cried to the LORD in their distress;
      from their straits he rescued them.
And he led them by a direct way
      to reach an inhabited city.—℟.

Let them give thanks to the LORD for his mercy
    and his wondrous deeds to the children of men,
Because he satisfied the longing soul
    and filled the hungry soul with good things.—℟.

All rise.

PRAYER   [God Restores]

Let us pray.

Lord, God of power,
who restore what has fallen
and preserve what you have restored,
increase, we pray, the peoples
to be renewed by the sanctification of your name,
that all who are washed clean by holy Baptism
may always be directed by your prompting.
Through Christ our Lord.
℟. **Amen.** ↓

OR

O God, who have brought us to rebirth by the word of
    life,
pour out upon us your Holy Spirit,
that, walking in oneness of faith,
we may attain in our flesh
the incorruptible glory of the resurrection.
Through Christ our Lord.
℟. **Amen.** ↓

OR

May your people exult for ever, O God,
in renewed youthfulness of spirit,
so that, rejoicing now in the restored glory of our
    adoption,
we may look forward in confident hope
to the rejoicing of the day of resurrection.
Through Christ our Lord.
℟. **Amen.** ↓

FOURTH READING

See p. 402, D. ↓

RESPONSORIAL PSALM Ps 104   [Send Out Your Spirit]

See p. 403. ↓

All rise.

PRAYER   [Witnesses]

Let us pray.

Fulfill for us your gracious promise,
O Lord, we pray, so that by his coming
the Holy Spirit may make us witnesses before the
    world
to the Gospel of our Lord Jesus Christ.
Who lives and reigns for ever and ever.
℟. **Amen.** ↓

Then the Priest intones the hymn Gloria in excelsis Deo *(Glory
to God in the highest).*

COLLECT   [Heavenly Grace]

Almighty ever-living God,
who willed the Paschal Mystery
to be encompassed as a sign in fifty days,
grant that from out of the scattered nations
the confusion of many tongues
may be gathered by heavenly grace
into one great confession of your name.
Through our Lord Jesus Christ, your Son,
who lives and reigns with you in the unity of the Holy
    Spirit,
God, for ever and ever. ℟. **Amen.** ↓

EPISTLE

See p. 404, Second Reading.

The Mass continues as in the Simple Form (pp. 404-405).

———————

AT THE MASS DURING THE DAY

ENTRANCE ANT. Wis 1:7   [The Spirit in the World]

The Spirit of the Lord has filled the whole world and that which contains all things understands what is said, alleluia.

OR Rom 5:5; cf. 8:11   [God's Love for Us]

The love of God has been poured into our hearts through the Spirit of God dwelling within us, alleluia.
→ No. 2, p. 10

COLLECT   [Gifts of the Spirit]

O God, who by the mystery of today's great feast
sanctify your whole Church in every people and nation,
pour out, we pray, the gifts of the Holy Spirit
across the face of the earth
and, with the divine grace that was at work
when the Gospel was first proclaimed,
fill now once more the hearts of believers.
Through our Lord Jesus Christ, your Son,
who lives and reigns with you in the unity of the Holy
    Spirit,
God, for ever and ever. ℟. **Amen.** ↓

FIRST READING Acts 2:1-11   [Coming of the Spirit]

As promised by Jesus, the Holy Spirit fills the faithful and, inspired, they proclaim the good news.

A reading from the Acts of the Apostles

WHEN the time for Pentecost was fulfilled, they were all in one place together. And suddenly there came from the sky a noise like a strong driving wind, and it filled the entire house in which they were. Then there appeared to them tongues as of fire, which parted and came to rest on each of them. And they were all filled with the Holy Spirit and began to speak in different tongues, as the Spirit enabled them to proclaim.

Now there were devout Jews from every nation under heaven staying in Jerusalem. At this sound, they gathered in a large crowd, but they were confused because each one heard them speaking in his own language. They were astounded, and in amazement they asked, "Are not all these people who are speaking Galileans? Then how does each of us hear them in his native language? We are Parthians, Medes, and Elamites, inhabitants of Mesopotamia, Judea and Cappadocia, Pontus and Asia, Phrygia and Pamphylia, Egypt, and the districts of Libya near Cyrene, as well as travelers from Rome, both Jews and converts to Judaism, Cretans and Arabs, yet we hear them speaking in our own tongues of the mighty acts of God."—The word of the Lord. ℟. **Thanks be to God.** ↓

RESPONSORIAL PSALM Ps 104   [Renewal by the Spirit]

℟. Lord, send out your Spir - it, and re-new the face of the earth.

Or: ℟. **Alleluia.**

Bless the LORD, O my soul!
    O LORD, my God, you are great indeed!
How manifold are your works, O LORD!
    the earth is full of your creatures.

℟. **Lord, send out your Spirit, and renew the face of the earth.**

Or: ℟. **Alleluia.**

May the glory of the LORD endure forever,
    may the LORD be glad in his works!
Pleasing to him be my theme;
    I will be glad in the LORD.

℟. **Lord, send out your Spirit, and renew the face of the earth.**

Or: ℟. **Alleluia.**

If you take away their breath, they perish
 and return to their dust.
When you send forth your spirit, they are created,
 and you renew the face of the earth.

℟. **Lord, send out your Spirit, and renew the face of
the earth.**

Or: ℟. **Alleluia.**↓

SECOND READING 1 Cor 12:3b-7, 12-13   [Grace of the Spirit]

 **The gifts of the Spirit are not exclusive but for all. The Spirit
brings a radical uniting that overcomes all distinctions.**

A reading from the first Letter of Saint Paul
to the Corinthians

BROTHERS and sisters: No one can say: "Jesus is
Lord," except by the Holy Spirit.

 There are different kinds of spiritual gifts but the same
Spirit; there are different forms of service but the same
Lord; there are different workings but the same God who
produces all of them in everyone. To each individual the
manifestation of the Spirit is given for some benefit.

 As a body is one though it has many parts, and all the
parts of the body, though many, are one body, so also
Christ. For in one Spirit we were all baptized into one
body, whether Jews or Greeks, slaves or free persons,
and we are all given to drink of one Spirit.—The word of
the Lord. ℟. **Thanks be to God.** ↓

SEQUENCE *(Veni, Sancte Spiritus)* [Come, Holy Spirit]

 Come, Holy Spirit, come!
 And from your celestial home
  Shed a ray of light divine!
 Come, Father of the poor!
 Come, source of all our store!
  Come, within our bosoms shine!
 You, of comforters the best;
 You, the soul's most welcome guest;
  Sweet refreshment here below;

In our labor, rest most sweet;
Grateful coolness in the heat;
  Solace in the midst of woe.
O most blessed Light divine,
Shine within these hearts of yours,
  And our inmost being fill!
Where you are not, we have naught,
Nothing good in deed or thought,
  Nothing free from taint of ill.
Heal our wounds, our strength renew;
On our dryness pour your dew;
  Wash the stains of guilt away:
Bend the stubborn heart and will;
Melt the frozen, warm the chill;
  Guide the steps that go astray.
On the faithful, who adore
And confess you, evermore
  In your sevenfold gift descend;
Give them virtue's sure reward;
Give them your salvation, Lord;
  Give them joys that never end. Amen.
  Alleluia. ↓

ALLELUIA   [Fire of God's Love]
℟. Alleluia, alleluia.
Come, Holy Spirit, fill the hearts of your faithful
and kindle in them the fire of your love.
℟. Alleluia, alleluia. ↓

GOSPEL Jn 20:19-23   [Christ Imparts the Spirit]
    Jesus gives the blessing of peace and bestows his author-
    ity on the disciples as he confers on them the Holy Spirit.

℣. The Lord be with you. ℟. **And with your spirit.**
✠ A reading from the holy Gospel according to John.
℟. **Glory to you, O Lord.**

O N the evening of that first day of the week, when the
  doors were locked, where the disciples were, for fear

of the Jews, Jesus came and stood in their midst and said
to them, "Peace be with you." When he had said this, he
showed them his hands and his side. The disciples
rejoiced when they saw the Lord. Jesus said to them
again, "Peace be with you. As the Father has sent me, so
I send you." And when he had said this, he breathed on
them and said to them, "Receive the Holy Spirit. Whose
sins you forgive are forgiven them, and whose sins you
retain are retained."—The Gospel of the Lord. ℟. **Praise
to you, Lord Jesus Christ.**   → No. 15, p. 18

PRAYER OVER THE OFFERINGS   [All Truth]

Grant, we pray, O Lord,
that, as promised by your Son,
the Holy Spirit may reveal to us more abundantly
the hidden mystery of this sacrifice
and graciously lead us into all truth.
Through Christ our Lord. ℟. **Amen.** ↓

PREFACE (P 28)   [Coming of the Spirit]

℣. The Lord be with you. ℟. **And with your spirit.**
℣. Lift up your hearts. ℟. **We lift them up to the Lord.**
℣. Let us give thanks to the Lord our God. ℟. **It is right
and just.**

It is truly right and just, our duty and our salvation,
always and everywhere to give you thanks,
Lord, holy Father, almighty and eternal God.

For, bringing your Paschal Mystery to completion,
you bestowed the Holy Spirit today
on those you made your adopted children
by uniting them to your Only Begotten Son.
This same Spirit, as the Church came to birth,
opened to all peoples the knowledge of God
and brought together the many languages of the earth
in profession of the one faith.

Therefore, overcome with paschal joy,
every land, every people exults in your praise
and even the heavenly Powers, with the angelic hosts,
sing together the unending hymn of your glory,
as they acclaim: ➜ No. 23, p. 23

When the Roman Canon is used, the proper form of the Communicantes *(In communion with those) is said.*

COMMUNION ANT. Acts 2:4, 11   [Filled with the Spirit]
They were all filled with the Holy Spirit and spoke of the marvels of God, alleluia. ↓

PRAYER AFTER COMMUNION   [Safeguard Grace]
O God, who bestow heavenly gifts upon your Church,
safeguard, we pray, the grace you have given,
that the gift of the Holy Spirit poured out upon her
may retain all its force
and that this spiritual food
may gain her abundance of eternal redemption.
Through Christ our Lord.
℟. **Amen.**   ➜ No. 30, p. 77

Optional Solemn Blessings, p. 97, and Prayers over the People, p. 105

(At the end of the Dismissal the people respond: **"Thanks be to God, alleluia, alleluia."***)*

With Easter Time now concluded, the paschal candle is extinguished. It is desirable to keep the paschal candle in the baptistery with due honor so that it is lit at the celebration of Baptism and the candles of those baptized are lit from it.

*"Blest be God the Father, and the Only Begotten
Son of God, and also the Holy Spirit."*

JUNE 4

THE MOST HOLY TRINITY

Solemnity

ENTRANCE ANT. [Blessed Trinity]

Blest be God the Father, and the Only Begotten Son of God, and also the Holy Spirit, for he has shown us his merciful love. → No. 2, p. 10

COLLECT [Witnessing to the Trinity]

God our Father, who by sending into the world
the Word of truth and the Spirit of sanctification
made known to the human race your wondrous mystery,
grant us, we pray, that in professing the true faith,
we may acknowledge the Trinity of eternal glory
and adore your Unity, powerful in majesty.
Through our Lord Jesus Christ, your Son,
who lives and reigns with you in the unity of the Holy
    Spirit,
God, for ever and ever. ℟. **Amen.** ↓

FIRST READING Ex 34:4b-6, 8-9 [The One God]

Moses takes two stone tablets up on Mount Sinai. He
bows down in worship, asking the Lord to be with his people and to pardon their sins and offenses.

418

A reading from the Book of Exodus

EARLY in the morning Moses went up Mount Sinai as the LORD had commanded him, taking along the two stone tablets.

Having come down in a cloud, the LORD stood with him there and proclaimed his name, "LORD." Thus the LORD passed before him and cried out, "The LORD, the LORD, a merciful and gracious God, slow to anger and rich in kindness and fidelity." Moses at once bowed down to the ground in worship. Then he said, "If I find favor with you, O LORD, do come along in our company. This is indeed a stiff-necked people; yet pardon our wickedness and sins, and receive us as your own."
—The word of the Lord. ℟. **Thanks be to God.** ↓

RESPONSORIAL PSALM Dn 3   [Praise the Lord]

℟. Glo - ry and praise for   ev - er!

Blessed are you, O Lord, the God of our fathers,
    praiseworthy and exalted above all forever;
and blessed is your holy and glorious name,
    praiseworthy and exalted above all for all ages.

℟. **Glory and praise for ever!**

Blessed are you in the temple of your holy glory,
    praiseworthy and glorious above all forever.

℟. **Glory and praise for ever!**

Blessed are you on the throne of your kingdom,
    praiseworthy and exalted above all forever.

℟. **Glory and praise for ever!**

Blessed are you who look into the depths
    from your throne upon the cherubim,
    praiseworthy and exalted above all forever.

℟. **Glory and praise for ever!** ↓

SECOND READING 2 Cor 13:11-13

[God's Grace, Love, and Fidelity]

Paul encourages the Corinthians to live in harmony, peace, and love in the fellowship of the Holy Spirit, that is, showing the love of God among them.

A reading from the second Letter of Saint Paul
to the Corinthians

BROTHERS and sisters, rejoice. Mend your ways, encourage one another, agree with one another, live in peace, and the God of love and peace will be with you. Greet one another with a holy kiss. All the holy ones greet you.

The grace of the Lord Jesus Christ and the love of God and the fellowship of the Holy Spirit be with all of you.—The word of the Lord. ℟. **Thanks be to God.** ↓

ALLELUIA Cf. Rv 1:8   [Triune God]

℟. **Alleluia, alleluia.**
Glory to the Father, the Son, and the Holy Spirit:
to God who is, who was, and who is to come.
℟. **Alleluia, alleluia.** ↓

GOSPEL Jn 3:16-18   [God's Love]

God sent his Son into the world that whoever would believe would therefore have eternal life.

℣. The Lord be with you. ℟. **And with your spirit.**
✠ A reading from the holy Gospel according to John.
℟. **Glory to you, O Lord.**

GOD so loved the world that he gave his only Son, so that everyone who believes in him might not perish but might have eternal life. For God did not send his Son into the world to condemn the world, but that the world might be saved through him. Whoever believes in him will not be condemned, but whoever does not believe has already been condemned, because he has not believed in the name of the only

Son of God.—The Gospel of the Lord. ℟. **Praise to you, Lord Jesus Christ.**   ➜ No. 15, p. 18

PRAYER OVER THE OFFERINGS   [Eternal Offering]

Sanctify by the invocation of your name,
we pray, O Lord our God,
this oblation of our service,
and by it make of us an eternal offering to you.
Through Christ our Lord. ℟. **Amen.** ↓

PREFACE (P 43)   [Mystery of the One Godhead]

℣. The Lord be with you. ℟. **And with your spirit.**
℣. Lift up your hearts. ℟. **We lift them up to the Lord.**
℣. Let us give thanks to the Lord our God. ℟. **It is right and just.**

It is truly right and just, our duty and our salvation,
always and everywhere to give you thanks,
Lord, holy Father, almighty and eternal God.

For with your Only Begotten Son and the Holy Spirit
you are one God, one Lord:
not in the unity of a single person,
but in a Trinity of one substance.

For what you have revealed to us of your glory
we believe equally of your Son
and of the Holy Spirit,
so that, in the confessing of the true and eternal Godhead,
you might be adored in what is proper to each Person,
their unity in substance,
and their equality in majesty.

For this is praised by Angels and Archangels,
Cherubim, too, and Seraphim,
who never cease to cry out each day,
as with one voice they acclaim: ➜ No. 23, p. 23

COMMUNION ANT. Gal 4:6   [Abba, Father]

**Since you are children of God, God has sent into your
hearts the Spirit of his Son, the Spirit who cries out:
Abba, Father.** ↓

PRAYER AFTER COMMUNION   [Eternal Trinity]

May receiving this Sacrament, O Lord our God,
bring us health of body and soul,
as we confess your eternal holy Trinity and undivided
   Unity.
Through Christ our Lord.
℟. **Amen.**   ➜ No. 30, p. 77

Optional Solemn Blessings, p. 97, and Prayers over the People, p. 105

"This is my Body. . . ."

JUNE 11
THE MOST HOLY BODY AND BLOOD
OF CHRIST
(CORPUS CHRISTI)
Solemnity

ENTRANCE ANT. Cf. Ps 81 (80):17 [Finest Wheat and Honey]

**He fed them with the finest wheat and satisfied them
with honey from the rock.**   ➜ No. 2, p. 10

COLLECT [Memorial of Christ's Passion]

O God, who in this wonderful Sacrament
have left us a memorial of your Passion,
grant us, we pray,
so to revere the sacred mysteries of your Body and
  Blood
that we may always experience in ourselves
the fruits of your redemption.
Who live and reign with God the Father
in the unity of the Holy Spirit,
God, for ever and ever. ℟. **Amen.** ↓

FIRST READING Dt 8:2-3, 14b-16a [Manna in the Desert]

Moses reminds the Israelites that although God let them
hunger, still he fed them with manna, a food unknown. He
brought them out of the slavery of Egypt and cared for them.

A reading from the Book of Deuteronomy

MOSES said to the people: "Remember how for
forty years now the LORD, your God, has directed
all your journeying in the desert, so as to test you by
affliction and find out whether or not it was your
intention to keep his commandments. He therefore let
you be afflicted with hunger, and then fed you with
manna, a food unknown to you and your fathers, in
order to show you that not by bread alone does one
live, but by every word that comes forth from the
mouth of the LORD.

"Do not forget the LORD, your God, who brought you
out of the land of Egypt, that place of slavery; who
guided you through the vast and terrible desert with its
saraph serpents and scorpions, its parched and water-
less ground; who brought forth water for you from the
flinty rock and fed you in the desert with manna, a
food unknown to your fathers."—The word of the
Lord. ℟. **Thanks be to God.** ↓

RESPONSORIAL PSALM Ps 147   [The Best of Wheat]

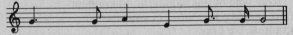

℟. **Praise   the Lord,   Je - ru - sa - lem.**

Or: ℟. **Alleluia.**

Glorify the LORD, O Jerusalem;
  praise your God, O Zion.
For he has strengthened the bars of your gates;
  he has blessed your children within you.

℟. **Praise the Lord, Jerusalem.**
Or: ℟. **Alleluia.**

He has granted peace in your borders;
  with the best of wheat he fills you.
He sends forth his command to the earth;
  swiftly runs his word!

℟. **Praise the Lord, Jerusalem.**
Or: ℟. **Alleluia.**

He has proclaimed his word to Jacob,
  his statutes and his ordinances to Israel.
He has not done thus for any other nation;
  his ordinances he has not made known to them.
    Alleluia.

℟. **Praise the Lord, Jerusalem.**
Or: ℟. **Alleluia.** ↓

SECOND READING 1 Cor 10:16-17   [Body and Blood]
In the one bread and sharing the one cup, we are united in the Body and Blood of Jesus. We, though many, are still one body in Jesus.

A reading from the first Letter of Saint Paul
to the Corinthians

Brothers and sisters: The cup of blessing that we bless, is it not a participation in the blood of Christ?

The bread that we break, is it not a participation in the body of Christ? Because the loaf of bread is one, we, though many, are one body, for we all partake of the one loaf.—The word of the Lord. ℟. **Thanks be to God.** ↓

SEQUENCE *(Lauda Sion)*   [Praise of the Eucharist]

The Sequence Laud, O Zion (Lauda Sion), *or the Shorter Form beginning with the verse* Lo! the angel's food is given, *may be sung optionally before the Alleluia.*

Laud, O Zion, your salvation,
Laud with hymns of exultation,
  Christ, your king and shepherd true:

Bring him all the praise you know,
He is more than you bestow.
  Never can you reach his due.

Special theme for glad thanksgiving
Is the quick'ning and the living
  Bread today before you set:

From his hands of old partaken,
As we know, by faith unshaken,
  Where the Twelve at supper met.

Full and clear ring out your chanting,
Joy nor sweetest grace be wanting,
  From your heart let praises burst:

For today the feast is holden,
When the institution olden
  Of that supper was rehearsed.

Here the new law's new oblation,
By the new king's revelation,
  Ends the form of ancient rite:

Now the new the old effaces,
Truth away the shadow chases,
  Light dispels the gloom of night.

What he did at supper seated,
Christ ordained to be repeated,
  His memorial ne'er to cease:

And his rule for guidance taking,
Bread and wine we hallow, making
  Thus our sacrifice of peace.

This truth each Christian learns,
Bread into his flesh he turns,
  To his precious blood the wine:

Sight has fail'd, nor thought conceives,
But a dauntless faith believes,
  Resting on a pow'r divine.

Here beneath these signs are hidden
Priceless things to sense forbidden;
  Signs, not things are all we see:

Blood is poured and flesh is broken,

Yet in either wondrous token
 Christ entire we know to be.

Whoso of this food partakes,
Does not rend the Lord nor
  breaks;
 Christ is whole to all that
  taste:

Thousands are, as one, re-
  ceivers,
One, as thousands of be-
  lievers,
 Eats of him who cannot waste.

Bad and good the feast are
  sharing,
Of what divers dooms prepar-
  ing,
 Endless death, or endless life.

Life to these, to those damna-
  tion,
See how like participation
 Is with unlike issues rife.

When the sacrament is broken,
Doubt not, but believe 'tis spoken,
 That each sever'd outward
  token
 doth the very whole contain.

Nought the precious gift di-
  vides,
Breaking but the sign betides,
 Jesus still the same abides,
  still unbroken does remain.

The Shorter Form of the Sequence begins here.

Lo! the angel's food is given
To the pilgrim who has striven;
 See the children's bread from
  heaven,
  which on dogs may not be
  spent.

Truth the ancient types fulfilling,
Isaac bound, a victim willing,
 Paschal lamb, its lifeblood
  spilling,
 manna to the fathers sent.

Very bread, good shepherd,
  tend us,

Jesu, of your love befriend us,
 You refresh us, you defend us,
 Your eternal goodness send us
In the land of life to see.

You who all things can and
  know,
Who on earth such food bestow,
 Grant us with your saints,
  though lowest,
 Where the heav'nly feast you
  show,
Fellow heirs and guests to be.
 Amen. Alleluia. ↓

ALLELUIA Jn 6:51   [Bread from Heaven]

℟. **Alleluia, alleluia.** •
I am the living bread that came down from heaven,
 says the Lord;

whoever eats this bread will live forever.
℞. **Alleluia, alleluia.** ↓

GOSPEL Jn 6:51-58   [Living Bread]
> Jesus speaks of his Body and Blood in the Holy Eucharist.
> Whoever receives the Holy Eucharist will be raised up on
> the last day; whoever eats this bread will live forever.

℣. The Lord be with you. ℞. **And with your spirit.**
✝ A reading from the holy Gospel according to John.
℞. **Glory to you, O Lord.**

JESUS said to the Jewish crowds: "I am the living
bread that came down from heaven; whoever eats
this bread will live forever; and the bread that I will
give is my flesh for the life of the world."
  The Jews quarreled among themselves, saying, "How
can this man give us his flesh to eat?" Jesus said to them,
"Amen, amen, I say to you, unless you eat the flesh of the
Son of Man and drink his blood, you do not have life
within you. Whoever eats my flesh and drinks my blood
has eternal life, and I will raise him on the last day. For
my flesh is true food, and my blood is true drink.
Whoever eats my flesh and drinks my blood remains in
me, and I in him. Just as the living Father sent me and I
have life because of the Father, so also the one who feeds
on me will have life because of me. This is the bread that
came down from heaven. Unlike your ancestors who ate
and still died, whoever eats this bread will live forever."—
The Gospel of the Lord. ℞. **Praise to you, Lord Jesus
Christ.**
                                            → No. 15, p. 18

PRAYER OVER THE OFFERINGS   [Unity and Peace]
Grant your Church, O Lord, we pray,
the gifts of unity and peace,
whose signs are to be seen in mystery
in the offerings we here present.
Through Christ our Lord.
℞. **Amen.**   → No. 21, p. 22 (Pref. P 47-48)

COMMUNION ANT. Jn 6:57   [Eucharistic Life]

Whoever eats my flesh and drinks my blood remains in me and I in him, says the Lord. ↓

PRAYER AFTER COMMUNION   [Divine Life]

Grant, O Lord, we pray,
that we may delight for all eternity
in that share in your divine life,
which is foreshadowed in the present age
by our reception of your precious Body and Blood.
Who live and reign for ever and ever.
℞. **Amen.**   → No. 30, p. 77

Optional Solemn Blessings, p. 97, and Prayers over the People, p. 105

*"Without cost you have received;
without cost you are to give."*

JUNE 18

11th SUNDAY IN ORDINARY TIME

ENTRANCE ANT. Cf. Ps 27 (26):7, 9   [Hear My Voice]

O Lord, hear my voice, for I have called to you; be my help. Do not abandon or forsake me, O God, my Savior!   → No. 2, p. 10

COLLECT   [Following God's Commands]

O God, strength of those who hope in you,
graciously hear our pleas,
and, since without you mortal frailty can do nothing,
grant us always the help of your grace,
that in following your commands
we may please you by our resolve and our deeds.
Through our Lord Jesus Christ, your Son,
who lives and reigns with you in the unity of the Holy
  Spirit,
God, for ever and ever. ℟. **Amen.** ↓

FIRST READING Ex 19:2-6a   [A Holy Nation]

God assures the Israelites of his special concern for them. They are his people. He led them from Egypt and cared for them. They are to be a holy nation.

A reading from the book of Exodus

IN those days, the Israelites came to the desert of Sinai and pitched camp. While Israel was encamped here in front of the mountain, Moses went up the mountain to God. Then the Lord called to him and said, "Thus shall you say to the house of Jacob; tell the Israelites: You have seen for yourselves how I treated the Egyptians and how I bore you up on eagle wings and brought you here to myself. Therefore, if you hearken to my voice and keep my covenant, you shall be my special possession, dearer to me than all other people, though all the earth is mine. You shall be to me a kingdom of priests, a holy nation."—The word of the Lord.
℟. **Thanks be to God.** ↓

RESPONSORIAL PSALM Ps 100   [God's Kindness]

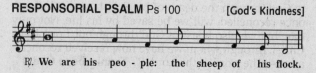

℟. We are his peo - ple: the sheep of his flock.

Sing joyfully to the LORD, all you lands;
  serve the LORD with gladness;
  come before him with joyful song.

℟. **We are his people: the sheep of his flock.**

Know that the LORD is God;
  he made us, his we are;
  his people, the flock he tends.

℟. **We are his people: the sheep of his flock.**

The LORD is good:
  his kindness endures forever,
  and his faithfulness, to all generations.

℟. **We are his people: the sheep of his flock.** ↓

SECOND READING Rom 5:6-11   [God's Love for Us]

God sent Jesus, his Son, into the world. Jesus showed his
extreme love for all human beings by offering his life for
them. Those who have been reconciled to God are to be
saved through Jesus' suffering and Death.

A reading from the Letter of Saint Paul to the Romans

BROTHERS and sisters: Christ, while we were still
helpless, yet died at the appointed time for the
ungodly. Indeed, only with difficulty does one die for a
just person, though perhaps for a good person one
might even find courage to die. But God proves his love
for us in that while we were still sinners Christ died for
us. How much more then, since we are now justified by
his blood, will we be saved through him from the wrath.
Indeed, if, while we were enemies, we were reconciled
to God through the death of his Son, how much more,
once reconciled, will we be saved by his life. Not only
that, but we also boast of God through our Lord Jesus
Christ, through whom we have now received reconciliation.—The word of the Lord. ℟. **Thanks be to God.** ↓

ALLELUIA Mk 1:15   [Repent and Believe]

℟. **Alleluia, alleluia.**
The kingdom of God is at hand.
Repent and believe in the Gospel.
℟. **Alleluia, alleluia.** ↓

GOSPEL Mt 9:36—10:8   [Commission of the Twelve]
Jesus felt compassion for the crowds and so sent the
Apostles to minister spiritually to them. During the Lord's
public ministry, this mission was confined to the people of
Israel. After his Resurrection, it was extended—under the
guidance of the Holy Spirit—to all people.

℣. The Lord be with you. ℟. **And with your spirit.**
✠ A reading from the holy Gospel according to Matthew.
℟. **Glory to you, O Lord**.

AT the sight of the crowds, Jesus' heart was moved
with pity for them because they were troubled
and abandoned, like sheep without a shepherd. Then
he said to his disciples, "The harvest is abundant but
the laborers are few; so ask the master of the harvest
to send out laborers for his harvest."

Then he summoned his twelve disciples and gave
them authority over unclean spirits to drive them out
and to cure every disease and every illness. The
names of the twelve apostles are these: first, Simon
called Peter, and his brother Andrew; James, the son
of Zebedee, and his brother John; Philip and
Bartholomew, Thomas and Matthew the tax collector;
James, the son of Alphaeus, and Thaddeus; Simon
from Cana, and Judas Iscariot who betrayed him.

Jesus sent out these twelve after instructing them
thus, "Do not go into pagan territory or enter a
Samaritan town. Go rather to the lost sheep of the
house of Israel. As you go, make this proclamation:
'The kingdom of heaven is at hand.' Cure the sick,

raise the dead, cleanse lepers, drive out demons. Without cost you have received; without cost you are to give."—The Gospel of the Lord. ℟. **Praise to you, Lord Jesus Christ.** → No. 15, p. 18

PRAYER OVER THE OFFERINGS [Needs of Human Nature]

O God, who in the offerings presented here
provide for the twofold needs of human nature,
nourishing us with food
and renewing us with your Sacrament,
grant, we pray,
that the sustenance they provide
may not fail us in body or in spirit.
Through Christ our Lord.
℟. **Amen.** → No. 21, p. 22 (Pref. P 29-36)

COMMUNION ANT. Ps 27 (26):4   [Living with the Lord]

There is one thing I ask of the Lord, only this do I seek: to live in the house of the Lord all the days of my life. ↓

OR Jn 17:11   [One with God]

Holy Father, keep in your name those you have given me, that they may be one as we are one, says the Lord. ↓

PRAYER AFTER COMMUNION   [Church Unity]

As this reception of your Holy Communion, O Lord,
foreshadows the union of the faithful in you,
so may it bring about unity in your Church.
Through Christ our Lord.
℟. **Amen.** → No. 30, p. 77

Optional Solemn Blessings, p. 97, and Prayers over the People, p. 105

———————————

"What I say to you in the darkness, speak in the light."

JUNE 25

12th SUNDAY IN ORDINARY TIME

ENTRANCE ANT. Cf. Ps 28 (27):8-9   [Saving Refuge]

The Lord is the strength of his people, a saving refuge for the one he has anointed. Save your people, Lord, and bless your heritage, and govern them for ever.

➔ No. 2, p. 10

COLLECT   [Foundation of God's Love]

Grant, O Lord,
that we may always revere and love your holy name,
for you never deprive of your guidance
those you set firm on the foundation of your love.
Through our Lord Jesus Christ, your Son,
who lives and reigns with you in the unity of the Holy
   Spirit,
God, for ever and ever. ℟. **Amen.** ↓

FIRST READING Jer 20:10-13   [The Lord Our Champion]

Jeremiah, a man chosen by God, tells how threatened his life is. His enemies lurk on every side, anxious to take vengeance on him. The Lord will protect him and confound the evildoers.

A reading from the Book of the Prophet Jeremiah

JEREMIAH said:
"Yes, I hear the whisperings of many:
    'Terror on every side!
      Denounce! let us denounce him!'
All those who were my friends
    are on the watch for any misstep of mine.
'Perhaps he will be trapped; then we can prevail,
    and take our vengeance on him.'
But the LORD is with me, like a mighty champion:
    my persecutors will stumble, they will not triumph.
In their failure they will be put to utter shame,
    to lasting, unforgettable confusion.
O LORD of hosts, you who test the just,
    who probe mind and heart,
let me witness the vengeance you take on them,
    for to you I have entrusted my cause.
Sing to the LORD,
    praise the LORD,
for he has rescued the life of the poor
    from the power of the wicked!"
The word of the Lord. ℟. **Thanks be to God.** ↓

RESPONSORIAL PSALM Ps 69   [The Lord's Kindness]

℟. Lord, in your great love, an - swer me.

For your sake I bear insult,
    and shame covers my face.
I have become an outcast to my brothers,
    a stranger to my mother's children,
because zeal for your house consumes me,
    and the insults of those who blaspheme you fall
      upon me.

℟. **Lord, in your great love, answer me.**

I pray to you, O LORD,
    for the time of your favor, O God!
In your great kindness answer me
    with your constant help.
Answer me, O LORD, for bounteous is your kindness;
    in your great mercy turn toward me.

℟. **Lord, in your great love, answer me.**

"See, you lowly ones, and be glad;
    you who seek God, may your hearts revive!
For the LORD hears the poor,
    and his own who are in bonds he spurns not.
Let the heavens and the earth praise him,
    the seas and whatever moves in them!"

℟. **Lord, in your great love, answer me.** ↓

SECOND READING Rom 5:12-15   [The Grace of God]

Through the sin of Adam, death and the consequences of sin came into the world. But through Jesus Christ, the grace of God abounds in the world.

A reading from the Letter of Saint Paul to the Romans

BROTHERS and sisters: Through one man sin entered the world, and through sin, death, and thus death came to all men, inasmuch as all sinned—for up to the time of the law, sin was in the world, though sin is not accounted when there is no law. But death reigned from Adam to Moses, even over those who did not sin after the pattern of the trespass of Adam, who is the type of the one who was to come.

But the gift is not like the transgression. For if by the transgression of the one the many died, how much more did the grace of God and the gracious gift of the one man Jesus Christ overflow for the many.—The word of the Lord. ℟. **Thanks be to God.** ↓

ALLELUIA Jn 15:26b, 27a   [God's Truth]

℟. **Alleluia, alleluia.**

The Spirit of truth will testify to me, says the Lord;
and you also will testify.

℟. **Alleluia, alleluia.** ↓

GOSPEL Mt 10:26-33   [Witnesses for Christ]

Jesus directs his Apostles to fear no human beings. All
truth will become known. He describes people's worth in
the eyes of God who knows all things. Whoever confesses Jesus before others will be acknowledged before God in
heaven.

℣. The Lord be with you. ℟. **And with your spirit.**

✠ A reading from the holy Gospel according to Matthew.

℟. **Glory to you, O Lord.**

JESUS said to the Twelve: "Fear no one. Nothing is
concealed that will not be revealed, nor secret that
will not be known. What I say to you in the darkness,
speak in the light; what you hear whispered, proclaim
on the housetops. And do not be afraid of those who
kill the body but cannot kill the soul; rather, be afraid
of the one who can destroy both soul and body in
Gehenna. Are not two sparrows sold for a small coin?
Yet not one of them falls to the ground without your
Father's knowledge. Even all the hairs of your head
are counted. So do not be afraid; you are worth more
than many sparrows. Everyone who acknowledges
me before others I will acknowledge before my heavenly Father. But whoever denies me before others, I
will deny before my heavenly Father."—The Gospel of
the Lord. ℟. **Praise to you, Lord Jesus Christ.**

→ No. 15, p. 18

PRAYER OVER THE OFFERINGS   [Pleasing Offering]

Receive, O Lord, the sacrifice of conciliation and
praise

and grant that, cleansed by its action,
we may make offering of a heart pleasing to you.
Through Christ our Lord.
℟. **Amen.**   → No. 21, p. 22 (Pref. P 29-36)

COMMUNION ANT. Ps 145 (144):15   [Divine Food]
**The eyes of all look to you, Lord, and you give them
their food in due season.** ↓

OR Jn 10:11, 15   [The Good Shepherd]
**I am the Good Shepherd, and I lay down my life for
my sheep, says the Lord.** ↓

PRAYER AFTER COMMUNION   [Pledge of Redemption]
Renewed and nourished
by the Sacred Body and Precious Blood of your Son,
we ask of your mercy, O Lord,
that what we celebrate with constant devotion
may be our sure pledge of redemption.
Through Christ our Lord.
℟. **Amen.**   → No. 30, p. 77

Optional Solemn Blessings, p. 97, and Prayers over the People, p. 105

"Whoever does not take up his cross and follow after me is not worthy of me."

JULY 2

13th SUNDAY IN ORDINARY TIME

ENTRANCE ANT. Ps 47 (46):2   **[Shouts of Joy]**

All peoples, clap your hands. Cry to God with shouts of joy! → No. 2, p. 10

COLLECT   **[Children of Light]**

O God, who through the grace of adoption
chose us to be children of light,
grant, we pray,
that we may not be wrapped in the darkness of error
but always be seen to stand in the bright light of truth.
Through our Lord Jesus Christ, your Son,
who lives and reigns with you in the unity of the Holy
   Spirit,
God, for ever and ever. ℟. **Amen.** ↓

FIRST READING 2 Kgs 4:8-11, 14-16a
      [Rewards of Hospitality]
A woman in Shunem recognized Elisha as a holy man. This
woman and her husband fixed a guest room for Elisha

438

whenever he was passing by. Gehazi confided to Elisha that the wife was barren, whereupon Elisha promised that within a year she would have a son.

A reading from the second Book of Kings

ONE day Elisha came to Shunem, where there was a woman of influence, who urged him to dine with her. Afterward, whenever he passed by, he used to stop there to dine. So she said to her husband, "I know that he is a holy man of God. Since he visits us often, let us arrange a little room on the roof and furnish it for him with a bed, table, chair, and lamp, so that when he comes to us he can stay there." Sometime later Elisha arrived and stayed in the room overnight.

Later Elisha asked, "Can something be done for her?" His servant Gehazi answered, "Yes! She has no son, and her husband is getting on in years." Elisha said, "Call her." When the woman had been called and stood at the door, Elisha promised, "This time next year you will be fondling a baby son."—The word of the Lord. ℟. **Thanks be to God.** ↓

RESPONSORIAL PSALM Ps 89   [Eternal Gratitude]

℟. For ev - er I will sing the good-ness of the Lord.

The promises of the LORD I will sing forever;
    through all generations my mouth shall proclaim
      your faithfulness.
For you have said, "My kindness is established for-
    ever";
    in heaven you have confirmed your faithfulness.

℟. **For ever I will sing the goodness of the Lord.**

Blessed the people who know the joyful shout;
   in the light of your countenance, O LORD, they walk.
At your name they rejoice all the day,
   and through your justice they are exalted.

℟. **For ever I will sing the goodness of the Lord.**

For you are the splendor of their strength,
   and by your favor our horn is exalted.
For to the LORD belongs our shield,
   and to the Holy One of Israel, our king.

℟. **For ever I will sing the goodness of the Lord.** ↓

SECOND READING Rom 6:3-4, 8-11   [Baptized into Christ]

Through the waters of Baptism, we rise to a new life of grace in Jesus who was buried and rose from the dead. In the same way, we who were dead to sin become alive for God in Jesus.

A reading from the Letter of Saint Paul to the Romans

BROTHERS and sisters: Are you unaware that we who were baptized into Christ Jesus were baptized into his death? We were indeed buried with him through baptism into death, so that, just as Christ was raised from the dead by the glory of the Father, we too might live in newness of life.

If, then, we have died with Christ, we believe that we shall also live with him. We know that Christ, raised from the dead, dies no more; death no longer has power over him. As to his death, he died to sin once and for all; as to his life, he lives for God. Consequently, you too must think of yourselves as dead to sin and living for God in Christ Jesus.—The word of the Lord. ℟. **Thanks be to God.** ↓

ALLELUIA 1 Pt 2:9   [Praise God]

℟. **Alleluia, alleluia.**
You are a chosen race, a royal priesthood, a holy nation;

announce the praises of him who called you out of darkness into his wonderful light.
℟. **Alleluia, alleluia.** ↓

GOSPEL Mt 10:37-42   [Welcoming Christ's Workers]
To follow Jesus, we must be ready to give of ourselves totally.

℣. The Lord be with you. ℟. **And with your spirit.**
✛ A reading from the holy Gospel according to Matthew.
℟. **Glory to you, O Lord.**

JESUS said to his apostles: "Whoever loves father or mother more than me is not worthy of me, and whoever loves son or daughter more than me is not worthy of me; and whoever does not take up his cross and follow after me is not worthy of me. Whoever finds his life will lose it, and whoever loses his life for my sake will find it. Whoever receives you receives me, and whoever receives me receives the one who sent me.

"Whoever receives a prophet because he is a prophet will receive a prophet's reward, and whoever receives a righteous man because he is a righteous man will receive a righteous man's reward. And whoever gives only a cup of cold water to one of these little ones to drink because the little one is a disciple—amen, I say to you, he will surely not lose his reward."—The Gospel of the Lord. ℟. **Praise to you, Lord Jesus Christ.**

→ No. 15, p. 18

PRAYER OVER THE OFFERINGS   [Serving God]

O God, who graciously accomplish
the effects of your mysteries,
grant, we pray,
that the deeds by which we serve you
may be worthy of these sacred gifts.
Through Christ our Lord.
℟. **Amen.**   → No. 21, p. 22 (Pref. P 29-36)

COMMUNION ANT. Cf. Ps 103 (102):1   [Bless the Lord]

Bless the Lord, O my soul, and all within me, his holy name. ↓

OR Jn 17:20-21   [One in God]

O Father, I pray for them, that they may be one in us, that the world may believe that you have sent me, says the Lord. ↓

PRAYER AFTER COMMUNION   [Lasting Charity]

May this divine sacrifice we have offered and received
fill us with life, O Lord, we pray,
so that, bound to you in lasting charity,
we may bear fruit that lasts for ever.
Through Christ our Lord.
℟. **Amen.**   → No. 30, p. 77

Optional Solemn Blessings, p. 97, and Prayers over the People, p. 105

*"Come to me, all you who labor and are burdened,
and I will give you rest."*

JULY 9

14th SUNDAY IN ORDINARY TIME

ENTRANCE ANT. Cf. Ps 48 (47):10-11 [God's Love and Justice]
**Your merciful love, O God, we have received in the
midst of your temple. Your praise, O God, like your
name, reaches the ends of the earth; your right hand
is filled with saving justice.**   → No. 2, p. 10

COLLECT   [Holy Joy]
O God, who in the abasement of your Son
have raised up a fallen world,
fill your faithful with holy joy,
for on those you have rescued from slavery to sin
you bestow eternal gladness.
Through our Lord Jesus Christ, your Son,
who lives and reigns with you in the unity of the Holy
    Spirit,
God, for ever and ever. ℟. **Amen.** ↓

FIRST READING Zec 9:9-10　　[Portrait of the Messiah]

> Zechariah foretells the coming of the Messiah. Rejoicing shall come to Jerusalem. He shall bring peace to all nations and rule over them.

A reading from the Book of the Prophet Zechariah

THUS says the LORD:
　Rejoice heartily, O daughter Zion,
　　shout for joy, O daughter Jerusalem!
See, your king shall come to you;
　a just savior is he,
meek, and riding on an ass,
　on a colt, the foal of an ass.
He shall banish the chariot from Ephraim,
　and the horse from Jerusalem;
the warrior's bow shall be banished,
　and he shall proclaim peace to the nations.
His dominion shall be from sea to sea,
　and from the River to the ends of the earth.
The word of the Lord. ℟. **Thanks be to God.** ↓

RESPONSORIAL PSALM Ps 145　　[God's Mercy]

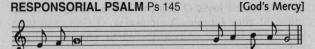

　℟. I will praise your name for ever,　my king and my God.

Or: ℟. **Alleluia.**

I will extol you, O my God and King,
　and I will bless your name forever and ever.
Every day will I bless you,
　and I will praise your name forever and ever.

℟. **I will praise your name for ever, my king and my
　God.**

Or: ℟. **Alleluia.**

The LORD is gracious and merciful,
　slow to anger and of great kindness.

The LORD is good to all
   and compassionate toward all his works.

℟. **I will praise your name for ever, my king and my God.**

Or: ℟. **Alleluia.**

Let all your works give you thanks, O LORD,
   and let your faithful ones bless you.
Let them discourse of the glory of your kingdom
   and speak of your might.

℟. **I will praise your name for ever, my king and my God.**

Or: ℟. **Alleluia.**

The LORD is faithful in all his words
   and holy in all his works.
The LORD lifts up all who are falling
   and raises up all who are bowed down.

℟. **I will praise your name for ever, my king and my God.**

Or: ℟. **Alleluia.** ↓

SECOND READING Rom 8:9, 11-13   [The Spirit of Christ]

Although we are both flesh and spirit, we must live according to the Spirit of God who dwells in us. This is a pledge for life if we die to sin and live by the Spirit.

A reading from the Letter of Saint Paul to the Romans

BROTHERS and sisters: You are not in the flesh; on the contrary, you are in the spirit, if only the Spirit of God dwells in you. Whoever does not have the Spirit of Christ does not belong to him. If the Spirit of the one who raised Jesus from the dead dwells in you, the one who raised Christ from the dead will give life to your mortal bodies also, through his Spirit that dwells in you. Consequently, brothers and sisters, we are not debtors to the flesh, to live according to the

flesh. For if you live according to the flesh, you will die, but if by the Spirit you put to death the deeds of the body, you will live.—The word of the Lord.
℟. **Thanks be to God.** ↓

ALLELUIA Cf. Mt 11:25   [Revealed to Little Ones]

℟. **Alleluia, alleluia.**
Blessed are you, Father, Lord of heaven and earth;
you have revealed to little ones the mysteries of the
   kingdom.
℟. **Alleluia, alleluia.** ↓

GOSPEL Mt 11:25-30   [Solace in Christ]

Jesus gives praise to his Father. No one knows the Son but the Father and those to whom the Father reveals this truth. Jesus calls to himself those who are troubled and weary that they may find refreshment.

℣. The Lord be with you. ℟. **And with your spirit.**
✤ A reading from the holy Gospel according to Matthew.
℟. **Glory to you, O Lord.**

AT that time Jesus exclaimed:"I give praise to you, Father, Lord of heaven and earth, for although you have hidden these things from the wise and the learned you have revealed them to little ones. Yes, Father, such has been your gracious will. All things have been handed over to me by my Father. No one knows the Son except the Father, and no one knows the Father except the Son and anyone to whom the Son wishes to reveal him.

   "Come to me, all you who labor and are burdened, and I will give you rest. Take my yoke upon you and learn from me, for I am meek and humble of heart; and you will find rest for yourselves. For my yoke is easy, and my burden light."—The Gospel of the Lord.
℟. **Praise to you, Lord Jesus Christ.**   ➔ No. 15, p. 18

PRAYER OVER THE OFFERINGS   [Purify Us]

May this oblation dedicated to your name
purify us, O Lord,
and day by day bring our conduct
closer to the life of heaven.
Through Christ our Lord.
℞. **Amen.**   ➙ No. 21, p. 22 (Pref. P 29-36)

COMMUNION ANT. Ps 34 (33):9   [The Lord's Goodness]

**Taste and see that the Lord is good; blessed the man
who seeks refuge in him.** ↓

OR Mt 11:28   [God Refreshes]

**Come to me, all who labor and are burdened, and I
will refresh you, says the Lord.** ↓

PRAYER AFTER COMMUNION   [Salvation and Praise]

Grant, we pray, O Lord,
that, having been replenished by such great gifts,
we may gain the prize of salvation
and never cease to praise you.
Through Christ our Lord.
℞. **Amen.**   ➙ No. 30, p. 77

Optional Solemn Blessings, p. 97, and Prayers over the People, p. 105

"A sower went out to sow. . . ."

JULY 16

15th SUNDAY IN ORDINARY TIME

ENTRANCE ANT. Cf. Ps 17 (16):15   [God's Face]

As for me, in justice I shall behold your face; I shall be filled with the vision of your glory.   ➜ No. 2, p. 10

COLLECT   [Right Path]

O God, who show the light of your truth
to those who go astray,
so that they may return to the right path,
give all who for the faith they profess
are accounted Christians
the grace to reject whatever is contrary to the name of
    Christ
and to strive after all that does it honor.
Through our Lord Jesus Christ, your Son,
who lives and reigns with you in the unity of the Holy
    Spirit,
God, for ever and ever. ℞. **Amen.** ↓

FIRST READING Is 55:10-11   [God's Fruitful Word]

Isaiah uses the example of rain and snow seeping into the ground to make it fertile to show how the word of God filters into the hearts of men. It shall not be void and empty.

448

A reading from the Book of the Prophet Isaiah

THUS says the LORD:
Just as from the heavens
    the rain and snow come down
and do not return there
    till they have watered the earth,
        making it fertile and fruitful,
giving seed to the one who sows
    and bread to the one who eats,
so shall my word be
    that goes forth from my mouth;
my word shall not return to me void,
    but shall do my will,
        achieving the end for which I sent it.

The word of the Lord. ℟. **Thanks be to God.** ↓

RESPONSORIAL PSALM Ps 65   [A Fruitful Harvest]

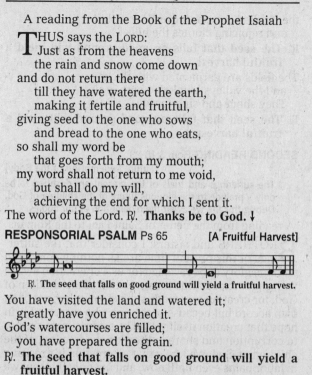

℟. **The seed that falls on good ground will yield a fruitful harvest.**

You have visited the land and watered it;
    greatly have you enriched it.
God's watercourses are filled;
    you have prepared the grain.

℟. **The seed that falls on good ground will yield a fruitful harvest.**

Thus have you prepared the land: drenching its furrows,
    breaking up its clods,
softening it with showers,
    blessing its yield.

℟. **The seed that falls on good ground will yield a fruitful harvest.**

You have crowned the year with your bounty,
    and your paths overflow with a rich harvest;

the untilled meadows overflow with it,
　　and rejoicing clothes the hills.

℟. **The seed that falls on good ground will yield a
　fruitful harvest.**

The fields are garmented with flocks
　　and the valleys blanketed with grain.
　　They shout and sing for joy.

℟. **The seed that falls on good ground will yield a
　fruitful harvest.** ↓

SECOND READING Rom 8:18-23

[Future Redemption of the Body]

**The sufferings and trials of the present are destined to be
only a prelude to the glorious future of the children of God.
During this life we await the redemption of our bodies.**

A reading from the Letter of Saint Paul to the Romans

Brothers and sisters: I consider that the sufferings of this present time are as nothing compared with the glory to be revealed for us. For creation awaits with eager expectation the revelation of the children of God; for creation was made subject to futility, not of its own accord but because of the one who subjected it, in hope that creation itself would be set free from slavery to corruption and share in the glorious freedom of the children of God. We know that all creation is groaning in labor pains even until now; and not only that, but we ourselves, who have the firstfruits of the Spirit, we also groan within ourselves as we wait for adoption, the redemption of our bodies.—The word of the Lord. ℟.
Thanks be to God. ↓

ALLELUIA

℟. **Alleluia, alleluia.**
The seed is the word of God, Christ is the sower.
All who come to him have life forever.
℟. **Alleluia, alleluia.** ↓

GOSPEL Mt 13:1-23 or 13:1-9   [Parable of the Sower]

Jesus teaches in parables that can be easily understood. He speaks of sowing the message of salvation that by some is heeded for a while, or ignored. Others, however, listen intently and try to live according to the will of God. Jesus explains this parable in detail.

[If the "Shorter Form" is used, the indented text in brackets is omitted.]

℣. The Lord be with you. ℟. **And with your spirit.**
✛ A reading from the holy Gospel according to Matthew.
℟. **Glory to you, O Lord.**

ON that day, Jesus went out of the house and sat down by the sea. Such large crowds gathered around him that he got into a boat and sat down, and the whole crowd stood along the shore. And he spoke to them at length in parables, saying: "A sower went out to sow. And as he sowed, some seed fell on the path, and birds came and ate it up. Some fell on rocky ground, where it had little soil. It sprang up at once because the soil was not deep, and when the sun rose it was scorched, and it withered for lack of roots. Some seed fell among thorns, and the thorns grew up and choked it. But some seed fell on rich soil, and produced fruit, a hundred or sixty or thirtyfold. Whoever has ears ought to hear."

[The disciples approached him and said, "Why do you speak to them in parables?" He said to them in reply, "Because knowledge of the mysteries of the kingdom of heaven has been granted to you, but to them it has not been granted. To anyone who has, more will be given and he will grow rich; from anyone who has not, even what he has will be taken away. This is why I speak to them in parables, because *they look but do not see and hear but do not listen or understand.* Isaiah's prophecy is fulfilled in them, which says:

You shall indeed hear but not understand,
   you shall indeed look but never see.
Gross is the heart of this people,
   they will hardly hear with their ears,
   they have closed their eyes,
   lest they see with their eyes
   and hear with their ears
and understand with their hearts and be converted,
   and I heal them.

"But blessed are your eyes, because they see, and your ears, because they hear. Amen, I say to you, many prophets and righteous people longed to see what you see but did not see it, and to hear what you hear but did not hear it.

"Hear then the parable of the sower. The seed sown on the path is the one who hears the word of the kingdom without understanding it, and the evil one comes and steals away what was sown in his heart. The seed sown on rocky ground is the one who hears the word and receives it at once with joy. But he has no root and lasts only for a time. When some tribulation or persecution comes because of the word, he immediately falls away. The seed sown among thorns is the one who hears the word, but then worldly anxiety and the lure of riches choke the word and it bears no fruit. But the seed sown on rich soil is the one who hears the word and understands it, who indeed bears fruit and yields a hundred or sixty or thirtyfold."]

The Gospel of the Lord. ℟. **Praise to you, Lord Jesus Christ.**   → No. 15, p. 18

PRAYER OVER THE OFFERINGS   [Greater Holiness]

Look upon the offerings of the Church, O Lord,
as she makes her prayer to you,
and grant that, when consumed by those who believe,
they may bring ever greater holiness.
Through Christ our Lord.
℞. **Amen.**   → No. 21, p. 22 (Pref. P 29-36)

COMMUNION ANT. Cf. Ps 84 (83):4-5   [The Lord's House]

**The sparrow finds a home, and the swallow a nest for
her young: by your altars, O Lord of hosts, my King
and my God. Blessed are they who dwell in your
house, for ever singing your praise.** ↓

OR Jn 6:57   [Remain in Jesus]

**Whoever eats my flesh and drinks my blood remains
in me and I in him, says the Lord.** ↓

PRAYER AFTER COMMUNION   [Saving Effects]

Having consumed these gifts, we pray, O Lord,
that, by our participation in this mystery,
its saving effects upon us may grow.
Through Christ our Lord.
℞. **Amen.**   → No. 30, p. 77

Optional Solemn Blessings, p. 97, and Prayers over the People, p. 105

"His enemy came and sowed weeds all through the wheat."

JULY 23

16th SUNDAY IN ORDINARY TIME

ENTRANCE ANT. Ps 54 (53):6, 8   [God Our Help]

See, I have God for my help. The Lord sustains my soul. I will sacrifice to you with willing heart, and praise your name, O Lord, for it is good.   ➡ No. 2, p. 10

COLLECT   [Keeping God's Commands]

Show favor, O Lord, to your servants
and mercifully increase the gifts of your grace,
that, made fervent in hope, faith and charity,
they may be ever watchful in keeping your commands.
Through our Lord Jesus Christ, your Son,
who lives and reigns with you in the unity of the Holy
   Spirit,
God, for ever and ever. ℟. **Amen.** ↓

FIRST READING Wis 12:13, 16-19   [God's Mercy]

The real source of might and power is justice. Through justice a man becomes master of his power. He can become lenient and kind and encourage repentance for sin.

A reading from the Book of Wisdom

THERE is no god besides you who have the care
of all,
  that you need show you have not unjustly condemned.
For your might is the source of justice;
  your mastery over all things makes you lenient
to all.
For you show your might when the perfection of
your power is disbelieved;
  and in those who know you, you rebuke temerity.
But though you are master of might, you judge
with clemency,
  and with much lenience you govern us;
  for power, whenever you will, attends you.
And you taught your people, by these deeds,
  that those who are just must be kind;
and you gave your children good ground for hope
  that you would permit repentance for their sins.
The word of the Lord. ℟. **Thanks be to God.** ↓

RESPONSORIAL PSALM Ps 86   [Kindness and Fidelity]

℟. Lord, you are good and for - giv - ing.

You, O LORD, are good and forgiving,
  abounding in kindness to all who call upon you.
Hearken, O LORD, to my prayer
  and attend to the sound of my pleading.

℟. **Lord, you are good and forgiving.**

All the nations you have made shall come
  and worship you, O LORD,
  and glorify your name.
For you are great, and you do wondrous deeds;
  you alone are God.

℟. **Lord, you are good and forgiving.**

You, O LORD, are a God merciful and gracious,
  slow to anger, abounding in kindness and fidelity.
Turn toward me, and have pity on me;
  give your strength to your servant.

℟. **Lord, you are good and forgiving.** ↓

SECOND READING Rom 8:26-27 [Intercession of the Spirit]

Through the Spirit, our weakness in prayer is overcome. He searches our hearts and makes true intercessions in our behalf.

A reading from the Letter of Saint Paul to the Romans

BROTHERS and sisters: The Spirit comes to the aid of our weakness; for we do not know how to pray as we ought, but the Spirit himself intercedes with inexpressible groanings. And the one who searches hearts knows what is the intention of the Spirit, because he intercedes for the holy ones according to God's will.—The word of the Lord. ℟. **Thanks be to God.** ↓

ALLELUIA Cf. Mt 11:25   [Revealed to Little Ones]

℟. **Alleluia, alleluia.**
Blessed are you, Father, Lord of heaven and earth;
you have revealed to little ones the mysteries of the
  kingdom.
℟. **Alleluia, alleluia.** ↓

GOSPEL Mt 13:24-43 or 13:24-30   [Parable of the Weeds]

Jesus teaches about God's Kingdom in parables. His Kingdom is like a field in which good grain and weeds grow. At harvest time the good will be sorted from the bad. God's Kingdom is also like a mustard plant reaching out to embrace all as it grows.

[If the "Shorter Form" is used, the indented text in brackets is omitted.]

℣. The Lord be with you. ℟. **And with your spirit.**
✤ A reading from the holy Gospel according to Matthew.
℟. **Glory to you, O Lord.**

JESUS proposed another parable to the crowds, saying: "The kingdom of heaven may be likened to a man who sowed good seed in his field. While everyone was asleep his enemy came and sowed weeds all through the wheat, and then went off. When the crop grew and bore fruit, the weeds appeared as well. The slaves of the householder came to him and said, 'Master, did you not sow good seed in your field? Where have the weeds come from?' He answered, 'An enemy has done this.' His slaves said to him, 'Do you want us to go and pull them up?' He replied, 'No, if you pull up the weeds you might uproot the wheat along with them. Let them grow together until harvest; then at harvest time I will say to the harvesters, "First collect the weeds and tie them in bundles for burning; but gather the wheat into my barn."'"

[He proposed another parable to them. "The kingdom of heaven is like a mustard seed that a person took and sowed in a field. It is the smallest of all the seeds, yet when full-grown it is the largest of plants. It becomes a large bush, and the 'birds of the sky come and dwell in its branches.'"

He spoke to them another parable. "The kingdom of heaven is like yeast that a woman took and mixed with three measures of wheat flour until the whole batch was leavened."

All these things Jesus spoke to the crowds in parables. He spoke to them only in parables, to fulfill what had been said through the prophet:

"I will open my mouth in parables,
I will announce what has lain hidden from
the foundation of the world."

Then, dismissing the crowds, he went into the house. His disciples approached him and said, "Explain to us the parable of the weeds in the field." He said in reply, "He who sows good seed is the Son of Man, the field is the world, the good seed the children of the kingdom. The weeds are the children of the evil one, and the enemy who sows them is the devil. The harvest is the end of the age, and the harvesters are angels. Just as weeds are collected and burned up with fire, so will it be at the end of the age. The Son of Man will send his angels, and they will collect out of his kingdom all who cause others to sin and all evildoers. They will throw them into the fiery furnace, where there will be wailing and grinding of teeth. Then the righteous will shine like the sun in the kingdom of their Father. Whoever has ears ought to hear."]

The Gospel of the Lord. ℟. **Praise to you, Lord Jesus Christ.**   ➜ No. 15, p. 18

PRAYER OVER THE OFFERINGS   [Saving Offerings]

O God, who in the one perfect sacrifice
brought to completion varied offerings of the law,
accept, we pray, this sacrifice from your faithful
    servants
and make it holy, as you blessed the gifts of Abel,
so that what each has offered to the honor of your
    majesty
may benefit the salvation of all.
Through Christ our Lord.
℟. **Amen.**   ➜ No. 21, p. 22 (Pref. P 29-36)

COMMUNION ANT. Ps 111 (110):4-5   [Jesus Gives]
The Lord, the gracious, the merciful, has made a memorial of his wonders; he gives food to those who fear him. ↓

OR Rev 3:20   [Jesus Knocks]

Behold, I stand at the door and knock, says the Lord.
If anyone hears my voice and opens the door to me, I
will enter his house and dine with him, and he with
me. ↓

PRAYER AFTER COMMUNION   [New Life]

Graciously be present to your people, we pray, O Lord,
and lead those you have imbued with heavenly
   mysteries
to pass from former ways to newness of life.
Through Christ our Lord.
R̸. **Amen.**   ➜ No. 30, p. 77

Optional Solemn Blessings, p. 97, and Prayers over the People, p. 105

"The kingdom of heaven is like a treasure buried in a field. . . ."

JULY 30

17th SUNDAY IN ORDINARY TIME

ENTRANCE ANT. Cf. Ps 68 (67):6-7, 36 [God Our Strength]

God is in his holy place, God who unites those who
dwell in his house; he himself gives might and
strength to his people.   ➜ No. 2, p. 10

COLLECT   [Enduring Things]

O God, protector of those who hope in you,
without whom nothing has firm foundation, nothing is
   holy,
bestow in abundance your mercy upon us
and grant that, with you as our ruler and guide,
we may use the good things that pass
in such a way as to hold fast even now
to those that ever endure.
Through our Lord Jesus Christ, your Son,
who lives and reigns with you in the unity of the Holy
   Spirit,
God, for ever and ever. ℟. **Amen.** ↓

FIRST READING 1 Kgs 3:5, 7-12   [The Gift of Understanding]
   Solomon prays for wisdom to lead the people of God. God is
   pleased that Solomon asked above all else to know right
   from wrong. God promises him wisdom and understanding
   that will be unequaled either in times past or in the future.

A reading from the first Book of Kings

THE LORD appeared to Solomon in a dream at
   night. God said, "Ask something of me and I will
give it to you." Solomon answered: "O LORD, my God,
you have made me, your servant, king to succeed my
father David; but I am a mere youth, not knowing at
all how to act. I serve you in the midst of the people
whom you have chosen, a people so vast that it cannot be numbered or counted. Give your servant,
therefore, an understanding heart to judge your people and to distinguish right from wrong. For who is
able to govern this vast people of yours?"

The LORD was pleased that Solomon made this
request. So God said to him: "Because you have asked
for this—not for a long life for yourself, nor for riches, nor for the life of your enemies, but for understanding so that you may know what is right—I do as

you requested. I give you a heart so wise and understanding that there has never been anyone like you
up to now, and after you there will come no one to
equal you."—The word of the Lord. ℟. **Thanks be to
God.** ↓

RESPONSORIAL PSALM Ps 119   [The Lord's Decrees]

℟. Lord,   I love   your com - mands.

I have said, O LORD, that my part
  is to keep your words.
The law of your mouth is to me more precious
  than thousands of gold and silver pieces.

℟. **Lord, I love your commands.**

Let your kindness comfort me
  according to your promise to your servants.
Let your compassion come to me that I may live,
  for your law is my delight.

℟. **Lord, I love your commands.**

For I love your commands
  more than gold, however fine.
For in all your precepts I go forward;
  every false way I hate.

℟. **Lord, I love your commands.**

Wonderful are your decrees;
  therefore I observe them.
The revelation of your words sheds light,
  giving understanding to the simple.

℟. **Lord, I love your commands.** ↓

SECOND READING Rom 8:28-30 [All Things Work for Good]
  God makes all his works of creation fit into his divine plan.
  He planned to share the image of his Son with us so that
  we might be justified and thereby enter into eternal glory.

A reading from the Letter of Saint Paul to the Romans

BROTHERS and sisters: We know that all things work for good for those who love God, who are called according to his purpose. For those he foreknew he also predestined to be conformed to the image of his Son, so that he might be the firstborn among many brothers and sisters. And those he predestined he also called; and those he called he also justified; and those he justified he also glorified.— The word of the Lord. ℟. **Thanks be to God.** ↓

ALLELUIA Cf. Mt 11:25   [Revealed to Little Ones]
℟. **Alleluia, alleluia.**
Blessed are you, Father, Lord of heaven and earth;
for you have revealed to little ones the mysteries of the
    kingdom.
℟. **Alleluia, alleluia.** ↓

GOSPEL Mt 13:44-52 or 13:44-46   [The Kingdom of God]
   Jesus compares the value of the Kingdom of God to a hidden treasure, to a most valuable pearl, to a dragnet. It is beyond human comprehension. In the end, God's angels will sort out those who have lived good lives from unrepentant sinners.

[If the "Shorter Form" is used, the indented text in brackets is omitted.]

℣. The Lord be with you. ℟. **And with your spirit.**
✠ A reading from the holy Gospel according to Matthew.
℟. **Glory to you, O Lord.**

JESUS said to his disciples: "The kingdom of heaven is like a treasure buried in a field, which a person finds and hides again, and out of joy goes and sells all that he has and buys that field. Again, the kingdom of heaven is like a merchant searching for fine pearls. When he finds a pearl of great price, he goes and sells all that he has and buys it.

[Again, the kingdom of heaven is like a net thrown into the sea, which collects fish of every kind. When it is full they haul it ashore and sit down to put what is good into buckets. What is bad they throw away. Thus it will be at the end of the age. The angels will go out and separate the wicked from the righteous and throw them into the fiery furnace, where there will be wailing and grinding of teeth.

"Do you understand all these things?" They answered, "Yes." And he replied, "Then every scribe who has been instructed in the kingdom of heaven is like the head of a household who brings from his storeroom both the new and the old."]

The Gospel of the Lord. ℟. **Praise to you, Lord Jesus Christ.**   ➛ No. 15, p. 18

PRAYER OVER THE OFFERINGS   [Sanctifying Mysteries]

Accept, O Lord, we pray, the offerings
which we bring from the abundance of your gifts,
that through the powerful working of your grace
these most sacred mysteries may sanctify our present
  way of life
and lead us to eternal gladness.
Through Christ our Lord.
℟. **Amen.**   ➛ No. 21, p. 22 (Pref. P 29-36)

COMMUNION ANT. Ps 103 (102):2   [Bless the Lord]

Bless the Lord, O my soul, and never forget all his benefits. ↓

OR Mt 5:7-8   [Blessed the Clean of Heart]

Blessed are the merciful, for they shall receive mercy. Blessed are the clean of heart, for they shall see God. ↓

PRAYER AFTER COMMUNION   [Memorial of Christ]

We have consumed, O Lord, this divine Sacrament,
the perpetual memorial of the Passion of your Son;
grant, we pray, that this gift,
which he himself gave us with love beyond all telling,
may profit us for salvation.
Through Christ our Lord.
℟. **Amen.**   → No. 30, p. 77

Optional Solemn Blessings, p. 97, and Prayers over the People, p. 105

"He was transfigured before them."

AUGUST 6

THE TRANSFIGURATION OF THE LORD

Feast
(18th Sunday in Ordinary Time)

ENTRANCE ANT. Cf. Mt 17:5   [Father, Son, and Spirit]

**In a resplendent cloud the Holy Spirit appeared. The
Father's voice was heard: This is my beloved Son, with
whom I am well pleased. Listen to him.** → No. 2, p. 10

COLLECT   [Listening to Christ]

O God, who in the glorious Transfiguration
of your Only Begotten Son

confirmed the mysteries of faith by the witness of the
   Fathers
and wonderfully prefigured our full adoption to
   sonship,
grant, we pray, to your servants,
that, listening to the voice of your beloved Son,
we may merit to become co-heirs with him.
Who lives and reigns with you in the unity of the Holy
   Spirit,
God, for ever and ever. ℟. **Amen.** ↓

FIRST READING Dn 7:9-10, 13-14   [Clothing White As Snow]

   Daniel's vision portrays the Son of man who has power,
   glory, and dominion. Thousands minister to him. His dominion is everlasting.

   A reading from the Book of the Prophet Daniel

AS I watched:
   Thrones were set up
      and the Ancient One took his throne.
His clothing was snow bright,
      and the hair on his head as white as wool;
His throne was flames of fire,
      with wheels of burning fire.
A surging stream of fire
      flowed out from where he sat;
Thousands upon thousands were ministering to him,
      and myriads upon myriads attended him.
The court was convened and the books were opened.
As the visions during the night continued, I saw
   One like a Son of man coming,
      on the clouds of heaven;
When he reached the Ancient One
      and was presented before him,
The one like a Son of man received dominion, glory,
         and kingship;
      all peoples, nations, and languages serve him.

His dominion is an everlasting dominion
    that shall not be taken away,
    his kingship shall not be destroyed.
The word of the Lord. ℟. **Thanks be to God.** ↓

RESPONSORIAL PSALM Ps 97   [The Lord Most High]

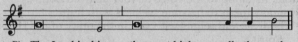

℟. **The Lord is king, the most high over all the earth.**

The LORD is king; let the earth rejoice;
    let the many islands be glad.
Clouds and darkness are round about him,
    justice and judgment are the foundation of his throne.

℟. **The Lord is king, the most high over all the earth.**

The mountains melt like wax before the LORD,
    before the LORD of all the earth.
The heavens proclaim his justice,
    and all peoples see his glory.

℟. **The Lord is king, the most high over all the earth.**

Because you, O LORD, are the Most High over all the
    earth,
    exalted far above all gods.

℟. **The Lord is king, the most high over all the earth.** ↓

SECOND READING 2 Pt 1:16-19   [Peter, an Eyewitness]

**Peter was an eyewitness of the Transfiguration of the Lord
Jesus in power and glory. He proclaims Jesus' message
with authority; his teaching is trustworthy and reliable.**

A reading from the second Letter of Saint Peter

BELOVED: We did not follow cleverly devised
myths when we made known to you the power and
coming of our Lord Jesus Christ, but we had been eye-
witnesses of his majesty. For he received honor and
glory from God the Father when that unique declara-

tion came to him from the majestic glory, "This is my
Son, my beloved, with whom I am well pleased." We
ourselves heard this voice come from heaven while we
were with him on the holy mountain. Moreover, we possess the prophetic message that is altogether reliable.
You will do well to be attentive to it, as to a lamp shining in a dark place, until day dawns and the morning
star rises in your hearts.—The word of the Lord. ℟.
Thanks be to God. ↓

ALLELUIA Mt 17:5c   [Listen to Him]

℟. **Alleluia, alleluia.**
This is my beloved Son with whom I am well pleased;
listen to him.
℟. **Alleluia, alleluia.** ↓

GOSPEL Mt 17:1-9   [Face Like the Sun]

**Jesus becomes transfigured before Peter, James, and John.
God speaks to us: "This is my beloved Son, . . . listen to
him."**

℣. The Lord be with you. ℟. **And with your spirit.**
✠ A reading from the holy Gospel according to Matthew.
℟. **Glory to you, O Lord.**

JESUS took Peter, James, and his brother, John, and
led them up a high mountain by themselves. And he
was transfigured before them; his face shone like the
sun and his clothes became white as light. And behold,
Moses and Elijah appeared to them, conversing with
him. Then Peter said to Jesus in reply, "Lord, it is good
that we are here. If you wish, I will make three tents
here, one for you, one for Moses, and one for Elijah."
While he was still speaking, behold, a bright cloud cast
a shadow over them, then from the cloud came a voice
that said, "This is my beloved Son, with whom I am
well pleased; listen to him." When the disciples heard
this, they fell prostrate and were very much afraid. But

Jesus came and touched them, saying, "Rise, and do not be afraid." And when the disciples raised their eyes, they saw no one else but Jesus alone.

As they were coming down from the mountain, Jesus charged them, "Do not tell the vision to anyone until the Son of Man has been raised from the dead."—The Gospel of the Lord. ℟. **Praise to you, Lord Jesus Christ.**

→ No. 15, p. 18

PRAYER OVER THE OFFERINGS   [Cleanse Us from Sin]

Sanctify, O Lord, we pray,
these offerings here made to celebrate
the glorious Transfiguration of your Only Begotten Son,
and by his radiant splendor
cleanse us from the stains of sin.
Through Christ our Lord. ℟. **Amen.** ↓

PREFACE (P 50)   [Sharing Christ's Glory]

℣. The Lord be with you. ℟. **And with your spirit.**
℣. Lift up your hearts. ℟. **We lift them up to the Lord.**
℣. Let us give thanks to the Lord our God. ℟. **It is right and just.**

It is truly right and just, our duty and our salvation,
always and everywhere to give you thanks,
Lord, holy Father, almighty and eternal God,
through Christ our Lord.

For he revealed his glory in the presence of chosen
   witnesses
and filled with the greatest splendor that bodily form
which he shares with all humanity,
that the scandal of the Cross
might be removed from the hearts of his disciples
and that he might show

how in the Body of the whole Church is to be fulfilled
what so wonderfully shone forth first in its Head.

And so, with the Powers of heaven,
we worship you constantly on earth,
and before your majesty
without end we acclaim: ➔ No. 23, p. 23

COMMUNION ANT. Cf. 1 Jn 3:2   [Vison of Christ]
**When Christ appears, we shall be like him, for we
shall see him as he is.** ↓

PRAYER AFTER COMMUNION   [In Christ's Likeness]
May the heavenly nourishment we have received,
O Lord, we pray,
transform us into the likeness of your Son,
whose radiant splendor you willed to make manifest
in his glorious Transfiguration.
Who lives and reigns for ever and ever.
℟. **Amen.**   ➔ No. 30, p. 77

Optional Solemn Blessings, p. 97, and Prayers over the People, p. 105

"It is I; do not be afraid."

AUGUST 13

19th SUNDAY IN ORDINARY TIME

ENTRANCE ANT. Cf. Ps 74 (73):20, 19, 22, 23

[Arise, O God]

Look to your covenant, O Lord, and forget not the life of your poor ones for ever. Arise, O God, and defend your cause, and forget not the cries of those who seek you. → No. 2, p. 10

COLLECT [Spirit of Adoption]

Almighty ever-living God,
whom, taught by the Holy Spirit,
we dare to call our Father,
bring, we pray, to perfection in our hearts
the spirit of adoption as your sons and daughters,
that we may merit to enter into the inheritance
which you have promised.
Through our Lord Jesus Christ, your Son,
who lives and reigns with you in the unity of the Holy
    Spirit,
God, for ever and ever. R. **Amen.** ↓

470

FIRST READING 1 Kgs 19:9a, 11-13a [Coming of the Lord]

The Lord tells Elijah to await him on the mountain. Elijah's faith is tried as he witnesses a devastating wind, an earthquake, and a fire. After these, the Lord speaks to Elijah in a tiny whispering sound.

A reading from the first Book of Kings

AT the mountain of God, Horeb, Elijah came to a cave where he took shelter. Then the LORD said to him, "Go outside and stand on the mountain before the LORD; the LORD will be passing by." A strong and heavy wind was rending the mountains and crushing rocks before the LORD—but the LORD was not in the wind. After the wind there was an earthquake—but the LORD was not in the earthquake. After the earthquake there was fire—but the LORD was not in the fire. After the fire there was a tiny whispering sound. When he heard this, Elijah hid his face in his cloak and went and stood at the entrance of the cave.—The word of the Lord. ℟. **Thanks be to God.** ↓

RESPONSORIAL PSALM Ps 85   [Truth and Justice]

℟. Lord, let us see your kind-ness, and grant us your sal-va-tion.

I will hear what God proclaims;
   the LORD—for he proclaims peace.
Near indeed is his salvation to those who fear him,
   glory dwelling in our land.
℟. **Lord, let us see your kindness, and grant us your salvation.**

Kindness and truth shall meet;
   justice and peace shall kiss.

Truth shall spring out of the earth,
  and justice shall look down from heaven.

℟. **Lord, let us see your kindness, and grant us your salvation.**

The Lord himself will give his benefits;
  our land shall yield its increase.
Justice shall walk before him,
  and prepare the way of his steps.

℟. **Lord, let us see your kindness, and grant us your salvation.** ↓

SECOND READING Rom 9:1-5   [Blessed Be God]

Paul admits that grief is in his heart. He would even accept separation from Jesus if it would help his brothers and sisters who have been privileged to know the revelation of God through the ages. Blessed be God forever.

A reading from the Letter of Saint Paul to the Romans

BROTHERS and sisters: I speak the truth in Christ, I do not lie; my conscience joins with the Holy Spirit in bearing me witness that I have great sorrow and constant anguish in my heart. For I could wish that I myself were accursed and cut off from Christ for the sake of my own people, my kindred according to the flesh. They are Israelites; theirs the adoption, the glory, the covenants, the giving of the law, the worship, and the promises; theirs the patriarchs, and from them, according to the flesh, is the Christ, who is over all, God blessed forever. Amen. —The word of the Lord. ℟. **Thanks be to God.** ↓

ALLELUIA Cf. Ps 130:5   [Hope and Trust]

℟. **Alleluia, alleluia.**
I wait for the Lord;
  my soul waits for his word.
℟. **Alleluia, alleluia.** ↓

GOSPEL Mt 14:22-33   [Jesus Walks on Water]

Jesus feeds the crowds and then withdraws to pray. His disciples want to cross the lake, but a threatening storm arises. Jesus appears and Peter gets out of the boat to walk to him, but because Peter doubts, he begins to sink. Jesus saves him and admonishes him for his little faith. Then Jesus calms the storm.

℣. The Lord be with you. ℟. **And with your spirit.**
✛ A reading from the holy Gospel according to Matthew.
℟. **Glory to you, O Lord.**

AFTER he had fed the people, Jesus made the disciples get into a boat and precede him to the other side, while he dismissed the crowds. After doing so, he went up on the mountain by himself to pray. When it was evening he was there alone. Meanwhile the boat, already a few miles offshore, was being tossed about by the waves, for the wind was against it. During the fourth watch of the night, he came toward them walking on the sea. When the disciples saw him walking on the sea they were terrified. "It is a ghost," they said, and they cried out in fear. At once Jesus spoke to them, "Take courage, it is I; do not be afraid." Peter said to him in reply, "Lord, if it is you, command me to come to you on the water." He said, "Come." Peter got out of the boat and began to walk on the water toward Jesus. But when he saw how strong the wind was he became frightened; and, beginning to sink, he cried out, "Lord, save me!" Immediately Jesus stretched out his hand and caught Peter, and said to him, "O you of little faith, why did you doubt?" After they got into the boat, the wind died down. Those who were in the boat did him homage, saying, "Truly, you are the Son of God."—The Gospel of the Lord. ℟. **Praise to you, Lord Jesus Christ.**

➜ No. 15, p. 18

PRAYER OVER THE OFFERINGS   [Mystery of Salvation]

Be pleased, O Lord, to accept the offerings of your
   Church,
for in your mercy you have given them to be offered
and by your power you transform them
into the mystery of our salvation.
Through Christ our Lord.
℟. **Amen.**   → No. 21, p. 22 (Pref. P 29-36)

COMMUNION ANT. Ps 147 (146):12,14   [Glorify the Lord]
**O Jerusalem, glorify the Lord, who gives you your fill
of finest wheat.** ↓

OR Cf. Jn 6:51   [The Flesh of Jesus]
**The bread that I will give, says the Lord, is my flesh
for the life of the world.** ↓

PRAYER AFTER COMMUNION [Confirm Us in God's Truth]

May the communion in your Sacrament
that we have consumed, save us, O Lord,
and confirm us in the light of your truth.
Through Christ our Lord.
℟. **Amen.**   → No. 30, p. 77

Optional Solemn Blessings, p. 97, and Prayers over the People, p. 105

"Alleluia. Mary is taken up to heaven."

AUGUST 15

THE ASSUMPTION OF
THE BLESSED VIRGIN MARY

Solemnity

AT THE VIGIL MASS (August 14)

ENTRANCE ANT. [Mary Exalted]

Glorious things are spoken of you, O Mary, who today were exalted above the choirs of Angels into eternal triumph with Christ. ➔ No. 2, p. 10

COLLECT [Crowned with Glory]

O God, who, looking on the lowliness of the Blessed
    Virgin Mary,
raised her to this grace,
that your Only Begotten Son was born of her according
    to the flesh
and that she was crowned this day with surpassing
    glory,
grant through her prayers,
that, saved by the mystery of your redemption,
we may merit to be exalted by you on high.
Through our Lord Jesus Christ, your Son,

who lives and reigns with you in the unity of the Holy
  Spirit,
God, for ever and ever. ℟. **Amen.** ↓

FIRST READING 1 Chr 15:3-4, 15-16; 16:1-2

[Procession of Glory]

**Under David's direction the Israelites brought the Ark of
the Lord to the tent prepared for it. They showed great
respect for it. They offered holocausts and peace offerings.
This becomes a figure of Mary who bore the Son of God.**

A reading from the first Book of Chronicles

DAVID assembled all Israel in Jerusalem to bring the
ark of the LORD to the place which he had prepared
for it. David also called together the sons of Aaron and
the Levites.

The Levites bore the ark of God on their shoulders
with poles, as Moses had ordained according to the
word of the LORD.

David commanded the chiefs of the Levites to appoint
their kinsmen as chanters, to play on musical instruments, harps, lyres, and cymbals, to make a loud sound
of rejoicing.

They brought in the ark of God and set it within the
tent which David had pitched for it. Then they offered
up burnt offerings and peace offerings to God. When
David had finished offering up the burnt offerings and
peace offerings, he blessed the people in the name of the
LORD.—The word of the Lord. ℟. **Thanks be to God.** ↓

RESPONSORIAL PSALM Ps 132   [Mary, Ark of God]

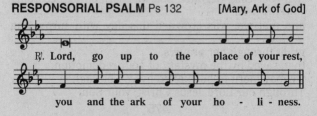

℟. Lord, go up to the place of your rest,

you and the ark of your ho - li - ness.

Behold, we heard of it in Ephrathah;
  we found it in the fields of Jaar.
Let us enter into his dwelling,
  let us worship at his footstool.

℟. **Lord, go up to the place of your rest, you and the ark of your holiness.**

May your priests be clothed with justice;
  let your faithful ones shout merrily for joy.
For the sake of David your servant,
  reject not the plea of your anointed.

℟. **Lord, go up to the place of your rest, you and the ark of your holiness.**

For the LORD has chosen Zion;
  he prefers her for his dwelling.
"Zion is my resting place forever;
  in her will I dwell, for I prefer her."

℟. **Lord, go up to the place of your rest, you and the ark of your holiness.** ↓

SECOND READING 1 Cor 15:54b-57   [Victory over Death]
  Paul reminds the Corinthians that in life after death there is victory. Through his love for us, God has given victory over sin and death in Jesus, his Son.

A reading from the first Letter of Saint Paul
to the Corinthians

BROTHERS and sisters: When that which is mortal clothes itself with immortality, then the word that is written shall come about:
  Death is swallowed up in victory.
  Where, O death, is your victory?
  Where, O death, is your sting?
The sting of death is sin, and the power of sin is the law. But thanks be to God who gives us the victory through our Lord Jesus Christ.—The word of the Lord.
℟. **Thanks be to God.** ↓

ALLELUIA Lk 11:28   [Doers of God's Word]

℟. **Alleluia, alleluia.**
Blessed are they who hear the word of God
and observe it.
℟. **Alleluia, alleluia.** ↓

GOSPEL Lk 11:27-28   [Keeping God's Word]

Mary's relationship as the Mother of Jesus is unique in all of history. But Jesus reminds us that those who keep his word are most pleasing to God. In this Mary has set an example.

℣. The Lord be with you. ℟. **And with your spirit.**
✛ A reading from the holy Gospel according to Luke.
℟. **Glory to you, O Lord.**

WHILE Jesus was speaking, a woman from the crowd called out and said to him, "Blessed is the womb that carried you and the breasts at which you nursed." He replied, "Rather, blessed are those who hear the word of God and observe it."—The Gospel of the Lord. ℟. **Praise to you, Lord Jesus Christ.**

→ No. 15, p. 18

PRAYER OVER THE OFFERINGS   [Sacrifice of Praise]

Receive, we pray, O Lord,
the sacrifice of conciliation and praise,
which we celebrate on the Assumption of the holy
   Mother of God,
that it may lead us to your pardon
and confirm us in perpetual thanksgiving.
Through Christ our Lord. ℟. **Amen.**

→ Pref. P 59, p. 483

COMMUNION ANT. Cf. Lk 11:27   [Mary Carried Christ]

Blessed is the womb of the Virgin Mary, which bore the Son of the eternal Father. ↓

PRAYER AFTER COMMUNION   [Beseech God's Mercy]

Having partaken of this heavenly table,
we beseech your mercy, Lord our God,
that we, who honor the Assumption of the Mother of
    God,
may be freed from every threat of harm.
Through Christ our Lord.
R︦. **Amen.**   ➙ No. 30, p. 77

Optional Solemn Blessings, p. 97, and Prayers over the People, p. 105

AT THE MASS DURING THE DAY

ENTRANCE ANT. Cf. Rev 12:1   [Mary's Glory]

**A great sign appeared in heaven: a woman clothed
with the sun, and the moon beneath her feet, and on
her head a crown of twelve stars.**   ➙ No. 2, p. 10

OR   [Joy in Heaven]

**Let us all rejoice in the Lord, as we celebrate the feast
day in honor of the Virgin Mary, at whose Assumption
the Angels rejoice and praise the Son of God.**
    ➙ No. 2, p. 10

COLLECT   [Sharing Mary's Glory]

Almighty ever-living God,
who assumed the Immaculate Virgin Mary, the Mother
    of your Son,
body and soul into heavenly glory,
grant, we pray,
that, always attentive to the things that are above,
we may merit to be sharers of her glory.
Through our Lord Jesus Christ, your Son,
who lives and reigns with you in the unity of the Holy
    Spirit,
God, for ever and ever. R︦. **Amen.** ↓

FIRST READING Rv 11:19a; 12:1-6a, 10ab   [Mary, the Ark]

The appearance of the Ark in this time of retribution indicates that God is now accessible—no longer hidden, but present in the midst of his people. Filled with hatred, the devil spares no pains to destroy Christ and his Church. The dragon seeks to destroy the celestial woman and her Son. Its hatred is futile.

A reading from the Book of Revelation

GOD'S temple in heaven was opened, and the ark of his covenant could be seen in the temple. A great sign appeared in the sky, a woman clothed with the sun, with the moon beneath her feet, and on her head a crown of twelve stars. She was with child and wailed aloud in pain as she labored to give birth. Then another sign appeared in the sky; it was a huge red dragon, with seven heads and ten horns, and on its heads were seven diadems. Its tail swept away a third of the stars in the sky and hurled them down to the earth. Then the dragon stood before the woman about to give birth, to devour her child when she gave birth. She gave birth to a son, a male child, destined to rule all the nations with an iron rod. Her child was caught up to God and his throne. The woman herself fled into the desert where she had a place prepared by God.

Then I heard a loud voice in heaven say:
  "Now have salvation and power come,
      and the Kingdom of our God
      and the authority of his Anointed One."
The word of the Lord. ℟. **Thanks be to God.** ↓

RESPONSORIAL PSALM Ps 45   [Mary the Queen]

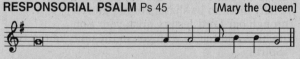

℟. **The queen stands at your right hand, ar-rayed in gold.**

The queen takes her place at your right hand in gold
 of Ophir.

℞. **The queen stands at your right hand, arrayed in
 gold.**

Hear, O daughter, and see; turn your ear,
 forget your people and your father's house.

℞. **The queen stands at your right hand, arrayed in
 gold.**

So shall the king desire your beauty;
 for he is your lord.

℞. **The queen stands at your right hand, arrayed in
 gold.**

They are borne in with gladness and joy;
 they enter the palace of the king.

℞. **The queen stands at your right hand, arrayed in
 gold.** ↓

SECOND READING 1 Cor 15:20-27   [Christ the King]

**The offering of the firstfruits was the symbol of the dedication
of the entire harvest to God. So the Resurrection of Christ
involves the resurrection of all who are in him. Since his glorious Resurrection, Christ reigns in glory; he is the Lord.**

A reading from the first Letter of Saint Paul
to the Corinthians

BROTHERS and sisters: Christ has been raised from
the dead, the firstfruits of those who have fallen
asleep. For since death came through man, the resurrection of the dead came also through man. For just as
in Adam all die, so too in Christ shall all be brought to
life, but each one in proper order: Christ the firstfruits;
then, at his coming, those who belong to Christ; then
comes the end, when he hands over the Kingdom to his
God and Father, when he has destroyed every sovereignty and every authority and power. For he must
reign until he has put all his enemies under his feet.

The last enemy to be destroyed is death, for "he subjected everything under his feet."—The word of the Lord. ℟. **Thanks be to God.** ↓

ALLELUIA   [Mary in Heaven]

Alleluia, alleluia.
Mary is taken up to heaven;
a chorus of angels exults.
℟. **Alleluia, alleluia.** ↓

GOSPEL Lk 1:39-56   [Blessed among Women]

Mary visits her kinswoman. Mary's song of thanksgiving, often called the "Magnificat," has been put together from many Old Testament phrases. The sum of Mary's spirituality is the best and most abundant gift of grace of the Incarnation of God's Son. Her spirit is filled with goodness and humility.

℣. The Lord be with you. ℟. **And with your spirit.**
✝ A reading from the holy Gospel according to Luke.
℟. **Glory to you, O Lord.**

MARY set out and traveled to the hill country in haste to a town of Judah, where she entered the house of Zechariah and greeted Elizabeth. When Elizabeth heard Mary's greeting, the infant leaped in her womb, and Elizabeth, filled with the Holy Spirit, cried out in a loud voice and said, "Blessed are you among women, and blessed is the fruit of your womb. And how does this happen to me, that the mother of my Lord should come to me? For at the moment the sound of your greeting reached my ears, the infant in my womb leaped for joy. Blessed are you who believed that what was spoken to you by the Lord would be fulfilled."

And Mary said:
"My soul proclaims the greatness of the Lord;
    my spirit rejoices in God my Savior
    for he has looked with favor upon his lowly servant.

From this day all generations will call me blessed:
the Almighty has done great things for me,
and holy is his Name.
He has mercy on those who fear him
in every generation.
He has shown the strength of his arm,
and has scattered the proud in their conceit.
He has cast down the mighty from their thrones,
and has lifted up the lowly.
He has filled the hungry with good things,
and the rich he has sent away empty.
He has come to the help of his servant Israel
for he has remembered his promise of mercy,
the promise he made to our fathers,
to Abraham and his children for ever."

Mary remained with her about three months and then returned to her home.—The Gospel of the Lord.
℟. **Praise to you, Lord Jesus Christ.**   ➔ No. 15, p. 18

PRAYER OVER THE OFFERINGS   [Longing for God]

May this oblation, our tribute of homage,
rise up to you, O Lord,
and, through the intercession of the most Blessed
Virgin Mary,
whom you assumed into heaven,
may our hearts, aflame with the fire of love,
constantly long for you.
Through Christ our Lord. ℟. **Amen.** ↓

PREFACE (P 59)   [Assumption—Sign of Hope]

℣. The Lord be with you. ℟. **And with your spirit.**
℣. Lift up your hearts. ℟. **We lift them up to the Lord.**
℣. Let us give thanks to the Lord our God. ℟. **It is right and just.**

It is truly right and just, our duty and our salvation,
always and everywhere to give you thanks,

Lord, holy Father, almighty and eternal God,
through Christ our Lord.

For today the Virgin Mother of God
was assumed into heaven
as the beginning and image
of your Church's coming to perfection
and a sign of sure hope and comfort to your pilgrim
    people;
rightly you would not allow her
to see the corruption of the tomb
since from her own body she marvelously brought forth
your incarnate Son, the Author of all life.

And so, in company with the choirs of Angels,
we praise you, and with joy we proclaim:

➔ No. 23, p. 23

COMMUNION ANT. Lk 1:48-49   [Blessed Is Mary]
**All generations will call me blessed, for he who is
mighty has done great things for me.** ↓

PRAYER AFTER COMMUNION   [Mary's Intercession]
Having received the Sacrament of salvation,
we ask you to grant, O Lord,
that, through the intercession of the Blessed Virgin
    Mary,
whom you assumed into heaven,
we may be brought to the glory of the resurrection.
Through Christ our Lord.
℟. **Amen.**   ➔ No. 30, p. 77

Optional Solemn Blessings, p. 97, and Prayers over the People, p. 105

"O woman, great is your faith! Let it be done for you as you wish."

AUGUST 20

20th SUNDAY IN ORDINARY TIME

ENTRANCE ANT. Ps 84 (83):10-11   [God Our Shield]

Turn your eyes, O God, our shield; and look on the face of your anointed one; one day within your courts is better than a thousand elsewhere. → No. 2, p. 10

COLLECT   [Attaining God's Promises]

O God, who have prepared for those who love you
good things which no eye can see,
fill our hearts, we pray, with the warmth of your love,
so that, loving you in all things and above all things,
we may attain your promises,
which surpass every human desire.
Through our Lord Jesus Christ, your Son,
who lives and reigns with you in the unity of the Holy
   Spirit,
God, for ever and ever. ℟. **Amen.** ↓

FIRST READING Is 56:1, 6-7   [Justice and Salvation for All]

> The prophet warns his people that for salvation, they must do what is just, love the Lord, and keep the sabbath. God will then lead them to his mountain and accept their sacrifices.

A reading from the Book of the Prophet Isaiah

THUS says the LORD:
   Observe what is right, do what is just;
      for my salvation is about to come,
      my justice, about to be revealed.

The foreigners who join themselves to the LORD,
      ministering to him,
loving the name of the LORD,
      and becoming his servants—
all who keep the sabbath free from profanation
      and hold to my covenant,
them I will bring to my holy mountain
      and make joyful in my house of prayer;
their holocausts and sacrifices
      will be acceptable on my altar,
for my house shall be called
      a house of prayer for all peoples.

The word of the Lord. ℞. **Thanks be to God.** ↓

RESPONSORIAL PSALM Ps 67   [Praise for the Lord]

℞. **O God, let all the nations praise you!**

May God have pity on us and bless us;
   may he let his face shine upon us.
So may your way be known upon earth;
   among all nations, your salvation.

℞. **O God, let all the nations praise you!**

May the nations be glad and exult
   because you rule the peoples in equity;
   the nations on the earth you guide.

℟. **O God, let all the nations praise you!**

May the peoples praise you, O God;
    may all the peoples praise you!
May God bless us,
    and may all the ends of the earth fear him!

℟. **O God, let all the nations praise you!** ↓

SECOND READING Rom 11:13-15, 29-32

[Irrevocable Gifts and Call]

Paul is proud of his ministry and he is anxious to lead his Jewish brothers and sisters to reconciliation with God. In spite of their disobedience, God has been merciful toward them.

A reading from the Letter of Saint Paul to the Romans

B ROTHERS and sisters: I am speaking to you Gentiles. Inasmuch as I am the apostle to the Gentiles, I glory in my ministry in order to make my race jealous and thus save some of them. For if their rejection is the reconciliation of the world, what will their acceptance be but life from the dead?

For the gifts and the call of God are irrevocable. Just as you once disobeyed God but have now received mercy because of their disobedience, so they have now disobeyed in order that, by virtue of the mercy shown to you, they too may now receive mercy. For God delivered all to disobedience, that he might have mercy upon all.— The word of the Lord. ℟. **Thanks be to God.** ↓

ALLELUIA Cf. Mt 4:23

[Jesus Heals]

℟. **Alleluia, alleluia.**
Jesus proclaimed the Gospel of the kingdom
and cured every disease among the people.
℟. **Alleluia, alleluia.** ↓

GOSPEL Mt 15:21-28

[Reward of Faith]

A Canaanite woman whose daughter is possessed comes to Jesus and asks for a favor with perseverance. Jesus commends her great faith and cures her daughter.

℣. The Lord be with you. ℟. **And with your spirit.**
✛ A reading from the holy Gospel according to Matthew.
℟. **Glory to you, O Lord.**

AT that time, Jesus withdrew to the region of Tyre and Sidon. And behold, a Canaanite woman of that district came and called out, "Have pity on me, Lord, Son of David! My daughter is tormented by a demon." But Jesus did not say a word in answer to her. Jesus' disciples came and asked him, "Send her away, for she keeps calling out after us." He said in reply, "I was sent only to the lost sheep of the house of Israel." But the woman came and did Jesus homage, saying, "Lord, help me." He said in reply, "It is not right to take the food of the children and throw it to the dogs." She said, "Please, Lord, for even the dogs eat the scraps that fall from the table of their masters." Then Jesus said to her in reply, "O woman, great is your faith! Let it be done for you as you wish." And the woman's daughter was healed from that hour.— The Gospel of the Lord. ℟. **Praise to you, Lord Jesus Christ.** → No. 15, p. 18

PRAYER OVER THE OFFERINGS   [Glorious Exchange]

Receive our oblation, O Lord,
by which is brought about a glorious exchange,
that, by offering what you have given,
we may merit to receive your very self.
Through Christ our Lord.
℟. **Amen.** → No. 21, p. 22 (Pref. P 29-36)

COMMUNION ANT. Ps 130 (129):7   [Plentiful Redemption]
With the Lord there is mercy; in him is plentiful redemption. ↓

OR Jn 6:51   [Eternal Life]

I am the living bread that came down from heaven, says the Lord. Whoever eats of this bread will live for ever. ↓

PRAYER AFTER COMMUNION   [Coheirs in Heaven]

Made partakers of Christ through these Sacraments,
we humbly implore your mercy, Lord,
that, conformed to his image on earth,
we may merit also to be his coheirs in heaven.
Who lives and reigns for ever and ever.
℞. **Amen.**   → No. 30, p. 77

Optional Solemn Blessings, p. 97, and Prayers over the People, p. 105

"You are Peter, and upon this rock I will build my Church."

AUGUST 27

21st SUNDAY IN ORDINARY TIME

ENTRANCE ANT. Cf. Ps 86 (85):1-3   [Save Us]

Turn your ear, O Lord, and answer me; save the servant who trusts in you, my God. Have mercy on me, O Lord, for I cry to you all the day long. → No. 2, p. 10

COLLECT   [One in Mind and Heart]

O God, who cause the minds of the faithful
to unite in a single purpose,
grant your people to love what you command
and to desire what you promise,
that, amid the uncertainties of this world,
our hearts may be fixed on that place
where true gladness is found.
Through our Lord Jesus Christ, your Son,
who lives and reigns with you in the unity of the Holy
    Spirit,
God, for ever and ever. ℟. **Amen.** ↓

FIRST READING Is 22:19-23   [The Gift of Authority]

Eliakim is given the leadership of the Israelites. He is to
become the father of the Jewish people. He shall have the
key of the House of David. He is to have a place of honor
for his family.

   A reading from the Book of the Prophet Isaiah

THUS says the LORD, to Shebna, master of the
    palace:
"I will thrust you from your office
      and pull you down from your station.
On that day I will summon my servant
      Eliakim, son of Hilkiah;
I will clothe him with your robe,
      and gird him with your sash,
      and give over to him your authority.
He shall be a father to the inhabitants of Jerusalem,
      and to the house of Judah.
I will place the key of the House of David on
      Eliakim's shoulder;
   when he opens, no one shall shut,
   when he shuts, no one shall open.

I will fix him like a peg in a sure spot,
  to be a place of honor for his family."
The word of the Lord. ℞. **Thanks be to God.** ↓

RESPONSORIAL PSALM Ps 138   [God's Eternal Love]

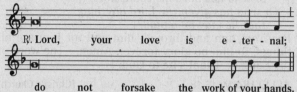

℞. **Lord,   your   love   is   e - ter - nal;
do   not   forsake   the   work of your hands.**

I will give thanks to you, O Lord, with all my heart,
  for you have heard the words of my mouth;
in the presence of the angels I will sing your praise;
  I will worship at your holy temple.

℞. **Lord, your love is eternal; do not forsake the work
  of your hands.**

I will give thanks to your name,
  because of your kindness and your truth:
when I called, you answered me;
  you built up strength within me.

℞. **Lord, your love is eternal; do not forsake the work
  of your hands.**

The Lord is exalted, yet the lowly he sees,
  and the proud he knows from afar.
Your kindness, O Lord, endures forever;
  forsake not the work of your hands.

℞. **Lord, your love is eternal; do not forsake the work
  of your hands.** ↓

SECOND READING Rom 11:33-36   [Eternal Glory]

**Paul offers a description of God, noting his infinite wisdom.
God's ways are unsearchable, and no one can really measure
the mind of God. But in him all things have their being.**

A reading from the Letter of Saint Paul to the Romans

OH, the depth of the riches and wisdom and knowledge of God! How inscrutable are his judgments and how unsearchable his ways!

For who has known the mind of the Lord
or who has been his counselor?
Or who has given the Lord anything
that he may be repaid?

For from him and through him and for him are all things. To him be glory forever. Amen.—The word of the Lord. ℟. **Thanks be to God.** ↓

ALLELUIA Mt 16:18   [Christ's Church]

℟. **Alleluia, alleluia.**
You are Peter and upon this rock I will build my Church
and the gates of the netherworld shall not prevail against it.
℟. **Alleluia, alleluia.** ↓

GOSPEL Mt 16:13-20   [The First Pope]

Peter acknowledges that Jesus is the Messiah. Jesus, in turn, declares Peter the rock upon which his Church is to be built. He also gives Peter the power of the keys.

℣. The Lord be with you. ℟. **And with your spirit.**
✤ A reading from the holy Gospel according to Matthew.
℟. **Glory to you, O Lord.**

JESUS went into the region of Caesarea Philippi and he asked his disciples, "Who do people say that the Son of Man is?" They replied, "Some say John the Baptist, others Elijah, still others Jeremiah or one of the prophets." He said to them, "But who do you say that I am?" Simon Peter said in reply, "You are the Christ, the Son of the living God." Jesus said to him in reply, "Blessed are you, Simon son of Jonah. For flesh and blood has not revealed this to you, but my heavenly Father. And so I say to you, you are Peter, and upon this rock I will build my church, and the gates

of the netherworld shall not prevail against it. I will
give you the keys to the kingdom of heaven.
Whatever you bind on earth shall be bound in heaven;
and whatever you loose on earth shall be loosed in
heaven."Then he strictly ordered his disciples to tell
no one that he was the Christ.—The Gospel of the
Lord. ℟. **Praise to you, Lord Jesus Christ.**

➜ No. 15, p. 18

PRAYER OVER THE OFFERINGS   [Unity and Peace]

O Lord, who gained for yourself a people by adoption
through the one sacrifice offered once for all,
bestow graciously on us, we pray,
the gifts of unity and peace in your Church.
Through Christ our Lord.
℟. **Amen.**   ➜ No. 21, p. 22 (Pref. P 29-36)

COMMUNION ANT. Cf. Ps 104 (103):13-15

[Sacred Bread and Wine]

**The earth is replete with the fruits of your work, O
Lord; you bring forth bread from the earth and wine
to cheer the heart.** ↓

OR Cf. Jn 6:54   [Eternal Life]

**Whoever eats my flesh and drinks my blood has eter-
nal life, says the Lord, and I will raise him up on the
last day.** ↓

PRAYER AFTER COMMUNION   [Pleasing God]

Complete within us, O Lord, we pray,
the healing work of your mercy
and graciously perfect and sustain us,
so that in all things we may please you.
Through Christ our Lord.
℟. **Amen.**   ➜ No. 30, p. 77

Optional Solemn Blessings, p. 97, and Prayers over the People, p. 105

"You are thinking not as God does, but as human beings do."

SEPTEMBER 3

22nd SUNDAY IN ORDINARY TIME

ENTRANCE ANT. Cf. Ps 86 (85):3, 5   [Call Upon God]

Have mercy on me, O Lord, for I cry to you all the day long. O Lord, you are good and forgiving, full of mercy to all who call to you.   ➙ No. 2, p. 10

COLLECT   [God's Watchful Care]

God of might, giver of every good gift,
put into our hearts the love of your name,
so that, by deepening our sense of reverence,
you may nurture in us what is good
and, by your watchful care,
keep safe what you have nurtured.
Through our Lord Jesus Christ, your Son,
who lives and reigns with you in the unity of the Holy
    Spirit,
God, for ever and ever. ℟. **Amen.** ↓

FIRST READING Jer 20:7-9   [Power of God's Word]

Jeremiah admits that he has become a mockery for the Lord. He is derided and reproached, but he cannot help but speak the word of the Lord.

494

A reading from the Book of the Prophet Jeremiah

Y OU duped me, O LORD, and I let myself be duped;
you were too strong for me, and you triumphed.
All the day I am an object of laughter;
everyone mocks me.

Whenever I speak, I must cry out,
violence and outrage is my message;
the word of the LORD has brought me
derision and reproach all the day.

I say to myself, I will not mention him,
I will speak in his name no more.
But then it becomes like fire burning in my heart,
imprisoned in my bones;
I grow weary holding it in, I cannot endure it.
The word of the Lord. ℟. **Thanks be to God.** ↓

RESPONSORIAL PSALM Ps 63   [Thirsting for God]

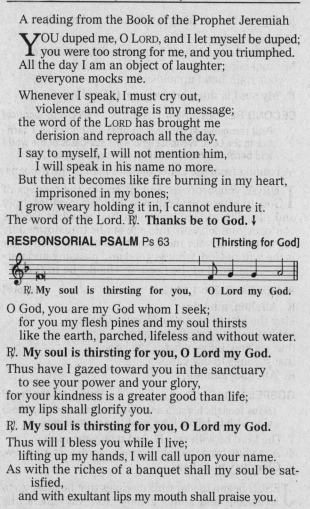

℟. My soul is thirsting for you,   O Lord my God.

O God, you are my God whom I seek;
for you my flesh pines and my soul thirsts
like the earth, parched, lifeless and without water.

℟. **My soul is thirsting for you, O Lord my God.**

Thus have I gazed toward you in the sanctuary
to see your power and your glory,
for your kindness is a greater good than life;
my lips shall glorify you.

℟. **My soul is thirsting for you, O Lord my God.**

Thus will I bless you while I live;
lifting up my hands, I will call upon your name.
As with the riches of a banquet shall my soul be satisfied,
and with exultant lips my mouth shall praise you.

℟. **My soul is thirsting for you, O Lord my God.**

You are my help,
   and in the shadow of your wings I shout for joy.
My soul clings fast to you;
   your right hand upholds me.
℟. **My soul is thirsting for you, O Lord my God.** ↓

SECOND READING Rom 12:1-2   [A Living Sacrifice]

   **Paul recommends sacrifice, to offer our bodies as a sacri-
   fice to the Lord. We must ignore the standards of the world
   and become renewed in spirit to be pleasing to God.**

A reading from the Letter of Saint Paul to the Romans

I URGE you, brothers and sisters, by the mercies of
   God, to offer your bodies as a living sacrifice, holy
and pleasing to God, your spiritual worship. Do not
conform yourselves to this age but be transformed by
the renewal of your mind, that you may discern what
is the will of God, what is good and pleasing and perfect.—The word of the Lord. ℟. **Thanks be to God.** ↓

ALLELUIA Cf. Eph 1:17-18   [Hope]

℟. **Alleluia, alleluia.**
May the Father of our Lord Jesus Christ
enlighten the eyes of our hearts,
that we may know what is the hope
that belongs to our call.
℟. **Alleluia, alleluia.** ↓

GOSPEL Mt 16:21-27   [Taking Up the Cross]

   **Jesus foretells his suffering, Passion, and Death. All those
   who wish to follow Jesus must take up their cross.**

℣. The Lord be with you. ℟. **And with your spirit.**
✠ A reading from the holy Gospel according to Matthew.
℟. **Glory to you, O Lord.**

JESUS began to show his disciples that he must go to
   Jerusalem and suffer greatly from the elders, the

chief priests, and the scribes, and be killed and on the third day be raised. Then Peter took Jesus aside and began to rebuke him, "God forbid, Lord! No such thing shall ever happen to you." He turned and said to Peter, "Get behind me, Satan! You are an obstacle to me. You are thinking not as God does, but as human beings do."

Then Jesus said to his disciples, "Whoever wishes to come after me must deny himself, take up his cross, and follow me. For whoever wishes to save his life will lose it, but whoever loses his life for my sake will find it. What profit would there be for one to gain the whole world and forfeit his life? Or what can one give in exchange for his life? For the Son of Man will come with his angels in his Father's glory, and then he will repay all according to his conduct."—The Gospel of the Lord.
℟. **Praise to you, Lord Jesus Christ.**   ➔ No. 15, p. 18

PRAYER OVER THE OFFERINGS   [Blessing of Salvation]

May this sacred offering, O Lord,
confer on us always the blessing of salvation,
that what it celebrates in mystery
it may accomplish in power.
Through Christ our Lord.
℟. **Amen.**   ➔ No. 21, p. 22 (Pref. P 29-36)

COMMUNION ANT. Ps 31 (30):20   [God's Goodness]

How great is the goodness, Lord, that you keep for those who fear you. ↓

OR Mt 5:9-10   [Blessed the Peacemakers]

Blessed are the peacemakers, for they shall be called children of God. Blessed are they who are persecuted for the sake of righteousness, for theirs is the Kingdom of Heaven. ↓

PRAYER AFTER COMMUNION   [Serving God in Neighbor]

Renewed by this bread from the heavenly table,
we beseech you, Lord,

that, being the food of charity,
it may confirm our hearts
and stir us to serve you in our neighbor.
Through Christ our Lord.
℟. **Amen.**   ➜ No. 30, p. 77

Optional Solemn Blessings, p. 97, and Prayers over the People, p. 105

*"Where two or three are gathered together in my name,
there am I in the midst of them."*

SEPTEMBER 10

23rd SUNDAY IN ORDINARY TIME

ENTRANCE ANT. Ps 119 (118):137, 124   [Plea for Mercy]
**You are just, O Lord, and your judgment is right; treat
your servant in accord with your merciful love.**

➜ No. 2, p. 10

COLLECT   [Christian Freedom]
O God, by whom we are redeemed and receive adoption,
look graciously upon your beloved sons and daughters,
that those who believe in Christ
may receive true freedom
and an everlasting inheritance.
Through our Lord Jesus Christ, your Son,

who lives and reigns with you in the unity of the Holy
  Spirit,
God, for ever and ever. ℟. **Amen.** ↓

FIRST READING Ez 33:7-9   [Warning the Wicked]

**Ezekiel is charged to dissuade evildoers from their faults.
If evildoers do not heed this warning, then they will die for
their guilt.**

A reading from the Book of the Prophet Ezekiel

THUS says the LORD: You, son of man, I have
  appointed watchman for the house of Israel;
when you hear me say anything, you shall warn them
for me. If I tell the wicked, "O wicked one, you shall
surely die," and you do not speak out to dissuade the
wicked from his way, [the wicked] shall die for his
guilt, but I will hold you responsible for his death. But
if you warn the wicked, trying to turn him from his
way, and he refuses to turn from his way, he shall die
for his guilt, but you shall save yourself.—The word of
the Lord. ℟. **Thanks be to God.** ↓

RESPONSORIAL PSALM Ps 95   [Answering the Lord's Call]

℟. **If today you hear his voice, harden not your hearts.**

Come, let us sing joyfully to the LORD;
  let us acclaim the rock of our salvation.
Let us come into his presence with thanksgiving;
  let us joyfully sing psalms to him.

℟. **If today you hear his voice, harden not your hearts.**

Come, let us bow down in worship;
  let us kneel before the LORD who made us.
For he is our God,
  and we are the people he shepherds, the flock he
    guides.

℟. **If today you hear his voice, harden not your hearts.**

Oh, that today you would hear his voice:
"Harden not your hearts as at Meribah,
as in the day of Massah in the desert,
where your fathers tempted me;
they tested me though they had seen my works."

℟. **If today you hear his voice, harden not your hearts.** ↓

SECOND READING Rom 13:8-10   [Love of Neighbor]

All who love their neighbors truly fulfill the law. The commandments forbidding adultery, stealing, murder, and coveting are all summed up in this law of laws.

A reading from the Letter of Saint Paul to the Romans

BROTHERS and sisters: Owe nothing to anyone, except to love one another; for the one who loves another has fulfilled the law. The commandments, "You shall not commit adultery; you shall not kill; you shall not steal; you shall not covet," and whatever other commandment there may be, are summed up in this saying, namely, "You shall love your neighbor as yourself." Love does no evil to the neighbor; hence, love is the fulfillment of the law.—The word of the Lord. ℟. **Thanks be to God.** ↓

ALLELUIA 2 Cor 5:19   [Reconciliation]

℟. **Alleluia, alleluia.**
God was reconciling the world to himself in Christ and entrusting to us the message of reconciliation.
℟. **Alleluia, alleluia.** ↓

GOSPEL Mt 18:15-20   [Communal Correction and Prayer]

To correct another person's fault, first speak to him or her. If this fails, invite a witness or two. But if the person continues in this fault, note it before the church assembly. Pray together and make your petitions in the name of Jesus.

℣. The Lord be with you. ℟. **And with your spirit.**

✤ A reading from the holy Gospel according to Matthew.
℟. **Glory to you, O Lord.**

JESUS said to his disciples: "If your brother sins against you, go and tell him his fault between you and him alone. If he listens to you, you have won over your brother. If he does not listen, take one or two others along with you, so that 'every fact may be established on the testimony of two or three witnesses.' If he refuses to listen to them, tell the church. If he refuses to listen even to the church, then treat him as you would a Gentile or a tax collector. Amen, I say to you, whatever you bind on earth shall be bound in heaven, and whatever you loose on earth shall be loosed in heaven. Again, amen, I say to you, if two of you agree on earth about anything for which they are to pray, it shall be granted to them by my heavenly Father. For where two or three are gathered together in my name, there am I in the midst of them."—The Gospel of the Lord. ℟. **Praise to you, Lord Jesus Christ.**   ➜ No. 15, p. 18

PRAYER OVER THE OFFERINGS   [True Prayer and Peace]

O God, who give us the gift of true prayer and of peace,
graciously grant that through this offering,
we may do fitting homage to your divine majesty
and, by partaking of the sacred mystery,
we may be faithfully united in mind and heart.
Through Christ our Lord.
℟. **Amen.**   ➜ No. 21, p. 22 (Pref. P 29-36)

COMMUNION ANT. Cf. Ps 42 (41):2-3   [Yearning for God]

Like the deer that yearns for running streams, so my soul is yearning for you, my God; my soul is thirsting for God, the living God. ↓

OR Jn 8:12   [The Light of Life]

I am the light of the world, says the Lord; whoever follows me will not walk in darkness, but will have the light of life. ↓

PRAYER AFTER COMMUNION   [Word and Sacrament]

Grant that your faithful, O Lord,
whom you nourish and endow with life
through the food of your Word and heavenly Sacrament,
may so benefit from your beloved Son's great gifts
that we may merit an eternal share in his life.
Who lives and reigns for ever and ever.
℞. **Amen.**   → No. 30, p. 77

Optional Solemn Blessings, p. 97, and Prayers over the People, p. 105

"His master handed him over to the torturers."

SEPTEMBER 17

24th SUNDAY IN ORDINARY TIME

ENTRANCE ANT. Cf. Sir 36:18   **[God's Peace]**
Give peace, O Lord, to those who wait for you, that
your prophets be found true. Hear the prayers of your
servant, and of your people Israel.   → No. 2, p. 10

COLLECT   **[Serving God]**
Look upon us, O God,
Creator and ruler of all things,
and, that we may feel the working of your mercy,
grant that we may serve you with all our heart.
Through our Lord Jesus Christ, your Son,
who lives and reigns with you in the unity of the Holy
   Spirit,
God, for ever and ever. ℟. **Amen.** ↓

FIRST READING Sir 27:30—28:7 **[The Need for Forgiveness]**
   The sinner abounds in wrath. It is the Lord who punishes,
   and we are to forgive injustice and be merciful. We should
   think of our last days.

A reading from the Book of Sirach

503

WRATH and anger are hateful things,
  yet the sinner hugs them tight.
The vengeful will suffer the LORD'S vengeance,
    for he remembers their sins in detail.
Forgive your neighbor's injustice;
    then when you pray, your own sins will be for-
      given.
Could anyone nourish anger against another
    and expect healing from the LORD?
Could anyone refuse mercy to another like himself,
    can he seek pardon for his own sins?
If one who is but flesh cherishes wrath,
    who will forgive his sins?
Remember your last days, set enmity aside;
    remember death and decay, and cease from sin!
Think of the commandments, hate not your neighbor;
    remember the Most High's covenant, and over-
      look faults.

The word of the Lord. ℟. **Thanks be to God.** ↓

RESPONSORIAL PSALM Ps 103   [God's Mercy]

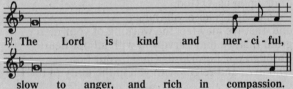

℟. The Lord is kind and mer - ci - ful,

slow to anger, and rich in compassion.

Bless the LORD, O my soul;
  and all my being, bless his holy name.
Bless the LORD, O my soul,
  and forget not all his benefits.

℟. **The Lord is kind and merciful, slow to anger, and
  rich in compassion.**

He pardons all your iniquities,
  heals all your ills,

He redeems your life from destruction,
  crowns you with kindness and compassion.

℟. **The Lord is kind and merciful, slow to anger, and
  rich in compassion.**

He will not always chide,
  nor does he keep his wrath forever.
Not according to our sins does he deal with us,
  nor does he requite us according to our crimes.

℟. **The Lord is kind and merciful, slow to anger, and
  rich in compassion.**

For as the heavens are high above the earth,
  so surpassing is his kindness toward those who
    fear him.
As far as the east is from the west,
  so far has he put our transgressions from us.

℟. **The Lord is kind and merciful, slow to anger, and
  rich in compassion.** ↓

SECOND READING Rom 14:7-9   [God's Partners]

> **We are not our own master since we belong to Jesus. This
> is true in life and in death.**

A reading from the Letter of Saint Paul
to the Romans

BROTHERS and sisters: None of us lives for oneself, and no one dies for oneself. For if we live, we
live for the Lord, and if we die, we die for the Lord; so
then, whether we live or die, we are the Lord's. For
this is why Christ died and came to life, that he might
be Lord of both the dead and the living. —The word
of the Lord. ℟. **Thanks be to God.** ↓

ALLELUIA Jn 13:34   [Love One Another]
℟. **Alleluia, alleluia.**
I give you a new commandment, says the Lord;

love one another as I have loved you.
℟. **Alleluia, alleluia.** ↓

GOSPEL Mt 18:21-35   [Forgiving Our Neighbor]

Jesus answers Peter that we are to forgive our neighbor's faults without any limit. Jesus tells the parable of the unjust steward who was forgiven a large debt by his master but refused to forgive a small debt owed to himself.

℣. The Lord be with you. ℟. **And with your spirit.**
✝ A reading from the holy Gospel according to Matthew.
℟. **Glory to you, O Lord.**

PETER approached Jesus and asked him, "Lord, if my brother sins against me, how often must I forgive? As many as seven times?" Jesus answered, "I say to you, not seven times but seventy-seven times. That is why the kingdom of heaven may be likened to a king who decided to settle accounts with his servants. When he began the accounting, a debtor was brought before him who owed him a huge amount. Since he had no way of paying it back, his master ordered him to be sold, along with his wife, his children, and all his property, in payment of the debt. At that, the servant fell down, did him homage, and said, 'Be patient with me, and I will pay you back in full.' Moved with compassion the master of that servant let him go and forgave him the loan. When that servant had left, he found one of his fellow servants who owed him a much smaller amount. He seized him and started to choke him, demanding, 'Pay back what you owe.' Falling to his knees, his fellow servant begged him, 'Be patient with me, and I will pay you back.' But he refused. Instead, he had the fellow servant put in prison until he paid back the debt. Now when his fellow servants saw what had happened, they were deeply disturbed, and went to their master and reported the whole affair. His master summoned him and said to him, 'You wicked servant! I forgave you your entire debt because you begged me to. Should you not have had pity on your fellow servant, as I had pity on you?' Then in anger his master handed him over to the torturers until he should pay back the whole debt. So will my heavenly Father do to you, unless each of you forgives your brother from your heart."—The Gospel of the Lord. ℟. **Praise to you, Lord Jesus Christ.** ➜ No. 15, p. 18

PRAYER OVER THE OFFERINGS [Accept Our Offerings]

Look with favor on our supplications, O Lord,
and in your kindness accept these, your servants' offerings,
that what each has offered to the honor of your name
may serve the salvation of all.
Through Christ our Lord.
℟. **Amen.** ➜ No. 21, p. 22 (Pref. P 29-36)

COMMUNION ANT. Cf. Ps 36 (35):8 [God's Mercy]

How precious is your mercy, O God! The children of men seek shelter in the shadow of your wings. ↓

OR Cf. 1 Cor 10:16 [Share of Christ]

The chalice of blessing that we bless is a communion in the Blood of Christ; and the bread that we break is a sharing in the Body of the Lord. ↓

PRAYER AFTER COMMUNION [Heavenly Gift]

May the working of this heavenly gift, O Lord, we pray,
take possession of our minds and bodies,
so that its effects, and not our own desires,
may always prevail in us.
Through Christ our Lord.
℟. **Amen.** ➜ No. 30, p. 77

Optional Solemn Blessings, p. 97, and Prayers over the People, p. 105

"The last will be first, and the first will be last."

SEPTEMBER 24

25th SUNDAY IN ORDINARY TIME

ENTRANCE ANT. [Salvation of People]

I am the salvation of the people, says the Lord. Should they cry to me in any distress, I will hear them, and I will be their Lord for ever. → No. 2, p. 10

COLLECT [Attaining Eternal Life]

O God, who founded all the commands of your sacred Law
upon love of you and of our neighbor,
grant that, by keeping your precepts,
we may merit to attain eternal life.
Through our Lord Jesus Christ, your Son,
who lives and reigns with you in the unity of the Holy Spirit,
God, for ever and ever. ℟. **Amen.** ↓

FIRST READING Is 55:6-9 [Seek the Lord]

Seek the Lord. His ways are far above human ways. The thoughts of God are not the thoughts of human beings. God is rich in forgiving.

A reading from the Book of the Prophet Isaiah

SEEK the LORD while he may be found,
call him while he is near.
Let the scoundrel forsake his way,
    and the wicked his thoughts:
let him turn to the LORD for mercy;
    to our God, who is generous in forgiving.
For my thoughts are not your thoughts,
    nor are your ways my ways, says the LORD.
As high as the heavens are above the earth,
    so high are my ways above your ways
    and my thoughts above your thoughts.
The word of the Lord. ℟. **Thanks be to God.** ↓

RESPONSORIAL PSALM Ps 145   [The Nearness of God]

℟. **The Lord is near to all who call up-on him.**

Every day will I bless you,
    and I will praise your name forever and ever.
Great is the LORD and highly to be praised;
    his greatness is unsearchable.

℟. **The Lord is near to all who call upon him.**

The LORD is gracious and merciful,
    slow to anger and of great kindness.
The LORD is good to all
    and compassionate toward all his works.

℟. **The Lord is near to all who call upon him.**

The LORD is just in all his ways
    and holy in all his works.
The LORD is near to all who call upon him,
    to all who call upon him in truth.

℟. **The Lord is near to all who call upon him.** ↓

SECOND READING Phil 1:20c-24, 27a   [Life in Christ]

**Paul notes that whether he lives or dies, his life belongs to
Christ. It would be more beneficial for the Philippians for**

Paul to continue living in the flesh to bring them the message of Jesus.

A reading from the Letter of Saint Paul
to the Philippians

BROTHERS and sisters: Christ will be magnified in my body, whether by life or by death. For to me life is Christ, and death is gain. If I go on living in the flesh, that means fruitful labor for me. And I do not know which I shall choose. I am caught between the two. I long to depart this life and be with Christ, for that is far better. Yet that I remain in the flesh is more necessary for your benefit.

Only, conduct yourselves in a way worthy of the gospel of Christ. —The word of the Lord. ℟. **Thanks be to God.** ↓

ALLELUIA Cf. Acts 16:14b   [Listen to Jesus]

℟. **Alleluia, alleluia.**
Open our hearts, O Lord,
to listen to the words of your Son.
℟. **Alleluia, alleluia.** ↓

GOSPEL Mt 20:1-16   [The Workers in the Vineyard]

Jesus teaches that the Kingdom of God is like the landowner who hires early in the morning, again at midmorning, at noon, and in midafternoon. At payment time, all the workers receive the same wage. How just and generous God is!

℣. The Lord be with you. ℟. **And with your spirit.**
✙ A reading from the holy Gospel according to Matthew.
℟. **Glory to you, O Lord.**

JESUS told his disciples this parable: "The kingdom of heaven is like a landowner who went out at dawn to hire laborers for his vineyard. After agreeing with them for the usual daily wage, he sent them into his vineyard. Going out about nine o'clock, the landowner saw others standing idle in the marketplace, and he said to them, 'You too go into my vineyard, and I will give you what is just.' So they went off. And he went out again around noon, and around three o'clock, and did likewise. Going out about five o'clock, the landowner found others standing around, and said to them, 'Why do you stand here idle all day?' They answered, 'Because no one has hired us.' He said to them, 'You too go into my vineyard.' When it was evening the owner of the vineyard said to his foreman, 'Summon the laborers and give them their pay, beginning with the last and ending with the first.' When those who had started about five o'clock came, each received the usual daily wage. So when the first came, they thought that they would receive more, but each of them also got the usual wage. And on receiving it they grumbled against the landowner, saying, 'These last ones worked only one hour, and you have made them equal to us, who bore the day's burden and the heat.' He said to one of them in reply, 'My friend, I am not cheating you. Did you not agree with me for the usual daily wage? Take what is yours and go. What if I wish to give this last one the same as you? Or am I not free to do as I wish with my own money? Are you envious because I am generous?' Thus, the last will be first, and the first will be last."—The Gospel of the Lord. ℟. **Praise to you, Lord Jesus Christ.**

➜ No. 15, p. 18

PRAYER OVER THE OFFERINGS   [Devotion and Faith]

Receive with favor, O Lord, we pray,
the offerings of your people,
that what they profess with devotion and faith
may be theirs through these heavenly mysteries.
Through Christ our Lord.
℟. **Amen.**   ➜ No. 21, p. 22 (Pref. P 29-36)

COMMUNION ANT. Ps 119 (118):4-5

[Keeping God's Statutes]

You have laid down your precepts to be carefully kept; may my ways be firm in keeping your statutes. ↓

OR Jn 10:14   [The Good Shepherd]

I am the Good Shepherd, says the Lord; I know my sheep, and mine know me. ↓

PRAYER AFTER COMMUNION   [Possessing Redemption]

Graciously raise up, O Lord,
those you renew with this Sacrament,
that we may come to possess your redemption
both in mystery and in the manner of our life.
Through Christ our Lord.
℟. **Amen.**   ➜ No. 30, p. 77

Optional Solemn Blessings, p. 97, and Prayers over the People, p. 105

"Tax collectors and prostitutes are entering the kingdom of God before you."

OCTOBER 1

26th SUNDAY IN ORDINARY TIME

ENTRANCE ANT. Dn 3:31, 29, 30, 43, 42   [God's Mercy]

All that you have done to us, O Lord, you have done with true judgment, for we have sinned against you and not obeyed your commandments. But give glory to your name and deal with us according to the bounty of your mercy.   ➔ No. 2, p. 10

COLLECT   [God's Pardon]

O God, who manifest your almighty power
above all by pardoning and showing mercy,
bestow, we pray, your grace abundantly upon us
and make those hastening to attain your promises
heirs to the treasures of heaven.
Through our Lord Jesus Christ, your Son,
who lives and reigns with you in the unity of the Holy
   Spirit,
God, for ever and ever. ℞. **Amen.** ↓

FIRST READING Ez 18:25-28 [The Virtuous Man Shall Live]

The Lord's way is fair and just. It is when sinners repent from their faults and do what is right that they are to live. Because of this reform, they deserve to live.

A reading from the Book of the Prophet Ezekiel

THUS says the LORD: You say, "The LORD's way is not fair!" Hear now, house of Israel: Is it my way that is unfair, or rather, are not your ways unfair? When someone virtuous turns away from virtue to commit iniquity, and dies, it is because of the iniquity he committed that he must die. But if he turns from the wickedness he has committed, and does what is right and just, he shall preserve his life; since he has turned away from all the sins that he committed, he shall surely live, he shall not die.—The word of the Lord. ℟. **Thanks be to God.** ↓

RESPONSORIAL PSALM Ps 25   [God's Compassion]

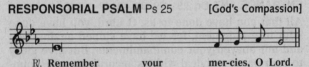

℟. **Remember   your   mer-cies, O Lord.**

Your ways, O LORD, make known to me;
   teach me your paths,
guide me in your truth and teach me,
   for you are God my savior.

℟. **Remember your mercies, O Lord.**

Remember that your compassion, O LORD,
   and your love are from of old.
The sins of my youth and my frailties remember not;
   in your kindness remember me,
      because of your goodness, O LORD.

℟. **Remember your mercies, O Lord.**

Good and upright is the LORD;
   thus he shows sinners the way.

He guides the humble to justice,
  he teaches the humble his way.·

℟. **Remember your mercies, O Lord. ↓**

SECOND READING Phil 2:1-11 or 2:1-5   [Jesus Is Lord]
**Paul encourages us to unify, to be of one heart and mind,
to possess a single love for one another. We should adopt
the attitude of Jesus. At his name every knee should bend.**

*[If the "Shorter Form" is used, the indented text in brackets is
omitted.]*

A reading from the Letter of Saint Paul
to the Philippians

BROTHERS and sisters: If there is any encouragement in Christ, any solace in love, any participation in the Spirit, any compassion and mercy, complete
my joy by being of the same mind, with the same love,
united in heart, thinking one thing. Do nothing out of
selfishness or out of vainglory; rather, humbly regard
others as more important than yourselves, each looking out not for his own interests, but also for those of
others. Have in you the same attitude that is also in
Christ Jesus,
    [Who, though he was in the form of God,
        did not regard equality with God
        something to be grasped.
    Rather, he emptied himself,
        taking the form of a slave,
        coming in human likeness;
        and found human in appearance,
        he humbled himself,
        becoming obedient to the point of death,
        even death on a cross.
    Because of this, God greatly exalted him
        and bestowed on him the name
        which is above every name,
        that at the name of Jesus

every knee should bend,
of those in heaven and on earth and under
    the earth,
and every tongue confess that
Jesus Christ is Lord,
to the glory of God the Father.]

The word of the Lord. ℟. **Thanks be to God.** ↓

ALLELUIA Jn 10:27   [Listen]

℟. **Alleluia, alleluia.**
My sheep hear my voice, says the Lord;
I know them, and they follow me.
℟. **Alleluia, alleluia.** ↓

GOSPEL Mt 21:28-32   [Obeying God's Will]

Jesus cites an example of a son who after having second
thoughts obeyed his father. Even sinners, once they repent
and sincerely search after God, will be saved.

℣. The Lord be with you. ℟. **And with your spirit.**
✠ A reading from the holy Gospel according to Matthew.
℟. **Glory to you, O Lord.**

JESUS said to the chief priests and elders of the
people: "What is your opinion? A man had two
sons. He came to the first and said, 'Son, go out and
work in the vineyard today.' He said in reply, 'I will
not,' but afterwards changed his mind and went. The
man came to the other son and gave the same order.
He said in reply, 'Yes, sir,' but did not go. Which of the
two did his father's will?" They answered, "The first."
Jesus said to them, "Amen, I say to you, tax collectors
and prostitutes are entering the kingdom of God
before you. When John came to you in the way of
righteousness, you did not believe him; but tax collectors and prostitutes did. Yet even when you saw that,
you did not later change your minds and believe
him."—The Gospel of the Lord. ℟. **Praise to you, Lord
Jesus Christ.**   ➜ No. 15, p. 18

PRAYER OVER THE OFFERINGS   [Offering as a Blessing]

Grant us, O merciful God,
that this our offering may find acceptance with you
and that through it the wellspring of all blessing
may be laid open before us.
Through Christ our Lord.
℟. **Amen.**   ➜ No. 21, p. 22 (Pref. P 29-36)

COMMUNION ANT. Cf. Ps 119 (118):49-50 [Words of Hope]

**Remember your word to your servant, O Lord, by
which you have given me hope. This is my comfort
when I am brought low.** ↓

OR 1 Jn 3:16   [Offering of Self]

**By this we came to know the love of God: that Christ
laid down his life for us; so we ought to lay down our
lives for one another.** ↓

PRAYER AFTER COMMUNION   [Coheirs with Christ]

May this heavenly mystery, O Lord,
restore us in mind and body,
that we may be coheirs in glory with Christ,
to whose suffering we are united
whenever we proclaim his Death.
Who lives and reigns for ever and ever.
℟. **Amen.**   ➜ No. 30, p. 77

Optional Solemn Blessings, p. 97, and Prayers over the People, p. 105

*"The stone that the builders rejected
has become the cornerstone."*

OCTOBER 8

27th SUNDAY IN ORDINARY TIME

ENTRANCE ANT. Cf. Est 4:17   **[Lord of All]**

**Within your will, O Lord, all things are established,
and there is none that can resist your will. For you
have made all things, the heaven and the earth, and all
that is held within the circle of heaven; you are the
Lord of all.**   → No. 2, p. 10

COLLECT   **[Mercy and Pardon]**

Almighty ever-living God,
who in the abundance of your kindness
surpass the merits and the desires of those who
    entreat you,
pour out your mercy upon us
to pardon what conscience dreads
and to give what prayer does not dare to ask.
Through our Lord Jesus Christ, your Son,
who lives and reigns with you in the unity of the Holy
    Spirit,
God, for ever and ever. ℟. **Amen.** ↓

FIRST READING Is 5:1-7   [The Lord's Vineyard]

Isaiah uses the story of a vineyard to show how the Lord respects his people. The vineyard is well cultivated, but it does not produce. The vineyard of the Lord is the house of Israel and the people of Judah his cherished plants.

A reading from the Book of the Prophet Isaiah

L ET me now sing of my friend,
my friend's song concerning his vineyard.
My friend had a vineyard
    on a fertile hillside;
he spaded it, cleared it of stones,
    and planted the choicest vines;
within it he built a watchtower,
    and hewed out a wine press.
Then he looked for the crop of grapes,
    but what it yielded was wild grapes.

Now, inhabitants of Jerusalem and people of Judah,
    judge between me and my vineyard:
What more was there to do for my vineyard
    that I had not done?
Why, when I looked for the crop of grapes,
    did it bring forth wild grapes?
Now, I will let you know
    what I mean to do to my vineyard:
take away its hedge, give it to grazing,
    break through its wall, let it be trampled!
Yes, I will make it a ruin:
    it shall not be pruned or hoed,
    but overgrown with thorns and briers;
I will command the clouds
    not to send rain upon it.
The vineyard of the LORD of hosts is the house of
        Israel,
    and the people of Judah are his cherished plant;

he looked for judgment, but see, bloodshed!
>   for justice, but hark, the outcry!
The word of the Lord. ℞. **Thanks be to God.** ↓

RESPONSORIAL PSALM Ps 80   [Safety in the Lord]

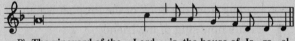

℞. The vineyard of the   Lord   is the house of Is - ra - el.

A vine from Egypt you transplanted;
>   you drove away the nations and planted it.
It put forth its foliage to the Sea,
>   its shoots as far as the River.

℞. **The vineyard of the Lord is the house of Israel.**

Why have you broken down its walls,
>   so that every passer-by plucks its fruit,
the boar from the forest lays it waste,
>   and the beasts of the field feed upon it?

℞. **The vineyard of the Lord is the house of Israel.**

Once again, O Lord of hosts,
>   look down from heaven, and see;
take care of this vine,
>   and protect what your right hand has planted
>   the son of man whom you yourself made strong.

℞. **The vineyard of the Lord is the house of Israel.**

Then we will no more withdraw from you;
>   give us new life, and we will call upon your name.
O Lord of hosts, restore us;
>   if your face shine upon us, then we shall be saved.

℞. **The vineyard of the Lord is the house of Israel.** ↓

SECOND READING Phil 4:6-9   [Wholesome Thoughts]
>   Pray to God for your needs. God will guard over you.
>   Discern what is true, noble, and good and pure, loved and

honored, virtuous or worthy of praise. God's peace will be with you.

A reading from the Letter of Saint Paul
to the Philippians

Brothers and sisters: Have no anxiety at all, but in everything, by prayer and petition, with thanksgiving, make your requests known to God. Then the peace of God that surpasses all understanding will guard your hearts and minds in Christ Jesus.

Finally, brothers and sisters, whatever is true, whatever is honorable, whatever is just, whatever is pure, whatever is lovely, whatever is gracious, if there is any excellence and if there is anything worthy of praise, think about these things. Keep on doing what you have learned and received and heard and seen in me. Then the God of peace will be with you.—The word of the Lord. ℟. **Thanks be to God.** ↓

ALLELUIA Cf. Jn 15:16   [Bear Fruit]

℟. **Alleluia, alleluia.**
I have chosen you from the world, says the Lord,
to go and bear fruit that will remain.
℟. **Alleluia, alleluia.** ↓

GOSPEL Mt 21:33-43   [The Tenant Farmers]

Jesus uses the parable of a vineyard owner. Salvation is offered to all. The chosen who reject Christ are really turning him over to the whole world. The vineyard will be leased to others. The Kingdom of God will produce fruit.

℣. The Lord be with you. ℟. **And with your spirit.**
✝ A reading from the holy Gospel according to Matthew.
℟. **Glory to you, O Lord.**

Jesus said to the chief priests and the elders of the people:"Hear another parable.There was a landowner who planted a vineyard, put a hedge around it, dug a wine press in it, and built a tower. Then he leased it to tenants and went on a journey. When vintage time drew near, he sent his servants to the tenants to obtain his produce. But the tenants seized the servants and one they beat, another they killed, and a third they stoned. Again he sent other servants, more numerous than the first ones, but they treated them in the same way. Finally, he sent his son to them, thinking, 'They will respect my son.' But when the tenants saw the son, they said to one another, 'This is the heir. Come, let us kill him and acquire his inheritance.' They seized him, threw him out of the vineyard, and killed him. What will the owner of the vineyard do to those tenants when he comes?" They answered him, "He will put those wretched men to a wretched death and lease his vineyard to other tenants who will give him the produce at the proper times." Jesus said to them, "Did you never read in the Scriptures:

The stone that the builders rejected
    has become the cornerstone;
by the Lord has this been done,
    and it is wonderful in our eyes?

Therefore, I say to you, the kingdom of God will be taken away from you and given to a people that will produce its fruit."—The Gospel of the Lord. ℟. **Praise to you, Lord Jesus Christ.**   → No. 15, p. 18

PRAYER OVER THE OFFERINGS   [Sanctifying Work]

Accept, O Lord, we pray,
the sacrifices instituted by your commands
and, through the sacred mysteries,
which we celebrate with dutiful service,
graciously complete the sanctifying work
by which you are pleased to redeem us.
Through Christ our Lord.
℟. **Amen.**   → No. 21, p. 22 (Pref. P 29-36)

COMMUNION ANT. Lam 3:25　　　[Hope in the Lord]
The Lord is good to those who hope in him, to the soul that seeks him. ↓

OR Cf. 1 Cor 10:17　　　[One Bread, One Body]
Though many, we are one bread, one body, for we all partake of the one Bread and one Chalice. ↓

PRAYER AFTER COMMUNION　　[Nourished by Sacrament]
Grant us, almighty God,
that we may be refreshed and nourished
by the Sacrament which we have received,
so as to be transformed into what we consume.
Through Christ our Lord.
℟. **Amen.**　　　　　　　　　　➜　No. 30, p. 77

Optional Solemn Blessings, p. 97, and Prayers over the People, p. 105

"Many are invited, but few are chosen."

OCTOBER 15

28th SUNDAY IN ORDINARY TIME

ENTRANCE ANT. Ps 130 (129):3-4   [A Forgiving God]

If you, O Lord, should mark iniquities, Lord, who could stand? But with you is found forgiveness, O God of Israel.   ➙ No. 2, p. 10

COLLECT   [Good Works]

May your grace, O Lord, we pray,
at all times go before us and follow after
and make us always determined
to carry out good works.
Through our Lord Jesus Christ, your Son,
who lives and reigns with you in the unity of the Holy
    Spirit,
God, for ever and ever. ℟. **Amen.** ↓

FIRST READING Is 25:6-10a   [God as Savior]

    The Lord will set up a sumptuous feast for his people. He
    will wipe away their tears. Then the people will recognize
    him as their Lord and God.

A reading from the Book of the Prophet Isaiah

ON this mountain the LORD of hosts
　will provide for all peoples
a feast of rich food and choice wines,
　　juicy, rich food and pure, choice wines.
On this mountain he will destroy
　　the veil that veils all peoples,
the web that is woven over all nations;
　　he will destroy death forever.
The Lord GOD will wipe away
　　the tears from every face;
the reproach of his people he will remove
　　from the whole earth; for the LORD has spoken.
　　On that day it will be said:
"Behold our God, to whom we looked to save us!
　　This is the LORD for whom we looked;
　　let us rejoice and be glad that he has saved us!"
For the hand of the LORD will rest on this mountain.
The word of the Lord. ℟. **Thanks be to God.** ↓

RESPONSORIAL PSALM Ps 23　　[Dwelling with the Lord]

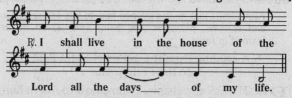

℟. I shall live in the house of the Lord all the days of my life.

The LORD is my shepherd; I shall not want.
　In verdant pastures he gives me repose;
beside restful waters he leads me;
　he refreshes my soul.

℟. **I shall live in the house of the Lord all the days of
　my life.**

He guides me in right paths
　for his name's sake.
Even though I walk in the dark valley
　I fear no evil; for you are at my side

with your rod and your staff
  that give me courage.

℟. **I shall live in the house of the Lord all the days of
  my life.**

You spread the table before me
  in the sight of my foes;
you anoint my head with oil;
  my cup overflows.

℟. **I shall live in the house of the Lord all the days of
  my life.**

Only goodness and kindness follow me
  all the days of my life;
and I shall dwell in the house of the LORD
  for years to come.

℟. **I shall live in the house of the Lord all the days of
  my life.** ↓

SECOND READING Phil 4:12-14, 19-20 [Sharing in Hardships]

Paul admits that he has learned how to live and accept joy
and sorrows, pleasures and pain. This lesson he has
learned in Jesus.

A reading from the Letter of Saint Paul
to the Philippians

B ROTHERS and sisters: I know how to live in humble circumstances; I know also how to live with
abundance. In every circumstance and in all things I
have learned the secret of being well fed and of going
hungry, of living in abundance and of being in need.
I can do all things in him who strengthens me. Still, it
was kind of you to share in my distress.

My God will fully supply whatever you need, in
accord with his glorious riches in Christ Jesus. To our
God and Father, glory forever and ever. Amen.—The
word of the Lord. ℟. **Thanks be to God.** ↓

ALLELUIA Cf. Eph 1:17-18   [Hope]

℟. **Alleluia, alleluia.**
May the Father of our Lord Jesus Christ
enlighten the eyes of our hearts,
so that we may know what is the hope
that belongs to our call.
℟. **Alleluia, alleluia.** ↓

GOSPEL Mt 22:1-14 or 22:1-10   [The Wedding Banquet]

> Jesus teaches using the parable of a king who gave a wed-
> ding banquet. Invited guests refused to come or mistreated
> his servants. The king destroyed these and invited the poor
> and simple. Even one of these did not accept his kindness.

*[If the "Shorter Form" is used, the indented text in brackets is
omitted.]*

℣. The Lord be with you. ℟. **And with your spirit.**
✢ A reading from the holy Gospel according to Matthew.
℟. **Glory to you, O Lord.**

JESUS again in reply spoke to the chief priests and
elders of the people in parables, saying, "The kingdom of heaven may be likened to a king who gave a
wedding feast for his son. He dispatched his servants
to summon the invited guests to the feast, but they
refused to come. A second time he sent other servants,
saying, 'Tell those invited: "Behold, I have prepared my
banquet, my calves and fattened cattle are killed, and
everything is ready; come to the feast." ' Some
ignored the invitation and went away, one to his farm,
another to his business. The rest laid hold of his servants, mistreated them, and killed them. The king was
enraged and sent his troops, destroyed those murder-
ers, and burned their city. Then he said to his servants, 'The feast is ready, but those who were invited
were not worthy to come. Go out, therefore, into the
main roads and invite to the feast whomever you
find.' The servants went out into the streets and

gathered all they found, bad and good alike, and the hall was filled with guests.

[But when the king came in to meet the guests, he saw a man there not dressed in a wedding garment. The king said to him, 'My friend, how is it that you came in here without a wedding garment?' But he was reduced to silence. Then the king said to his attendants, 'Bind his hands and feet, and cast him into the darkness outside, where there will be wailing and grinding of teeth.' Many are invited, but few are chosen.]"

The Gospel of the Lord. ℟. **Praise to you, Lord Jesus Christ.**   ➔ No. 15, p. 18

PRAYER OVER THE OFFERINGS   [Devotedness]

Accept, O Lord, the prayers of your faithful
with the sacrificial offerings,
that, through these acts of devotedness,
we may pass over to the glory of heaven.
Through Christ our Lord.
℟. **Amen.**   ➔ No. 21, p. 22 (Pref. P 29-36)

COMMUNION ANT. Cf. Ps 34 (33):11   [God's Providence]

The rich suffer want and go hungry, but those who seek the Lord lack no blessing. ↓

OR 1 Jn 3:2   [Vision of God]

When the Lord appears, we shall be like him, for we shall see him as he is. ↓

PRAYER AFTER COMMUNION   [Christ's Divine Nature]

We entreat your majesty most humbly, O Lord,
that, as you feed us with the nourishment
which comes from the most holy Body and Blood of
    your Son,
so you may make us sharers of his divine nature.

Who lives and reigns for ever and ever.
R̞. **Amen.**   ➜ No. 30, p. 77

Optional Solemn Blessings, p. 97, and Prayers over the People, p. 105

*"Repay to Caesar what belongs to Caesar and to God
what belongs to God."*

OCTOBER 22

29th SUNDAY IN ORDINARY TIME

ENTRANCE ANT. Cf. Ps 17 (16):6, 8   [Refuge in God]
**To you I call; for you will surely heed me, O God; turn
your ear to me; hear my words. Guard me as the apple
of your eye; in the shadow of your wings protect me.**
   ➜ No. 2, p. 10

COLLECT   [Sincerity of Heart]
Almighty ever-living God,
grant that we may always conform our will to yours
and serve your majesty in sincerity of heart.
Through our Lord Jesus Christ, your Son,
who lives and reigns with you in the unity of the Holy
   Spirit,
God, for ever and ever. R̞. **Amen.** ↓

FIRST READING Is 45:1, 4-6   [One God]

For the sake of the Israelites, the Lord calls Cyrus. He gives him a title. It is the Lord who arms him, and through him all people will know that there is only one Lord.

A reading from the Book of the Prophet Isaiah

THUS says the LORD to his anointed, Cyrus,
   whose right hand I grasp,
subduing nations before him,
   and making kings run in his service,
opening doors before him
   and leaving the gates unbarred:
For the sake of Jacob, my servant,
   of Israel, my chosen one,
I have called you by your name,
   giving you a title, though you knew me not.
I am the LORD and there is no other,
   there is no God besides me.
It is I who arm you, though you know me not,
   so that toward the rising and the setting of the sun
   people may know that there is none besides me.
I am the LORD, there is no other.

The word of the Lord. ℟. **Thanks be to God. ↓**

RESPONSORIAL PSALM Ps 96   [The Lord Is King]

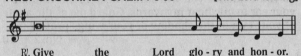

℟. Give   the   Lord   glo - ry and hon - or.

Sing to the LORD a new song;
   sing to the LORD, all you lands.
Tell his glory among the nations;
   among all peoples, his wondrous deeds.

℟. **Give the Lord glory and honor.**

For great is the LORD and highly to be praised;
   awesome is he, beyond all gods.

For all the gods of the nations are things of nought,
   but the LORD made the heavens.

℟. **Give the Lord glory and honor.**

Give to the LORD, you families of nations,
   give to the LORD glory and praise;
   give to the LORD the glory due his name!
Bring gifts, and enter his courts.

℟. **Give the Lord glory and honor.**

Worship the LORD, in holy attire.
   Tremble before him, all the earth;
say among the nations: The LORD is king,
   he governs the peoples with equity.

℟. **Give the Lord glory and honor.** ↓

SECOND READING 1 Thes 1:1-5b   [Preaching the Gospel]

Paul writes to the Thessalonians to encourage them. He prays for them constantly as they prove their faith through works of love, for God has chosen them.

A reading from the first Letter of Saint Paul
to the Thessalonians

PAUL, Silvanus, and Timothy to the church of the Thessalonians in God the Father and the Lord Jesus Christ: grace to you and peace. We give thanks to God always for all of you, remembering you in our prayers, unceasingly calling to mind your work of faith and labor of love and endurance in hope of our Lord Jesus Christ, before our God and Father, knowing, brothers and sisters loved by God, how you were chosen. For our gospel did not come to you in word alone, but also in power and in the Holy Spirit and with much conviction.—The word of the Lord.

℟. **Thanks be to God.** ↓

ALLELUIA Phil 2:15d, 16a   [Word of Life]

℟. **Alleluia, alleluia.**
Shine like lights in the world
as you hold on to the word of life.
℟. **Alleluia, alleluia.** ↓

GOSPEL Mt 22:15-21   [Lawful Taxes]

The Pharisees try to confound Jesus. They ask about a possible conflict of giving tribute to Caesar and God. Jesus asks for a coin which has Caesar's inscription. Jesus responds that both Caesar and God should each be given his due.

℣. The Lord be with you. ℟. **And with your spirit.**

✜ A reading from the holy Gospel according to Matthew.
℟. **Glory to you, O Lord.**

THE Pharisees went off and plotted how they might entrap Jesus in speech. They sent their disciples to him, with the Herodians, saying, "Teacher, we know that you are a truthful man and that you teach the way of God in accordance with the truth. And you are not concerned with anyone's opinion, for you do not regard a person's status. Tell us, then, what is your opinion: Is it lawful to pay the census tax to Caesar or not?" Knowing their malice, Jesus said, "Why are you testing me, you hypocrites? Show me the coin that pays the census tax." Then they handed him the Roman coin. He said to them, "Whose image is this and whose inscription?" They replied, "Caesar's." At that he said to them, "Then repay to Caesar what belongs to Caesar and to God what belongs to God."—The Gospel of the Lord. ℟. **Praise to you, Lord Jesus Christ.**   → No. 15, p. 18

PRAYER OVER THE OFFERINGS   [Respect Gifts]

Grant us, Lord, we pray,
a sincere respect for your gifts,

that, through the purifying action of your grace,
we may be cleansed by the very mysteries we serve.
Through Christ our Lord.
℟. **Amen.**   ➜ No. 21, p. 22 (Pref. P 29-36)

COMMUNION ANT. Cf. Ps 33 (32):18-19 [Divine Protection]
**Behold, the eyes of the Lord are on those who fear
him, who hope in his merciful love, to rescue their
souls from death, to keep them alive in famine.** ↓

OR Mk 10:45   [Christ Our Ransom]
**The Son of Man has come to give his life as a ransom
for many.** ↓

PRAYER AFTER COMMUNION   [Eternal Gifts]
Grant, O Lord, we pray,
that, benefiting from participation in heavenly things,
we may be helped by what you give in this present age
and prepared for the gifts that are eternal.
Through Christ our Lord.
℟. **Amen.**   ➜ No. 30, p. 77

Optional Solemn Blessings, p. 97, and Prayers over the People, p. 105

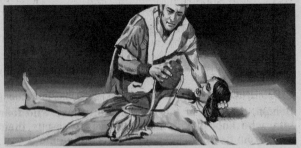
"You shall love your neighbor as yourself."

OCTOBER 29
30th SUNDAY IN ORDINARY TIME

ENTRANCE ANT. Cf. Ps 105 (104):3-4   [Seek the Lord]
Let the hearts that seek the Lord rejoice; turn to the Lord and his strength; constantly seek his face.

→ No. 2, p. 10

COLLECT   [Increase Virtues]
Almighty ever-living God,
increase our faith, hope and charity,
and make us love what you command,
so that we may merit what you promise.
Through our Lord Jesus Christ, your Son,
who lives and reigns with you in the unity of the Holy
   Spirit,
God, for ever and ever. ℟. **Amen.** ↓

FIRST READING Ex 22:20-26   [Kindness to Others]
The Lord warns his people neither to oppress foreigners nor to harm widows or orphans. Consideration for the poor and needy should be a prime concern.

A reading from the Book of Exodus

THUS says the LORD: "You shall not molest or oppress an alien, for you were once aliens yourselves in the land of Egypt. You shall not wrong any widow or orphan. If ever you wrong them and they cry out to me, I will surely hear their cry. My wrath will flare up, and I will kill you with the sword; then your own wives will be widows, and your children orphans.

"If you lend money to one of your poor neighbors among my people, you shall not act like an extortioner toward him by demanding interest from him. If you take your neighbor's cloak as a pledge, you shall return it to him before sunset; for this cloak of his is the only covering he has for his body. What else has he to sleep in? If he cries out to me, I will hear him; for I am compassionate."—The word of the Lord. ℟. **Thanks be to God.** ↓

RESPONSORIAL PSALM Ps 18   [God Our Rock]

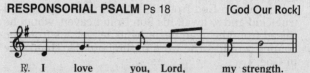

℟. I   love   you, Lord,   my strength.

I love you, O LORD, my strength,
    O LORD, my rock, my fortress, my deliverer.

℟. **I love you, Lord, my strength.**

My God, my rock of refuge,
    my shield, the horn of my salvation, my stronghold!
Praised be the LORD, I exclaim,
    and I am safe from my enemies.

℟. **I love you, Lord, my strength.**

The LORD lives and blessed be my rock!
    Extolled be God my savior,
you who gave great victories to your king
    and showed kindness to your anointed.

℟. **I love you, Lord, my strength.** ↓

SECOND READING 1 Thes 1:5c-10   [Imitating Christ]

You received the word of the Lord in spite of great hardships. You then became model Christians for your neighbors. You turned from idols to worship the true God.

A reading from the first Letter of Saint Paul
to the Thessalonians

Brothers and sisters: You know what sort of people we were among you for your sake. And you became imitators of us and of the Lord, receiving the word in great affliction, with joy from the Holy Spirit, so that you became a model for all the believers in Macedonia and in Achaia. For from you the word of the Lord has sounded forth not only in Macedonia and in Achaia, but in every place your faith in God has gone forth, so that we have no need to say anything. For they themselves openly declare about us what sort of reception we had among you, and how you turned to God from idols to serve the living and true God and to await his Son from heaven, whom he raised from the dead, Jesus, who delivers us from the coming wrath.—The word of the Lord. ℟. **Thanks be to God.** ↓

ALLELUIA Jn 14:23   [Keep My Word]

℟. **Alleluia, alleluia.**
Whoever loves me will keep my word, says the Lord, and my Father will love him and we will come to him.
℟. **Alleluia, alleluia.** ↓

GOSPEL Mt 22:34-40   [The Greatest Commandment]

Jesus tells the scholar of the law that the greatest of all the commandments is love—to love God with all your being and your neighbor as yourself. This sums up the whole law.

℣. The Lord be with you. ℟. **And with your spirit.**
✚ A reading from the holy Gospel according to Matthew.
℟. **Glory to you, O Lord.**

WHEN the Pharisees heard that Jesus had silenced the Sadducees, they gathered together, and one of them, a scholar of the law, tested him by asking, "Teacher, which commandment in the law is the greatest?" He said to him, "You shall love the Lord, your God, with all your heart, with all your soul, and with all your mind. This is the greatest and the first commandment. The second is like it: You shall love your neighbor as yourself. The whole law and the prophets depend on these two commandments."—The Gospel of the Lord.

℟. **Praise to you, Lord Jesus Christ.**   ➜ No. 15, p. 18

PRAYER OVER THE OFFERINGS   [Glorifying God]

Look, we pray, O Lord,
on the offerings we make to your majesty,
that whatever is done by us in your service
may be directed above all to your glory.
Through Christ our Lord.

℟. **Amen.**   ➜ No. 21, p. 22 (Pref. P 29-36)

COMMUNION ANT. Cf. Ps 20 (19):6   [Saving Help]

We will ring out our joy at your saving help and exult in the name of our God. ↓

OR Eph 5:2   [Christ's Offering for Us]

Christ loved us and gave himself up for us, as a fragrant offering to God. ↓

PRAYER AFTER COMMUNION   [Celebrate in Signs]

May your Sacraments, O Lord, we pray,
perfect in us what lies within them,
that what we now celebrate in signs
we may one day possess in truth.
Through Christ our Lord.

℟. **Amen.**   ➜ No. 30, p. 77

Optional Solemn Blessings, p. 97, and Prayers over the People, p. 105

"Blessed are the clean of heart, for they will see God."

NOVEMBER 1

ALL SAINTS

Solemnity

ENTRANCE ANT.   [Honoring All the Saints]

Let us all rejoice in the Lord, as we celebrate the feast day in honor of all the Saints, at whose festival the Angels rejoice and praise the Son of God. → No. 2, p. 10

COLLECT   [Reconciliation]

Almighty ever-living God,
by whose gift we venerate in one celebration
the merits of all the Saints,
bestow on us, we pray,
through the prayers of so many intercessors,
an abundance of the reconciliation with you
for which we earnestly long.
Through our Lord Jesus Christ, your Son,
who lives and reigns with you in the unity of the Holy
    Spirit,
God, for ever and ever. ℟. **Amen.** ↓

FIRST READING Rv 7:2-4, 9-14　　[A Huge Crowd of Saints]

The elect give thanks to God and the Lamb who saved them. The whole court of heaven joins the acclamation of the Saints.

A reading from the Book of Revelation

I, JOHN, saw another angel come up from the East, holding the seal of the living God. He cried out in a loud voice to the four angels who were given power to damage the land and the sea, "Do not damage the land or the sea or the trees until we put the seal on the foreheads of the servants of our God." I heard the number of those who had been marked with the seal, one hundred and forty-four thousand marked from every tribe of the children of Israel.

After this I had a vision of a great multitude, which no one could count, from every nation, race, people, and tongue. They stood before the throne and before the Lamb, wearing white robes and holding palm branches in their hands. They cried out in a loud voice:

"Salvation comes from our God, who is seated on the throne,
　　and from the Lamb."

All the angels stood around the throne and around the elders and the four living creatures. They prostrated themselves before the throne, worshiped God, and exclaimed:

"Amen. Blessing and glory, wisdom and thanksgiving,
　　honor, power, and might
　　be to our God forever and ever. Amen."

Then one of the elders spoke up and said to me, "Who are these wearing white robes, and where did they come from?" I said to him, "My lord, you are the one who knows." He said to me, "These are the ones who have survived the time of great distress; they have washed their robes and made them white in the Blood of the Lamb."—The word of the Lord. ℟. **Thanks be to God.** ↓

RESPONSORIAL PSALM Ps 24   [Longing To See God]

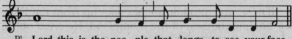

℟. **Lord, this is the peo - ple that longs to see your face.**

The LORD's are the earth and its fullness;
    the world and those who dwell in it.
For he founded it upon the seas
    and established it upon the rivers.

℟. **Lord, this is the people that longs to see your face.**

Who can ascend the mountain of the LORD?
    or who may stand in his holy place?
One whose hands are sinless, whose heart is clean,
    who desires not what is vain.

℟. **Lord, this is the people that longs to see your face.**

He shall receive a blessing from the LORD,
    a reward from God his Savior.
Such is the race that seeks for him,
    that seeks the face of the God of Jacob.

℟. **Lord, this is the people that longs to see your face.** ↓

SECOND READING 1 Jn 3:1-3   [We Shall See God]

God's gift of love has been the gift of his only Son as Savior of the world. It is this gift that has made it possible for us to be called the children of God.

A reading from the first Letter of Saint John

BELOVED: See what love the Father has bestowed on us that we may be called the children of God. Yet so we are. The reason the world does not know us is that it did not know him. Beloved, we are God's children now; what we shall be has not yet been revealed. We do know that when it is revealed we shall be like him, for we shall see him as he is. Everyone who has this hope based on him makes himself pure, as he is pure.—The word of the Lord. ℟. **Thanks be to God.** ↓

ALLELUIA Mt 11:28   [Rest in the Lord]

℟. **Alleluia, alleluia.**
Come to me, all you that labor and are burdened,
and I will give you rest, says the Lord.
℟. **Alleluia, alleluia.** ↓

GOSPEL Mt 5:1-12a   [The Beatitudes]

Jesus is meant to be the new Moses, proclaiming the new revelation on a new Mount Sinai. This is the proclamation of the good news. Blessings are pronounced on those who do not share the values of the world.

℣. The Lord be with you. ℟. **And with your spirit.**
✝ A reading from the holy Gospel according to Matthew.
℟. **Glory to you, O Lord.**

WHEN Jesus saw the crowds, he went up the mountain, and after he had sat down, his disciples came to him. He began to teach them, saying:
"Blessed are the poor in spirit,
    for theirs is the Kingdom of heaven.
Blessed are they who mourn,
    for they will be comforted.
Blessed are the meek,
    for they will inherit the land.
Blessed are they who hunger and thirst for righteousness,
    for they will be satisfied.
Blessed are the merciful,
    for they will be shown mercy.

Blessed are the clean of heart,
for they will see God.
Blessed are the peacemakers,
for they will be called children of God.
Blessed are they who are persecuted for the sake
of righteousness,
for theirs is the Kingdom of heaven.
Blessed are you when they insult you and persecute
you and utter every kind of evil against you falsely
because of me. Rejoice and be glad, for your reward
will be great in heaven."—The Gospel of the Lord.
℞. **Praise to you, Lord Jesus Christ.**   → No. 15, p. 18

PRAYER OVER THE OFFERINGS
[The Saints' Concern for Us]

May these offerings we bring in honor of all the Saints
be pleasing to you, O Lord,
and grant that, just as we believe the Saints
to be already assured of immortality,
so we may experience their concern for our salvation.
Through Christ our Lord. ℞. **Amen.** ↓

PREFACE (P 71)   [Strength and Example]

℣. The Lord be with you. ℞. **And with your spirit.**
℣. Lift up your hearts. ℞. **We lift them up to the Lord.**
℣. Let us give thanks to the Lord our God. ℞. **It is right and just.**

It is truly right and just, our duty and our salvation,
always and everywhere to give you thanks,
Lord, holy Father, almighty and eternal God.

For today by your gift we celebrate the festival of your
city,
the heavenly Jerusalem, our mother,
where the great array of our brothers and sisters
already gives you eternal praise.

Towards her, we eagerly hasten
  as pilgrims advancing by faith,
rejoicing in the glory bestowed upon those exalted
  members of the Church
through whom you give us, in our frailty, both strength
  and good example.

And so, we glorify you with the multitude of Saints
  and Angels,
as with one voice of praise we acclaim: ➡ No. 23, p. 23

COMMUNION ANT. Mt 5:8-10   [The Saints: Children of God]

**Blessed are the clean of heart, for they shall see God.
Blessed are the peacemakers, for they shall be called
children of God. Blessed are they who are persecuted
for the sake of righteousness, for theirs is the
Kingdom of Heaven.** ↓

PRAYER AFTER COMMUNION   [Heavenly Homeland]

As we adore you, O God, who alone are holy
and wonderful in all your Saints,
we implore your grace,
so that, coming to perfect holiness in the fullness of
  your love,
we may pass from this pilgrim table
to the banquet of our heavenly homeland.
Through Christ our Lord.
℟. **Amen.**   ➡ No. 30, p. 77

Optional Solemn Blessings, p. 97, and Prayers over the People, p. 105

"Whoever exalts himself will be humbled; but whoever humbles himself will be exalted."

NOVEMBER 5

31st SUNDAY IN ORDINARY TIME

ENTRANCE ANT. Cf. Ps 38 (37):22-23

[Call for God's Help]

Forsake me not, O Lord, my God; be not far from me! Make haste and come to my help, O Lord, my strong salvation! ➜ No. 2, p. 10

COLLECT [Praiseworthy Service]

Almighty and merciful God,
by whose gift your faithful offer you
right and praiseworthy service,
grant, we pray,
that we may hasten without stumbling
to receive the things you have promised.
Through our Lord Jesus Christ, your Son,
who lives and reigns with you in the unity of the Holy
Spirit,
God, for ever and ever. ℟. **Amen**. ↓

FIRST READING Mal 1:14b—2:2b, 8-10

[Violating the Covenant]

I have sent a curse upon you, says the Lord, since you have turned from me. You have not kept my ways. Only one God has created us. Why do we break faith with one another?

A reading from the Book of the Prophet Malachi

A GREAT King am I, says the LORD of hosts,
   and my name will be feared among the nations.
And now, O priests, this commandment is for you:
   If you do not listen,
if you do not lay it to heart,
   to give glory to my name, says the LORD of hosts,
I will send a curse upon you
   and of your blessing I will make a curse.
You have turned aside from the way,
   and have caused many to falter by your instruc-
      tion;
you have made void the covenant of Levi,
   says the LORD of hosts.
I, therefore, have made you contemptible
   and base before all the people,
since you do not keep my ways,
   but show partiality in your decisions.
Have we not all the one Father?
   Has not the one God created us?
Why then do we break faith with one another,
   violating the covenant of our fathers?
The word of the Lord. ℟. **Thanks be to God.** ↓

RESPONSORIAL PSALM Ps 131   [Peace in the Lord]

℟. In you, Lord, I have found my peace.

O LORD, my heart is not proud,
  nor are my eyes haughty;
I busy not myself with great things,
  nor with things too sublime for me.

R̸. **In you, Lord, I have found my peace.**

Nay rather, I have stilled and quieted
  my soul like a weaned child.
Like a weaned child on its mother's lap,
  so is my soul within me.

R̸. **In you, Lord, I have found my peace.**

O Israel, hope in the LORD,
  both now and forever.

R̸. **In you, Lord, I have found my peace.** ↓

SECOND READING 1 Thes 2:7b-9, 13 [God's Good Tidings]

> **Paul tells the Thessalonians how he wanted to share the teachings of Jesus with them as well as his own life. He works day and night for them. The word of God works in those who believe.**

A reading from the first Letter of Saint Paul
to the Thessalonians

BROTHERS and sisters: We were gentle among you, as a nursing mother cares for her children. With such affection for you, we were determined to share with you not only the gospel of God, but our very selves as well, so dearly beloved had you become to us. You recall, brothers and sisters, our toil and drudgery. Working night and day in order not to burden any of you, we proclaimed to you the gospel of God.

And for this reason we too give thanks to God unceasingly, that, in receiving the word of God from hearing us, you received not a human word but, as it truly is, the word of God, which is now at work in you who believe.—The word of the Lord. ℞. **Thanks be to God.** ↓

ALLELUIA Mt 23:9b, 10b   [One Father]

℞. **Alleluia, alleluia.**
You have but one Father in heaven
and one master, the Christ.
℞. **Alleluia, alleluia.** ↓

GOSPEL Mt 23:1-12   [The Virtue of Humility]

Jesus warns that the Pharisees speak many words boldy, admonishing others to observe the Law but their deeds fail in fulfilling the Law. They act only to be seen. Only the humble will be exalted.

℣. The Lord be with you. ℞. **And with your spirit.**
✝ A reading from the holy Gospel according to Matthew.
℞. **Glory to you, O Lord**.

JESUS spoke to the crowds and to his disciples, saying, "The scribes and the Pharisees have taken their seat on the chair of Moses. Therefore, do and observe all things whatsoever they tell you, but do not follow their example. For they preach but they do not practice. They tie up heavy burdens hard to carry and lay them on people's shoulders, but they will not lift a finger to move them. All their works are performed to be seen. They widen their phylacteries and lengthen their tassels. They love places of honor at banquets, seats of honor in synagogues, greetings in marketplaces, and the salutation 'Rabbi.' As for you, do not be called 'Rabbi.'You have but one teacher, and you are all brothers. Call no one on earth your father; you have but one Father in heaven. Do not be called 'Master'; you have but one master, the Christ.The greatest among you must be your servant. Whoever exalts himself will be humbled; but whoever humbles himself will be exalted."

—The Gospel of the Lord. ℟. **Praise to you, Lord Jesus Christ.**   ➜ No. 15, p. 18

PRAYER OVER THE OFFERINGS   [God's Mercy]

May these sacrificial offerings, O Lord,
become for you a pure oblation,
and for us a holy outpouring of your mercy.
Through Christ our Lord.
℟. **Amen.**   ➜ No. 21, p. 22 (Pref. P 29-36)

COMMUNION ANT. Cf. Ps 16 (15):11   [Joy]

You will show me the path of life, the fullness of joy in your presence, O Lord. ↓

OR Jn 6:58   [Life]

Just as the living Father sent me and I have life because of the Father, so whoever feeds on me shall have life because of me, says the Lord. ↓

PRAYER AFTER COMMUNION   [Renewal]

May the working of your power, O Lord,
increase in us, we pray,
so that, renewed by these heavenly Sacraments,
we may be prepared by your gift
for receiving what they promise.
Through Christ our Lord.
℟. **Amen.**   ➜ No. 30, p. 77

Optional Solemn Blessings, p. 97, and Prayers over the People, p. 105

"The bridegroom came and [the bridesmaids] who were ready went into the wedding feast with him."

NOVEMBER 12

32nd SUNDAY IN ORDINARY TIME

ENTRANCE ANT. Cf. Ps 88 (87):3   [Answer to Prayer]

Let my prayer come into your presence. Incline your ear to my cry for help, O Lord.   → No. 2, p. 10

COLLECT   [Freedom of Heart]

Almighty and merciful God,
graciously keep from us all adversity,
so that, unhindered in mind and body alike,
we may pursue in freedom of heart
the things that are yours.
Through our Lord Jesus Christ, your Son,
who lives and reigns with you in the unity of the Holy
    Spirit,
God, for ever and ever. ℟. **Amen.** ↓

FIRST READING Wis 6:12-16   [Love of Wisdom]

Wisdom is found by those who seek after it. Those who watch for wisdom shall find it. Wisdom graciously appears.

549

A reading from the Book of Wisdom

RESPLENDENT and unfading is wisdom,
    and she is readily perceived by those who love her,
    and found by those who seek her.
She hastens to make herself known in anticipation of
        their desire;
    whoever watches for her at dawn shall not be
        disappointed,
    for he shall find her sitting by his gate.
For taking thought of wisdom is the perfection of
        prudence,
    and whoever for her sake keeps vigil
    shall quickly be free from care;
because she makes her own rounds, seeking those
        worthy of her,
    and graciously appears to them in the ways,
    and meets them with all solicitude.
The word of the Lord. ℟. **Thanks be to God.** ↓

RESPONSORIAL PSALM Ps 63   [Seeking the Lord]

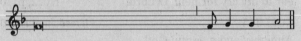

℟. My soul is thirsting for you, O Lord my God.

O God, you are my God whom I seek;
    for you my flesh pines and my soul thirsts
    like the earth, parched, lifeless and without water.

℟. **My soul is thirsting for you, O Lord my God.**

Thus have I gazed toward you in the sanctuary
    to see your power and your glory,
for your kindness is a greater good than life;
    my lips shall glorify you.

℟. **My soul is thirsting for you, O Lord my God.**

Thus will I bless you while I live;
    lifting up my hands, I will call upon your name.

As with the riches of a banquet shall my soul be satisfied,
  and with exultant lips my mouth shall praise you.

℟. **My soul is thirsting for you, O Lord my God.**

I will remember you upon my couch,
  and through the night-watches I will meditate on
   you:
you are my help,
  and in the shadow of your wings I shout for joy.

℟. **My soul is thirsting for you, O Lord my God.** ↓

SECOND READING 1 Thes 4:13-18 or 4:13-14
[Rising from the Dead]

> **Those who die believing in Jesus will rise with him. They
> will in the Last Judgment rise first to enjoy God's life with
> Jesus.**

*[If the "Shorter Form" is used, the indented text in brackets is
omitted.]*

A reading from the first Letter of Saint Paul
to the Thessalonians

WE do not want you to be unaware, brothers and
 sisters, about those who have fallen asleep, so
that you may not grieve like the rest, who have no
hope. For if we believe that Jesus died and rose, so too
will God, through Jesus, bring with him those who
have fallen asleep.

[Indeed, we tell you this, on the word of the Lord,
that we who are alive, who are left until the coming of the Lord, will surely not precede those
who have fallen asleep. For the Lord himself,
with a word of command, with the voice of an
archangel and with the trumpet of God, will
come down from heaven, and the dead in Christ
will rise first. Then we who are alive, who are

left, will be caught up together with them in the clouds to meet the Lord in the air. Thus we shall always be with the Lord. Therefore, console one another with these words.]

The word of the Lord. ℟. **Thanks be to God.** ↓

ALLELUIA Mt 24:42a, 44   [Be Ready]

℟. **Alleluia, alleluia.**

Stay awake and be ready!

For you do not know on what day your Lord will come.

℟. **Alleluia, alleluia.** ↓

GOSPEL Mt 25:1-13   [The Need for Watchfulness]

Jesus compares heaven to the five wise and five foolish bridesmaids awaiting the master. Only those who are ever watchful will be ready to meet him.

℣. The Lord be with you. ℟. **And also with you.**

✦ A reading from the holy Gospel according to Matthew.

℟. **Glory to you, O Lord.**

JESUS told his disciples this parable: "The kingdom of heaven will be like ten virgins who took their lamps and went out to meet the bridegroom. Five of them were foolish and five were wise. The foolish ones, when taking their lamps, brought no oil with them, but the wise brought flasks of oil with their lamps. Since the bridegroom was long delayed, they all became drowsy and fell asleep. At midnight, there was a cry, 'Behold, the bridegroom! Come out to meet him!' Then all those virgins got up and trimmed their lamps. The foolish ones said to the wise, 'Give us some of your oil, for our lamps are going out.' But the wise ones replied, 'No, for there may not be enough for us and you. Go instead to the merchants and buy some for yourselves.' While they went off to buy it, the bridegroom came and those who were ready went

into the wedding feast with him. Then the door was locked. Afterwards the other virgins came and said, 'Lord, Lord, open the door for us!' But he said in reply, 'Amen, I say to you, I do not know you.' Therefore, stay awake, for you know neither the day nor the hour."—The Gospel of the Lord. ℟. **Praise to you, Lord Jesus Christ.**
→ No. 15, p. 18

PRAYER OVER THE OFFERINGS   [Celebrating the Passion]

Look with favor, we pray, O Lord,
upon the sacrificial gifts offered here,
that, celebrating in mystery the Passion of your Son,
we may honor it with loving devotion.
Through Christ our Lord.
℟. **Amen.**   → No. 21, p. 22 (Pref. P 29-36)

COMMUNION ANT. Cf. Ps 23 (22):1-2 [The Lord Our Shepherd]

The Lord is my shepherd; there is nothing I shall want. Fresh and green are the pastures where he gives me repose, near restful waters he leads me. ↓

OR Cf. Lk 24:35   [Jesus in the Eucharist]

The disciples recognized the Lord Jesus in the breaking of bread. ↓

PRAYER AFTER COMMUNION   [Outpouring of the Spirit]

Nourished by this sacred gift, O Lord,
we give you thanks and beseech your mercy,
that, by the pouring forth of your Spirit,
the grace of integrity may endure
in those your heavenly power has entered.
Through Christ our Lord.
℟. **Amen.**   → No. 30, p. 77

Optional Solemn Blessings, p. 97, and Prayers over the People, p. 105

"Master, you gave me five talents. See, I have made five more."

NOVEMBER 19

33rd SUNDAY IN ORDINARY TIME

ENTRANCE ANT. Jer 29:11, 12, 14   [God Hears Us]

The Lord said: I think thoughts of peace and not of affliction. You will call upon me, and I will answer you, and I will lead back your captives from every place.

→ No. 2, p. 10

COLLECT   [Glad Devotion]

Grant us, we pray, O Lord our God,
the constant gladness of being devoted to you,
for it is full and lasting happiness
to serve with constancy
the author of all that is good.
Through our Lord Jesus Christ, your Son,
who lives and reigns with you in the unity of the Holy
     Spirit,
God, for ever and ever. ℟. **Amen.** ↓

FIRST READING Prv 31:10-13, 19-20, 30-31   [A Worthy Wife]

A true wife is valued beyond all pearls. She brings good to
her husband. She works for the household. She helps the
poor. She fears the Lord. She deserves her reward.

554

A reading from the Book of Proverbs

WHEN one finds a worthy wife,
    her value is far beyond pearls.
Her husband, entrusting his heart to her,
    has an unfailing prize.
She brings him good, and not evil,
    all the days of her life.
She obtains wool and flax
    and works with loving hands.
She puts her hands to the distaff,
    and her fingers ply the spindle.
She reaches out her hands to the poor,
    and extends her arms to the needy.
Charm is deceptive and beauty fleeting;
    the woman who fears the LORD is to be praised.
Give her a reward for her labors,
    and let her works praise her at the city gates.
The word of the Lord. ℟. **Thanks be to God.** ↓

RESPONSORIAL PSALM Ps 128   [Fear of the Lord]

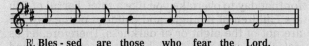

℟. **Bles - sed   are   those   who   fear   the   Lord.**

Blessed are you who fear the LORD,
    who walk in his ways!
For you shall eat the fruit of your handiwork;
    blessed shall you be, and favored.

℟. **Blessed are those who fear the Lord.**

Your wife shall be like a fruitful vine
    in the recesses of your home;
your children like olive plants
    around your table.

℟. **Blessed are those who fear the Lord.**

Behold, thus is the man blessed
  who fears the LORD.
The LORD bless you from Zion:
  may you see the prosperity of Jerusalem
  all the days of your life.

℟. **Blessed are those who fear the Lord.** ↓

SECOND READING 1 Thes 5:1-6   [The Day of the Lord]

The Day of the Lord will come like a thief in the night. It will be sudden. There will be no escape.

A reading from the first Letter of Saint Paul
to the Thessalonians

CONCERNING times and seasons, brothers and
sisters, you have no need for anything to be written to you. For you yourselves know very well that the day of the Lord will come like a thief at night. When people are saying, "Peace and security," then sudden disaster comes upon them, like labor pains upon a pregnant woman, and they will not escape.

But you, brothers and sisters, are not in darkness, for that day to overtake you like a thief. For all of you are children of the light and children of the day. We are not of the night or of darkness. Therefore, let us not sleep as the rest do, but let us stay alert and sober.—The word of the Lord. ℟. **Thanks be to God.** ↓

ALLELUIA Jn 15:4a, 5b   [Live in Christ]

℟. **Alleluia, alleluia.**
Remain in me as I remain in you, says the Lord.
Whoever remains in me bears much fruit.
℟. **Alleluia, alleluia.** ↓

GOSPEL Mt 25:14-30 or 25:14-15, 19-21   [The Faithful Servant]

Jesus speaks of the master who is going on a journey. He entrusts his property to three servants. Upon his return,

the first two are rewarded for their work; the third who did not increase his wealth is chastised and punished.

[If the "Shorter Form" is used, the indented text in brackets is omitted.]

℣. The Lord be with you. ℟. **And with your spirit.**

✛ A reading from the holy Gospel according to Matthew.
℟. **Glory to you, O Lord.**

JESUS told his disciples this parable: "A man going on a journey called in his servants and entrusted his possessions to them. To one he gave five talents; to another, two; to a third, one—to each according to his ability. Then he went away.

[Immediately the one who received five talents went and traded with them, and made another five. Likewise, the one who received two made another two. But the man who received one went off and dug a hole in the ground and buried his master's money.]

"After a long time the master of those servants came back and settled accounts with them. The one who had received five talents came forward bringing the additional five. He said, 'Master, you gave me five talents. See, I have made five more.' His master said to him, 'Well done, my good and faithful servant. Since you were faithful in small matters, I will give you great responsibilities. Come, share your master's joy.'

[Then the one who had received two talents also came forward and said, 'Master, you gave me two talents. See, I have made two more.' His master said to him, 'Well done, my good and faithful servant. Since you were faithful in small matters, I will give you great responsibilities. Come, share your master's joy.' Then the one who had received the one talent came forward and said,

'Master, I knew you were a demanding person, harvesting where you did not plant and gathering where you did not scatter; so out of fear I went off and buried your talent in the ground. Here it is back.' His master said to him in reply, 'You wicked, lazy servant! So you knew that I harvest where I did not plant and gather where I did not scatter? Should you not then have put my money in the bank so that I could have got it back with interest on my return? Now then! Take the talent from him and give it to the one with ten. For to everyone who has, more will be given and he will grow rich; but from the one who has not, even what he has will be taken away. And throw this useless servant into the darkness outside, where there will be wailing and grinding of teeth']."

The Gospel of the Lord. ℟. **Praise to you, Lord Jesus Christ.**   ➜ No. 15, p. 18

PRAYER OVER THE OFFERINGS   [Everlasting Happiness]

Grant, O Lord, we pray,
that what we offer in the sight of your majesty
may obtain for us the grace of being devoted to you
and gain us the prize of everlasting happiness.
Through Christ our Lord.
℟. **Amen.**   ➜   No. 21, p. 22 (Pref. P 29-36)

COMMUNION ANT. Ps 73 (72):28   [Hope in God]

To be near God is my happiness, to place my hope in God the Lord. ↓

OR Mk 11:23-24   [Believing Prayer]

Amen, I say to you: Whatever you ask in prayer, believe that you will receive, and it shall be given to you, says the Lord. ↓

PRAYER AFTER COMMUNION [Growth in Charity]

We have partaken of the gifts of this sacred mystery,
humbly imploring, O Lord,
that what your Son commanded us to do
in memory of him
may bring us growth in charity.
Through Christ our Lord.
℟. **Amen.** → No. 30, p. 77

Optional Solemn Blessings, p. 97, and Prayers over the People, p. 105

"The Son of Man . . . will sit upon his glorious throne. . . ."

NOVEMBER 26

Last Sunday in Ordinary Time
OUR LORD JESUS CHRIST, KING OF THE UNIVERSE

Solemnity

ENTRANCE ANT. Rev 5:12; 1:6   [Christ's Glory]

How worthy is the Lamb who was slain, to receive power and divinity, and wisdom and strength and honor. To him belong glory and power for ever and ever.   → No. 2, p. 10

COLLECT   [King of the Universe]

Almighty ever-living God,
whose will is to restore all things
in your beloved Son, the King of the universe,
grant, we pray,
that the whole creation, set free from slavery,
may render your majesty service
and ceaselessly proclaim your praise.
Through our Lord Jesus Christ, your Son,

who lives and reigns with you in the unity of the Holy
  Spirit,
God, for ever and ever. ℟. **Amen.** ↓

FIRST READING Ez 34:11-12, 15-17   [The Lord's Care]

**The Lord looks after his own flock. He takes them to pas-
ture and rescues them. He goes after those who are lost.
He also will judge them.**

A reading from the Book of the Prophet Ezekiel

T HUS says the Lord GOD: I myself will look after and
  tend my sheep. As a shepherd tends his flock when
he finds himself among his scattered sheep, so will I
tend my sheep. I will rescue them from every place
where they were scattered when it was cloudy and
dark. I myself will pasture my sheep; I myself will give
them rest, says the Lord GOD. The lost I will seek out,
the strayed I will bring back, the injured I will bind up,
the sick I will heal, but the sleek and the strong I will
destroy, shepherding them rightly.

  As for you, my sheep, says the Lord GOD, I will judge
between one sheep and another, between rams and
goats.—The word of the Lord. ℟. **Thanks be to God.** ↓

RESPONSORIAL PSALM Ps 23   [The Good Shepherd]

℟. **The Lord is my shep-herd; there is noth-ing I shall want.**

The LORD is my shepherd; I shall not want.
  In verdant pastures he gives me repose.

℟. **The Lord is my shepherd; there is nothing I shall
  want.**

Beside restful waters he leads me;
  he refreshes my soul.
He guides me in right paths
  for his name's sake.

℟. **The Lord is my shepherd; there is nothing I shall want.**

You spread the table before me
  in the sight of my foes;
you anoint my head with oil;
  my cup overflows.

℟. **The Lord is my shepherd; there is nothing I shall want.**

Only goodness and kindness follow me
  all the days of my life;
and I shall dwell in the house of the LORD
  for years to come.

℟. **The Lord is my shepherd; there is nothing I shall want.** ↓

SECOND READING 1 Cor 15:20-26, 28 [Christ the Firstfruits]

Christ has risen, and he is the firstfruits of the dead. All have
life in him. He will reign and all will be subjected to him.

A reading from the first Letter of Saint Paul
to the Corinthians

BROTHERS and sisters: Christ has been raised
from the dead, the firstfruits of those who have
fallen asleep. For since death came through man, the
resurrection of the dead came also through man. For
just as in Adam all die, so too in Christ shall all be
brought to life, but each one in proper order: Christ
the firstfruits; then, at his coming, those who belong
to Christ; then comes the end, when he hands over
the kingdom to his God and Father, when he has
destroyed every sovereignty and every authority and
power. For he must reign until he has put all his enemies under his feet. The last enemy to be destroyed is
death. When everything is subjected to him, then the
Son himself will also be subjected to the one who

subjected everything to him, so that God may be all in all.—The word of the Lord. ℟. **Thanks be to God.** ↓

ALLELUIA Mk 11:9, 10　　　　　　　　　　[Son of David]

℟. **Alleluia, alleluia.**
Blessed is he who comes in the name of the Lord!
Blessed is the kingdom of our father David that is to
　come!
℟. **Alleluia, alleluia.** ↓

GOSPEL Mt 25:31-46　　　　　　　　　[The Last Judgment]

All people will be judged by the Son of Man who will be seated on his royal throne. The sheep will be on his right, the goats on his left. He will reward all good and punish all evil.

℣. The Lord be with you. ℟. **And with your spirit.**
✚ A reading from the holy Gospel according to Matthew.
℟. **Glory to you, O Lord.**

JESUS said to his disciples: "When the Son of Man comes in his glory, and all the angels with him, he will sit upon his glorious throne, and all the nations will be assembled before him. And he will separate them one from another, as a shepherd separates the sheep from the goats. He will place the sheep on his right and the goats on his left. Then the king will say to those on his right, 'Come, you who are blessed by my Father. Inherit the kingdom prepared for you from the foundation of the world. For I was hungry and you gave me food, I was thirsty and you gave me drink, a stranger and you welcomed me, naked and you clothed me, ill and you cared for me, in prison and you visited me.' Then the righteous will answer him and say, 'Lord, when did we see you hungry and feed you, or thirsty and give you drink? When did we see you a stranger and welcome you, or naked and clothe you? When did we see you ill or in prison, and visit you?' And the king will say to them in reply, 'Amen, I say to you, whatever you did for one of the least brothers of mine, you did for me.' Then he will say to those on his left, 'Depart from me, you accursed, into the eternal fire prepared for the devil and his angels. For I was hungry and you gave me no food, I was thirsty and you gave me no drink, a stranger and you gave me no welcome, naked and you gave me no clothing, ill and in prison, and you did not care for me.' Then they will answer and say, 'Lord, when did we see you hungry or thirsty or a stranger or naked or ill or in prison, and not minister to your needs?' He will answer them, 'Amen, I say to you, what you did not do for one of these least ones, you did not do for me.' And these will go off to eternal punishment, but the righteous to eternal life."—The Gospel of the Lord. ℟. **Praise to you, Lord Jesus Christ.**

➛ No. 15, p. 18

PRAYER OVER THE OFFERINGS   [Unity and Peace]

As we offer you, O Lord, the sacrifice
by which the human race is reconciled to you,
we humbly pray
that your Son himself may bestow on all nations
the gifts of unity and peace.
Through Christ our Lord. ℟. **Amen.** ↓

PREFACE (P 51)   [Marks of Christ's Kingdom]

℣. The Lord be with you. ℟. **And with your spirit.**
℣. Lift up your hearts. ℟. **We lift them up to the Lord.**
℣. Let us give thanks to the Lord our God. ℟. **It is right and just.**

It is truly right and just, our duty and our salvation,
always and everywhere to give you thanks,
Lord, holy Father, almighty and eternal God.

For you anointed your Only Begotten Son,
our Lord Jesus Christ, with the oil of gladness
as eternal Priest and King of all creation,

so that, by offering himself on the altar of the Cross
as a spotless sacrifice to bring us peace,
he might accomplish the mysteries of human
    redemption
and, making all created things subject to his rule,
he might present to the immensity of your majesty
an eternal and universal kingdom,
a kingdom of truth and life,
a kingdom of holiness and grace,
a kingdom of justice, love and peace.

And so, with Angels and Archangels,
with Thrones and Dominions,
and with all the hosts and Powers of heaven,
we sing the hymn of your glory,
as without end we acclaim: ➜ No. 23, p. 23

COMMUNION ANT. Ps 29 (28):10-11   [Blessing of Peace]
**The Lord sits as King for ever. The Lord will bless his
people with peace.** ↓

PRAYER AFTER COMMUNION   [Christ's Eternal Kingdom]

Having received the food of immortality,
we ask, O Lord,
that, glorying in obedience
to the commands of Christ, the King of the universe,
we may live with him eternally in his heavenly
    Kingdom.
Who lives and reigns for ever and ever.
℟. **Amen.**   ➜ No. 30, p. 77

Optional Solemn Blessings, p. 97, and Prayers over the People, p. 105

Saint Joseph

HYMNAL

1   Praise My Soul, the King of Heaven

F. Lyte

John Goss

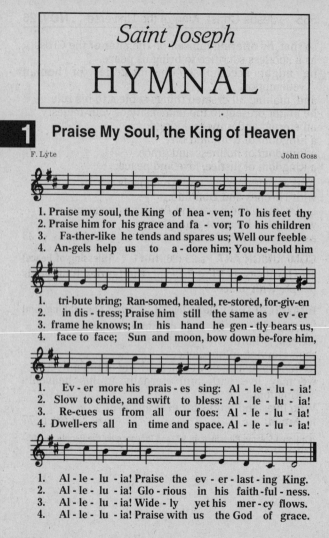

1. Praise my soul, the King of hea - ven; To his feet thy
2. Praise him for his grace and fa - vor; To his children
3.   Fa - ther - like he tends and spares us; Well our feeble
4.   An - gels help us to a - dore him; You be - hold him

1.   tri - bute bring; Ran - somed, healed, re - stored, for - giv - en
2.   in dis - tress; Praise him still the same as ev - er
3. frame he knows; In his hand he gen - tly bears us,
4.   face to face; Sun and moon, bow down be - fore him,

1.   Ev - er more his prais - es sing: Al - le - lu - ia!
2.   Slow to chide, and swift to bless: Al - le - lu - ia!
3.   Re - cues us from all our foes: Al - le - lu - ia!
4. Dwell - ers all in time and space. Al - le - lu - ia!

1.   Al - le - lu - ia! Praise the ev - er - last - ing King.
2.   Al - le - lu - ia! Glo - rious in his faith - ful - ness.
3.   Al - le - lu - ia! Wide - ly yet his mer - cy flows.
4.   Al - le - lu - ia! Praise with us the God of grace.

Praise to the Lord

1. Praise to the Lord,
   The almighty, the King of creation;
   O my soul, praise him,
   For he is our health and salvation;
   Hear the great throng,
   Joyous with praises and song,
   Sounding in glad adoration.

2. Praise to the Lord,
   Who doth prosper thy way and defend thee;
   Surely his goodness
   And mercy shall ever attend thee;
   Ponder anew
   What the almighty can do,
   Who with his love doth befriend thee.

3. Praise to the Lord,
   O let all that is in me adore him!
   All that hath breath join
   In our praises now to adore him!
   Let the "Amen"
   Sung by all people again
   Sound as we worship before him. Amen.

Eye Has Not Seen

3

Tune: Marty Haugen, b. 1950

Text: 1 Corinthians 2:9-10;
Marty Haugen, b. 1950

Refrain

Eye has not seen, ear has not heard what God has read-y for those who love him; Spir-it of love, come, give us the mind of Je - sus, teach us the wis-dom of God.

Verses 1-3

1. When pain and sor-row weigh us down, be near to us, O Lord, for - give the weak - ness of our faith, and bear us up with-in your peace-ful word.

2. Our lives are but a sin-gle breath, we flow-er and we fade, yet all our days are in your hands, so we re-turn in love what love has made.

3. To those who see with eyes of faith, the Lord is ev - er near, re - flect-ed in the fac - es of all the poor and low-ly of the world.

Verse 4

4. We sing a mys-t'ry from the past in halls where saints have

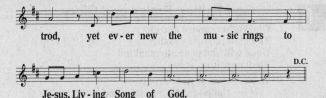

trod, yet ev-er new the mu-sic rings to

D.C.

Je-sus, Liv-ing Song of God.

Praise God from Whom All Blessings Flow 4

1. Praise God, from whom all blessings flow;
   Praise him, all creatures here below;
   Praise him above, ye heav'nly host:
   Praise Father, Son, and Holy Ghost.

2. All people that on earth do dwell.
   Sing to the Lord with cheerful voice;
   Him serve with mirth, his praise forth tell,
   Come ye before him and rejoice.

3. Know that the Lord is God indeed;
   Without our aid he did us make;
   We are his flock, he doth us feed.
   And for his sheep he doth us take.

4. O enter then his gates with praise,
   Approach with joy his courts unto;
   Praise, laud, and bless his name always,
   For it is seemly so to do. Amen.

Faith of Our Fathers 5

1. Faith of our fathers! living still,
   In spite of dungeon, fire, and sword;
   O how our hearts beat high with joy,
   Whene'er we hear that glorious word!

   Refrain: Faith of our fathers holy faith,
   We will be true to thee till death.

2. Faith of our fathers! We will love
   Both friend and foe in all our strife,
   And preach thee too, as love knows how,
   By kindly words and virtuous life.

3. Faith of our fathers! Mary's prayers
   Shall keep our country close to thee;
   And through the truth that comes from God,
   O we shall prosper and be free.

569

6 God Father, Praise and Glory

1. God Father, praise and glory
   Thy children bring to thee.
   Good will and peace to mankind
   Shall now forever be.

Refrain: O most Holy Trinity,
   Undivided Unity; Holy God,
   Mighty God, God immortal be adored.

2. And thou, Lord Coeternal.
   God's sole begotten Son;
   O Jesus, King anointed,
   Who hast redemption won.—*Refrain*

3. O Holy Ghost, Creator.
   Thou gift of God most high;
   Life, love and sacred Unction
   Our weakness thou supply.—*Refrain*

7 Praise the Lord of Heaven

Praise the Lord of Heaven,
Praise Him in the height.
Praise Him all ye angels,
Praise Him stars and light;
Praise Him skies and waters
   which above the skies
When His word commanded,
Mighty did arise,

Praise Him man and maiden,
Princes and all kings,
Praise Him hills and mountains,
All created things;
Heav'n and earth He fashioned
   mighty oceans raised;
This day and forever
His name shall be praised.

8 Holy, Holy, Holy

1. Holy, holy, holy! Lord God almighty.
   Early in the morning our song shall rise to thee:
   Holy, holy, holy! Merciful and mighty,
   God in three persons, blessed Trinity.

2. Holy, holy, holy! Lord God almighty.
   All thy works shall praise thy name in earth and sky
      and sea;
   Holy, holy, holy! Merciful and mighty,
   God in three persons, blessed Trinity.

3. Holy, holy, holy! All thy saints adore thee,
   Praising thee in glory, with thee to ever be;
   Cherubim and Seraphim, falling down before thee,
   Which wert and art and evermore shall be.

Now Thank We All Our God

9

1. Now thank we all our God,
   With heart and hands and voices,
   Who wondrous things hath done,
   In whom the world rejoices;
   Who from our mother's arms
   Hath blessed us on our way
   With countless gifts of love,
   And still is ours today.

2. All praise and thanks to God,
   The Father now be given,
   The Son, and him who reigns
   With them in highest heaven,
   The one eternal God
   Whom earth and heav'n adore;
   For thus it was, is now,
   And shall be ever more.

The Church's One Foundation

10

1

The Church's one foundation
Is Jesus Christ her Lord.
She is his new creation,
By water and the Word;
From heav'n he came and sought her,
To be his holy bride;
With his own blood he bought her,
And for her life he died.

2

Elect from ev'ry nation,
Yet one o'er all the earth.
Her charter of salvation,
One Lord, one faith, one birth;
One holy Name she blesses,
Partakes one holy food;
And to one hope she presses,
With ev'ry grace endued.

3

Mid toil and tribulation,
And tumult of her war.
She waits the consummation
Of peace for evermore;
Till with the vision glorious
Her loving eyes are blest,
And the great Church victorious
Shall be the Church at rest.

11 Awake, Awake and Greet the New Morn

Tune: REJOICE, REJOICE, 9 8 9 8 8 7 8 9;
Marty Haugen, b. 1950

Text: Marty Haugen, b. 1950

1. A - wake! a - wake, and greet the new morn, For
2. To us, to all in sor - row and fear, Em -
3. In dark - est night his com - ing shall be, When
4. Re - joice, re - joice, take heart in the night, Though

an - gels her-ald its dawn-ing, Sing out your joy, for
man - u - el comes a - sing-ing, His hum-ble song is
all the world is de - spair-ing, As morn-ing light so
dark the win - ter and cheer-less, The ris - ing sun shall

now* he is born, Be - hold! the Child of our long - ing.
qui - et and near, Yet fills the earth with its ring - ing;
qui - et and free, So warm and gen - tle and car - ing.
crown you with light, Be strong and lov - ing and fear - less;

Come as a ba - by weak and poor, To bring all hearts to-
Mu - sic to heal the bro-ken soul And hymns of lov - ing
Then shall the music break forth in song, The lame shall leap in
Love be our song and love our prayer, And love our end - less

geth - er, He o - pens wide the heav'n - ly door And
kind - ness, The thun - der of his an - thems roll To
won - der, The weak be raised a - bove the strong, And
sto - ry, May God fill ev - 'ry day we share, And

lives now in - side us for ev - er.
shat - ter all ha - tred and blind - ness.
weap - ons be bro - ken a - sun - der.
bring us at last in - to glo - ry.

* During Advent: "soon"

Rejoice, the Lord Is King

C. Wesley, alt.

J. Darwall, 1770

1. Re - joice, the Lord is King! Your Lord and King a-
2. The Lord, the Sav - ior reigns, The God of truth and
3. His king-dom can - not fail; He rules o'er earth and

1. dore! Let all give thanks and sing, And tri - umph
2. love, When he had purged our stains, He took his
3. heav'n; The King of vic - t'ry hail, all praise to

Refrain

1. ev - er more. Lift up your heart! Lift
2. seat a - bove.
3. Christ be giv'n.

up your voice! Re - joice! a-gain I say re - joice!

We Gather Together

(Same Melody as Hymn No. 14)

1. We gather together to ask the Lord's blessing;
   He chastens and hastens his will to make known;
   The wicked oppressing now cease from distressing;
   Sing praises to his name; he forgets not his own.

2. Beside us to guide us, our God with us joining,
   Ordaining, maintaining his kingdom divine;
   So from the beginning the fight we were winning;
   Thou Lord, wast at our side: all glory be thine.

3. We all do extol thee, thou leader triumphant,
   And pray that thou still our defender wilt be.
   Let thy congregation escape tribulation:
   Thy name be ever praised! O Lord, make us free!

14 We Praise Thee, O God, Our Redeemer

Ps 26:12
Tr. Julia B. Cady

E. Kremser

1. We praise Thee, O God, our Re-
2. We wor-ship Thee, God of our
3. With voic-es u-nit-ed our

deem-er, Cre-a-tor, In grate-ful de-
fa-thers, we bless Thee; Thro' trou-ble and
prais-es we of-fer, To Thee, great Je-

vo-tion our trib-ute we bring; We
tem-pest our Guide hast Thou been; When
ho-vah, glad an-thems we raise. Thy

lay it be-fore Thee, we kneel and a-
per-ils o'er-take us, es-cape Thou wilt
strong arm will guide us, our God is be-

dore Thee, We bless Thy ho-ly name, glad
make us, And with Thy help, O Lord, our
side us, To Thee, our great Re-deem-er for-

prais-es we sing.
bat-tles we win.
ev-er be praise. A-men.

Crown Him with Many Crowns

15

1. Crown him with many crowns,
The Lamb upon his throne;
Hark how the heav'nly anthem drowns
All music but its own;

 Awake my soul, and sing
Of him who died for thee,
And hail him as thy matchless King
Through all eternity.

2. Crown him of lords the Lord,
Who over all doth reign,
Who once on earth, the incarnate Word,
For ransomed sinners slain.

 Now lives in realms of light,
Where saints with angels sing
Their songs before him day and night,
Their God, Redeemer, King.

O Perfect Love

16

1. O perfect Love, all human thought transcending.
Lowly we kneel in prayer before thy throne,
That theirs may be the love that knows no ending,
Whom thou for evermore dost join in one.

2. O perfect Life, be thou their full assurance
Of tender charity and steadfast faith,
Of patient hope, and quiet, brave endurance,
With child-like trust that fears not pain nor death.

On Jordan's Bank

17

1. On Jordan's bank the Baptist's cry
Announces that the Lord is nigh,
Awake and hearken, for he brings
Glad tidings of the King of Kings.

2. Then cleansed be ev'ry breast from sin;
Make straight the way of God within,
Oh, let us all our hearts prepare
For Christ to come and enter there.

18 Gather Us In

Tune: GATHER US IN, Irreg.,
Marty Haugen, b. 1950

Text: Marty Haugen, b. 1950

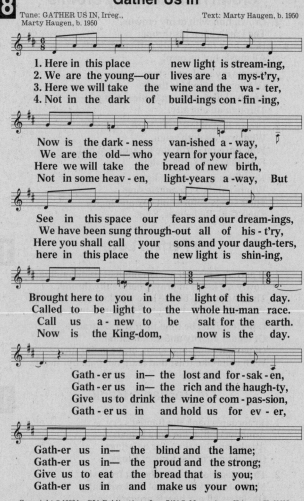

1. Here in this place new light is stream-ing,
2. We are the young—our lives are a mys-t'ry,
3. Here we will take the wine and the wa - ter,
4. Not in the dark of build-ings con-fin -ing,

Now is the dark - ness van-ished a - way,
We are the old— who yearn for your face,
Here we will take the bread of new birth,
Not in some heav - en, light-years a -way, But

See in this space our fears and our dream-ings,
We have been sung through-out all of his - t'ry,
Here you shall call your sons and your daugh-ters,
here in this place the new light is shin-ing,

Brought here to you in the light of this day.
Called to be light to the whole hu-man race.
Call us a - new to be salt for the earth.
Now is the King-dom, now is the day.

Gath - er us in— the lost and for - sak - en,
Gath - er us in— the rich and the haugh-ty,
Give us to drink the wine of com - pas-sion,
Gath - er us in and hold us for ev - er,

Gath-er us in— the blind and the lame;
Gath-er us in— the proud and the strong;
Give us to eat the bread that is you;
Gath-er us in and make us your own;

Call to us now, and we shall a-wak-en,
Give us a heart so meek and so low-ly,
Nour-ish us well, and teach us to fash-ion
Gath-er us in— all peo-ples to-geth-er,

We shall a-rise at the sound of our name.
Give us the cour-age to en-ter the song.
Lives that are ho-ly and hearts that are true.
Fire of love in our flesh and our bone.

Confitemini Domino / Come and Fill

19

Tune: Jacques Berthier, 1923-1994

Text: Psalm 137,
Give thanks to the Lord for he is good;
Taizé Community, 1982

Ostinato Refrain

Con - fi - te - mi - ni   Do - mi - no
Come and fill our hearts   with your peace.

quo - ni - am   bo-nus. Con - fi - te - mi - ni
You a - lone, O Lord, are ho-ly. Come and fill our hearts

Do - mi - no,   Al - le - lu - ia!
with your peace,   Al - le - lu - ia!

20 Come All You People

Tune: Alexander Gondo;
arr. by John L. Bell, b. 1949

Text: Alexander Gondo

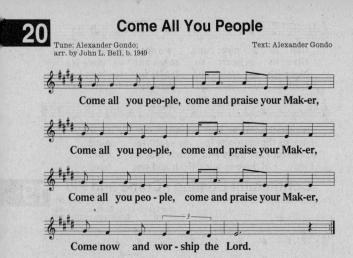

Come all you peo-ple, come and praise your Mak-er,

Come all you peo-ple, come and praise your Mak-er,

Come all you peo - ple, come and praise your Mak-er,

Come now and wor - ship the Lord.

21 To Jesus Christ, Our Sovereign King

1. To Jesus Christ, our sov'reign King,
   Who is the world's Salvation,
   All praise and homage do we bring
   And thanks and adoration.

2. Your reign extend, O King benign,
   To ev'ry land and nation;
   For in your kingdom, Lord divine,
   Alone we find salvation.

3. To you and to your Church, great King,
   We pledge our heart's oblation;
   Until before your throne we sing
   In endless jubilation.

   Refrain:
   Christ Jesus, Victor! Christ Jesus, Ruler!
   Christ Jesus, Lord and Redeemer!

Hark, a Mystic Voice Is Sounding

22

Tr. E. Caswall, 1849

En Clara Vox
R.L. de Pearsall, 1795-1856

1.

Hark, a mystic voice is sounding;
"Christ is nigh," It seems to say;
"Cast away the dreams of darkness,
O ye children of the day."

2.

Startled at the solemn warning,
Let the earthbound soul arise;

Christ her sun, all sloth dispelling,
Shines upon the morning skies.

3.

Lo, the Lamb so long expected
Comes with pardon down from heav'n;
Let us haste, with tears of sorrow,
One and all, to be forgiv'n.

The Coming of Our God

23

1.

The coming of our Lord
Our thought must now employ;
Then let us meet him on the road.
With song of holy joy.

2.

The co-eternal Son
A maiden's offspring see;

A servant's form Christ putteth on;
To set his people free.

3.

Daughter of Sion, rise
To greet thine Infant King;
Not let thy thankless heart despise
The pardon he doth bring.

O Come, Divine Messiah

Anne Pellegrin, 1663-1745
Sr. St. Mary of St. Philip

Venez Divin Messie
16th Century French
Harm. G. Ridout, 1971

O come, divine Messiah!
The world in silence waits the day
When hope shall sing its triumph,
And sadness flee away.

Chorus: Sweet Saviour, haste,
Come, come to earth:
Dispel the night, and show thy face,
And bid us hail the dawn of grace.
O come, divine Messiah,
The world in silence waits the day
When hope shall sing its triumph,
And sadness flee away.

25   O Come, O Come, Emmanuel

John M. Neal, Tr.

Melody adapted by T. Helmore

O come, O come, Emmanuel,
And ransom captive Israel,
That mourns in lowly exile here,
Until the Son of God appear.

Refrain: Rejoice! Rejoice! O Israel,
To thee shall come Emmanuel.

26   Come, Thou Long Expected Jesus

1. Come, thou long expected Jesus,
   Born to set thy people free;
   From our sins and fears release us,
   Let us find our rest in thee.

2. Israel's strength and consolation,
   Hope of all the earth thou art;
   Dear desire of every nation,
   Joy of every longing heart.

3. Born thy people to deliver,
   Born a child and yet a king.
   Born to reign in us for ever,
   Now thy gracious kingdom bring.

27   O Come Little Children

O come little children, O come one and all
Draw near to the crib here in Bethlehem's stall
And see what a bright ray of heaven's delight,
Our Father has sent on this thrice holy night.

He lies there, O children, on hay and straw,
Dear Mary and Joseph regard HIm with awe,
The shepherds, adoring, how humbly in pray'r
Angelical choirs with song rend the air.

O children bend low and adore Him today,
O lift up your hands like the shepherds, and pray
Sing joyfully children, with hearts full of love
In jubilant song join the angels above.

O Come, All Ye Faithful

1. O come, all ye faithful, joyful and triumphant,
   O come ye, O come ye to Bethlehem;
   Come and behold Him born, the King of angels.

   Refrain:
   O come, let us adore Him,
   O come, let us adore Him,
   O come, let us adore Him, Christ the Lord.

2. Sing choirs of angels, Sing in exultation.
   Sing all ye citizens of Heav'n above;
   Glory to God, Glory to the highest.—*Refrain*

3. Yea, Lord, we greet thee, born this happy morning,
   Jesus to thee be all glory giv'n;
   Word of the Father, now in flesh appearing.—*Refrain*

The First Noel

1. The first Noel the angel did say,
   Was to certain poor shepherds in fields as they lay;
   In fields where they lay keeping their sheep
   On a cold winter's night that was so deep.

   Refrain:
   Noel, Noel, Noel, Noel,
   Born is the King of Israel.

2. They looked up and saw a star,
   Shining in the east, beyond them far,
   And to the earth it gave great light,
   And so it continued both day and night.—*Refrain*

3. This star drew nigh to the northwest,
   O'er Bethlehem it took its rest,
   And there it did stop and stay,
   Right over the place where Jesus lay.—*Refrain*

4. Then entered in those wise men three,
   Full reverently upon their knee,
   And offered there, in his presence,
   Their gold and myrrh and frankincense.—*Refrain*

30

A Child Is Born in Bethlehem
Three Magi Kings

Carlton

1. A Child is born in Beth-le-hem, al-
2. Though found with-in a man-ger poor, al-
3. O let us sing in one ac-cord, al-
1. Three Ma-gi Kings came from a-far, al-
2. Their pre-cious gifts to Him they bring, al-

1. le-lu-ia; O come, re-joice Je-ru-
2. le-lu-ia; His King-dom shall for-e'er
3. le-lu-ia; And bless, for-ev-er Christ
1. le-lu-ia; Led by a light, the Christ-
2. le-lu-ia; An of-f'ring to the In-

1. sa-lem, al-le-lu-ia, al-le-lu-ia.
2. en-dure, al-le-lu-ia, al-le-lu-ia.
3. the Lord, al-le-lu-ia, al-le-lu-ia.
1. mas star, al-le-lu-ia, al-le-lu-ia.
2. fant King, al-le-lu-ia, al-le-lu-ia.

Responsory: All

Let grate-ful hearts now sing, A song

of joy and ho-ly praise to Christ the new-born King.

Silent Night

31

Silent night, holy night!
All is calm, all is bright.
'Round yon Virgin Mother and Child,
Holy Infant so tender and mild:
Sleep in heavenly peace,
Sleep in heavenly peace.

Silent night, holy night!
Shepherds quake at the sight!
Glories stream from heaven afar,
Heav'nly hosts sing Alleluia:
Christ, the Savior is born,
Christ, the Savior is born!

582

3. Silent night, holy night!
   Son of God, love's pure light.
   Radiant beams from thy holy face,
   With the dawn of redeeming grace,
   Jesus, Lord, at thy birth,
   Jesus, Lord, at thy birth.

Hark! The Herald Angels Sing

1. Hark! The herald angels sing.
   "Glory to the new-born King.
   Peace on earth, and mercy mild
   God and sinners reconciled."
   Joyful all ye nations rise,
   Join the triumph of the skies.
   With th' angelic host proclaim,
   "Christ is born in Bethlehem."

   Refrain:
   Hark! The herald angels sing,
   "Glory to the new-born King."

2. Christ, by highest heaven adored,
   Christ, the everlasting Lord.
   Late in time behold Him come,
   Off-spring of a virgin's womb.
   Veiled in flesh, the God-head see;
   Hail th' incarnate Deity!
   Pleased as Man with men to appear,
   Jesus, our Immanuel here!—*Refrain*

O Sing a Joyous Carol

33

1. O sing a joyous carol
   Unto the Holy Child,
   And praise with gladsome
      voices
   His mother undefiled.
   Our gladsome voices greeting
   Shall hail our Infant King;
   And our sweet Lady listens
   When joyful voices sing.

2. Who is there meekly lying
   In yonder stable poor?
   Dear children, it is Jesus;
   He bids you now adore.
   Who is there kneeling by him
   In virgin beauty fair?
   It is our Mother Mary,
   She bids you all draw near.

34 Good Christian Men Rejoice

Tr. John Mason Neale

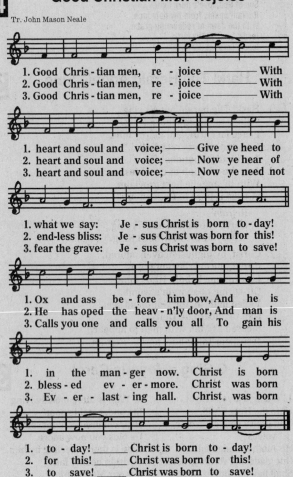

1. Good Chris-tian men, re - joice ——— With
2. Good Chris-tian men, re - joice ——— With
3. Good Chris-tian men, re - joice ——— With

1. heart and soul and voice; ——— Give ye heed to
2. heart and soul and voice; ——— Now ye hear of
3. heart and soul and voice; ——— Now ye need not

1. what we say: Je - sus Christ is born to - day!
2. end-less bliss: Je - sus Christ was born for this!
3. fear the grave: Je - sus Christ was born to save!

1. Ox and ass be - fore him bow, And he is
2. He has oped the heav - n'ly door, And man is
3. Calls you one and calls you all To gain his

1. in the man - ger now. Christ is born
2. bless - ed ev - er - more. Christ was born
3. Ev - er - last - ing hall. Christ was born

1. to - day! _____ Christ is born to - day!
2. for this! _____ Christ was born for this!
3. to save! _____ Christ was born to save!

Angels We Have Heard on High

35

1. Angels we have heard on high,
   Sweetly singing o'er the plains,
   And the mountains in reply
   Echoing their joyous strains.

   Refrain: Gloria in excelsis Deo. (Repeat)

2. Shepherds, why this jubilee,
   Why your rapturous song prolong?
   What the gladsome tidings be
   Which inspire your heav'nly song?—*Refrain*

3. Come to Bethlehem and see
   Him whose birth the angels sing;
   Come, adore on bended knee
   Christ the Lord, the new-born King.—*Refrain*

Away in a Manger

36

1. Away in a manger, no crib for his bed,
   The little Lord Jesus laid down his sweet head.
   The stars in the bright sky looked down where he lay,
   The little Lord Jesus asleep on the hay.

2. The cattle are lowing, the baby awakes,
   But little Lord Jesus no crying he makes.
   I love thee, Lord Jesus! Look down from the sky,
   And stay by my side until morning is nigh.

3. Be near me Lord Jesus, I ask thee to stay
   Close by me forever, and love me I pray.
   Bless all the dear children in thy tender care,
   And fit us for heaven to live with thee there.

O Little Town of Bethlehem

37

O little town of Bethlehem,
How still we see thee lie!
Above the deep and dreamless sleep
The silent stars go by;
Yet in the dark streets shineth
The everlasting Light;
The hopes and fears of all the years
Are met in thee tonight.

For Christ is born of Mary,
And gathered all above,
While mortals sleep, the angels keep
Their watch of wondering love.
O morning stars, together
Proclaim the holy birth!
And praising sing to God the King
And peace to men on earth.

O holy Child of Bethlehem!
Descend on us we pray;
Cast out our sin, and enter in,
Be born in us today.
We hear the Christmas angels,
The great glad tidings tell;
O come to us, abide with us,
Our Lord Emmanuel.

38

What Child Is This?

What child is this, who laid to rest,
On Mary's lap is sleeping?
Whom angels greet with anthems sweet,
While shepherds watch are keeping?

> *Refrain:*
> This, this is Christ the King,
> Whom shepherds guard and angels sing;
> Haste, haste to bring him laud,
> The Babe, the Son of Mary.

Why lies he in such mean estate
Where ox and ass are feeding?
Good Christian fear, for sinners here
The silent Word is pleading.—*Refrain*

So bring him incense, gold, and myrrh,
Come peasant, king to own him,
The King of kings salvation brings,
Let loving hearts enthrone him.—*Refrain*

We Three Kings

1. We three kings of Orient are
   Bearing gifts we traverse afar,
   Field and fountain, moor and mountain,
   Following yonder star.

   Refrain:
   O Star of wonder, Star of night,
   Star with royal beauty bright,
   Westward leading, still proceeding,
   Guide us to thy perfect light.

2. Born a king on Bethlehem's plain,
   Gold I bring to crown Him again,
   King forever, ceasing never,
   Over us all to reign.—*Refrain*

3. Frankincense to offer have I
   Incense owns a Deity high,
   Prayer and praising, all men raising,
   Worship Him, God most High.—*Refrain*

4. Myrrh is mine, its bitter perfume
   Breathes a life of gathering gloom:
   Sorrowing, sighing, bleeding, dying,
   Sealed in the stone-cold tomb.—*Refrain*

5. Glorious now behold Him arise,
   King and God and Sacrifice,
   Alleluia, Alleluia,
   Earth to the heavens replies.—*Refrain*

Holy God, We Praise Thy Name

1. Holy God, we praise Thy Name!
   Lord of all, we bow before Thee!
   All on earth Thy sceptre claim,
   All in heaven above adore Thee.
   Infinite Thy vast domain,
   Everlasting is Thy reign. *Repeat last two lines*

2. Hark! the loud celestial hymn,
   Angel choirs above are raising;
   Cherubim and seraphim,
   In unceasing chorus praising,
   Fill the heavens with sweet accord;
   Holy, holy, holy Lord! *Repeat last two lines*

41 Lord, Who throughout These 40 Days

1. Lord, who throughout these forty days
   For us did fast and pray,
   Teach us with you to mourn our sins,
   And close by you to stay.

2. And through these days of penitence,
   And through your Passiontide,
   Yea, evermore, in life and death,
   Jesus! with us abide.

3. Abide with us, that so, this life
   Of suff'ring over past,
   An Easter of unending joy
   We may attain at last. Amen.

42 When I Behold the Wondrous Cross

1. When I be-hold the won-drous cross
2. For-bid it, Lord, that I should boast,
3. See from his head, his hands, his feet,
4. Were all the realms of na-ture mine,

1. On which the prince of glo-ry died,
2. Save in the death of Christ, my God;
3. What grief and love flow min-gled down;
4. It would be off-'ring far too small;

1. My rich-est gain I count but loss,
2. The vain things that at-tract me most,
3. Did e'er such love that sor-row meet,
4. Love so a-maz-ing, so di-vine,

1. And pour con-tempt on all my pride.
2. I sac-ri-fice them to his blood.
3. Or thorns com-pose so rich a crown?
4. De-mands my soul, my life, my all.

Jesus, Remember Me

Tune: Jacques Berthier, 1923-1994
Text: Luke 23:42
Taizé Community, 1981

Ostinato Refrain

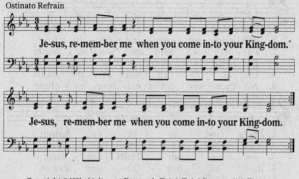

Je-sus, re-mem-ber me when you come in-to your King-dom.

Je-sus, re-mem-ber me when you come in-to your King-dom.

O Sacred Head Surrounded

1. O sacred Head surrounded
   By crown of piercing thorn!
   O bleeding Head, so wounded,
   Reviled, and put to scorn!
   Death's pallid hue comes ov'r you,
   The glow of life decays,
   Yet angel hosts adore you,
   And tremble as they gaze.

2. I see your strength and vigor
   All fading in the strife,
   And death with cruel rigor,
   Bereaving you of life.
   O agony and dying!
   O love to sinners free!
   Jesus, all grace supplying,
   O turn your face on me.

Where Charity and Love Prevail

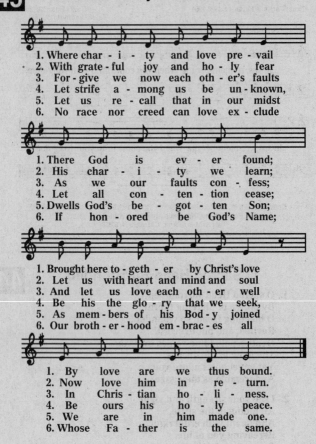

1. Where char - i - ty and love pre - vail
2. With grate - ful joy and ho - ly fear
3. For - give we now each oth - er's faults
4. Let strife a - mong us be un - known,
5. Let us re - call that in our midst
6. No race nor creed can love ex - clude

1. There God is ev - er found;
2. His char - i - ty we learn;
3. As we our faults con - fess;
4. Let all con - ten - tion cease;
5. Dwells God's be - got - ten Son;
6. If hon - ored be God's Name;

1. Brought here to - geth - er by Christ's love
2. Let us with heart and mind and soul
3. And let us love each oth - er well
4. Be his the glo - ry that we seek,
5. As mem - bers of his Bod - y joined
6. Our broth - er - hood em - brac - es all

1. By love are we thus bound.
2. Now love him in re - turn.
3. In Chris - tian ho - li - ness.
4. Be ours his ho - ly peace.
5. We are in him made one.
6. Whose Fa - ther is the same.

O Faithful Cross

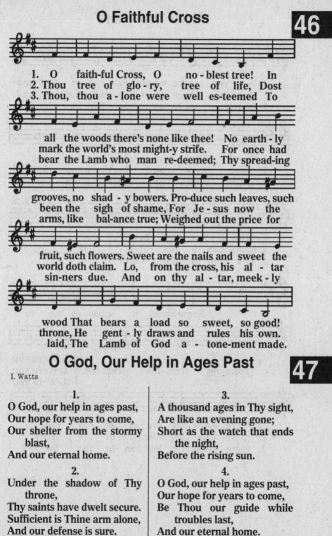

1. O   faith-ful Cross, O   no - blest tree! In
2. Thou   tree of glo - ry,   tree of life, Dost
3. Thou, thou a - lone were well es-teemed To

all the woods there's none like thee! No earth - ly
mark the world's most might-y strife.   For once had
bear the Lamb who man re-deemed; Thy spread-ing

grooves, no shad - y bowers. Pro-duce such leaves, such
been the sigh of shame, For Je - sus now the
arms, like bal-ance true; Weighed out the price for

fruit, such flowers. Sweet are the nails and sweet the
world doth claim. Lo, from the cross, his al - tar
sin-ners due. And on thy al - tar, meek - ly

wood That bears a load so sweet, so good!
throne, He gent - ly draws and rules his own.
laid, The Lamb of God a - tone-ment made.

O God, Our Help in Ages Past

I. Watts

1.
O God, our help in ages past,
Our hope for years to come,
Our shelter from the stormy
    blast,
And our eternal home.

2.
Under the shadow of Thy
    throne,
Thy saints have dwelt secure.
Sufficient is Thine arm alone,
And our defense is sure.

3.
A thousand ages in Thy sight,
Are like an evening gone;
Short as the watch that ends
    the night,
Before the rising sun.

4.
O God, our help in ages past,
Our hope for years to come,
Be Thou our guide while
    troubles last,
And our eternal home.

Were You There

1. Were you there when they cru - ci - fied my
2. Were you there when they nailed him to the
3. Were you there when they laid him in the

1. Lord? Were you there when they
2. tree? Were you there when they
3. tomb? Were you there when they

1. cru - ci - fied my Lord?
2. nailed him to the tree?   Oh_____
3. laid him in the tomb?

Some-times it caus - es me to

trem-ble, trem - ble trem-ble.
1. Were you
2. Were you
3. Were you

1. there when they cru - ci - fied my Lord?
2. there when they nailed him to the tree?
3. there when they laid him in the tomb?

At the Cross Her Station Keeping

49

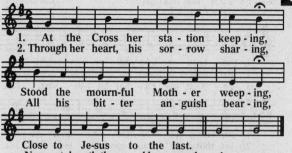

1. At the Cross her sta-tion keep-ing,
2. Through her heart, his sor-row shar-ing,

Stood the mourn-ful Moth-er weep-ing,
All his bit-ter an-guish bear-ing,

Close to Je-sus to the last.
Now at length the sword has passed. A - men.

3. Oh, how sad and sore distressed
Was that Mother highly blessed
Of the sole begotten One!

4. Christ above in torment hangs,
She beneath beholds the pangs
Of her dying, glorious Son.

5. Is there one who would not weep
'Whelmed in miseries so deep
Christ's dear Mother to behold?

6. Can the human heart refrain
From partaking in her pain,
In that mother's pain untold?

7. Bruised, derided, cursed, defiled,
She beheld her tender Child,
All with bloody scourges rent.

8. For the sins of His own nation
Saw Him hang in desolation
Till His spirit forth He sent.

9. O sweet Mother! fount of love,
Touch my spirit from above,
Make my heart with yours accord.

10. Make me feel as you have felt.
Make my soul to glow and melt
With the love of Christ, my Lord.

11. Holy Mother, pierce me through,
In my heart each wound renew
Of my Savior crucified.

12. Let me share with you His pain,
Who for all our sins was slain,
Who for me in torments died.

13. Let me mingle tears with you
Mourning Him Who mourned for me,
All the days that I may live.

14. By the Cross with you to stay,
There with you to weep and pray,
Is all I ask of you to give.

15. Virgin of all virgins blest!
Listen to my fond request.
Let me share your grief divine.

16. Let me, to my latest breath
In my body bear the death
Of that dying Son of yours.

17. Wounded with His every wound,
Steep my soul till it has swooned
In His very blood away.

18. Be to me, O Virgin, nigh,
Lest in flames I burn and die,
In His awful judgment day.

19. Christ, when You shall call me hence
Be Your Mother my defense.
Be Your Cross my victory.

20. While my body here decays,
May my soul Your goodness praise
Safe in heaven eternally.
Amen. Alleluia.

50 That Eastertide with Joy Was Bright

Verses 1, 2: tr. J.M. Neale, 1851
Verse 3: tr. J. Chambers, 1857, alt.

Lasst Uns Erfreuen
Geistliches Kirchengesang, 1623

1. That East-er-tide with joy was bright, The
2. He showed to them his hands, his side, Where
3. To God the Fa-ther let us sing, To

1. sun shone out with fair-er light, Al-le-
2. yet those glo-rious wounds a - bide, Al-le-
3. God the Son, our ris-en King, Al-le-

1. lu - ia, al-le-lu-ia, When, to their long-
2. lu - ia, al-le-lu-ia, The to-kens true
3. lu - ia, al-le-lu-ia, And e-qual-ly

1. ing eyes re-stored, The glad a-pos-tles saw their
2. which made it plain. Their Lord in-deed was ris'n a-
3. let us a-dore The Ho-ly Spir-it ev-er-

1. Lord, Al-le-lu-ia, al-le-lu-ia, Al-le-
2. gain, Al-le-lu-ia, al-le-lu-ia, Al-le-
3. more, Al-le-lu-ia, al-le-lu-ia, Al-le-

1. lu - ia, al-le-lu-ia, al-le-lu - ia!
2. lu - ia, al-le-lu-ia, al-le-lu - ia!
3. lu - ia, al-le-lu-ia, al-le-lu - ia!

594

O Lord, Hear My Prayer

Tune: Jacques Berthier, 1923-1994

Text: Psalm 102
Taizé Community, 1982

Ostinato Chorale

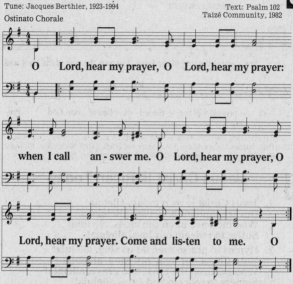

O Lord, hear my prayer, O Lord, hear my prayer:

when I call an-swer me. O Lord, hear my prayer, O

Lord, hear my prayer. Come and lis-ten to me. O

Stay Here and Keep Watch

Tune: Jacques Berthier, 1923-1994

Text: from Matthew 26;
Taizé Community

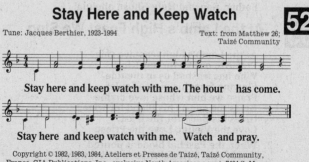

Stay here and keep watch with me. The hour has come.

Stay here and keep watch with me. Watch and pray.

53   Prepare the Way of the Lord

Tune: Jacques Berthier, 1923-1994

Text: Luke 3:4, 6;
Taizé Community

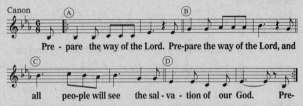

Canon

Pre - pare the way of the Lord. Pre-pare the way of the Lord, and
all peo-ple will see the sal - va - tion of our God. Pre-

54   Jesus Christ Is Risen Today

1. Jesus Christ is ris'n today, alleluia!
   Our triumphant holy day, alleluia!
   Who did once upon the cross, alleluia!
   Suffer to redeem our loss, alleluia!

2. Hymns of praise then let us sing, alleluia!
   Unto Christ our heav'nly King, alleluia!
   Who endured the cross and grave, alleluia!
   Sinners to redeem and save, alleluia!

3. Sing we to our God above, alleluia!
   Praise eternal as his love, alleluia!
   Praise him, all ye heav'nly host, alleluia!
   Father, Son and Holy Ghost, alleluia!

55   At the Lamb's High Feast We Sing

1. At the Lamb's high feast we sing
   Praise to our victor'ous King,
   Who has washed us in the tide
   Flowing from his pierced side;
   Praise we him whose love divine
   Gives the guests his Blood for wine,
   Gives his Body for the feast,
   Love the Victim, Love the Priest.

2. When the Paschal blood is poured,
   Death's dark Angel sheathes his sword;
   Israel's hosts triumphant go
   Through the wave that drowns the foe.

Christ, the Lamb whose Blood was shed,
Paschal victim, Paschal bread;
With sincerity and love
Eat we Manna from above.

Christ the Lord Is Risen Today

Tr. Jane E. Leeson, 1807-1882   Traditional

1. Christ, the Lord is risn' to-day,
2. Christ, the Vic-tim un-de-filed,
3. Christ, Who once for sin-ners bled,

Chris-tians, haste your vows to pay; Of-fer ye your
Man to God hath re-con-ciled; When in strange and
Now the first born of the dead, Thron'd in end-less

prais-es meet At the Pas-chal Vic-tim's feet.
aw-ful strife Met to-geth-er death and life;
might and pow'r, Lives and reigns for-ev-er more.

For the sheep the Lamb hath bled; Sin-less in the
Chris-tians on this hap-py day Haste with joy your
Hail, e-ter-nal Hope on high! Hail, Thou King of

sin-ner's stead; Christ, the Lord, is ris'n on high;
vows to pay. Christ, the Lord, is ris'n on high;
Vic-to-ry! Hail, Thou Prince of Life a-dored!

Now He lives no— more to die!
Now He lives no— more to die!
Help and save us— gra-cious Lord. 597

57. All Glory, Laud, and Honor

Tr. John Mason Neale, 1851

Melchior Teschner, pub. 1615

1. All glo - ry, laud, and hon - or To
3. The com - pa - ny of an - gels Are
5. To thee be - fore thy Pas - sion They

1. thee, Re-deem-er, King! To whom the lips of
3. prais-ing thee on high; And mor-tal men and
5. sang their hymns of praise: To thee, now nigh ex-

1. chil - dren Made glad ho - san- nas ring.
3. all things Cre - a - ted make re - ply. ★
5. alt - ed, Our mel - o - dy we raise. ★

2. Thou art the King of Is - ra - el, Thou
4. The peo - ple of the He - brews With
6. Thou didst ac - cept their prais - es: Ac-

2. Dav - id's roy - al Son, Who in the Lord's Name
4. palms be-fore thee went: Our praise and prayer and
6 cept the praise we bring, Who in all good de-

2. com - est, The King and Bless- ed One. ★
4. an - thems Be - fore thee we pre - sent. ★
6 light - est, thou good and gra-cious King. ★

★ *Refrain:* after each stanza except the first.

The Strife Is O'er

Alleluia! Alleluia! Alleluia!

1. The strife is o'er, the battle done!
   The victory of life is won!
   The song of triumph has begun! Alleluia!

2. The powers of death have done their worst,
   But Christ their legions has dispersed;
   Let shouts of holy joy outburst! Alleluia!

3. The three sad days are quickly sped,
   He rises glor'ous from the dead;
   All glory to our risen Head! Alleluia!

4. He closed the yawning gates of hell;
   The bars from heaven's high portals fell;
   Let hymns of praise His triumph tell! Alleluia!

O Sons and Daughters, Let Us Sing!

Alleluia! Alleluia! Alleluia!

1. O sons and daughters, let us sing!
   The King of heav'n, the glorious King,
   Today is ris'n and triumphing. Alleluia!

2. On Easter morn, at break of day,
   The faithful women went their way
   To seek the tomb where Jesus lay. Alleluia!

3. An angel clad in white they see,
   Who sat and spoke unto the three,
   "Your Lord doth go to Galilee." Alleluia!

4. On this most holy day of days,
   To you our hearts and voice we raise,
   In laud and jubilee and praise. Alleluia!

5. Glory to Father and to Son,
   Who has for us the vict'ry won
   And Holy Ghost; blest Three in One. Alleluia!

60 Christ the Lord Is Risen Again

1. Christ the Lord is ris'n a-gain!
2. He who gave for us his life,
3. He who bore all pain and loss

Christ has bro-ken ev-'ry chain!
Who for us en-dured the strife,
Com-fort-less up-on the Cross,

Hark, the an-gels shout for joy,
Is our Pas-chal Lamb to-day!
Lives in glo-ry now on high,

Sing-ing ev-er more on high,_
We too sing for joy and say,_
Pleads for us and hears our cry,_

Al-le-lu-ia. Al-le-lu-

ia. Al-le-lu-ia.

61 Creator Spirit, Lord of Grace

Creator Spirit, Lord of Grace,
Make thou our hearts thy dwelling place;
And, with thy might celestial, aid
The souls of those whom thou hast made.

O to our souls thy light impart,
And give thy love to every heart;
Turn all our weakness into might,
O thou the source of life and light.

Come, Holy Ghost, Creator Blest

1. Come, Holy Ghost, Creator blest,
   And in our hearts take up thy rest;
   Come with thy grace and heav'nly aid
   To fill the hearts which thou hast made,
   To fill the hearts which thou hast made.

2. O Comforter, to thee we cry,
   Thou heav'nly gift of God most high;
   Thou fount of life and fire of love
   And sweet anointing from above,
   And sweet anointing from above.

3. Praise we the Father, and the Son,
   And the blest Spirit with them one;
   And may the Son on us bestow
   The gifts that from the Spirit flow,
   The gifts that from the Spirit flow.

O God of Loveliness

1. O God of loveliness, O Lord of Heav'n above,
   How worthy to possess my heart's devoted love!
   So sweet Thy Countenance, so gracious to behold,
   That one, and only glance to me were bliss untold.

2. Thou are blest Three in One, yet undivided still;
   Thou art that One alone whose love my heart can fill,
   The heav'ns and earth below, were fashioned by Thy
       Word;
   How amiable art Thou, my ever dearest Lord!

3. O loveliness supreme, and beauty infinite
   O everflowing Stream, and Ocean of delight;
   O life by which I live, my truest life above,
   To You alone I give my undivided love.

Come Down, O Love Divine

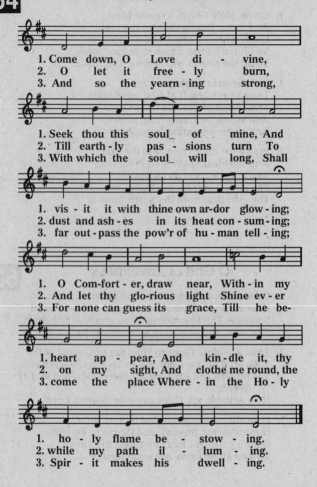

1. Come down, O Love di - vine,
2. O let it free - ly burn,
3. And so the yearn - ing strong,

1. Seek thou this soul_ of mine, And
2. Till earth - ly pas - sions turn To
3. With which the soul_ will long, Shall

1. vis - it it with thine own ar-dor glow-ing;
2. dust and ash - es in its heat con - sum - ing;
3. far out-pass the pow'r of hu - man tell - ing;

1. O Com-fort - er, draw near, With - in my
2. And let thy glo-rious light Shine ev - er
3. For none can guess its grace, Till he be-

1. heart ap - pear, And kin - dle it, thy
2. on my sight, And clothe me round, the
3. come the place Where - in the Ho - ly

1. ho - ly flame be - stow - ing.
2. while my path il - lum - ing.
3. Spir - it makes his dwell - ing.

When Morning Gilds the Skies

E. Caswall, Tr.   Traditional

1. When morn - ing gilds the skies My
2. Be   this, while life is   mine, My
3. To   God, the Word, on   high   The
4. Let   earth's wide cir - cle round In

1. heart a - wak-ing cries; May Je - sus Christ be
2. cant - i - cle di - vine; May Je - sus Christ be
3. hosts of an - gels cry; May Je - sus Christ be
4. joy - ful song re - sound; May Je - sus Christ be

1. praised! A - like at work and   prayer To
2. praised! Be   our e - ter - nal   song, Through
3. praised! Let na-tions too   up - raise Their
4. praised! Let air, and sea, and   sky, Through

1. Je - sus I   re - pair: May Je-sus Christ be
2. all the a - ges   long. May Je-sus Christ be
3. voice in hymns of   praise: May Je-sus Christ be
4. depth and height re - ply   May Je-sus Christ be

1. praised! May Je - sus Christ be   praised!
2. praised! May Je - sus Christ be   praised!
3. praised! May Je - sus Christ be   praised!
4. praised! May Je - sus Christ be   praised!

66 Psalm 23: Shepherd Me, O God

Music: Marty Haugen   Text: Psalm 23; Marty Haugen

Refrain

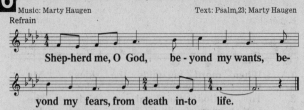

Shep-herd me, O God, be-yond my wants, be-yond my fears, from death in-to life.

Verses

1. God is my shepherd, so nothing shall I want,
   I rest in the meadows of faithfulness and love,
   I walk by the quiet waters of peace.

2. Gently you raise me and heal my weary soul,
   you lead me by pathways of righteousness and truth,
   my spirit shall sing the music of your name.

3. Though I should wander the valley of death,
   I fear no evil, for you are at my side, your rod and your
   staff,
   my comfort and my hope.

4. Surely your kindness and mercy follow me all the days
   of my life;
   I will dwell in the house of my God for evermore.

67 Eat This Bread

Tune: Jacques Berthier, 1923-1994 Text: John 6; adapt. by Robert J. Batastini, b. 1942
and the Taizé Community

Refrain

Eat this bread, drink this cup, come to him and nev-er be hun-gry.

Eat this bread, drink this cup, trust in him and you will not thirst.

Taste and See

Tune: James E. Moore, Jr., b. 1951

Text: Psalm 34;
James E. Moore, Jr., b. 1951

Refrain

Taste and see, taste and see the good-ness of the

Lord. O taste and see, taste and see the

good - ness of the Lord, of the Lord.

Verses

1. I will bless the Lord at all times.
2. Glo - ri - fy the Lord with me,
3. Wor-ship the Lord, all you peo-ple.

Praise shall al-ways be on my lips;
To-geth-er let us all praise God's name.
You'll want for noth-ing if you ask.

my soul shall glo-ry in the Lord
I called the Lord who an - swered me;
Taste and see that the Lord is good;

D.C.

for God has been so good to me.
from all my tou-bles I was set free.
in God we need put all our trust.

Loving Shepherd of Your Sheep

1. Lov - ing Shep - herd of your sheep,
2. Lov - ing Shep - herd you did give,
3. Lov - ing Shep - herd ev - er near,

Keep us Lord in safe - ty keep;
Your own life that we might live;
Teach us still your voice to hear;

Noth - ing can your pow'r with - stand,
May we love you day by day,
Suf - fer not our steps to stray

None can pluck us from your hand.
Glad - ly your sweet Will o - bey.
From the straight and nar - row way.

Good Shep - herd, shield us.
Good Shep - herd, shield us.
Good Shep - herd, shield us.

In the Lord's Atoning Grief

1. In the Lord's atoning grief
   Be our rest and sweet relief;
   Deep within our hearts we'll store
   Those dear pains and wrongs he bore.

2. Thorns and cross and nail and spear,
   Wounds that faithful hearts revere,
   Vinegar and gall and reed
   And the pang his soul that freed.

3. Crucified we thee adore,
   Thee with all our hearts implore;
   With the saints our soul unite,
   In the realms of heav'nly light.

Ubi Caritas

Tune: Jacques Berthier 1923-1994   Text: 1 Corinthians 13:2-8

U - bi ca - ri - tas   et a - mor,
Live in char - i - ty   and stead - fast love,

u - bi ca - ri - tas   De - us i - bi est.
live in char - i - ty;   God will dwell with you.

72 I Am the Bread of Life

Tune: BREAD OF LIFE, Irreg with refrain;
Suzanne Toolan, SM, b. 1927.

Text: John 6;
Suzanne Toolan, SM, b. 1927

1. ___ I am the Bread of life. You who
2. The bread that___ I will give is my
3. Un - less___ you eat of the
4. ___ I am the Res - ur - rec - tion,___
5. Yes, Lord,___ I be - lieve that___

1. Yo soy el pan de vi - da. El que
2. El pan que___ yo da - ré___ es mi
3. ___ Mien - tras no co-mas el___
4. ___ Yo soy la re - su - rrec - ción.___
5. ___ Sí, Se - ñor, yo cre - o que___

come to me shall not hun - ger;___ and who be-
flesh for the life of the world,___ and if you
flesh of the Son of Man and___
I___ am the life.___ If you be -
you___ are the Christ,___ the___

vie - ne_a mí no ten-drá ham - bre.___ El que
cuer - po vi - da del mun - do, y el que
cuer-po del hi-jo del hom-bre,___ y___
Yo___ soy la vi - da.___ El que
tú e - res el Cris - to, ___ El

lieve in me shall not thirst.___ No one can come to
eat___ of this bread,___ you shall__ live for
drink___ of his blood,__ and drink___ of his
lieve ___ in ___ me, ___ e-ven__ though you
Son of__ God, Who has__

cree_en mí no ten-drá sed.___ Na - die__ vie - ne_a
co - ma__ de mi car-ne___ ten-drá__ vi - da_e-
be - bas __ de su san-gre y be-bas__ de su
cree___ en___ mí,___ aun-que__ mu - rie-
Hi - jo de Dios,___ que vi - no al

me   un-less   the__ Fa - ther   beck-ons.
ev - er,_____   you   shall__ live   for   ev - er.
blood,   you shall   not have life   with - in you.
die,_____   you   shall__ live   for   ev - er.
come   in - to_____ the____   world.___
mí_____   mien - tras el Pa - dre   lla - me.
ter - na, _____   ten - drá__ vi - da e __ ter - na.
san - gre,   no   ten - drá   vi - da   en   ti.
ra,_____   ten - drá vi - da   e - ter - na.
mun-do_____   pa - ra sal-var-nos.

And   I   will   raise   you   up,   and   I   will
Yo   le   re - su - ci - ta - ré,   Yo   lo   re -

raise   you   up,   and   I   will   raise   you
su - ci - ta - ré,   Yo   lo   re - su - ci - ta -

up   on   the   last   day.
ré   el   di - a   de_El.

O Lord, I Am Not Worthy

73

1. **O Lord, I am not worthy,**
    That thou should come to me,
    But speak the word of comfort
    My spirit healed shall be.

2. **And humbly I'll receive thee,**
    The bridegroom of my soul,
    No more by sin to grieve thee
    Or fly thy sweet control.

3. **O Sacrament most holy,**
    O Sacrament divine,
    All praise and all thanksgiving
    Be every moment thine.

The Summons

Tune: KELVINGROVE, 7 6 7 6 777 6;
Scottish traditional; arr. by John L. Bell, b. 1949

Text: John L. Bell, b. 1949;

1. Will you come and fol-low me If I but call your name? Will you go where you don't know And nev-er be the same? Will you let my love be shown, Will you let my name be known, Will you let my life be grown In you and you in me?

2. Will you leave your-self be-hind If I but call your name? Will you care for cruel and kind And nev-er be the same? Will you risk the hos-tile stare Should your life at-tract or scare? Will you let me an-swer prayer In you and you in me?

3. Will you let the blind-ed see If I but call your name? Will you set the pris-'ners free And nev-er be the same? Will you kiss the lep-er clean, And do such as this un-seen, And ad-mit to what I mean In you and you in me?

4. Will you love the 'you' you hide If I but call your name? Will you quell the fear in-side And nev-er be the same? Will you use the faith you've found To re-shape the world a-round, Through my sight and touch and sound In you and you in me?

We Walk by Faith

Tune: SHANTI, CM;
Marty Haugen, b. 1950

Text: Henry Alford, 1810-1871, alt.

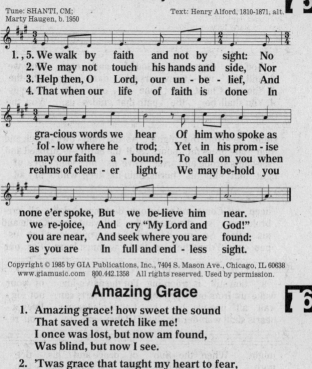

1., 5. We walk by faith and not by sight: No
2. We may not touch his hands and side, Nor
3. Help then, O Lord, our un-be-lief, And
4. That when our life of faith is done In

gra-cious words we hear Of him who spoke as
fol-low where he trod; Yet in his prom-ise
may our faith a-bound; To call on you when
realms of clear-er light We may be-hold you

none e'er spoke, But we be-lieve him near.
we re-joice, And cry "My Lord and God!"
you are near, And seek where you are found:
as you are In full and end-less sight.

Amazing Grace

1. Amazing grace! how sweet the sound
   That saved a wretch like me!
   I once was lost, but now am found,
   Was blind, but now I see.

2. 'Twas grace that taught my heart to fear,
   And grace my fears relieved;
   How precious did that grace appear
   The hour I first believed!

3. Through many dangers, toils, and snares,
   I have already come;
   'Tis grace hath brought me safe thus far,
   And grace will lead me home.

4. The Lord has promised good to me,
   His word my hope secures;
   He will my shield and portion be,
   As long as life endures.

77 God of Day and God of Darkness

Tune: BEACH SPRING, 8 7 8 7 D;
The Sacred Harp, 1844;
harm. by Marty Haugen, b. 1950

Text: Marty Haugen, b. 1950;

1. God of day and God of dark - ness, Now we
2. Still the na - tions curse the dark - ness, Still the
3. Show us Christ in one an - oth - er, Make us
4. You shall be the path that guides us, You the

stand be - fore the night; As the shad - ows stretch and
rich op - press the poor; Still the earth is bruised and
ser - vants strong and true; Give us all your love of
light that in us burns; Shin - ing deep with - in all

deep - en, Come and make our dark - ness bright. All cre-
brok - en By the ones who still want more. Come and
jus - tice So we do what you would do. Let us
peo - ple, Yours the love that we must learn, For our

a - tion still is groan - ing For the dawn - ing of your
wake us from our sleep - ing, So our hearts can - not ig-
call all peo - ple ho - ly, Let us pledge our lives a-
hearts shall wan - der rest - less 'Til they safe to you re-

might, When the Sun of peace and jus - tice
nore all your peo - ple lost and bro - ken,
new, Make us one with all the low - ly,
turn; Find - ing you in one an - oth - er,

Fills the earth with ra - diant light.
All your chil - dren at our door.
Let us all be one in you.
We shall all your face dis - cern.

Sing My Tongue the Savior's Glory

1. Sing my tongue, the Savior's glory,
   Of his flesh the mystr'y sing;
   Of the Blood all price exceeding,
   Shed by our immortal King,
   Destined for the world's redemption,
   From a noble womb to spring.

2. Of a pure and spotless Virgin
   Born for us on earth below,
   He, as Man, with man conversing,
   Stayed, the seeds of truth to sow;
   Then he closed in solemn order
   Wondrously his life of woe.

3. On the night of that Last Supper,
   Seated with his chosen band,
   He the Paschal victim eating,
   First fulfills the Law's command;
   Then as food to his Apostles
   Gives himself with his own hand.

4. Word made flesh the bread of nature
   By his word to Flesh he turns;
   Wine into his blood he changes
   What though sense no change discerns?
   Only be the heart in earnest,
   Faith her lesson quickly learns.

(Tantum ergo)

5. Down in adoration falling
   Lo! the sacred Host we hail,
   Lo! o'er ancient forms departing,
   Newer rites of grace prevail;
   Faith for all defects supplying,
   Where the feeble senses fail.

6. To the Everlasting Father,
   And the Son who reigns on high,
   With the Holy Ghost proceeding
   Forth from each eternally
   Be salvation, honor, blessing,
   Might, and endless majesty. Amen.

79 Immaculate Mary

1. Immaculate Mary, thy praises we sing,
   Who reignest in splendor with Jesus, our King.

   Refrain:
   Ave, ave, ave, Maria! Ave, ave, Maria!

2. In heaven, the blessed thy glory proclaim,
   On earth, we thy children invoke thy fair name.
   —*Refrain*

3. Thy name is our power, thy virtues our light,
   Thy love is our comfort, thy pleading our might.
   —*Refrain*

4. We pray for our mother, the Church upon earth,
   And bless, dearest Lady, the land of our birth.
   —*Refrain*

80 Hail, Holy Queen Enthroned Above

1. Hail, holy Queen enthroned above, O Maria!
   Hail, Mother of mercy and of love, O Maria!

   Refrain:
   Triumph, ail ye cherubim,
   Sing with us, ye seraphim,
   Heav'n and earth resound the hymn.
   Salve; salve, salve Regina.

2. Our life, our sweetness here below, O Maria!
   Our hope in sorrow and in woe, O Maria!
   —*Refrain*

3. To thee we cry, poor sons of Eve, O Maria!
   To thee we sigh, we mourn, we grieve, O Maria!
   —*Refrain*

4. Turn, then, most gracious Advocate, O Maria!
   Toward us thine eyes compassionate, O Maria!
   —*Refrain*

5. When this our exile's time is o'er, O Maria!
   Show us thy Son for evermore, O Maria!
   —*Refrain*

For All the Saints

William W. How
Moderately, in unison

R. Vaughan Williams, 1872-1958

1. For all the saints,
   who from their labors
   rest,
   Who Thee by faith
   before the world con-
   fessed,
   Thy Name, O Jesus, be
   for ever blest.
   Alleluia, alleluia!

2. O blest communion!
   fellowship divine!
   We feebly struggle,
   they in glory shine;
   Yet all are one in Thee,
   for all are Thine.
   Alleluia, alleluia!

3. From earth's wide
   bounds,
   from ocean's farthest
   coast,
   Through gates of pearl
   streams
   in the countless host,
   Singing to Father, Son
   and Holy Ghost.
   Alleluia, alleluia!

America

1.
My country, 'tis of thee,
Sweet land of liberty,
Of thee I sing;
Land where my fathers died,
Land of the pilgrim's pride
From ev'ry mountainside
Let freedom ring.

2.
My native country, thee,
Land of the noble free,
Thy name I love;
I love thy rocks and rills,
Thy woods and templed hills;
My heart with rapture thrills
Like that above.

America the Beautiful

1. O beautiful for spacious skies,
   For amber wave of grain,
   For purple mountain majesties
   Above the fruited plain.
   America! America! God shed his grace on thee.
   And crown thy good with brotherhood
   From sea to shining sea.

2. O beautiful for pilgrim feet
   Whose stern impassioned stress
   A thoroughfare for freedom beat
   Across the wilderness.
   America! America! God mend thy ev'ry flaw,
   Confirm thy soul in self control,
   Thy liberty in law.

HYMN INDEX

No.	Page
30 - A Child Is Born	582
57 - All Glory, Laud, and Honor	598
76 - Amazing Grace	611
82 - America	615
83 - America the Beautiful	615
35 - Angels We Have Heard	585
49 - At the Cross Her Station Keeping	593
55 - At the Lamb's High Feast	596
11 - Awake, Awake and Greet the New Morn	572
36 - Away in a Manger	585
60 - Christ the Lord Is Risen Again	600
56 - Christ the Lord Is Risen Today	597
20 - Come All You People	578
64 - Come Down, O Love Divine	602
62 - Come, Holy Ghost, Creator Blest	601
26 - Come, Thou Long Expected Jesus	580
19 - Confitemini Domino / Come and Fill	577
61 - Creator Spirit, Lord of Grace	600
15 - Crown Him with Many Crowns	575
67 - Eat This Bread	604
3 - Eye Has Not Seen	568
5 - Faith of Our Fathers	569
81 - For All the Saints	615
18 - Gather Us In	576
6 - God Father, Praise and Glory	570
77 - God of Day and God of Darkness	612
34 - Good Christian Men	584
80 - Hail, Holy Queen	614
22 - Hark, a Mystic Voice Is Sounding	579
32 - Hark! The Herald Angels Sing	583
40 - Holy God, We Praise Thy Name	587
8 - Holy, Holy, Holy	570
72 - I Am the Bread of Life	608
79 - Immaculate Mary	614
70 - In the Lord's Atoning Grief	607
54 - Jesus Christ Is Risen Today	596
43 - Jesus, Remember Me	589
41 - Lord, Who throughout These 40 Days	588
69 - Loving Shepherd	606
9 - Now Thank We All Our God	571
28 - O Come, All Ye Faithful	581
24 - O Come, Divine Messiah	579
27 - O Come Little Children	580
25 - O Come, O Come, Emmanuel	580
46 - O Faithful Cross	591
63 - O God of Loveliness	601

No.   Page

47 - O God, Our Help in
Ages Past 591

37 - O Little Town of Bethlehem 585

51 - O Lord, Hear My Prayer . . . 595

73 - O Lord, I Am Not Worthy . . 609

17 - On Jordan's Bank 575

16 - O Perfect Love 575

44 - O Sacred Head
Surrounded. 589

33 - O Sing a Joyous Carol 583

59 - O Sons and Daughters . . . 599

4 - Praise God from Whom All
Blessings Flow 569

1 - Praise My Soul 566

7 - Praise the Lord of Heaven . . 570

2 - Praise to the Lord 567

53 - Prepare the Way of the Lord. 596

12 - Rejoice, the Lord Is King . . 573

66 - Shepherd Me, O God 604

31 - Silent Night. 582

78 - Sing My Tongue 613

52 - Stay Here and Keep Watch 595

68 - Taste and See. 605

50 - That Eastertide with Joy
Was Bright 594

No.   Page

10 - The Church's One
Foundation 571

23 - The Coming of Our God . . . 579

29 - The First Noel 581

58 - The Strife Is O'er 599

74 - The Summons. 610

30 - Three Magi Kings 582

21 - To Jesus Christ, Our
Sovereign King 578

71 - Ubi Caritas 607

13 - We Gather Together. 573

14 - We Praise Thee, O God, Our
Redeemer 574

48 - Were You There 592

39 - We Three Kings 587

75 - We Walk by Faith. 611

38 - What Child Is This? 586

42 - When I Behold the
Wondrous Cross 588

65 - When Morning Gilds the
Skies. 603

45 - Where Charity and Love
Prevail 590

TREASURY OF PRAYERS

MORNING PRAYERS

Morning Offering

O Jesus, through the Immaculate Heart of Mary, I offer You my prayers, works, joys, and sufferings of this day for all the intentions of Your Sacred Heart, in union with the Holy Sacrifice of the Mass throughout the world, for the salvation of souls, the reparation of sins, the reunion of all Christians, and in particular for the intentions of the Holy Father this month.

Another Morning Offering

Most holy and adorable Trinity, one God in three Persons, I praise you and give you thanks for all the favors you have bestowed upon me. Your goodness has preserved me until now. I offer you my whole being and in particular all my thoughts, words and deeds, together with all the trials I may undergo this day. Give them your blessing. May your Divine Love animate them and may they serve your greater glory.

I make this morning offering in union with the Divine intentions of Jesus Christ who offers himself daily in the holy Sacrifice of the Mass, and in union with Mary, his Virgin Mother and our Mother, who was always the faithful handmaid of the Lord.

Glory be to the Father, and to the Son, and to the Holy Spirit. Amen.

Guardian Angel Prayer

Angel of God, my Guardian dear, to whom God's love commits me here. Ever this day be at my side, to light and guard, to rule and guide. Amen.

Prayers at the Beginning of the Day

Almighty God, you have given us this day: strengthen us with your power and keep us from falling into sin, so that whatever we say or think or do may be in your service and for the sake of your kingdom. We ask this through Christ our Lord. Amen. *Partial indulgence*

Lord, may everything we do begin with your inspiration and continue with your help, so that all our prayers and works may begin in you and by you be happily ended. We ask this through Christ our Lord. Amen. *Partial indulgence*

NIGHT PRAYERS

I adore you, my God, and thank you for having created me, for having made me a Christian and preserved me this day. I love you with all my heart and I am sorry for having sinned against you, because you are infinite Love and infinite Goodness. Protect me during my rest and may your love be always with me. Amen.

Eternal Father, I offer you the Precious Blood of Jesus Christ in atonement for my sins and for all the intentions of our Holy Church.

Holy Spirit, Love of the Father and the Son, purify my heart and fill it with the fire of your Love, so that I may be a chaste Temple of the Holy Trinity and be always pleasing to you in all things. Amen.

Plea for Divine Help

Hear us, Lord, and send your angel from heaven to visit and protect, to comfort and defend all who live in this house. Amen.   *Partial indulgence*

PRAYERS BEFORE HOLY COMMUNION

Act of Faith

Lord Jesus Christ, I firmly believe that you are present in this Blessed Sacrament as true God and true Man, with your Body and Blood, Soul and Divinity. My Redeemer and my Judge, I adore your Divine Majesty together with the angels and saints. I believe, O Lord; increase my faith.

Act of Hope

Good Jesus, in you alone I place all my hope. You are my salvation and my strength, the Source of all good. Through your mercy, through your Passion and Death, I hope to obtain the pardon of my sins, the grace of final perseverance and a happy eternity.

Act of Love

Jesus, my God, I love you with my whole heart and above all things, because you are the one supreme Good and an infinitely perfect Being. You have given your life for me, a poor sinner, and in your mercy you have even offered yourself as food for my soul. My God, I love you. Inflame my heart so that I may love you more.

Act of Contrition

O my Savior, I am truly sorry for having offended you because you are infinitely good and sin displeases you. I detest all the sins of my life and I desire to atone for them. Through the merits of your Precious Blood, wash from my soul all stain of sin, so that, cleansed in body and soul, I may worthily approach the Most Holy Sacrament of the Altar.

PRAYERS AFTER HOLY COMMUNION

Act of Faith

Jesus, I firmly believe that you are present within me as God and Man, to enrich my soul with graces and to fill my heart with the happiness of the blessed. I believe that you are Christ, the Son of the living God!

Act of Adoration

With deepest humility, I adore you, my Lord and God; you have made my soul your dwelling place. I adore you as my Creator from whose hands I came and with whom I am to be happy forever.

Act of Love

Dear Jesus, I love you with my whole heart, my whole soul, and with all my strength. May the love of your own Sacred Heart fill my soul and purify it so that I may die to the world for love of you, as you died on the Cross for love of me. My God, you are all mine; grant that I may be all yours in time and in eternity.

Act of Thanksgiving

From the depths of my heart I thank you, dear Lord, for your infinite kindness in coming to me. How good you are to me! With your most holy Mother and all the angels, I praise your mercy and generosity toward me, a poor sinner. I thank you for nourishing my soul with your Sacred Body and Precious Blood. I will try to show my gratitude to you in the Sacrament of your love, by obedience to your holy commandments, by fidelity to my duties, by kindness to my neighbor and by an earnest endeavor to become more like you in my daily conduct.

Act of Offering

Jesus, you have given yourself to me, now let me give myself to you; I give you my body, that it may be chaste and pure. I give you my soul, that it may be free from sin. I give you my heart, that it may always love you. I give you every thought, word, and deed of my life, and I offer all for your honor and glory.

Prayer to Christ the King

O Christ Jesus, I acknowledge you King of the universe. All that has been created has been made for you. Exercise upon me all your rights. I renew my baptismal promises, renouncing Satan and all his works and pomps. I promise to live a good Christian life and to do all in my power to procure the triumph of the rights of God and your Church.

Divine Heart of Jesus, I offer you my poor actions in order to obtain that all hearts may acknowledge your sacred Royalty, and that thus the reign of your peace may be established throughout the universe. Amen.

Indulgenced Prayer before a Crucifix

Look down upon me, good and gentle Jesus, while before your face I humbly kneel, and with a burning soul pray and beseech you to fix deep in my heart lively sentiments of faith, hope and charity, true contrition for my sins, and a firm purpose of amendment, while I contemplate with great love and tender pity your five wounds, pondering over them within me, calling to mind the words which David, your prophet, said of you, my good Jesus: "They have pierced my hands and my feet; they have numbered all my bones" (Ps 22:17-18).

On any Friday during Lent a *plenary indulgence* is granted the Christian faithful who, after communion, devoutly recite the above prayer before an image of Jesus Christ crucified. On other days of the year the indulgence is a *partial* one.

Prayer to Mary

O Jesus living in Mary, come and live in your servants, in the spirit of your holiness, in the fullness of your power, in the perfection of your ways, in the truth of your mysteries. Reign in us over all adverse powers by your Holy Spirit, and for the glory of the Father. Amen.

Anima Christi

Soul of Christ, sanctify me.
Body of Christ, save me.
Blood of Christ, inebriate me.
Water from the side of Christ, wash me.
Passion of Christ, strengthen me.
O good Jesus, hear me.
Within your wounds hide me.
Separated from you let me never be.
From the malignant enemy, defend me.
At the hour of death, call me.
And close to you bid me.
That with your saints I may be
Praising you, forever and ever. Amen.

Partial indulgence

THE SCRIPTURAL WAY OF THE CROSS

The Way of the Cross is a devotion in which we accompany, in spirit, our Blessed Lord in his sorrowful journey to Calvary, and devoutly meditate on his suffering and death.

A *plenary indulgence* is granted the Christian faithful who devoutly make the Stations of the Cross.

1. Jesus Is Condemned to Death—God so loved the world that he gave his only-begotten Son to save it (Jn 3:16).

2. Jesus Bears His Cross—If anyone wishes to come after me, let him deny himself, and take up his cross daily (Lk 9:23).

3. Jesus Falls the First Time—The Lord laid upon him the guilt of us all (Is 53:6).

4. Jesus Meets His Mother—Come, all you who pass by the way, look and see whether there is any suffering like my suffering (Lam 1:13).

5. Jesus Is Helped by Simon—As long as you did it for one of these, the least of my brethren, you did it for me (Mt 25:40).

6. Veronica Wipes the Face of Jesus—He who sees me, sees also the Father (Jn 14:9).

7. Jesus Falls a Second Time—Come to me, all you who labor, and are burdened, and I will give you rest (Mt 11:28).

8. Jesus Speaks to the Women—Daughters of Jerusalem, do not weep for me, but weep for yourselves and for your children (Lk 23:2).

9. Jesus Falls a Third Time—Everyone who exalts himself shall be humbled, and he who humbles himself shall be exalted (Lk 14:11).

10. Jesus Is Stripped of His Garments—Every one of you who does not renounce all that he possesses cannot be my disciple (Lk 14:33).

11. Jesus Is Nailed to the Cross—I have come down from heaven, not to do my own will, but the will of him who sent me (Jn 6:38).

12. Jesus Dies on the Cross—He humbled himself, becoming obedient to death, even to death on a cross. Therefore God has exalted him (Phil 2:8-9).

13. Jesus Is Taken Down from the Cross—Did not the Christ have to suffer those things before entering into his glory? (Lk 24:26).

14. Jesus Is Placed in the Tomb—Unless the grain of wheat falls into the ground and dies, it remains alone. But if it dies, it brings forth much fruit (Jn 12:24-25).

STATIONS
of the
CROSS

1. Jesus Is Condemned to Death

O Jesus, help me to appreciate Your sanctifying grace more and more.

2. Jesus Bears His Cross

O Jesus, You chose to die for me. Help me to love You always with all my heart.

3. Jesus Falls the First Time

O Jesus, make me strong to conquer my wicked passions, and to rise quickly from sin.

4. Jesus Meets His Mother

O Jesus, grant me a tender love for Your Mother, who offered You for love of me.

STATIONS
of the
CROSS

5. Jesus Is Helped by Simon

O Jesus, like Simon lead me ever closer to You through my daily crosses and trials.

6. Jesus and Veronica

O Jesus, imprint Your image on my heart that I may be faithful to You all my life.

7. Jesus Falls a Second Time

O Jesus, I repent for having offended You. Grant me forgiveness of all my sins.

8. Jesus Speaks to the Women

O Jesus, grant me tears of compassion for Your sufferings and of sorrow for my sins.

STATIONS
of the
CROSS

9. Jesus Falls a Third Time

O Jesus, let me never yield to despair. Let me come to You in hardship and spiritual distress.

10. He Is Stripped of His Garments

O Jesus, let me sacrifice all my attachments rather than imperil the divine life of my soul.

11. Jesus Is Nailed to the Cross

O Jesus, strengthen my faith and increase my love for You. Help me to accept my crosses.

12. Jesus Dies on the Cross

O Jesus, I thank You for making me a child of God. Help me to forgive others.

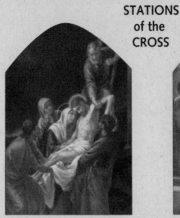

13. Jesus Is Taken Down from the Cross

O Jesus, through the intercession of Your holy Mother, let me be pleasing to You.

14. Jesus Is Laid in the Tomb

O Jesus, strengthen my will to live for You on earth and bring me to eternal bliss in heaven.

Prayer after the Stations

JESUS, You became an example of humility, obedience and patience, and preceded me on the way of life bearing Your Cross. Grant that, inflamed with Your love, I may cheerfully take upon myself the sweet yoke of Your Gospel together with the mortification of the Cross and follow You as a true disciple so that I may be united with You in heaven. Amen.

THE HOLY ROSARY

PRAYER BEFORE THE ROSARY

QUEEN of the Holy Rosary, you have deigned to come to Fatima to reveal to the three shepherd children the treasures of grace hidden in the Rosary. Inspire my heart with a sincere love of this devotion, in order that by meditating on the Mysteries of our Redemption which are recalled in it, I may be enriched with its fruits and obtain peace for the world, the conversion of sinners and of Russia, and the favor which I ask of you in this Rosary. *(Here mention your request.)* I ask it for the greater glory of God, for your own honor, and for the good of souls, especially for my own. Amen.

The Five *Joyful* Mysteries

Said on Mondays and Saturdays [except during Lent], and the Sundays from Advent to Lent.

3. The Nativity
For the spirit of poverty.

1. The Annunciation
For the love of humility.

4. The Presentation
For the virtue of obedience.

2. The Visitation
For charity toward my neighbor.

5. Finding in the Temple
For the virtue of piety.

The Five Luminous Mysteries*

Said on Thursdays [except during Lent].

*Added to the Mysteries of the Rosary by Pope John Paul II in his Apostolic Letter of October 16, 2002, entitled *The Rosary of the Virgin Mary.*

1. The Baptism of Jesus
For living my Baptismal Promises.

2. The Wedding at Cana
For doing whatever Jesus says.

4. The Transfiguration
Becoming a New Person in Christ.

3. Proclamation of the Kingdom
For seeking God's forgiveness.

5. Institution of the Eucharist
For active participation at Mass.

The Five Sorrowful Mysteries

Said on Tuesdays and Fridays throughout the year, and every day from Ash Wednesday until Easter.

1. Agony in the Garden
For true contrition.

2. Scourging at the Pillar
For the virtue of purity.

3. Crowning with Thorns
For moral courage.

4. Carrying of the Cross
For the virtue of patience.

5. The Crucifixion
For final perseverance.

The Five Glorious Mysteries

Said on Wednesdays [except during Lent], and the Sundays from Easter to Advent.

1. The Resurrection
For the virtue of faith.

2. The Ascension
For the virtue of hope.

4. Assumption of the BVM
For devotion to Mary.

3. Descent of the Holy Spirit
For love of God.

5. Crowning of the BVM
For eternal happiness.

THE HAIL! HOLY QUEEN

HAIL! Holy Queen, Mother of Mercy, our life, our sweetness, and our hope. To you do we cry, poor banished children of Eve. To you do we send up our sighs, mourning and weeping in this valley of tears. Turn then, O most gracious advocate, your eyes of mercy toward us; and after this our exile, show unto us the blessed fruit of your womb, Jesus. O clement! O loving! O sweet Virgin Mary!

℣. Pray for us, O Holy Mother of God. ℟. That we may be made worthy of the promises of Christ.

———————

PRAYER AFTER THE ROSARY

O GOD, Whose only-begotten Son, by His Life, Death, and Resurrection, has purchased for us the rewards of eternal life; grant, we beseech You, that, meditating upon these Mysteries of the Most Holy Rosary of the Blessed Virgin Mary, we may imitate what they contain and obtain what they promise, through the same Christ our Lord. Amen.

℣. May the divine assistance remain always with us. ℟. Amen.

℣. And may the souls of the faithful departed, through the mercy of God, rest in peace. ℟. Amen.

The Litany of Loreto

Lord, have mercy.
Christ, have mercy.
Lord, have mercy.
Christ, hear us.
Christ, graciously hear us.
God, the Father of heaven,
  have mercy on us.
God, the Son, Redeemer of the world,
  have mercy on us.
God, the Holy Spirit,
  have mercy on us.
Holy Trinity, one God,
  have mercy on us.
Holy Mary, *pray for us.**
Holy Mother of God,
Holy Virgin of virgins,
Mother of Christ,
Mother of the Church,
Mother of mercy,
Mother of Divine grace,
Mother of hope,
Mother most pure,
Mother most chaste,
Mother inviolate,
Mother undefiled,
Mother most amiable,
Mother most admirable,
Mother of good counsel,
Mother of our Creator,
Mother of our Savior,
Virgin most prudent,
Virgin most venerable,
Virgin most renowned,
Virgin most powerful,
Virgin most merciful,
Virgin most faithful,
Mirror of justice,
Seat of wisdom,
Cause of our joy,
Spiritual vessel,
Vessel of honor,
Singular vessel of devotion,
Mystical rose,
Tower of David,
Tower of ivory,
House of gold,
Ark of the covenant,
Gate of heaven,
Morning star,
Health of the sick,
Refuge of sinners,
Solace of migrants,
Comforter of the afflicted,
Help of Christians,
Queen of angels,
Queen of patriarchs,
Queen of prophets,

* *Pray for us* is repeated after each invocation.

Queen of apostles,

Queen of martyrs,

Queen of confessors,

Queen of virgins,

Queen of all saints,

Queen conceived without original sin,

Queen assumed into heaven,

Queen of the most holy Rosary,

Queen of families,

Queen of peace,

Lamb of God, You take away the sins of the world; *spare us, O Lord!*

Lamb of God, You take away the sins of the world; *graciously hear us, O Lord!*

Lamb of God, You take away the sins of the world; *have mercy on us.*

℣. Pray for us, O holy Mother of God.

℟. *That we may be made worthy of the promises of Christ.*

Let us pray.

Grant, we beg You, O Lord God,

that we Your servants

may enjoy lasting health of mind and body,

and by the glorious intercession

of the Blessed Mary, ever Virgin,

be delivered from present sorrow

and enter into the joy of eternal happiness.

Through Christ our Lord.

℟. *Amen.*

The Magnificat/The Canticle of Mary

My soul proclaims the greatness of the Lord,
my spirit rejoices in God my Savior
for he has looked with favor on his lowly servant.

From this day all generations will call me blessed:
the Almighty has done great things for me,
and holy is his Name.

He has mercy on those who fear him
in every generation.

He has shown the strength of his arm,
he has scattered the proud in their conceit.

He has cast down the mighty from their thrones,
and has lifted up the lowly.

He has filled the hungry with good things,
and the rich he has sent away empty.

He has come to the help of his servant Israel
for he has remembered his promise of mercy,
the promise he made to our fathers,
to Abraham and his children for ever.

PRAYERS FOR SPECIAL INTENTIONS

For the Sick

Father, your Son accepted our sufferings to teach us the virtue of patience in human illness. Hear the prayers we offer for our sick brothers and sisters. May all who suffer pain, illness or disease realize that they are chosen to be saints, and know that they are joined to Christ in his suffering for the salvation of the world, who lives and reigns with you and the Holy Spirit, one God, for ever and ever.

For Religious Vocations

Father, you call all who believe in you to grow perfect in love by following in the footsteps of Christ your Son. May those whom you have chosen to serve you as religious provide by their way of life a convincing sign of your kingdom for the Church and the whole world.

Prayer for Civil Authorities

Almighty and everlasting God, You direct the powers and laws of all nations; mercifully regard those who rule over us, that, by Your protecting right hand, the integrity of religion and the security of each country might prevail everywhere on earth. Through Christ our Lord. Amen.

Prayer for Health

O Sacred Heart of Jesus, I come to ask of Your infinite mercy the gift of health and strength that I may serve You more faithfully and love You more sincerely than in the past. I wish to be well and strong if this be Your good pleasure and for Your greater glory. Filled with high resolves and determined to perform my tasks most perfectly for love of You, I wish to be enabled to go back to my duties.

Prayer for Peace and Joy

Jesus, I want to rejoice in You always. You are near. Let me have no anxiety, but in every concern by prayer and supplication with thanksgiving I wish to let my petitions be made known in my communing with God.

May the peace of God, which surpasses all understanding, guard my heart and my thoughts in You.

Prayer to Know God's Will

God the Father of our Lord Jesus Christ, the Author of glory, grant me spiritual wisdom and revelation. Enlighten the eyes of my mind with a deep knowledge of You and Your holy will. May I understand of what nature is the hope to which You call me, what is the wealth of the splendor of Your inheritance among the Saints; and what is the surpassing greatness of Your power toward me.

Prayer for Eternal Rest

Eternal rest grant unto them, O Lord, and let perpetual light shine upon them. May the souls of the faithful departed, through the mercy of God, rest in peace. Amen.

ESSENTIAL CATHOLIC PRAYERS

Spiritual Communion Prayer

My Jesus, I believe that You are present in the most Blessed Sacrament. I love You above all things, and I desire to receive You into my soul. Since I cannot now receive You sacramentally, come at least spiritually into my heart. I embrace You as if You were already there and unite myself wholly to You. Never permit me to be separated from You. Amen.

Prayer to the Holy Spirit

Come, Holy Spirit, fill the hearts of Your faithful and kindle in them the fire of Your love.

℣. Send forth Your Spirit, and they shall be created.

℟. **And You shall renew the face of the earth.**

Let us pray. O God, Who did instruct the hearts of the faithful by the light of the Holy Spirit: grant that, by the gift of the same Spirit, we may be always truly wise, and ever rejoice in His consolation. Through Christ our Lord. Amen.

The Angelus

℣. The Angel of the Lord declared unto Mary.

℟. **And she conceived of the Holy Spirit.**

Hail Mary, etc.

℣. Behold the handmaid of the Lord.

℟. **Be it done unto me according to Your word.**

Hail Mary, etc.

℣. And the Word was made flesh.

℟. **And dwelt among us.**

Hail Mary, etc.

℣. Pray for us, O holy Mother of God.

℟. **That we may be made worthy of the promises of Christ.**

Let us pray. Pour forth, we beseech You, O Lord, Your grace into our hearts, that we to whom the Incarnation of Christ, Your Son, was made known by the message of an angel, may by His Passion and Cross be brought to the glory of His Resurrection, through the same Christ our Lord. Amen.

Regina Caeli

(Said during Easter Time instead of the Angelus)

Queen of heaven, rejoice, alleluia. For He Whom you merited to bear, alleluia. Has risen as He said, alleluia. Pray for us to God, alleluia.

℣. Rejoice and be glad, O Virgin Mary, alleluia.

℟. **Because the Lord is truly risen, alleluia.**

Let us pray. O God, Who by the Resurrection of Your Son, our Lord Jesus Christ, granted joy to the whole world, grant, we beg You, that, through the intercession of the Virgin Mary, His Mother, we may attain the joys of eternal life. Through the same Christ our Lord. Amen.

The Memorare

Remember, O most gracious Virgin Mary,
that never was it known
that anyone who fled to your protection,
implored your help, or sought your intercession
was left unaided.
Inspired by this confidence,
I fly unto you, O Virgin of virgins, my Mother;
to you do I come,
before you I stand, sinful and sorrowful.
O Mother of the Word Incarnate,
despise not my petitions,
but in your mercy hear and answer me. Amen.

Partial indulgence

PRAYERS TO AND FROM SAINTS

The Memorare to St. Joseph

Remember, O most chaste spouse of the Virgin Mary,
that never was it known
that anyone who implored your help and sought
     your intercession
was left unassisted.
Full of confidence in your power,
I fly unto you and beg your protection.
Despise not, O foster father of the Redeemer,
my humble supplication,
but in your bounty, hear and answer me.
Amen.

St. Francis' Prayer before the Crucifix

Most High, glorious God,
enlighten the darkness of my heart
and give me true faith, certain hope, and perfect
    charity,
sense and knowledge, Lord,
that I may carry out Your holy and true command.
Amen.

Prayer of Self-Offering/Suscipe

Take, Lord, and receive all my liberty,
my memory, my understanding,
and my entire will,
all I have and call my own.

You have given all to me.
To You, Lord, I return it.

Everything is Yours; do with it what You will.
Give me only Your love and Your grace,
that is enough for me.

St. Ignatius of Loyola

Prayer to St. Michael the Archangel

St. Michael the Archangel,
defend us in battle.
Be our protection against
the wickedness and snares of the devil.
May God rebuke him we humbly pray,
and do thou, O Prince of the Heavenly host,
by the power of God,
cast into hell Satan
and all the evil spirits
who prowl about the world
seeking the ruin of souls.
Amen.

From St. Patrick's Breastplate

Christ with me,
Christ before me,
Christ behind me,
Christ in me,
Christ beneath me,
Christ above me,
Christ on my right,
Christ on my left,
Christ when I lie down,
Christ when I sit down,
Christ when I arise,
Christ in the heart of everyone who thinks of me,
Christ in the mouth of everyone who speaks of me,
Christ in every eye that sees me,
Christ in every ear that hears me.

Prayer of St. Benedict

Gracious God our Father,
grant us the intellect
to understand you,
wisdom to discern you,
diligence to seek you,
desire to find you,
a spirit to know you,
a heart to love you.

May our ears hear you,
may our eyes behold you, and
may our tongues proclaim you.

Give us the grace that our way of life
may be pleasing to you,
that we may have the patience

to wait for you and the
perseverance to look for you.

Grant us the perfect gift
of your holy presence,
a blessed resurrection
and life everlasting.

We ask this through
Christ our Lord. Amen.

Prayer for the Help of the Holy Spirit

O God,
send forth Your Holy Spirit
into my heart that I may perceive,
into my mind that I may remember,
and into my soul that I may meditate.

Inspire me to speak with piety,
holiness, tenderness, and mercy.
Teach, guide, and direct my thoughts and senses
from the beginning to the end.

May Your grace ever help and correct me,
and may I be strengthened now
with wisdom from on high,
for the sake of Your infinite mercy.

St. Anthony of Padua

Prayer to Be Centered on Christ

LORD Jesus Christ, . . .
may my soul always revolve around You,
seek You,
and find You.
Help it to turn to You,
and reach You.
Let its every thought and word be centered
on You.

Grant that my soul may sing Your praise
and the glory of Your holy Name
with humility and reserve,
with love and joy,
with ease and gentleness,
with patience and tranquility,
with success and persistence
to the very end.

St. Bonaventure

Prayer to Do Always the Will of God

O Lord,
regulate all things by Your wisdom,
so that I may always serve You
in the manner that You will
rather than in the manner that I will.
Do not punish me
by granting what I will
if it offends against Your love,
for I want Your love to live always in me.
Help me to deny myself
in order that I may serve You.
Let me live for You—
Who in Yourself are the true life.

St. Teresa of Avila

Prayer of Trust in the Sacred Heart

O Heart of love,
I place all my trust in You.
I fear all things
from my own weakness,
but I hope for all things
from Your goodness.

St. Margaret Mary Alacoque

Prayer That God May Not Abandon Us in Affliction

O my God,
I beg You,
by Your loneliness,
not that You may spare me affliction,
but that You may not abandon me in it.
When I encounter affliction,
teach me to see You in it
as my sole comforter.
Let affliction strengthen my faith,
fortify my hope,
and purify my love.
Grant me the grace
to see Your hand in my affliction,
and to desire no other comforter but You.

St. Bernadette of Lourdes

Prayer of Our Love for God Alone

My God,
You know that I have always desired
to love You alone.
I seek no other glory.
Your love has preceded me
from the time of my childhood,
become greater with my youth,
and is presently an abyss
whose depth I cannot fathom.

St. Thérèse of Lisieux

Prayer to St. Anthony of Padua
Patron of Seekers of Lost Articles

Wonderful Saint and Doctor of the Church,
you are the patron of the poor
and the helper of all who seek lost articles.

Help me to find the object I have lost
so that I will be able to make better use
of the time that I will gain
for God's greater honor and glory.

Grant your gracious aid to all people
who seek what they have lost—
especially those who seek to regain God's grace.

Prayer to St. Catherine of Siena
Patroness against Miscarriages

Humble Virgin and Doctor of the Church,
in thirty-three years you achieved great perfection
and became the counselor of Popes.
You know the temptations of mothers today
as well as the dangers that await unborn infants.
Intercede for me that I may avoid miscarriage
and bring forth a healthy baby
who will become a true child of God.
Also pray for all mothers,
that they may not resort to abortion
but help bring a new life into the world.

Prayer to St. Jude
Patron of Desperate Cases

Dear Apostle and Martyr for Christ,
you left us an Epistle in the New Testament.
With good reason many invoke you
when illness is at a desperate stage.
We now recommend to your kindness
N. . . . who is in a critical condition.
May the cure of this patient increase
his/her faith and love for the Lord of Life,
for the glory of our merciful God.

Prayer to St. Peregrine
Patron of Cancer Patients

Dear Apostle of Emilia
and member of the Order of Mary,
you spread the Good News by your word
and by your life witnessed to its truth.
In union with Jesus crucified,
you endured excruciating sufferings so patiently
as to be healed miraculously of cancer in the leg.
If it is agreeable to God,
obtain relief and cure for N. . . .
and keep us all from the dread cancer of sin.

Prayer to St. Raphael
Patron of Travelers

Wondrous Archangel and dedicated guide,
your lovely name means "God heals."
The Lord sent you to young Tobiah
to guide him throughout a long journey.
Upon his return you taught him
how to cure his father's blindness.
How natural, therefore, for Christians
to pray for your powerful help
for safe travel and a happy return.
This is what we ask for ourselves
as well as for all who are far from home.

Prayer to St. Catherine of Siena
Patroness of Firefighters

Dominican Tertiary and Doctor of the Church,
you were full of wisdom, the special gift of God,
and you knew how to guide even Pontiffs,
as well as how to extinguish fiery passions
and restore true peace among people.

How inspiring your spiritual writings
and how heroic your abstemious life!
Fires are today unfortunately all too common—
some even caused by criminal persons.
Please protect and encourage firefighters
in their heroic efforts to save lives.

Prayer to St. Monica
Patroness of Mothers

Exemplary Mother of the great Augustine,
you perseveringly pursued your wayward son
not with wild threats
but with prayerful cries to heaven.
Intercede for all mothers in our day
so that they may learn to draw their children to God.
Teach them how to remain close to their children,
even the prodigal sons and daughters
who have sadly gone astray.

Prayer to St. Camillus of Lellis
Patron of Nurses and Hospital Workers

Wonderful Helper of souls and bodies,
your compassion for the sick and the dying
led you to found the Servants of the Sick.
As the Patron of nurses and hospital workers,
infuse in them your compassionate spirit.
Make hospitals resemble the inn in Christ's Parable
to which the Good Samaritan brought the wounded
     man,
saying: "Take care of him,
and I will repay you for it."

Prayer to St. Luke
Patron of Physicians

Most charming and saintly Physician,
you were animated by the heavenly Spirit of love.
In faithfully detailing the Humanity of Jesus,
you also showed His Divinity
and His genuine compassion for all human beings.

Inspire our physicians with your professionalism
and with the Divine compassion for their patients.
Enable them to cure the ills of both body and spirit
that afflict so many in our day.

Prayer to St. Michael
Patron of Police Officers

Dear Archangel and Warrior for God,
your name means, "Who is like God?"
and it indicates that you remained faithful
when others rebelled against God.

Help police officers in our day
who strive to stem the rebellion and evil
that are rampant on all sides.

Keep them faithful to their God
as well as to their country
and their fellow human beings.

LITANIES
Litany of the Blessed Sacrament
(For Private Devotion)

Lord, have mercy.
Christ, have mercy.
Lord, have mercy.
Christ, hear us.
Christ, graciously hear us.
God the Father of heaven, *have mercy on us.**
God the Son, Redeemer of the world,
God the Holy Spirit,
Holy Trinity, one God,
Living Bread, that came down from heaven,
Hidden God and Savior,
Corn of the elect,
Wine whose fruit are virgins,
Bread of fatness, and royal Dainties,
Perpetual Sacrifice,
Clean Oblation,
Lamb without spot,
Most pure Feast,
Food of Angels,
Hidden Manna,
Memorial of the wonders of God,
Super-substantial Bread,

Word made flesh, dwelling in us,
Sacred Host,
Chalice of benediction,
Mystery of faith,
Most high and adorable Sacrament,
Most holy of all sacrifices,
True Propitiation for the living and the dead,
Heavenly Antidote against the poison of sin,
Most wonderful of all miracles,
Most holy Commemoration of the Passion of Christ,
Gift transcending all fullness,
Special Memorial of Divine love,
Affluence of Divine bounty,
Most august and holy Mystery,
Medicine of immortality,
Tremendous and life-giving Sacrament,

* *Have mercy on us* is repeated after each invocation.

Bread made flesh by the omnipotence of the Word,

Unbloody Sacrifice,

Our Feast at once and our Fellow-guest,

Sweetest Banquet, at which Angels minister,

Sacrament of piety,

Bond of charity,

Priest and Victim,

Spiritual Sweetness tasted in its proper source,

Refreshment of holy souls,

Viaticum of such as die in the Lord,

Pledge of future glory,

Be merciful,
spare us, O Lord.

Be merciful,
graciously hear us, O Lord.

From an unworthy reception of Your Body and Blood,
*O Lord, deliver us.***

From the lust of the flesh,

From the lust of the eyes,

From the pride of life,

From every occasion of sin,

Through the desire, by which You desired to eat this Passover with Your disciples,

Through that profound humility, by which You washed their feet,

Through that ardent charity, by which You instituted this Divine Sacrament,

Through Your Precious Blood, that You have left us on our altars,

Through the Five Wounds of this Your most holy Body, that You received for us,

We sinners,
*we beseech You, hear us.****

That You would preserve and increase our faith, reverence, and devotion toward this admirable Sacrament,

---

** *O Lord, deliver us* is repeated after each invocation.
*** *We beseech You, hear us* is repeated after each invocation.

That You would conduct us, through a true confession of our sins, to a frequent reception of the Holy Eucharist,

That You would deliver us from all heresy, perfidy, and blindness of heart,

That You would impart to us the precious and heavenly fruits of this most holy Sacrament,

That at the hour of death You would strengthen and defend us by this heavenly Viaticum,

Son of God,

Lamb of God, You take away the sins of the world; *spare us, O Lord.*

Lamb of God, You take away the sins of the world; *graciously hear us, O Lord;*

Lamb of God, You take away the sins of the world; *have mercy on us.*

Christ, hear us. *Christ, graciously hear us.*

℣. You gave them Bread from heaven,

℟. *Containing in itself all sweetness.*

Let us pray.
O God,
in this wonderful Sacrament
You left us a memorial of Your Passion.
Grant us so to venerate the sacred mysteries
of Your Body and Blood
that we may ever continue to feel within us
the blessed fruit of Your redemption.
You live and reign for ever and ever.

Litany of the Most Holy Trinity

(For Private Devotion)

Lord, have mercy.
Christ, have mercy.
Lord, have mercy.
Blessed Trinity, hear us.
Adorable Unity, graciously hear us.
God the Father of heaven,
have mercy on us.
God the Son, Redeemer of the world,*
God the Holy Spirit,
Holy Trinity, one God,
Father, from Whom are all things,
Son, through Whom are all things,
Holy Spirit, in Whom are all things,
Holy and undivided Trinity,
Father everlasting,
Only-begotten Son of the Father,
Spirit, Who proceed from the Father and the Son,
Co-eternal Majesty of Three Divine Persons,
Father the Creator,
Son the Redeemer,
Holy Spirit the Comforter,
Holy, holy, holy Lord God of hosts,
Who are, Who were, and Who are to come,
God, Most High, Who inhabit eternity,
To Whom alone are due all honor and glory,
Who alone do great wonders,
Power infinite,
Wisdom incomprehensible,
Love unspeakable,
Be merciful, *spare us, O Holy Trinity.*
Be merciful, *graciously hear us, O Holy Trinity.*
From all evil, *deliver us, O Holy Trinity.*

* *Have mercy on us* is repeated after each invocation.

From all sin,**

From all pride,

From all love of riches,

From all uncleanness,

From all sloth,

From all inordinate affection,

From all envy and malice,

From all anger and impatience,

From every thought, word, and deed, contrary to Your holy law,

From Your everlasting malediction,

Through Your almighty power,

Through Your plenteous loving-kindness,

Through the exceeding treasures of Your goodness and love,

Through the depths of Your wisdom and knowledge,

Through all Your ineffable perfections,

We sinners,

we beseech You, hear us.

That we may ever serve You alone,***

That we may worship You in spirit and in truth,

That we may love You with all our heart, with all our soul, and with all our strength,

That, for Your sake, we may love our neighbor as ourselves,

That we may faithfully keep Your holy commandments,

That we may never defile our bodies and our souls with sin,

That we may go from grace to grace, and from virtue to virtue,

That we may finally enjoy the sight of You in glory,

That You would hear us, O blessed Trinity,

we beseech You, deliver us.

** *Deliver us, O Holy Trinity* is repeated after each invocation.

*** *We beseech You, hear us* is repeated after each invocation.

O blessed Trinity,
*we beseech You, save
   us.*
O blessed Trinity,
have mercy on us.
Lord, have mercy.
Christ, have mercy.
Lord, have mercy.

℣. Blessed are you, O
   Lord, in the firma-
   ment of heaven.

℟. *And worthy to be
   praised, and glorious,
   and highly exalted
   forever.*

Let us pray.
Almighty and everlasting God,
You have given us Your servants
grace by the profession of the true faith
to acknowledge the glory of the eternal Trinity
and in the power of Your Divine Majesty
to worship the Unity.
We beg You to grant that,
by our fidelity in this same faith,
we may always be defended from all dangers.

Litany of the Holy Spirit
(For Private Devotion)

Lord, have mercy.
Christ, have mercy.
Lord, have mercy.
Holy Spirit, hear us.
Holy Spirit, graciously hear us.
God, the Father of heaven, *have mercy on us.*
God, the Son, Redeemer of the world,*
God, the Holy Spirit,
Holy Trinity, one God,
Holy Spirit, Who proceed from the Father,
Holy Spirit, co-equal with the Father and the Son,
Promise of the Father, most bounteous,
Gift of God most high,
Ray of heavenly Light,
Author of all good,
Source of living Water,
Consuming Fire,
Burning Love,
Spiritual Unction,
Spirit of truth and power,
Spirit of wisdom and understanding,
Spirit of counsel and fortitude,
Spirit of knowledge and piety,
Spirit of fear of the Lord,
Spirit of compunction,
Spirit of grace and prayer,
Spirit of charity, peace, and joy,
Spirit of patience,
Spirit of longanimity and goodness,
Spirit of benignity and mildness,
Spirit of fidelity,
Spirit of modesty and continence,
Spirit of chastity,
Spirit of adoption of children of God,
Holy Spirit, comforter,
Holy Spirit, sanctifier,
You through Whom spoke holy men of God,

---

* *Have mercy on us* is repeated after each invocation.

You Who overshadowed Mary,

You by Whom Mary conceived Christ,

You Who descend upon human beings at Baptism,

You Who, on the Day of Pentecost, appeared through fiery tongues,

You by Whom we are reborn,

You Who dwell in us as in a temple,

You Who govern and animate the Church,

You Who fill the whole world,

That You may renew the face of the earth,

we beseech You, hear us.

That You may shed Your Light upon us,**

That You may pour Your Love into our hearts,

That You may inspire us to love our neighbor,

That You may teach us to ask for the graces we need,

That You may enlighten us with Your heavenly inspirations,

That You may guide us in the way of holiness,

That You may make us obedient to Your commandments,

That You may teach us how to pray,

That You may always pray with us,

That You may inspire us with horror for sin,

That You may direct us in the practice of virtue,

That You may make us persevere in a holy life,

That You may make us faithful to our vocation,

That You may grant us good priests and Bishops,

That You may give us good Christian families,

That You may grant us a spiritual renewal of the Church,

** *We beseech You, hear us* is repeated after each invocation.

That You may guide
and console the Holy
Father,

Lamb of God, You take
away the sins of the
world; *spare us, O
Lord.*

Lamb of God, You take
away the sins of the
world; *graciously hear
us, O Lord.*

Lamb of God, You take
away the sins of the
world; *have mercy on
us.*

Holy Spirit, hear us.
*Holy Spirit, graciously
hear us.*

Lord, have mercy.
Christ, have mercy.
Lord, have mercy.

℣. Create a clean heart
in us.

℟. *Renew a right spirit
in us.*

Let us pray.
O merciful Father,
grant that Your Divine Spirit
may cleanse, inflame, and enlighten our minds and
hearts.
Enable us to be fruitful in good works
for the glory of Your Majesty
and the spiritual and material well-being of all
people.
We ask this through Jesus Christ Your Son
and the Holy Spirit.

MAJOR PRACTICES

THE LITURGICAL YEAR

The Liturgical Year is the succession of Times and Feasts of the Church celebrated annually from Advent to Advent.

As presently constituted, the Liturgical Year has the following Times (divisions):

Advent: Beginning on the Sunday closest to November 30 (the Feast of St. Andrew), this period of preparation for the Nativity of the Lord extends over four Sundays.

Christmas Time: This Time begins with the Vigil Masses for the Solemnity of the Nativity of the Lord [Christmas] and concludes on the Feast of the Baptism of the Lord. The period from the end of Christmas Time until the beginning of Lent is included in Ordinary Time (see below).

Lent: The penitential season of Lent begins on Ash Wednesday and ends on Holy Thursday before the Mass of the Lord's Supper that evening. The final week, Holy Week, concludes with the Sacred Paschal Triduum, which takes place from the evening of Holy Thursday to the evening of Easter Sunday.

Easter Time: This Time spans a 50-day period, from the Solemnity of Easter to Pentecost. Its central theme is the Resurrection of Christ together with our resurrection from sin to the new life of grace.

Ordinary Time: This Time comprises the other 33 or 34 weeks of the Liturgical Year. It includes not only the period between the end of Christmas Time and the beginning of Lent but all Sundays and weekdays after Pentecost until the beginning of Advent. It is "ordinary" only by comparison, because the great Feasts of our Lord are prepared for and specially celebrated other times of the year.

Feasts: The first Christians knew only one Feast, Easter, the Feast of our Lord's Resurrection. But this they celebrated all the time, whenever they gathered for the Eucharist. In the Eucharistic celebration, every day and especially every Sunday became for them a little Easter. Easter, in fact, is the center in which all Mysteries of our Redemption merge.

Eventually, however, the Church began to celebrate many of these mysteries in their own right, with Feasts of their own, especially the Birth of our Lord, His Life and Death as well as His Resurrection and Glorification, and also the sending of the Holy Spirit and His work of grace in the soul. Gradually added were Feasts of the Blessed Mother Mary and the Saints.

The Liturgical Year, therefore, has had a long history of development. As early as the year 700, however, the Roman Liturgical Year was essentially as it is today, with two major cycles, Christmas with its Advent and Easter with its Lent, plus the Sundays in between.

HOLYDAYS OF OBLIGATION
Holydays in the United States

Solemnity of Mary, the Holy Mother
   of God.. January 1
Ascension of the Lord .... 40 days after Easter or
                  Sunday after the 6th Sunday of Easter
Assumption of the Blessed Virgin Mary........... August 15
All Saints .... November 1
Immaculate Conception of the Blessed
   Virgin Mary...December 8
Nativity of the Lord [Christmas]................. December 25

SPIRITUAL WORKS OF MERCY

1. To admonish the sinner (correct those who need it).
2. To instruct the ignorant (teach the ignorant).
3. To counsel the doubtful (give advice to those who need it).
4. To comfort the sorrowful (comfort those who suffer).
5. To bear wrongs patiently (be patient with others).
6. To forgive all injuries (forgive others who hurt you).
7. To pray for the living and the dead (pray for others).

CORPORAL WORKS OF MERCY

1. To feed the hungry.
2. To give drink to the thirsty.
3. To clothe the naked.
4. To visit the imprisoned.
5. To shelter the homeless.
6. To visit the sick.
7. To bury the dead.

THE TEN COMMANDMENTS

1. I, the Lord, am your God. You shall not have other gods besides Me.
2. You shall not take the name of the Lord, your God, in vain.
3. Remember to keep holy the Sabbath day.
4. Honor your father and your mother.
5. You shall not kill.
6. You shall not commit adultery.
7. You shall not steal.
8. You shall not bear false witness against your neighbor.
9. You shall not covet your neighbor's wife.
10. You shall not covet your neighbor's goods.

PRECEPTS OF THE CHURCH
(Traditional Form)

1. To participate at Mass on all Sundays and Holydays of Obligation.
2. To fast and to abstain on the days appointed.
3. To confess our sins at least once a year.
4. To receive Holy Communion during Easter Time.
5. To contribute to the support of the Church.
6. To observe the laws of the Church concerning marriage.

GUIDELINES FOR THE RECEPTION
OF COMMUNION

For Catholics

As Catholics, we fully participate in the celebration of the Eucharist when we receive Holy Communion. We are encouraged to receive Communion devoutly and frequently. In order to be properly disposed to receive Communion, participants should not be conscious of grave sin and normally should have fasted for one hour. A person who is conscious of grave sin is not to receive the Body and Blood of the Lord without prior sacramental confession except for a grave reason where there is no opportunity for confession. In this case, the person is to be mindful of the obligation to make an act of perfect contrition, including the intention of confessing as soon as possible (*Code of Canon Law, canon 916*). A frequent reception of the Sacrament of Penance is encouraged for all.

For Fellow Christians

We welcome our fellow Christians to this celebration of the Eucharist as our brothers and sisters. We pray that our common baptism and the action of the Holy Spirit in this Eucharist will draw us closer to one another and begin to dispel the sad divisions that separate us. We pray that these will lessen and finally disappear, in keeping with Christ's prayer for us "that they may all be one" (John 17:21).

Because Catholics believe that the celebration of the Eucharist is a sign of the reality of the oneness of faith, life, and worship, members of those churches with whom we are not yet fully united are ordinarily not admitted to Holy Communion. Eucharistic sharing in exceptional circumstances by other Christians requires permission according to the directives of the diocesan bishop and the provisions of canon law (*canon 844 § 4*). Members of the Orthodox Churches, the Assyrian Church of the East, and the Polish National Catholic Church are urged to respect the discipline of their own Churches. According to Roman Catholic discipline, the Code of Canon Law does not object to the reception of Communion by Christians of these Churches (*canon 844 § 3*).

For Those Not Receiving Holy Communion

All who are not receiving Holy Communion are encouraged to express in their hearts a prayerful desire for unity with the Lord Jesus and with one another.

For Non-Christians

We also welcome to this celebration those who do not share our faith in Jesus Christ. While we cannot admit them to Holy Communion, we ask them to offer their prayers for the peace and the unity of the human family.

RITE OF PENANCE

(Extracted from the Rite of Penance)

Texts for the Penitent

The penitent should prepare for the celebration of the sacrament by prayer, reading of Scripture, and silent reflection. The penitent should think over and should regret all sins since the last celebration of the sacrament.

RECEPTION OF THE PENITENT

The penitent enters the confessional or other place set aside for the celebration of the sacrament of penance. After the welcoming of the priest, the penitent makes the sign of the cross saying:

In the name of the Father, and of the Son, and of the Holy Spirit. Amen.

The penitent is invited to have trust in God and replies:

Amen.

READING OF THE WORD OF GOD

The penitent then listens to a text of Scripture which tells about God's mercy and calls man to conversion.

CONFESSION OF SINS AND ACCEPTANCE OF SATISFACTION

The penitent speaks to the priest in a normal, conversational fashion. The penitent tells when he or she last celebrated the sacrament and then confesses his or her sins. The penitent then listens to any advice the priest may give and accepts the satisfaction from the priest. The penitent should ask any appropriate questions.

PRAYER OF THE PENITENT AND ABSOLUTION
Prayer

Before the absolution is given, the penitent expresses sorrow for sins in these or similar words:

**My God,
I am sorry for my sins with all my heart.
In choosing to do wrong
and failing to do good,
I have sinned against you
whom I should love above all things.
I firmly intend, with your help,
to do penance,
to sin no more,
and to avoid whatever leads me to sin.
Our Savior Jesus Christ
suffered and died for us.
In his name, my God, have mercy.**

OR:

Remember that your compassion, O LORD,
   and your love are from of old.
In your kindness remember me,
   because of your goodness, O LORD.

OR:

Thoroughly wash me from my guilt
   and of my sin cleanse me.
For I acknowledge my offense,
   and my sin is before me always.

OR:

Father, I have sinned [. . .] against you.
I no longer deserve to be called your son.
Be merciful to me a sinner.

OR:

Father of mercy,
like the prodigal son
I return to you and say:
"I have sinned against you
and am no longer worthy to be called your son."
Christ Jesus, Savior of the world,
I pray with the repentant thief
to whom you promised Paradise:
"Lord, remember me in your kingdom."
Holy Spirit, fountain of love,
I call on you with trust:
"Purify my heart,
and help me to walk as a child of light."

OR:

Lord Jesus,
you opened the eyes of the blind,
healed the sick,
forgave the sinful woman,
and after Peter's denial confirmed him in your love.
Listen to my prayer:
forgive all my sins,
renew your love in my heart,
help me to live in perfect unity with my fellow Christians
that I may proclaim your saving power to all the world.

OR:

Lord Jesus,
you chose to be called the friend of sinners.
By your saving death and resurrection
free me from my sins.
May your peace take root in my heart

and bring forth a harvest
of love, holiness, and truth.

OR:

Lord Jesus Christ,
you are the Lamb of God;
you take away the sins of the world.
Through the grace of the Holy Spirit
restore me to friendship with your Father,
cleanse me from every stain of sin
in the blood you shed for me,
and raise me to new life
for the glory of your name.

OR:

Lord God,
in your goodness have mercy on me:
do not look on my sins,
but take away all my guilt.
Create in me a clean heart
and renew within me an upright spirit.

OR:

Lord Jesus, Son of God,
have mercy on me, a sinner.

ABSOLUTION

*If the penitent is not kneeling, he or she bows his or her head
as the priest extends his hands (or at least extends his right
hand).*

God, the Father of mercies,
through the death and resurrection of his Son
has reconciled the world to himself
and sent the Holy Spirit among us
for the forgiveness of sins;
through the ministry of the Church
may God give you pardon and peace,
and I absolve you from your sins
in the name of the Father, and of the Son, ✛
and of the Holy Spirit. Amen.

PROCLAMATION OF PRAISE OF GOD AND DISMISSAL

Penitent and priest give praise to God.

Priest: Give thanks to the Lord, for he is good.
Penitent: His mercy endures for ever.

Then the penitent is dismissed by the priest.

Form of Examination of Conscience

This suggested form for an examination of conscience should be completed and adapted to meet the needs of different individuals and to follow local usages.

In an examination of conscience, before the sacrament of penance, each individual should ask himself these questions in particular:

1. What is my attitude to the sacrament of penance? Do I sincerely want to be set free from sin, to turn again to God, to begin a new life, and to enter into a deeper friendship with God? Or do I look on it as a burden, to be undertaken as seldom as possible?

2. Did I forget to mention, or deliberately conceal, any grave sins in past confessions?

3. Did I perform the penance I was given? Did I make reparation for any injury to others? Have I tried to put into practice any resolution to lead a better life in keeping with the Gospel?

Each individual should examine his life in the light of God's word.

I. The Lord says: "You shall love the Lord your God with your whole heart."

1. Is my heart set on God, so that I really love him above all things and am faithful to his commandments, as a son loves his father? Or am I more concerned about the things of this world? Have I a right intention in what I do?

2. God spoke to us in his Son. Is my faith in God firm and secure? Am I wholehearted in accepting the Church's teaching? Have I been careful to grow in my understanding of the faith, to hear God's word, to listen to instructions on the faith, to avoid dangers to faith? Have I been always strong and fearless in professing my faith in God and the Church? Have I been willing to be known as a Christian in private and public life?

3. Have I prayed morning and evening? When I pray, do I really raise my mind and heart to God or is it a matter of words only? Do I offer God my difficulties, my joys, and my sorrows? Do I turn to God in time of temptation?

4. Have I love and reverence for God's name? Have I offended him in blasphemy, swearing falsely, or taking his name in vain? Have I shown disrespect for the Blessed Virgin Mary and the saints?

5. Do I keep Sundays and feast days holy by taking a full part, with attention and devotion, in the liturgy, and especially in the Mass? Have I fulfilled the precept of annual confession and of communion during the Easter season?

6. Are there false gods that I worship by giving them greater attention and deeper trust than I give to God: money, superstition, spiritism, or other occult practices?

II. The Lord says: "Love one another as I have loved you."

1. Have I a genuine love for my neighbors? Or do I use them for my own ends, or do to them what I would not want done to myself? Have I given grave scandal by my words or actions?

2. In my family life, have I contributed to the well-being and happiness of the rest of the family by patience and genuine love? Have I been obedient to parents, showing them proper respect and giving them help in their spiritual and material needs? Have I been careful to give a Christian upbringing to my children, and to help them by good example and by exercising authority as a parent? Have I been faithful to my husband/wife in my heart and in my relations with others?

3. Do I share my possessions with the less fortunate? Do I do my best to help the victims of oppression, misfortune, and poverty? Or do I look down on my neighbor, especially the poor, the sick, the elderly, strangers, and people of other races?

4. Does my life reflect the mission I received in confirmation? Do I share in the apostolic and charitable works of the Church and in the life of my parish? Have I helped to meet the needs of the Church and of the world and prayed for them: for unity in the Church, for the spread of the Gospel among the nations, for peace and justice, etc.?

5. Am I concerned for the good and prosperity of the human community in which I live, or do I spend my life caring only for myself? Do I share to the best of my ability in the work of promoting justice, morality, harmony, and love in human relations? Have I done my duty as a citizen? Have I paid my taxes?

6. In my work or profession am I just, hard-working, honest, serving society out of love for others? Have I paid a fair wage to my employees? Have I been faithful to my promises and contracts?

7. Have I obeyed legitimate authority and given it due respect?

8. If I am in a position of responsibility or authority, do I use this for my own advantage or for the good of others, in a spirit of service?

9. Have I been truthful and fair, or have I injured others by deceit, calumny, detraction, rash judgment, or violation of a secret?

10. Have I done violence to others by damage to life or limb, reputation, honor, or material possessions? Have I involved them in loss? Have I been responsible for advising an abortion or procuring one?

Have I kept up hatred for others? Am I estranged from others through quarrels, enmity, insults, anger? Have I been guilty of refusing to testify to the innocence of another because of selfishness?

11. Have I stolen the property of others? Have I desired it unjustly and inordinately? Have I damaged it? Have I made restitution of other people's property and made good their loss?

12. If I have been injured, have I been ready to make peace for the love of Christ and to forgive, or do I harbor hatred and the desire for revenge?

III. Christ our Lord says: "Be perfect as your Father is perfect."

1. Where is my life really leading me? Is the hope of eternal life my inspiration? Have I tried to grow in the life of the Spirit through prayer, reading the word of God and meditating on it, receiving the sacraments, self-denial? Have I been anxious to control my vices, my bad inclinations and passions, e.g., envy, love of food and drink? Have I been proud and boastful, thinking myself better in the sight of God and despising others as less important than myself? Have I imposed my own will on others, without respecting their freedom and rights?

2. What use have I made of time, of health and strength, of the gifts God has given to me to be used like the talents in the Gospel? Do I use them to become more perfect every day? Or have I been lazy and too much given to leisure?

3. Have I been patient in accepting the sorrows and disappointments of life? How have I performed mortification so as to "fill up what is wanting to the sufferings of Christ"? Have I kept the precept of fasting and abstinence?

4. Have I kept my senses and my whole body pure and chaste as a temple of the Holy Spirit consecrated for resurrection and glory, and as a sign of God's faithful love for men and women, a sign that is seen most perfectly in the sacrament of matrimony? Have I dishonored my body by fornication, impurity, unworthy conversation or thoughts, evil desires or actions? Have I given in to sensuality? Have I indulged in reading, conversation, shows, and entertainments that offend against Christian and human decency? Have I encouraged others to sin by my own failure to maintain these standards? Have I been faithful to the moral law in my married life?

5. Have I gone against my conscience out of fear or hypocrisy?

6. Have I always tried to act in the true freedom of the sons of God according to the law of the Spirit, or am I the slave of forces within me?